CHILDREN OF KATRINA

THE KATRINA BOOKSHELF

Kai Erikson, Series Editor

In 2005 Hurricane Katrina crashed into the Gulf Coast and precipitated the flooding of New Orleans. It was a towering catastrophe by any standard. Some 1,800 persons were killed outright. More than a million were forced to relocate, many for the remainder of their lives. A city of five hundred thousand was nearly emptied of life. The storm stripped away the surface of our social structure and showed us what lies beneath—a grim picture of race, class, and gender in these United States.

It is crucial to get this story straight so that we may learn from it and be ready for that stark inevitability, *the next time*. When seen through a social science lens, Katrina informs us of the real human costs of a disaster and helps prepare us for the events that we know are lurking just over the horizon. The Katrina Bookshelf is the result of a national effort to bring experts together in a collaborative program of research on the human costs of the disaster. The program was supported by the Ford, Gates, MacArthur, Rockefeller, and Russell Sage Foundations and sponsored by the Social Science Research Council. This is the most comprehensive social science coverage of a disaster to be found anywhere in the literature. It is also a deeply human story.

CHILDREN OF KATRINA

ALICE FOTHERGILL AND LORI PEEK

University of Texas Press

AUSTIN

First edition, 2015

Requests for permission to reproduce material from this work should be sent to:
Permissions
University of Texas Press
P.O. Box 7819
Austin, TX 78713–7819
http://utpress.utexas.edu/index.php/rp-form

♾ The paper used in this book meets the minimum requirements of
ANSI/NISO Z39.48–1992 (R1997) (Permanence of Paper).

LIBRARY OF CONGRESS CATALOGING-IN-PUBLICATION DATA
Fothergill, Alice, author.
Children of Katrina / Alice Fothergill and Lori Peek. — First edition.
    pages cm — (The Katrina bookshelf)
Includes bibliographical references and index.
ISBN 978-1-4773-0389-4 (cloth : alk. paper)
ISBN 978 1 4773 0546 1 (pbk. : alk. paper)
ISBN 978-1-4773-0390-0 (lib. e-book)
ISBN 978-1-4773-0391-7 (nonlib. e-book)
1. Hurricane Katrina, 2005—Social aspects. 2. Child disaster victims—
Louisiana—New Orleans—Social conditions. 3. Child disaster victims—
Louisiana—New Orleans—Psychological aspects. I. Peek, Lori A., author.
    II. Title. III. Series: Katrina bookshelf.
HV6362005.N4 F67 2015
363.34′922092530976335—dc23   2015009040
doi:10.7560/303894

For Joe, Maggie, and Jeff
–A. F.

For Mom and Dad
–L. P.

This book is dedicated in memory of
William A. Anderson (1937–2013),
a friend, mentor, leader,
and champion for research on children and disasters.

There is no trust more sacred than the one the world holds with children. There is no duty more important than ensuring that their rights are respected, that their welfare is protected, that their lives are free from fear and want, and that they can grow up in peace.

KOFI ANNAN

CONTENTS

FIGURES AND TABLES

FIGURES

TABLES

FOREWORD

When the late psychologist Norman Garmezy, a pioneer of the field of resilience, first began studying positive adaptation in children in the early 1970s, he sought out stories of children who had thrived despite being exposed to highly stressful environments, particularly those associated with poverty. "Who will fall to the ravaging effects of mental disorder," he declared to his colleagues at a 1970 conference, "or who will, despite stress and adversity, remain inviolate to psychopathology remains a problem of mystery and challenge."[1] Garmezy had already spent two decades studying war veterans, schizophrenics, and the children of schizophrenics. In each, he sought to illuminate the predictive path, those factors in people's lives that foreshadowed either positive or negative outcomes, that divided the successful from the unsuccessful, and the adaptive from the psychopathological.

At the start of his two-decades-long children's study, Garmezy visited public schools throughout Minnesota, asking the same question of the school principals, nurses, and social workers with whom he met: were there any children in the school whose background worried them when they first learned of them, but who now elicited pride when they walked the school halls because they had succeeded despite steep odds? Illustrations of resilience were often distilled in snapshots of a child's life. He learned of one nine-year-old boy who was being raised by a single mother, herself an alcoholic. The two of them often had little food in the house. Each day the boy would bring to school a "bread sandwich," two pieces of bread with nothing in between, in order to blend in with the other children bringing their lunches from home. He didn't want the other children to pity him, Garmezy learned, nor to know of his mother's failings. As Garmezy and his colleagues evolved their theories of resilience and adaptation they accumulated many such stories. Some were drawn from children who experienced cataclysmic events in their lives, others from children who lived the quieter lives of grinding desperation and poverty. "I have to think of a single great stressor and its consequences," Garmezy said, in recounting his life's work in 2002, "and I also think of the accumulation of stressors in which the environment, the family, and the background all add up to generate negative events and circumstances that ordinarily would bring a child down, but in many instances do not."[2]

In *Children of Katrina*, Alice Fothergill and Lori Peek use the backdrop of the catastrophic 2005 hurricane to advance our understanding of resilience and recovery even further. They have built on both the inductive power of that story-telling tradition, and upon several decades of psychological and sociological literatures of adaptation, resilience, and vulnerability. The stories they tell in this volume, drawn from the generation of children who experienced Hurricane Katrina along the U.S. Gulf Coast, bridge the acute traumatic stressors of the storm and displacement, and those that are more personal stressors common to those who live chaotic lives of broken homes, homelessness, and poverty. From among the 650 children they encountered in their research, Peek and Fothergill selected seven stories in particular with which to illuminate the pathways to recovery. They were careful to vary their selected children by age and gender, race, and social class. Much as Garmezy exhorted his colleagues to do, they have methodically explored the social, cultural, and economic forces in the lives of these seven children. From the data they collected over the span of seven years of observing and interviewing the children, their families, and their social networks, Fothergill and Peek have painted a picture of three recovery trajectories: one in which the child finds equilibrium, one in which the child fluctuates between positive and negative states, and one in which the child and the family are in decline. The individual stories are often heart-wrenching. The implications are enormous.

Katrina was momentous in its destruction and disruption. As many as 1.2 million residents of Louisiana and Mississippi evacuated their homes, approximately 500,000 people were displaced for at least four months, and of the 160,000 children who were displaced, only 60 percent had returned to their home communities two years later.[3] The images of Katrina splashed across the media reflected a city under water, a critical infrastructure devastated, and a vulnerability revealed. This was particularly damning coming only four short years after the terror attacks of 9/11, and the revelation that U.S. systems of response and recovery were so ill-prepared. A bipartisan congressional report labeled the response to Katrina a "failure of initiative."[4]

In many ways, though, the drama of the initial storm and response pales in comparison to the enormity of the recovery. Even today, nearly a decade after the hurricane, many Gulf Coast residents are still dealing with the economic and emotional legacy of Katrina. By documenting these recovery trajectories among the children and households they profile, Fothergill and Peek have underscored some of the key individual, familial, social, and structural characteristics that distinguish each of the recovery trajectories.

The world of disaster research is small, and that of those of us focused on disaster recovery is even more intimate, so our paths and academic interests have certainly crossed with those of Fothergill and Peek (and in the interest of full disclosure, have led to significant and ongoing collaborations with the latter). Our own quantitative work revealed that five years after the hurricane, children exposed to the storm were five times as likely as comparable "non-exposed" children to be suffering from Serious Emotional Disturbance. But this finding masked the nuances of the story. Not every child was suffering; after all, two-thirds were not. Why did some children fare well and others less so? What pieces of "ordinary magic," as Ann Masten has referred to the normative characteristics of resilience common to many children, were essential for those children who were able to experience better outcomes?[5]

In chapter 6, Fothergill and Peek offer the story of Cierra, 11 years old at the time of the hurricane, to illustrate a child who was able to regain and maintain her equilibrium. As the hurricane approached, Cierra and her mother, Debra, sheltered at the New Orleans hospital where Debra worked. When the levees broke the floodwaters rose quickly, and in short order the hospital was besieged by evacuees arriving at its doors by boat, the electricity failed, and patients decompensated and died around them. After days in the failing hospital, Cierra and Debra were shuttled to the Superdome and then to Lafayette, Louisiana. Their home was destroyed, and all their possessions gone. They started life anew first in a shelter and then in a FEMA trailer in Lafayette, where they lived for three years. Initially, when Fothergill and Peek interviewed Cierra, she was bereft at the loss of all that was familiar to her: "I was missing all my family and my friends and the people that were really close to me that loved me the most." But over time, Cierra flourished in her new surroundings. She developed a diverse and caring network of friends and adult supporters and she succeeded in school; she was even awarded a prestigious fellowship to travel to Washington, DC, as a student leader. Through the detailed and evocative story they tell of Cierra and Debra, Fothergill and Peek identify the many factors contributing to her finding equilibrium, most notably "the support and assistance of advocates and institutions, with her mother as the primary conduit to these resources." This led them to formulate a critical recovery model for the resource-poor, one which includes supportive advocates; strong social and civic institutions, such as schools, relief programs, and faith-based organizations; a competent and resourceful parent or guardian; and a child willing to be an active participant in his or her own recovery. "Without all of these factors simultaneously in play," they note, "Cierra may have not found equilibrium following Katrina."

Garmezy and his protégé Ann Masten and other resilience theorists developed a "short list" of psychological attributes that promoted positive adaptation among children. The list included intelligence, self-efficacy, executive control, and a good sense of humor, among others. In looking back over 30 years of resilience scholarship, Masten and her colleagues referred to this as the "first wave" of resilience research, in which they identified individual resilience factors. The second wave explored resilience processes within individuals and across social systems, the third wave examined interventions that might enhance or facilitate resilience, and the still-emerging fourth wave has focused upon a consideration of multiple system effects, encompassing biological and social systems.[6] Fothergill and Peek bring the sociological perspective to the space straddling the third and fourth waves. Their stories and insights articulate many of the psychological and social forces at play in children's lives, and their recovery models align with evolving policy prescriptions for child-serving institutions and more generally for systems of response and recovery. In the decade since Hurricane Katrina, this country has experienced a series of domestic disasters that have focused the research community on the impact of disasters on children—the Joplin, Missouri, and Moore, Oklahoma, tornadoes, the Deepwater Horizon oil spill, and the Sandy Hook Elementary School shootings in Connecticut, among others. In the tornadoes, the children lost peers and their schools; in the oil spill the children lost access to a recreational environment and to some extent to a way of life; and in the school shooting the children lost a sense of safety and security. Fothergill and Peek's model of finding equilibrium, with its emphasis on effective and compassionate advocates and institutions and on the way that social structures and conventions manifest themselves in children's lives, can offer some guideposts for policy-makers intent on helping children resist or recover from such disasters. It goes without saying, of course, that such disasters should be prevented in the first place.

Fundamentally, though, what Alice Fothergill and Lori Peek offer in this volume is an exceptionally well crafted and meticulously researched work that advances the *voice* and *agency* of children. Perhaps it was preordained. In the weeks before Katrina struck the two sociologists had been inspired by the words of Bill Anderson, a widely known disaster scholar and legendary former National Science Foundation program officer, who had challenged the field to consider the impact of disasters on children. Anderson posed three questions to frame the research: What do disasters do to children? What is done on behalf of children? And what can children do for themselves and others?[7] Fothergill and Peek discussed the ways that they, as two young sociology professors, could respond to that call. When Katrina hit, their answer was readily at hand and they moved quickly into the field, within weeks. They were intent on interviewing the children directly as a means of expressing the *voice* of children so often absent in research studies. And they were equally committed to understanding the role of children's participation in their own recovery, their *agency*.

What Fothergill and Peek have done in *Children of Katrina* is to expertly weave three approaches in responding to Anderson's three questions: the careful ethnographic methodology of Elliot Liebow's *Tally's Corner* and Kai Erikson's *Everything in Its Path*, the methodical long-form journalism exemplified by Jason DeParle's *American Dream*, and the clear and utter compassion for their subjects that is uniquely their own. Readers of this book should take note, in appendix B in particular, of how carefully and compassionately they navigated the relationships they fostered in conducting the research for this book. They empathized with their research participants, recognized the differences, and bridged them as they could. That appendix is, in itself, a master class on qualitative techniques, as well as a thoughtful discourse on some of the thorny ethical dilemmas confronted by social science researchers.

Lastly, the three trajectories—declining, finding equilibrium, and fluctuating—that Fothergill and Peek have advanced in this book are important to the field, as is their particular emphasis on social structure and youth engagement. Hurricane Katrina was a devastating event for the country, but it will not be the last; this volume speaks for the children of Katrina, and for the children of disasters yet to come. It is critical to those of us in the fields of disaster research, policy, and practice that we not only hear the voices of these children, but also attend to them, identifying and facilitating the resources for recovery they need within themselves, their families, and their communities.

David M. Abramson, PhD, MPH
Associate Professor
Global Institute of Public Health
New York University

Irwin Redlener, MD
Director
National Center for Disaster Preparedness at the Earth Institute
Professor of Health Policy and Management
Columbia University

ACKNOWLEDGMENTS

We owe thanks to many people who helped us to complete this book. First, we would like to acknowledge the children and youth who shared their thoughts and experiences with us. We understand that trusting us enough to tell us their stories required courage, and for that we are ever grateful. We would also like to thank the family members, teachers, school administrators, childcare providers, disaster relief workers, volunteers, and others who allowed us to interview them. We promised to keep our respondents' identities confidential, and thus have changed all names to pseudonyms and altered some identifying information throughout the book. This also means, of course, that we cannot thank each participant by name here. We hope, however, that those who so patiently answered our questions understand how much they contributed to our work and to our lives.

We relied on many persons in Louisiana as we conducted our fieldwork. Without the generosity of JoAnne DeRouen, the project never would have gotten off the ground. She invited us to stay with her after we found out there were no available motel or hotel rooms along the Gulf Coast after Katrina. She also provided several contacts to persons who would later become part of the study. John and Kathleen Maloney kindly allowed us to stay in their new home in Lafayette as well as in their old New Orleans home—which had flooded during Katrina and was slowly being rebuilt— during several of our later visits to the city. New Orleans scholars and Katrina survivors Pamela Jenkins, Dick Krajeski, Shirley Laska, Rachel Luft, and Kristina Peterson gave us advice, offered local insights, and took us on driving tours around New Orleans; it was absolutely invaluable for us to see and learn about the city through their eyes.

We owe a significant debt of gratitude to Kai Erikson, editor of the Katrina Bookshelf and chair of the Social Science Research Council (SSRC) Task Force on Hurricane Katrina, for his thoughtful guidance and enduring support for this project. Kai's insights, his lengthy and intellectually generous memos, and his meticulous edits have improved the overall contributions of the work as well as the structure, flow, and sensitivity of our arguments.

We have benefited immensely from our collaboration with the scholars who make up the Research Network on Persons Displaced by Katrina. Elizabeth Fussell, Cynthia Garza, Pamela Jenkins, Laura Lein, Jacquelyn Litt,

Rachel Luft, Beverly Mason, Lee Miller, Jessica Pardee, and Lynn Weber have each contributed to this work in countless ways.

We have been fortunate to have contact with outstanding mentors throughout our careers thus far. As the devastation that Katrina had wrought became apparent, we turned to our trusted former graduate school advisor, Dennis Mileti, who encouraged us to launch this project. William A. Anderson, who was one of the first to call for more sociological research on children and disaster, inspired us and provided key insights at critical moments as the project progressed. Sadly, he died suddenly as we were nearing completion of this book. His guidance and enduring support will be missed by us and so many others, but we know his legacy will continue through the recently created foundation in his name that will expand inclusive hazard and disaster planning for communities of color.

This manuscript has gone through many iterations, and it has been improved as a result of comments from Carole Bebelle, Andrew Beveridge, Cecilia Menjívar, Bill Quigley, and William Julius Wilson, who participated in a 2010 Katrina research workshop in New York City organized by the SSRC. David Abramson read a later draft of the book and offered comments that sharpened the core arguments. We are grateful for the thoughtful feedback offered by other Katrina Bookshelf authors and SSRC Task Force mentors: Vern Baxter, Katherine Browne, JoAnne DeRouen, Ron Eyerman, Robert Gramling, Pamela Jenkins, Steve Kroll-Smith, Shirley Laska, Keith Nicholls, J. Steven Picou, Lynn Weber, and George Wooddell.

Two graduate students at Colorado State University, Megan Underhill and Jennifer Tobin-Gurley, traveled with us to Louisiana on separate occasions and assisted with our fieldwork efforts. Michelle Meyer, also a graduate student at Colorado State University at the time, helped us with various parts of the book, including conducting literature searches, creating tables and figures, and developing summaries of our research findings. Her creativity—and her generosity of spirit—made a tremendous difference in the final product. Emily Albo, John Boyne, Sarah Carlson, Alyssa Dawson, Emily Doerr, Jennifer Lambrick, Becky Peters, Krista Richardson, Jessa Vonfeldt, and Jamica Zion, all students at Colorado State University, assisted with many additional research errands on our behalf.

Meghan Mordy, a doctoral candidate at Colorado State University, deserves special recognition for the herculean effort that she undertook as we were nearing completion of this manuscript. Meghan reviewed every chapter, offering careful and incisive comments that we might have expected to receive only from a much more seasoned editor. In addition, Meghan cross-checked all of the references and helped us to round out our reviews of relevant literature. In some cases, she identified obscure references, read them, and helped us to develop them into endnotes for the book. She did a spectacular job, and we owe her many thanks.

This project was supported by funding from the Quick Response Grant Program, sponsored by the National Science Foundation, at the Natural Hazards Center at the University of Colorado–Boulder; the Midwest Sociological Society; the Department of Sociology and College of Arts and Sciences at the University of Vermont; and the Department of Sociology and College of Liberal Arts at Colorado State University. In addition, funding from the American Sociological Association, the MacArthur Foundation, and the Rockefeller Foundation, as well as support from the SSRC, allowed us to attend Katrina-focused meetings and research workshops in Boston, Montreal, New Orleans, and New York City.

We have presented portions of our research at the Natural Hazards Workshop and at the annual meetings of the American Sociological Association, the International Sociological Association, the Midwest Sociological Society, and the National Women's Studies Association. In each instance, we benefited from feedback from colleagues who organized and participated in the sessions.

We would like to thank our editors at the University of Texas Press, Theresa May and Robert Devens, for their thoughtfulness, enthusiasm, and guidance. Sarah Rosen and Molly Frisinger, who are members of the editorial team at the Press, helped guide us through the publication process with skill and grace. We also gratefully acknowledge the feedback provided by the external reviewer for the Press. We offer our thanks to Sandy Grabowski for transcribing most of the interviews in this book and to Lisa Rivero who prepared the index.

We never could have finished this book without all of the help that we received from our families and friends. Alice would like to thank her husband, Jeff, for his never-ending support and enthusiasm, and her children, Joe and Maggie, who were only six and three years old at the start of the project. For nearly a decade of their childhood, they good-naturedly accepted their mother disappearing on trips to Louisiana and glued to her laptop when she returned. Maggie drew original art for the book, and Joe served as technical advisor. Lori would like to thank her mom and dad, Bud and Cathy Peek, as well as her three brothers, three sisters-in-law, and 10 nieces and nephews, for their unending and unconditional love. She is also grateful for the many colleagues, students, and friends who discussed the book and offered encouragement. Katherine Browne and Elke Weesjes stand out in this regard. Povilas Jocas deserves special recognition for all the support and care that he offered Lori.

A final few words: as with all of our work, this book was a true collaboration. All decisions—regardless of whether we were in the field or back at our home universities analyzing the data and writing up the results—were made collectively. We settled upon the author order based on alphabetical listing. We contributed equally to the research and writing represented herein. That means we get to take mutual credit for things that readers like but also that we must accept shared responsibility for any shortcomings.

CHILDREN OF KATRINA

THE YOUNGEST SURVIVORS

For Cierra, the sound of Katrina is the sound of "people screaming." She was only 11 years old when the hurricane hit. Years have now passed since "the awful storm," but she has not forgotten how the water looked as it kept rising, how dark it was at night when there were no lights in New Orleans, or how scared she felt.

We first met Cierra and her mother, Debra, at a large disaster evacuation shelter a few weeks after Katrina. They had just been notified that they had been assigned a new Federal Emergency Management Agency (FEMA) trailer in a park outside the low-lying city of Lafayette, Louisiana. After surviving the storm, enduring a second evacuation caused by Hurricane Rita, and living in the shelter for weeks, they wept with tears of joy when they heard the news of the trailer. But this was also the beginning of new challenges that we watched unfold over subsequent years.

On an October afternoon in 2005, Cierra and Debra sat down with us in a quiet corner of the shelter and shared how their ordeal began. Debra, a 45-year-old African American native of New Orleans with a gentle voice, was part of the janitorial staff at a hospital in the city. Although her supervisors had called her in to work the day before Katrina struck, Debra still described herself as "lucky" because the hospital allowed vital employees to bring their family members with them as part of the hospital emergency response plan. So Debra brought Cierra, her only child, with her.

As the storm intensified throughout the night and as the levees began to give way on that fateful Monday morning of August 29, 2005, the hospital lost electricity and the backup generators failed. The patients, staff, and visiting family members were left with no lights and no air-conditioning. The sticky summer heat was overwhelming, and the hospital started to feel less like a safe refuge and more like a prison surrounded by a moat of rising water on all four sides. Debra rushed around caring for ailing patients, as she also kept a watchful eye on her daughter. Cierra tried to help out in the hospital, too, but mostly she waited and watched and listened.

As the day progressed, Debra and Cierra started to notice more and more people passing by the hospital in boats and on other makeshift floating devices like mattresses and large pieces of cardboard, many of them yelling for help as they bobbed up and down in the murky brown floodwaters. Conditions were deteriorating inside the hospital as well: the lower floors flooded and the elevator stopped working; fresh water was in short supply and what food there was began to spoil; and frail elderly patients were dying from heat exhaustion, a lack of electricity to power their medical devices, insufficient medicine—and perhaps, Debra thought, from fear and hopelessness.

Debra, who was exhausted and stressed to the limit, asked Cierra to stay close by her side. Several times, however, as Debra tried to help staff and patients throughout the hospital, she was separated from her daughter in the darkness and chaos. This left her terrified and searching along pitch-black, sweltering hallways for Cierra. After those frightening moments, Debra had Cierra accompany her everywhere throughout the hospital. Cierra had to watch as hospital interns struggled to carry dying patients up several flights of stairs. She overheard a nurse saying that she should give a patient a big meal because "it would be his last." She cried when the hospital sign crashed through the enormous picture window at the front of the building, sending shattered glass sliding across the tile entryway.

Cierra and Debra spent four long days and three seemingly endless nights in the hospital. Then they were rescued by boat by fellow survivors who took them to the Superdome in the heart of New Orleans. They stayed in those desperate conditions for another day as they waited for transport out of the city. At last, a van arrived and shuttled them to Lafayette, about two hours west of New Orleans. Once there, they joined a wave of tens of thousands of Katrina survivors at the Cajundome, a sports arena that was converted to a temporary disaster relief shelter. At the Cajundome, evacuees entered through double doors with a metal detector and armed guards in camouflage fatigues. They slept on the stadium floor on rows and rows of fold-out cots. Adults stood in long lines waiting for food, medicine, and temporary housing information while shelter workers and other volunteers tried to keep the children busy with activities.

Debra and Cierra had never been outside New Orleans. They had no family or friends in Lafayette, and as they would learn over the coming weeks, the rest of their loved ones were scattered across several states: Cierra's dad and his family evacuated to Texas, while her favorite aunt, her uncle, and her grandmother were separated and relocated by the government to other parts of Texas, Louisiana, and Georgia. For the first time, Debra and Cierra were truly on their own. Their rental home in New Orleans was damaged beyond repair. All of their belongings and keepsakes, including photos and Cierra's childhood artwork, achievement ribbons, and trophies, were gone. Nothing could be salvaged. Cierra's school was not scheduled to reopen until January 2006, at the earliest, and Debra had no job to return to because the hospital where she had worked was closed indefinitely.

As they told their story, Debra's brown eyes filled with tears and Cierra spoke in barely a whisper as she remembered looking out at the "dirty water" that covered her city. Even after all that they had endured, Debra and Cierra, mother and daughter, buoyed by each other and their faith, remarked that they had been "blessed" to meet the "God-sent angels" at the Cajundome, the stadium staff and other volunteers who supported them after the storm.

At the end of the interview, Cierra gently asked if she could sing us a song. We told her we would love it if she did. It was "Amazing Grace."

Cierra was one of tens of thousands of children directly affected by Hurricane Katrina. We wanted to know: What happened to these children? What did they need during the emergency response and recovery periods? Who helped them? How did they help themselves and other young people? How did their lives unfold following the catastrophe and displacement?

To answer these questions, we spent seven years studying the experiences of children and youth in the aftermath of Katrina. (For a discussion of the complexity associated with defining children and youth, see appendix A, Who Counts as a Child?) This book draws on our observations of and interviews with a group of young people who were between the ages of 3 and 18 at the time of the storm. We also spent a great deal of time with their family members, teachers and other school personnel, childcare providers, shelter workers, and many additional persons tasked with caring for children. *Children of Katrina* presents the stories of some of the youngest survivors of the storm to describe what happened to them. We also draw upon official statistics and published studies to further explore the myriad ways that children's lives were shaped by Katrina.

MISPERCEPTIONS ABOUT CHILDREN, YOUTH, AND DISASTER

Children differ from one another in countless ways. Nevertheless, adults in our society often share preconceptions about children as a category. Thus, before we present the stories in this book, it is important for us to clear the blackboard of some of these misleading perceptions and portrayals of children.

First, many members of the public subscribe to the *resilience myth*. From this vantage point, children are seen as being blissfully unaware of, and mostly unaffected by, disasters. The assumption is that children, like little rubber balls, will "bounce back" quickly from the harmful effects of disaster, even with no outside support or assistance. In essence, no matter what happens, the belief is that they are somehow naturally resilient and will be okay.

A second misconception regarding children and disaster is in effect the opposite of the first. We refer to this as the *helpless victims myth*. This worldview casts children as powerless and fragile, always rendered completely incapable of acting in the face of disaster. As such, children are perceived as being in need of multiple specialized interventions to ensure their safety and recovery from catastrophe.

A third misconception, the *disasters as equal opportunity events myth*, paints extreme events as impacting all children equally. Those who subscribe to this myth fail to recognize that the youngest members of any given society, just like adults, face significant race, gender, and class inequalities that shape their everyday experiences and life chances. This viewpoint also ignores the variability among children, which is influenced by age and developmental processes as well as levels of cognitive and physical ability.

The danger of these misleading conceptions is that they may distort all that adults see—or do not see—when they attempt to assist, engage with, or study children and youth in the aftermath of disaster. Our research suggests that children's vulnerabilities as well as their capabilities are affected by an array of factors. Children do have unique needs that must be met in the aftermath of disaster. At the same time, they make important contributions and have many strengths, which are all too often misunderstood or overlooked altogether. In times of trouble, the fates of children are every bit as complex as those of adults.

OUR APPROACH

This book grew out of a commitment to listen carefully to children's voices to assure that those voices "contribute to discussions and interventions that affect their lives."[1] Prior to the 1980s, children were "written about but rarely consulted."[2] The sociology of childhood aims to correct this scholarly shortcoming by conceptualizing children as constructive members of society who both shape and are shaped by their social circumstances.[3] This perspective recognizes that children need to be listened to and responded to, but first, they must be encouraged to speak.[4]

Although the sociological study of children and youth has undergone a major paradigm shift over recent decades, much of the research on children and disaster continues to rely on parents', teachers', or clinicians' reports of children's well-being.[5] There is obviously value in these approaches to studying children in disaster contexts, yet there are many reasons to be cautious of relying solely on adults' answers to survey and interview questions about children's actions, attitudes, and overall health.[6]

Indeed, some adults' descriptions of children's behaviors are not rooted in systematic observation. Instead they may be based on vague impressions or generalized characterizations.[7] Moreover, how children act in the presence of their parents, teachers, or health care providers may be quite different than how they behave when they are not under the watchful supervision of adults. Children sometimes tell adults what they think they want to hear, rather than what they actually feel or believe. They may also withhold information to "protect" their parents. As a case in point, Mekana, one of the teens in our study, said she would "hide" her true emotions and hold her "feelings in" when she was around her mom. In the months following Katrina, her mother was angry and struggled with depression. Mekana eventually reached a point where she would simply tell her mother, "I do not feel like talking about this," so that she could avoid crying or "being all sad" in front of her. This example and the other aforementioned potential shortcomings of adult-centric research on children help explain, in part, why adults consistently underreport children's levels of post-disaster distress and underestimate children's preparedness levels and recovery needs.[8]

Our research adopts the basic premise that "the most direct way to learn *about* children is to learn *from* children."[9] We view children as capable actors who are the "best authorities on their own lives."[10] At the same time, we recognize and respect the need to seek information from the adults in children's lives who support, care for, raise, teach, and socialize them. Children are obviously strongly influenced by their families and the broader social contexts in which they live, and thus "a child's voice cannot be disembedded from the living world, it must be framed as part of the world."[11] With this admonition in mind, and recognizing the value of multiple viewpoints, we also draw on interviews and observations with numerous adults who helped or otherwise worked with children before and after Hurricane Katrina.

Hurricane Katrina is widely considered one of the worst disasters in our national experience. Even a brief accounting of the scope of physical destruction and human suffering inflicted by the storm helps explain why Katrina will likely long hold that grim distinction. Louisiana, Mississippi, Alabama, Georgia, and Florida were directly affected by the wind, rain, storm surge, and tornadoes that Katrina generated. The government declared 90,000 square miles—a stretch of land the size of Great Britain—a federal disaster area. Eighty percent of the city of New Orleans was submerged after sections of the inadequate levee system failed. Entire communities along the Mississippi Gulf Coast and in rural Louisiana were wiped off the map.

An estimated 1.2 to 1.5 million persons fled their homes in the days and hours preceding Katrina's landfall. In New Orleans, another 100,000 or so people were unable or unwilling to evacuate.[12] Many were eventually plucked from rooftops and highway overpasses amidst the floodwaters. Over 1,800 persons—most of them in Louisiana—died from drowning, exposure, or medical conditions that worsened lethally as already ailing individuals waited for help that never came.[13] Katrina remains the most costly U.S. disaster on record, generating over $135 billion in insured and uninsured losses across the affected region.[14] More than a million Gulf Coast housing units and at least 10,000 businesses sustained substantial damage or were completely destroyed.[15]

The vulnerability of children was starkly apparent in Hurricane Katrina. A dozen children in Louisiana perished in the hurricane itself.[16] An untold number lost loved ones, were orphaned, or were left homeless. Over 5,000 children were reported missing for a time, many of whom were separated from their family members for days or weeks and in some cases for months.[17] Children in foster care faced particular challenges, as often important records and parent contact information were lost or destroyed.[18] The U.S. Department of Education estimated that some 372,000 students were displaced from their home communities in the states directly affected by Katrina,[19] while 160,000 remained dislocated years after the storm.[20] Many of these displaced children were from New Orleans, where more than two-thirds of the school district's 300-plus buildings were considered to be in "poor" or "very poor" condition due to storm damage and long-neglected maintenance issues.[21] Research suggests that nearly half of all children in Louisiana who survived Katrina suffered from serious and ongoing mental health issues.[22] Officials in New Orleans also reported that drug-related deaths and suicides increased among young people as a consequence of the disaster.[23]

It is worth pausing for a moment to note that even as devastating as Katrina was, for many children along the Gulf Coast, the hurricane was not their first traumatic, stressful, dangerous, or life-threatening experience. In fact, tens of thousands of those children had experienced "daily disasters" associated with poverty, violence, failing schools, and other associated social problems well before Katrina. In Louisiana, nearly one-third of all children were living in poverty before the storm, with disproportionately high percentages of children of color living below the poverty line.[24]

One post-Katrina survey of 700 displaced children from New Orleans revealed that an astonishing 60 percent of these young people, most of whom were African American, had witnessed a shooting or a murder prior to the hurricane, almost half had seen a drug sale, and 42 percent had seen physical violence between a man and a woman.[25] Even before Katrina, New Orleans public schools were among the worst-performing in the nation. They were also highly segregated by race and class, enrolling five times more African American students than the national average (93.4 percent of New Orleans's public school students were African American at the time of Katrina) and twice as many low-income children (80 percent of the students were poor enough to meet eligibility requirements for free or reduced-cost lunch subsidies).[26]

These numbers depicting some aspects of life from both before and after Katrina are meant to give a general sense of the contours of the region and the persons most affected by the storm. But these statistics do not do justice to the full effect of the catastrophe. Facts and figures, printed dispassionately in black and white, do not convey what Katrina has meant to the people whose lives were upended, whose families were displaced, and whose homes and communities were changed forever.

It was against this backdrop that we began our study. We started our fieldwork in October 2005, just over a month after the storm came ashore. By that time, we were relatively seasoned observers of disaster. We had each conducted research in New York City after the 9/11 attacks, and one of us had studied flood-soaked communities in the Midwest. We were trained at the same university as sociologists and disaster researchers and we had worked closely together before.

Thus as we prepared to travel to Louisiana soon after Katrina, we had some idea what it is like to interview persons who have just experienced numbing losses, and we wanted to approach the research with the utmost sensitivity.

We were aware that past research had revealed that disaster studies rarely cause emotional burdens for the participants, and in fact, scholars have argued that disaster survivors may actually experience some benefits from telling their stories to researchers. Yet, we still gave careful thought to how our study would affect the children and families at the center of our inquiry. (For more discussion of these research and ethical issues, see appendix B, Studying Children and Youth in Disaster: A Note on Methods.)

With a sense of caution and these considerations in mind, we boarded planes in Vermont and Colorado, the states where we lived, and flew to Louisiana for the first of many field research trips. The ethical concerns, and the responsibility that we felt toward the children and adults who ultimately participated in our study, never went away, however.[27] We tried to always remain sensitive to this dynamic, while also adjusting our methods accordingly. We were committed from the beginning to studying children over the long term. Although the one-time case study method predominates in disaster research, we knew that if we wanted to understand how Katrina was influencing the lives of children, we would have to remain in the field for a longer period to develop enough trust to be granted permission to watch those processes unfold over time.[28]

We also wanted both breadth *and* depth in this research. Therefore, on the one hand, we sought out interviews from as broad an array of individuals as possible. We purposefully sampled children from diverse racial and ethnic backgrounds and of different social classes and included an equal number of boys and girls in our study. All totaled over the seven-year period of this research, we studied well over 650 children between the ages of 3 and 18 years old and interviewed approximately 100 adults. The sample of adults included family members, teachers, pastors, friends, neighbors, city officials, social workers, relief workers, American Red Cross volunteers, childcare center staff, school administrators such as principals and vice principals, and other school staff, such as nurses and custodians.

Because we had varying levels of contact with the children in the larger sample, we divide our youngest respondents into focal, core, secondary, and tertiary groups (see figure 1.1).

1. The *focal sample* includes seven young people whom we studied in the most depth (details are included below).
2. The *core sample* includes 25 children whom we formally interviewed and observed at multiple points in time over seven years.
3. The *secondary sample* includes 60 additional children whom we formally or informally interviewed and observed at one point in time.

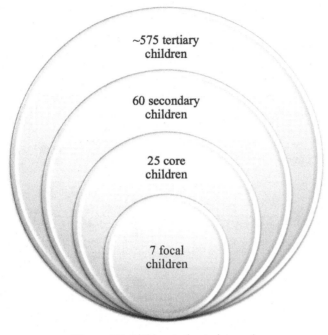

Figure 1.1. Children in the study sample

4. The *tertiary sample* includes a group of approximately 575 children whom we observed but did not interview formally. We watched them go about their lives and/or had informal conversations with them in classrooms, on playgrounds, in school lunchrooms, in disaster relief centers, and in public places such as shopping centers and restaurants.

Because so many families were displaced after the storm, our research took us not only to New Orleans, but also to Baton Rouge, Lafayette, New Iberia, and Scott in Louisiana and to Denver, Colorado, and Dallas, Texas (see figure 1.2). (It is important to underscore that the individuals in our sample evacuated and were temporarily displaced to many more locations than those listed here. These were the places where we were able to actually visit in order to collect data.) Traveling to these sites gave us more insight into the attitudes of the "receiving communities" toward the evacuees.[29] Some of these receiving communities were welcoming at first, but then relations became strained when the displaced stayed longer than expected and needed work, housing, public transportation, and social services.[30]

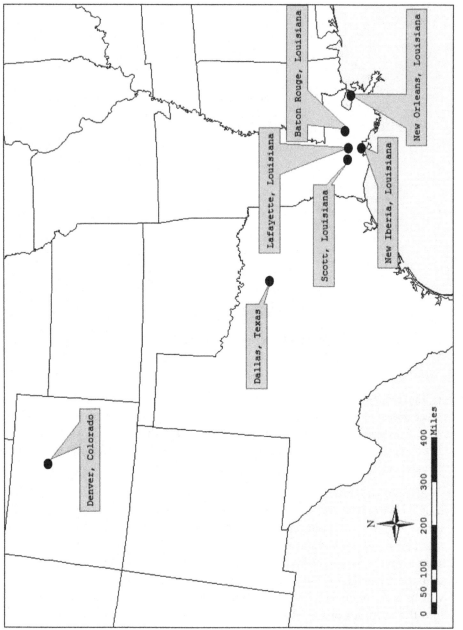

Figure 1.2. Field research locations

We made over a dozen field visits over the seven-year period of this research, which culminated in well over 1,000 hours in the field. We visited schools and childcare centers in all of the study locations so we could talk to teachers, counselors, school administrators, and childcare providers. We participated in youth-organized and youth-led community events such as a neighborhood community garden celebration and a forum to talk about police actions in public schools. We spent time in disaster shelters, emergency relief centers, FEMA trailer parks, and later in the temporary and permanent homes of evacuees. We observed hundreds of children going about their daily lives in disaster shelters, playing in school yards and parks, eating lunch in school cafeterias, and worshipping together during church services. The data that we accumulated allowed us to understand the broader context of Katrina.

In order to ensure depth in our research, we eventually identified a sample of 25 core children and their families whom we decided to follow closely over time—seven of whom we refer to as the "focal children" in this book. Drawing this smaller sample and engaging in what Annette Lareau calls "intensive immersion"[31] allowed us to more fully understand the experiences of boys and girls; children of differing racial and class[32] backgrounds with diverse family structures; and children and youth of a range of ages—from toddlers to teenagers and young adults—when Katrina happened.

We chose these focal children, in part, because of their dissimilar disaster experiences and the fact that they were subjected to differing degrees of loss and displacement as a consequence of Katrina. Each of the focal children and their families lived in New Orleans prior to Katrina. All families experienced some damage to their housing (ranging from minor water damage to complete destruction) and all were displaced for some length of time after the storm. Some returned to the city in the months or years after the storm, but some never did.

Between 2005 and 2012, we interviewed each of the seven focal children at least five times. We also interviewed their siblings, parents, grandparents, and other extended family members, friends, and staff from their schools, typically on multiple occasions as well. This involvement provided us with a deeper understanding of the many consequences of Katrina and of how dynamic post-disaster trajectories unfold over time.

Thus, the largest group, the tertiary sample, provided us with a strong sense of the population we were dealing with and the problems they were experiencing. Our job after that was to progressively zero in, to learn more about the themes identified. We began that process with more contact and conversations with 60 children selected for the purpose because they seemed to us reasonably representative of that larger population. We then turned to a core sample of 25 whom we interviewed and observed more closely, and finally we focused on 7 young people from the core sample because we felt that we had to get down to the personal grit so that we could convey the situation accurately. For us to discuss the circumstances of hundreds of young people would be to shift into a world of statistics and numbers. To get to know seven young people well and to be able to relate their stories is to get down to matters of *tone* and *texture* and *feeling*. In effect, then, the focal children who are centerpieces of this book are voices selected from a chorus of hundreds because their experiences reflect a much larger population. We tell their stories, but they are speaking for multitudes. Moreover, while they are exceptional young people in many ways, they are not the exception. Instead, we selected them for more in-depth study and research because their experiences represented the much broader sample.

In order to gain richer, more in-depth data, we used a number of prompts and methodological approaches with the young people in our study (see appendix B). For example, we had the children and youth work through a series of flash cards where they took the lead and guided us through key aspects of their lives and post-Katrina experiences. We asked some of the older children to trace their own or their siblings' recovery process, while we had the younger children draw pictures for us about their storm experiences (see figure 1.3).

This book is intended for interested general readers as well as for anyone who studies or wants to learn more about Katrina and the social impacts of disasters, the sociology of childhood, family studies, or qualitative research methods. Most broadly, this book is for anyone who is curious about how Katrina affected the lives, families, housing and educational contexts, and communities of the youngest survivors of the storm. It also is for those who hope to learn more about what helped or hindered children's recovery, as well as about the ways that children and youth were actively engaged in assisting after the storm.

We have organized the book primarily around the seven focal children and their post-disaster experiences. Before we share their stories, however, chapter 2 helps to place this study in a larger context; it offers an overview of what is currently known about children, youth, and disasters. We also introduce the theoretical perspectives that guide this work, as well as a number

Figure 1.3. Drawing of "what Katrina looked like," by Joseph, 10 years old

of concepts that we used or developed over the course of the research as we sought to make sense of the children's lived realities.

The main body of the book is divided into three parts, each with a section introduction. Those parts illustrate the three trajectories we identified in our research: the *declining trajectory*, the *finding-equilibrium trajectory*, and the *fluctuating trajectory*. The empirical chapters in each section describe the personal characteristics, pre- and post-disaster life circumstances, and experiences of the focal children and their families (table 1.1). In chapters 3 and 4, you will meet Daniel and Mekana, who represent the declining trajectory. Chapters 5 and 6 tell the stories of Zachary, Isabel, and Cierra, who fit the finding-equilibrium trajectory. The stories of Jerron and Clinton, whose recovery processes align with the fluctuating trajectory, are featured in chapters 7 and 8. In each of the focal children's chapters, we include observational and interview data with the children themselves, as well as with family members, peers, and with key adult figures such as teachers and pastors in their lives. In each instance, we detail the people and places that were most significant to the focal children. We also discuss various other factors, such as access to health care, religious or extracurricular involvement, and neighborhood context, which ultimately shaped the children's trajectories.

The book concludes with a summary of the key findings from this long-term study, with a special emphasis on the personal and social forces that increased children's vulnerability both before and after Katrina. We also discuss those factors that helped aid their recovery and describe the myriad

TABLE 1.1. Select characteristics of the seven focal children

Child's name	Gender	Race	Age on August 29, 2005	Class status	Family structure
Clinton	Male	Black	4 years old	Low income	Single mother, two siblings; father not involved
Jerron	Male	Black	6 years old	Working class	Single mother, one sibling, aunt, maternal grandmother; father and paternal grandmother highly involved
Zachary	Male	White	7 years old	Middle class	Parents not together; time split evenly between mother and father; no siblings
Isabel	Female	White	9 years old	Middle class	Two-parent household, two siblings
Cierra	Female	Black	11 years old	Working class	Single mother, no siblings; father not involved
Daniel	Male	Black	12 years old	Poor	Single mother, two siblings; father deceased
Mekana	Female	Black	15 years old	Working class	Single mother, one sibling; father minimally involved

ways that children helped themselves, as well as others, in the aftermath of the catastrophe.

We spent nearly a decade researching and writing this book. We learned a great deal along the way from the children and adults who were generous and trusting enough to share their stories with us. It is our sincere hope that readers, when they get to the end, will have a much better sense of what the children of Katrina experienced and how this catastrophic event affected their worldviews, their aspirations, their relationships, and their overall life circumstances.

2

CHILDREN, YOUTH, AND DISASTER

Clinton scoops up a handful of the purple play-dough that we had brought with us to the trailer park in Baton Rouge. He stares at it briefly and then begins to gently roll it in his small hands.

"How old are you now, Clinton?" "Five," he says quietly. He keeps his almond-shaped brown eyes cast downward, working intently on molding the dough. We had last seen him a year and a half earlier when he and his mother, Karen, were staying in a Baptist church shelter for Katrina survivors. It was now the spring of 2007, and they had been living in a two-bedroom trailer supplied by FEMA for just over a year. They gave us a tour of their trailer home, and then Lori interviewed Clinton at a small play table in the back bedroom while Alice caught up with Karen in the living room.

> LORI: Do you remember the church shelter where you and your mom stayed after Katrina?
> CLINTON: Yup.
> LORI: What was it like?
> CLINTON: It was good.
> LORI: Why was it good?
> CLINTON: Because it had all kinds of people. That was good.
> LORI: What kind of people?
> CLINTON: Good people, Miss Lori.

We continue on for a while, making shapes with our respective lumps of play-dough, talking a little, not rushing. "What do you think of this bird's nest?" Clinton looks up and thoughtfully examines the mushy purple figure. "I like the eggs," he notes in a matter-of-fact voice.

He does not say much, which is typical for the younger participants in our study, but some key things emerge: He likes the trailer home where he and his mother now live, and he especially appreciates having his own room.

He does not know where his dad is now, but thinks he might be in Texas. He misses his older brother, Aaron, who recently moved to Dallas to be closer to his girlfriend. Clinton's sister, Brandi, calls him every afternoon from her college dorm room "just to check in." He and his mom sometimes attend church services on Sunday mornings. His best friend is in his kindergarten class at his new school. They and the other children their age play a game called "Igloo" at recess and in the afternoons. And, these days, he has both good dreams and bad dreams.

After about 30 minutes, Clinton shows signs that he is winding down with the play-dough. "One last question: What did you need the most after Hurricane Katrina?" "Pancakes," he responds, totally straight-faced. Then he grins and laughs. This signaled that the interview was coming to an end. Clinton began taking stock of his creations—a sandwich, a snowman, taco shells, a snake, and a banana peel. After completing the inventory, we cleaned up the play-dough and put each bright color back in its container for Clinton to keep.

"I'll show you my room," Clinton volunteers, and so we walk to the back of the trailer toward a bedroom door on the left. It is a small room with a twin-size mattress on the floor, two narrow wooden dressers under the window, and a cardboard box in the bottom of the closet. Clinton shows off his Diego wall poster (a cartoon character from the popular children's television series *Dora the Explorer*) and the new Spiderman sheet set that covers his mattress and pillow.

Clinton describes the various items in his room, eventually pointing to a shiny gold medal that he recently won. "Is it okay to take a photo with you and your medal?" "Sure, that's okay," Clinton agrees, as he picks up the medal and holds it proudly in front of him. "Ready? One. Two. Three." After the flash goes off, Lori and Clinton put their heads together to view the image in the digital camera screen. Clinton offers an approving smile and a nod. He seems especially happy to know that we plan to send him and his mom prints of the shot. They lost all of their photos and other possessions in Katrina, so having such a gift has a new and special meaning.

When the interviews are finished, the four of us pile into our rental car and head out to visit Clinton's school. We also make a stop to see the convenience store where Karen works the night shift. We take them to an early dinner at a local Southern-food buffet restaurant, and afterward we drop them off at their trailer. Hugs all around as we say our good-byes and promise to come see them again soon.

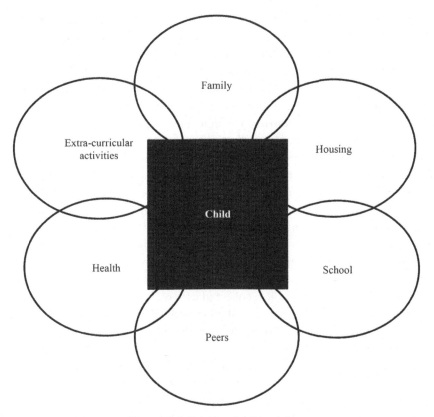

Figure 2.1. Spheres of children's lives

SPHERES OF CHILDREN'S LIVES

Over the years as we listened to Clinton and the other young people in our study, we learned a great deal about their lives and how they were disrupted as a consequence of Hurricane Katrina. To make sense of these various facets of their lives more fully and completely, we sought to understand their pre- and post-disaster experiences in context.[1]

Life is lived on a continuous field, but it is hard for observers like us to see the whole in its entirety or to convey it in words to others. So we have grouped the questions we asked and the answers we received into some of the spheres into which the flow of human life can be reasonably divided (see figure 2.1). We are not breaking the whole into distinct parts so much as locating centers of gravity, so to speak, in which social activities and things of meaning in children's lives tend to cluster.

Through interviewing the children and youth—as well as their family members, friends, teachers, and other caregivers—we sought to understand how the event affected children's individual health and well-being, family situations, housing and neighborhood contexts, schooling, peer relationships, and extracurricular activities. We asked all of our interviewees about their pre-event circumstances as well as about how things did, or did not, change after Hurricane Katrina. We offer some examples in the paragraphs below of the types of data we collected in an effort to understand spheres of children's lives in disaster recovery (also see appendix B).

To understand the *family sphere*, we examined the children's relationships with parents, siblings, grandparents, and other members of their extended family networks. We asked about how often the children saw or spoke with different family members and how that changed after Katrina. We explored how close they were with their family, how they spent their time together, how family members—including siblings—helped and supported each other, and how they coped with being separated from family in the Katrina aftermath. We also collected data on family structure, parental employment, social class status, and other important characteristics to help situate the family in the broader social landscape.

We explored the *housing and neighborhood context* in which the children and their families lived both before and after Katrina. We gathered data on housing type and location, finding out if it was owned, rented, or government subsidized, and whether it was transitional, temporary, or permanent. We inquired in interviews and observed firsthand the communities where the families lived, looking for the social and physical markers as to whether they were safe and child-friendly places with parks, open space, and other children nearby. For each family, we attempted to map the proximity of the household to important institutions and amenities, such as schools, churches, health care providers, grocery stores, and parents' workplaces. Because all of the children in our sample were displaced at least once, if not multiple times, after Katrina, we were able to compare housing and neighborhood contexts as families transitioned from one place to the next.

We gathered data on many aspects of the children's *educational experiences*, including information on how many schools they had attended pre-Katrina and during the post-disaster displacement and recovery period, what the demographics of those schools were, and how the children and their parents felt about the quality of the institution. We also asked about educational aspirations and collected school performance data based on children's grades and test scores. We visited the focal children's schools, as well as many other schools in the region, and observed how young people interacted with their peers and their teachers and school administrators, how the classrooms were arranged, and what resources were available. We kept track of how many and what school-sponsored activities children in the sample were involved in.

To understand the role of *peers and friends* in their lives, we visited children at school and at play, watched how they interacted with their fellow students, and asked them about their friendship groups. We explored how they were affected by leaving friends at one school and joining new peer groups at new schools after Katrina, and how they handled the long-term separation from pre-Katrina friends and classmates in New Orleans. Generally, we wanted to know how disruption to their established networks of friends affected their outlooks and other relationships, how peers influenced the recovery process for them, and how they helped and provided support to one another.

We also focused on children's *physical and emotional well-being.* We asked children and their parents how often they felt happy or sad, how they coped after Katrina, and who they turned to for emotional and instrumental support. We observed the children in many settings and took note of their engagement with others, their energy levels, and sociability. We tracked changes in health conditions we could see ourselves, such as obesity, and anything they, or their family members, seemed to be struggling with, such as depression or anxiety. We documented whether the children and their families had access to medical professionals and were able to receive regular care and treatment. In addition, in light of mounting evidence suggesting that a parent's mental health is one of the best predictors of a child's health and well-being, we collected data from the parents about their own health status and also interviewed health care providers in New Orleans to understand broader trends regarding post-Katrina health outcomes.[2]

The sixth area that we explored, *recreational and extracurricular activities*, encompassed things such as the children's interests and hobbies and their involvement in clubs, sports teams, religious institutions, employment, and other activities that were not necessarily school or family centered. We were interested in the role that children's participation, and their access to supportive mentors and positive peer influences through various activities, played in their recovery. We attended church services with them, observed their sporting events, watched their dance routines, and talked to them about their afterschool projects like chess club, 4-H, drama club, and flag football, among many others.

The most catastrophic events—like Hurricane Katrina—have the potential to simultaneously and seriously disrupt the "embedded, interdependent, and constantly interacting" spheres of children's lives.[3] As psychologists Carl Weems and Stacy Overstreet observe in reference to Hurricane Katrina and its aftermath, "Threats to basic needs emanated from every ecology surrounding the child, increasing the risk for negative developmental outcomes and mental health problems."[4]

With this in mind, we focus in the subsequent chapters on the factors and social forces that either encouraged or impeded children's post-disaster recovery experiences in each of the above areas or spheres. We also explore how the overlapping spheres surrounding the child might have shifted or expanded to absorb the shock of the disaster, as well as places where links between spheres were disrupted or destroyed altogether due to the loss and displacement.

CHILDREN, DISASTER, AND CUMULATIVE VULNERABILITY

Of all the media coverage of Hurricane Katrina, some of the most heart-wrenching and unforgettable images were those of children's suffering.[5] One widely reproduced photograph captured a young boy in Mississippi, sitting atop the flattened wreckage of his former home, head in his hands, crying. Another was an aerial photograph of a baby being rescued by helicopter. Tears streamed down the mother's face as she handed her diaper-clad infant off to a member of the U.S. Coast Guard. Television crews recorded a boy sobbing uncontrollably after National Guard troops refused to allow him to take his small dog with him as he boarded a bus out of New Orleans. Cameras rolled on as girls and boys in the Superdome joined adults in organizing and chanting "We Want Help! We Want Help!"

Child rights advocates have observed elsewhere that children's suffering is often used as a tool to increase media viewership and to garner financial support for disaster relief missions; yet, as Amer Jabry asserts in the report "After the Cameras Have Gone," there is rarely any sustained attention to children's ongoing needs. We worry, too, that fleeting images of children's sadness and loss can become so personal and individualizing that viewers may be overcome with sympathy, rarely pausing to ask: why was that child in harm's way when the disaster struck?

Those most vulnerable to disaster are those who have the fewest economic and social resources available to prepare for, respond to, and recover from extreme events.[6] A substantial body of research now exists clearly demonstrating that those who live at the margins of society suffer disproportionately negative consequences in disasters.[7] To date, scholarly research has focused primarily on racial and ethnic minorities,[8] low-income individuals and families,[9] and women[10] as the groups most prone to loss and harm in the context of disaster. Yet, it is also important to consider vulnerability that exists as a result of age.[11]

Globally, children make up approximately 50 percent of those who are affected by disasters,[12] and the risks they face are mounting. Overwhelming evidence suggests that climate change will lead to more frequent and severe weather-related disasters in the immediate future. This means that more children will be exposed to floods, droughts, windstorms, heat waves, and other extreme events. Children, who are more likely to be poor than any other group of people, also occupy some of the world's most dangerous spaces, with disproportionate numbers living in earthquake zones, on floodplains, and in coastal regions vulnerable to hurricanes, tsunamis, and sea level rise. The advocacy organization Save the Children estimates that during the 2010–2020 decade, as many as 175 million children every year are likely to be adversely affected by disasters.[13]

Although children in the least developed countries around the world are most at risk when disaster strikes, children (as well as adults) in the United States are also experiencing an escalation in disaster-related threats. Over the past five decades, the number of federal disaster declarations has tripled.[14] The United States now regularly experiences "billion-dollar disasters" that destroy homes, businesses, schools, and other critical infrastructure while displacing increasingly large numbers of people. The new century ushered in an era of catastrophe for Americans—from the 9/11 attacks, which claimed nearly 3,000 lives, to Hurricane Katrina, the most costly and the sixth deadliest disaster in national history.

When disasters occur, children may experience a range of vulnerabilities: psychological, physical, and educational.[15] These vulnerabilities tend to be interconnected and mutually reinforcing. Thus, for example, children who suffer physical injury or have their life threatened in disaster are more apt to experience emotional distress and to miss school.

In the most comprehensive review of the disaster mental health literature to date, Fran Norris and her colleagues report that children are more severely affected by disasters than adults: all of the school-age children surveyed in post-crisis settings experienced some level of mental health troubles after a disaster.[16] These effects differ by age and stage of development.[17] Toddlers and other young children may have nightmares, refuse to sleep alone, be irritable, and have temper tantrums. Adolescents and teens are more likely to engage in risky behaviors such as smoking or drinking after a disaster, to develop eating and sleep disorders, and to be less interested in social activities and school.[18] Children who are unable or unwilling to communicate their distress, and those with the least developed emotional coping skills, tend to suffer the most severe and prolonged traumatic reactions after disaster.[19]

Children, and especially those living in developing countries, are physically vulnerable to disaster, as evidenced by their disproportionate death and injury rates. In the 2010 Haiti earthquake, tens of thousands of children were killed, while hundreds more lost limbs crushed by buildings. The 2010 Pakistan flooding left millions of children homeless and at risk for disease outbreak. Many children around the world attend school in unsafe structures, as was tragically brought to light in the 2008 Sichuan, China, earthquake, which left perhaps as many as 80,000 children dead after their school buildings and homes collapsed. In the United States, children experience different levels of risk to different hazards at different ages: infants and children age 0–4 are most likely to die of exposure to extreme heat, those age 5–14 are most likely to die in cataclysmic storms and flood events, and teens and young adults age 15–24 are most likely to die of excessive cold.[20] In intentional acts of community violence or terrorist disasters, such as the 1995 Oklahoma City bombings, the 1999 Columbine High School shootings in Littleton, Colorado, and the 2012 Sandy Hook Elementary School shootings in Newtown, Connecticut, there were large numbers of fatalities among children and youth. Recent research has demonstrated that children both in the United States and abroad are at risk for abuse, violence,[21] and trafficking after disaster and in conflict settings.[22]

Disasters may disrupt children's educational process and diminish their long-term educational outcomes as well. Although educational vulnerability has received comparatively limited attention, this is a critically important area because it involves a particular risk that school-age children in disasters face that most adults do not. Children's intellectual growth is hindered when they miss school or cannot concentrate in the classroom, and children who have to change schools are more likely to drop out altogether.[23] Disasters may cause students to lose valuable instruction time, and when they fall behind in their academic work they may find it difficult, if not impossible, to catch up.[24] When teachers are overwhelmed, upset, and distracted, they may not be able to provide the care and support that are necessary for children's sense of safety and security within schools.

Age alone does not make a child vulnerable to disaster. Instead, age interacts with many other factors that may render children particularly at risk.[25] Moreover, vulnerability factors tend to build over time and cluster together, resulting in what we refer to as *cumulative vulnerability*. The disaster may be a stressor or crisis on top of other serious issues or constraints the child is already confronting. For instance, a racial minority child with a physical disability who lives in an impoverished household in a hazard-prone area will experience multiple, intersecting forms of social, environmental, physical, and economic vulnerability that will shape that child's experiences—and likelihood of survival—in a disaster. Thus, it is not solely age or race or ability status or poverty or hazards exposure, but how these risk factors *accumulate* in a child's life; it is as if each "piece" of vulnerability affects how the vulnerability puzzle connects and then is experienced by the child. The children with the highest levels of cumulative vulnerability are at greatest risk for a range of negative psychological, physical, and educational effects and have the hardest time rebounding from disaster.

To understand cumulative vulnerability in disaster, it is useful to examine the characteristics of children at three periods of time: before, during, and after a disaster (see figure 2.2). Again, a child's vulnerability is shaped by an array of personal and situational characteristics that render some children more vulnerable when a disaster occurs. Past research has found that these characteristics include gender, race, ethnicity, types of coping and communication skills, and family levels of income, wealth, and education. For example, being poor and a member of a racial minority increases a child's vulnerability, and globally, girl children are more likely to die in a disaster, while in the U.S. boys are more at risk for death.[26]

In addition to this array of personal characteristics, a child is situated in a "pre-disaster environment" that also partially determines disaster outcomes. As seen in the figure, vulnerability is increased by residing in poor neighborhoods, living and/or going to school in unsafe structures, living in a single-parent household, having limited or no access to health care, and being malnourished or having a poor diet.[27] A child's pre-disaster vulnerability is further intensified by residing in a particularly hazardous area such as in a floodplain, a coastal area vulnerable to sea level rise, or a seismically active zone.

When disaster strikes, a child who was vulnerable prior to the event is more at risk during the actual disaster. The child and his or her family are less likely to evacuate or to have a life-threatening evacuation. In the worst-case scenario, the child could perish during this period.[28] Those who survive the event are more likely to be separated from family members, to lose loved ones, to be injured, to endure the destruction of their home and community, and to witness death or other traumatic incidents. The extent and intensity of the child's exposure contributes to higher levels of immediate physical suffering and short- and long-term psychological distress.[29]

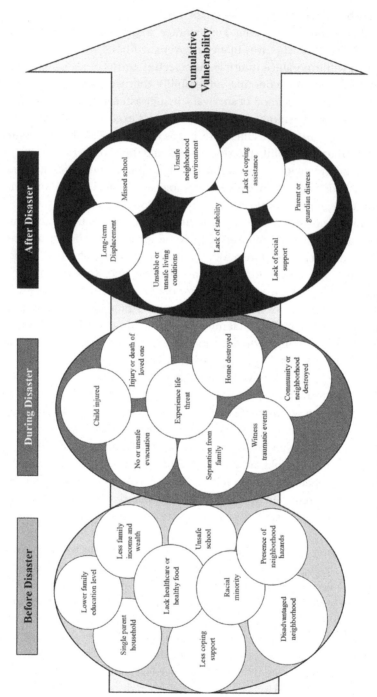

Figure 2.2. Cumulative vulnerability before, during, and after disaster

Finally, a child survivor may be vulnerable in the third stage, the aftermath of the disaster. The most at-risk children are more likely to be displaced after the event, to have family and friendship ties severed in the displacement, and to miss out on schooling. As illustrated in figure 2.2, other factors affecting children's post-disaster environment and potentially amplifying their vulnerability are associated with coping assistance, living conditions, levels of safety and protection, perceived and/or received social support, and the distress felt by parents or guardians.

In understanding the concept of cumulative vulnerability, it is important to keep in mind that it has a *temporal* component, in that vulnerability unfolds over time. But it also has an *additive* component: the more that risk factors accumulate, the more likely children are to experience developmental delays, poor mental or physical health, or negative educational outcomes. Thus, the children who experience the highest levels of cumulative vulnerability are most often the same children who suffer the most serious and enduring effects of disaster. In chapter 3, we tell the story of Daniel, who experienced high levels of pre- and post-disaster cumulative vulnerability, while in chapter 4, we focus on Mekana, a teen who experienced a serious "piling up" of vulnerability in the Katrina aftermath.

RESOURCE DEPTH AND RESOURCE MOBILIZATION

When we consider the vulnerability of children in disasters, it is also important to understand the ways in which some children are less vulnerable and are able to be shielded from some of the most serious and damaging effects. We found that children and families who either had more pre-disaster "resource depth" or who were able to engage in successful "resource mobilization" after the disaster were less vulnerable.

Helpful resources come in many forms—financial, social, cultural, educational, and personal. Wealth, high levels of education, and occupational status, for example, are resources that can also generate a familiarity and ease with bureaucratic institutions or the ability to easily gather information through professional networks. These resources, then, are related in important ways to what is called social and cultural capital.

The concept of social capital, as advanced by theorist Pierre Bourdieu, refers to the connections one has with other persons that can be counted on in times of trouble. In Bourdieu's words, social capital is "the aggregate of actual or potential resources which are linked to possession of a durable network of more or less institutionalized relationships of mutual acquaintance and recognition."[30] Thus, the amount of social capital individuals can potentially possess is determined not only by their total economic capital but also through other forms of capital linked to the person through their networks.[31] Put simply, one's social connections have value and can have real benefits, such as friends helping with employment opportunities.

Cultural capital, a related concept, addresses how families' and children's cultural know-how and habits shape their interactions with and evaluations by peers, teachers, doctors, and other people in the child's or family's social network.[32] Sociologists Annette Lareau and Elliot Weininger depart from prior definitions of cultural capital, which rely on measures such as how often families participate in high-brow cultural activities (for example, visiting museums, going to the theatre, reading literature, etc.). Instead, the authors argue that cultural capital is found in "micro-interactional processes whereby individuals' strategic use of knowledge, skills, and competence come into contact with institutionalized standards of evaluation."[33] In other words, cultural capital describes an individual's overall approach to interacting with others. It is an important concept for understanding why some individuals are able to get what they want out of interactions with authority figures or bureaucratic agents at institutions such as schools, employment agencies, or even disaster recovery offices.[34] Adults and children who are able to interact with authority figures in ways that the institution expects, prefers, or demands are more likely to be positively evaluated and achieve their ends. In schools, children's placement in groups organized by ability (such as reading groups), their treatment by staff and teachers, and the peer groups they form are some of the consequences of these interactions and evaluations.[35]

Disaster scholars have studied how structured inequality and a lack of social and cultural resources can constrain choices and be highly detrimental in a disaster situation.[36] Conversely, it is clear that financial resources are helpful in preparation, evacuation, and rebuilding, and social support and other less tangible, but still critically important, resources can assist survivors emotionally.[37] In this book, and especially in part II, we offer examples of how the depth of the resources that children and their families had available to them before Katrina was critical. It was not only the amount of resources that mattered, but also the degree to which people accessed and used them; this included their interactions with other people and institutions. Further, the durability of networks strengthened resources and often created more of them.

Resource depth is undoubtedly conditioned by demographic characteristics (social class, race, gender, etc.) that differentially shape children's and

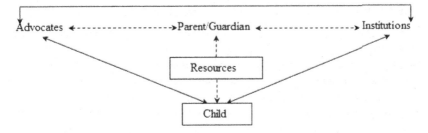

Figure 2.3. Model of mobilizing resources for children and youth

their families' capacity to respond and recover in disaster. In our analysis, the concept of resource depth includes, but goes beyond, what is traditionally seen as resources, such as savings or paychecks, and incorporates some of the ideas of social and cultural capital. For our purposes, we define *resource depth* in disasters as a generous amount of personally and socially valuable resources, coupled with the accessibility, transferability, longevity, and applicability of those resources.

Resource depth, therefore, is critical. The children in our sample who were most resilient to Katrina tended to have the greatest pre-disaster resource depth. That might sound obvious. Our job here is to show what the process was like—the *details* of it, the *tone* of it, the *feel* of it—for those who lived through it. Our job is also to explain the exceptions to the pattern. For example, a limited number of children and families whom we studied with little pre-disaster resource depth and limited social and cultural capital nonetheless were able to lessen their vulnerability post-disaster. They did this through effective resource mobilization. We found that mobilizing resources for the express benefit of children happened with the support and assistance of advocates and institutions and a parent or other adult as a primary conduit to these resources. With this combination, children experienced fewer damaging effects of the disaster.

In this model of *resource mobilization* (see figure 2.3), advocates, such as disaster shelter workers, teachers, and church pastors, and the resources and commitment of various institutions, such as integrated schools and housing programs and policies that assist the working poor, make a difference in disaster-affected children's lives. In addition, a child's parent or another caring adult may become an instrumental intermediary for locating and mobilizing resources for the child. This adult often serves as the critical link between the child and available resources.

As illustrated by the arrows shown in figure 2.3, post-disaster resources can flow in various directions. The initial move toward securing resources may begin with an advocate, parent, child, or an institution, or several of them together in a team-like fashion. In addition, the process of getting vital resources to the child may also take different paths. In some cases, the securing of resources may be ongoing, and the paths may look different over time. For example, the process could start with the parent, but then the advocates continue the process and thus the "flow" subsequently takes on a different path, perhaps directly from institution to child.

NOT HELPLESS VICTIMS: UNDERSTANDING CHILDREN'S CAPACITIES

During our first post-Katrina trip to Louisiana, we spent many hours at a large shelter for evacuated individuals and families. While we were there we observed thousands of people coming and going, security guards standing at the main door, Red Cross volunteers sitting at various tables, cots neatly made and lined up in every room, and bags and boxes with belongings on the floor.

As we spent more time there and in other shelters, one thing that struck us was the way in which older children took care of younger ones: how they held their hands, wiped their faces, bounced them on their laps, played games. We also watched children drawing pictures and writing in their journals—sometimes with adult prompting, and sometimes without—to make sense of the disaster. These boys and girls were *active agents*, not passive victims.[38] They were helping others and contributing to their own recovery.

The children we watched were certainly not totally helpless or incapable. Children—including those living in the most precarious environments— have considerable *capacities*, here defined as strengths, skills, knowledge, abilities, gifts, and aptitudes. Sociology of childhood scholars were among the first to point out that children help create their own social worlds while simultaneously influencing the larger society in many ways. Sociologist William Corsaro makes the case strongly: children are creative social beings who produce their own unique cultures and also add to the production of society as a whole.[39] Research on low-income children, for example, has documented the ways in which they engage in numerous self-care behaviors at young ages, and also take care of other children.[40]

Yet, to date, disaster research has been more likely to focus on children's vulnerability than on their capacities. In 2005, just before we began this research, William Anderson published an influential paper where he noted how invisible children have been in disaster research and challenged social scientists to more carefully consider young people's experiences in crises.[41] Anderson was one of the first disaster scholars to problematize the "children as vulnerable victims" paradigm. He hypothesized that children could use technology to communicate risk, could take protective actions, and could help themselves and others. Organizations such as UNICEF, Plan International, Save the Children, and World Vision have also promoted the idea that children are active agents and hence should participate in disaster planning, response, and recovery activities.[42] In 2011, the United Nations International Strategy for Disaster Risk Reduction organized their International Disaster Risk Reduction Day around the theme of encouraging and empowering children and youth to "step up for disaster risk reduction."[43]

Over the past several years, more reports and research studies have highlighted the important roles that children have played in warning and protecting others in disaster. A young girl from Britain, for example, persuaded adults to move to higher ground in the 2004 Indian Ocean tsunami. Her knowledge and action helped save many lives.[44] Similarly, in the 2011 Japan earthquake and tsunami, a student opened a window to establish an evacuation route for his classmates. When the trembling stopped, hundreds of children ran together to higher ground in anticipation of the dangerously high waves from the ocean that would follow.[45] Adolescents also assisted and comforted younger children during the event.[46] In Bangladesh following a slum fire in 2004, children who had previously formed a group called the "Child Brigade" helped to distribute food, provide medical assistance, and find affected children's families.[47] In Hurricane Katrina in 2005, second-generation Vietnamese American youth helped translate warnings and recovery information for their non-English-speaking family members.[48] After the 2010 Haiti earthquake, the *New York Times* reported that orphans were caring and cooking for other orphans in the wreckage of the disaster.[49]

We recorded many specific examples of children's capacities and contributions in our years of research. These included the case of one of the focal children in this study, Daniel, a 12-year-old African American boy from New Orleans. Daniel, his one-year-old sister, Alexandria, and his mother, Deirdre, were living far below the poverty line when Katrina made landfall. Deirdre had only a fourth-grade education and had long struggled with mental and physical health issues. Her husband (and the father of her children) had recently passed away after a battle with cancer and since his death she and the children had struggled to make it, moving in and out of homeless shelters and other temporary housing arrangements.

In August of 2005, the family was living in a government-subsidized housing complex on the outskirts of New Orleans. The three-story, nondescript white building was located on a busy four-lane road and was surrounded by fast-food restaurants, pawn shops, and other small businesses. As Katrina approached, the family had no family or friends nearby to rely on, no extra cash, and no car. The city provided no transportation to the thousands of residents who had no vehicles or other means to get to safety.[50] Daniel and his family had no place to go to escape the storm, and they had no way to make it to the Superdome, the "shelter of last resort."

Daniel explained to us how the night before the storm something "did not feel right" to him, so he suggested to his mother that the three of them move into the back room, which was away from the living room windows and thus, he felt, the safest room in the home. Here is how he told us the story:

> The night before the storm, it was raining and so stormy, I thought it was just like another storm, not Hurricane Cindy, but [Tropical] Storm Cindy, something like that. We survived Cindy before Hurricane Katrina.[51] I went to sleep that night, and something didn't feel right, so I said, "Mama, why don't we get up and move to the back room, put the mattress in the back room?" Because that's the safest place in the house.

The family awoke the next morning to the alarming sound of things falling outside. The floodwaters had already reached the apartment building and it was now evident that the family was going to have to flee to survive. But Deirdre was too scared to enter the water, fearing that loose electrical wires would electrocute them. Daniel, with his soothing voice and gentle demeanor, calmed her and explained how the maintenance man had turned off the electricity in advance of the storm.

As the water continued to rise, Daniel peered out the front door, saw the dark water rushing down the street, and knew he had to come up with a plan to escape with his mom and Alexandria. Improvising, he took a bed sheet, wrapped up his baby sister, and strapped her with the ends of the sheet to his mother's chest. Taking a deep breath, the three of them headed out, with Daniel in the lead. As they descended the outside staircase, part of the outside wall of the building crumbled down in their path. They kept going; they plowed through the waist-deep water, walked for many blocks, and got Alexandria safely to higher ground. This is where they would then spend days waiting to be evacuated from the flooded city. Daniel's courage and ingenuity helped to save his sister's, and perhaps his mother's, life.

Daniel's story—as well as many other examples that we uncovered in our research—reveals that children's knowledge and creativity could be better utilized during all phases of the disaster lifecycle. Moreover, if children were better integrated into disaster planning and response efforts, they could likely help reduce their own as well as others' vulnerability to disaster.[52] Children alone, however, cannot solely reduce the harmful effects of disaster. As can be seen in Daniel's evacuation story, his actions produced a positive outcome, and the family survived. But the story could easily have ended in tragedy, despite Daniel's efforts. City officials in New Orleans knew that many low-income and working-class families had no way to safely evacuate and yet did not carry out any comprehensive plan to keep them safe. As a result, Daniel and many other children were failed by this municipal policy collapse. As we discuss in subsequent chapters, children and youth need a web of protections: families with resources who support them, positive peer networks and strong school systems, sound government policies that encourage disaster mitigation and citizen engagement, access to health care, and well-prepared safe neighborhoods and communities that recognize their needs and capacities.

DYNAMIC POST-DISASTER TRAJECTORIES

Over the seven years of the study, we were often asked whether the children we were following had "recovered" from Katrina. What were their lives like now? Were they still suffering from the aftereffects? Were they better or worse off than before the storm?

These were difficult, if not impossible, questions to answer. Although recovery is often envisioned as an "outcome" or an "end point," we, like many others working in this field, view post-disaster recovery as a process. It is something that unfolds over time. It often occurs in uneven ways, with progress in some areas of life, and setbacks in others. Because recovery happens across time, space, and varying dimensions of social life, there is no simple way to declare when children, families, and communities have reached "recovery." Moreover, in an event as destructive and disruptive as Katrina, the effects may be lifelong and even transmitted across generations, thus further complicating our theoretical and applied understanding of recovery.

Because we maintained contact with the core sample and the focal children in our study and continued to observe and interview them over time, we were able to follow their life trajectories, to observe how others supported children to help them in their recovery path, and to understand the ways that children contributed to their own recovery. It is clear that children's recovery is a variable and complex phenomenon that involves the possibility of the accumulation of negative risk factors or positive adaptive qualities. Brenda Phillips, building on the work of Dennis Mileti, writes about recovery in terms of communities, defining recovery as a process of "putting a disaster-stricken community back together."[53] FEMA states that "recovery continues until all systems return to normal or better."[54] According to Daniel Aldrich, for individuals, recovery is the "gradual resumption of normal daily routines for survivors."[55]

For the purposes of this book, drawing from some of the aforementioned definitions, we conceptualize *children's recovery* as when a child has a semblance of stability, routine, well-being, and predictability in all spheres of life. With that in mind, we fully acknowledge that there are many children living at the margins of society before disaster strikes, who live a daily existence lacking any stability, sense of routine, or predictability. We also document, however, that disasters can and do open up windows of opportunity for change, but this takes time, care, effort, and dedicated resources. This is a challenge we return to in the conclusion of this book.

In our years of research, we identified three post-disaster patterns among the children whom we studied over time. Below, we describe what distinguishes these patterns. Before we proceed, it is important to emphasize that in all cases, the children in our sample went through some period of decline after Katrina: the disruption and destruction were so overwhelming that all participants experienced some negative effects. Indeed, because of the extensive flooding that New Orleans endured, all of the children in our study were displaced from their homes and had to evacuate their city and live in a strange place.

While every child experienced some level of decline, the depth of the decline, and the length of time that children struggled varied significantly. This is what made their post-disaster trajectories distinct. The vulnerabilities the children brought with them into the disaster strongly influenced their post-disaster trajectories, of course, but did not seal their fate. Some children had individual dispositions and capacities that helped them cope with the stress and rebound more quickly from the crisis. Other children received extra support in critical moments from concerned adults and advocates who took action on their behalf.

The three trajectories that we saw most often are defined below and shown in figure 2.4. In considering these trajectories, it is important to keep the following in mind. First, these three trajectories represent general trends and patterns in the post-disaster process. Second, and in light of this

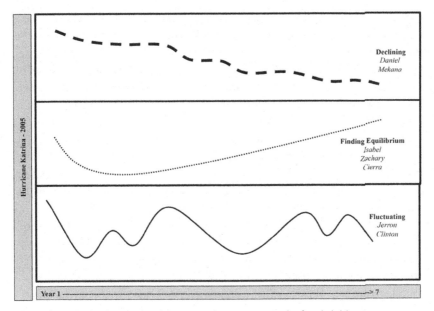

Figure 2.4. Post-disaster trajectories among the focal children

aforementioned point, the trajectory lines shown in figure 2.4—as well as the ones that appear in subsequent sections of the book—are meant to be illustrative of the general pattern and not to represent exact data points at exact moments in time. Third, each child we studied exhibited some individual variation from the pattern we have assigned him or her. This means that there was variation within the trajectories as well as across them. The trajectories are ideal types in that each one captures certain elements that were most common among the cases we observed. We discuss these trajectories in much greater detail in the following chapters in an attempt to underscore the commonalities and variance among children and youth who fit the same trajectory.

1. Declining trajectory. The lives of children we classified as "life trajectory in decline" had the highest levels of pre-disaster vulnerability and ongoing instability afterward. But we also observed children who were in more or less stable situations before the disaster whose post-disaster lives were marked by rapid increases in instability and vulnerability. Regardless of where they started, all of the children who fit this trajectory experienced an accumulation of risk factors and lost many protective support systems after the storm.

This trajectory strongly suggests that pre-disaster circumstances and children's class, race, and family structure matter. But these variables do not wholly explain or predict this particular trajectory. Children's exposure to the disaster as well as how their recovery unfolded over time also matter. When children were displaced multiple times to faraway places; when they were forced into unfamiliar and hostile new environments; and when their caregivers, siblings, or other family members began to struggle emotionally, economically, or otherwise after the storm, so too did the children. Moreover, their levels of vulnerability in all, or nearly all, aspects of their lives were serious and ongoing. What differentiated these children—and made them most vulnerable—was that they experienced simultaneous and ongoing disruptions in all the key spheres of their lives for years after the storm.

2. *Finding-equilibrium trajectory.* After an initial period of disruption and minor or even major decline, the children who fit into this classification either returned to a familiar stable place in their lives or were able to attain a new kind of stability with assistance from supportive adults, newfound advocates, and/or institutions dedicated to helping them. These children were likely to have the greatest resource depth to draw on in terms of personal, social, and financial support. Those who did not have high levels of resources within their own families received the most significant and meaningful post-disaster interventions, which helped them to mobilize resources and to progress on their recovery path.

3. *Fluctuating trajectory.* The children and youth who fit the fluctuating trajectory experienced a mixture of stability and instability, in two different patterns. Some children who did well in one critical area (such as schooling) but poorly in another (such as housing) would become unstable and problems would ripple through other areas of their lives, creating a lack of alignment across key spheres, with resultant instability. Other children and youth in this trajectory experienced an even more constant and rapid state of flux, shifting from decline to equilibrium in all spheres at the same time, in a wave-like motion. Importantly, one of the factors that kept the children who fit this trajectory from moving into a more sustained decline was the presence of an *anchor*, a consistent supportive and stabilizing force within their lives.

As figure 2.4 shows, the recovery process is dynamic. *Trajectories*, by our definition, entail active processes that unfold over time, at different speeds and rates, and across different dimensions of children's lives. In our work, we sought to determine how and why children followed different trajectories after Katrina. Since the children in our research were diverse in terms of their ages and their racial identities, social class backgrounds, gender, and family structures, we take into account how those factors influenced their trajectories. For instance, when the disaster happened, the children and youth were at different points in their lives and had differing amounts of social support.

In many ways, studying children and youth in a post-disaster setting is like studying something that is growing and changing before your eyes. Psychologist Bridget Franks found that disasters change the contexts in which children are developing, and those changed contexts can then alter the course of the children's development in a reciprocal fashion.[56] Yet, our knowledge of their pre-Katrina life circumstances enabled us to see how the catastrophe accelerated preexisting negative and positive trends, testing the children's capacity to cope, or, in some cases, providing them with resources and social ties to begin new, positive trajectories. The trajectories and the focal children's experiences are presented in the next three sections of the book.

DECLINING TRAJECTORY

For some children, disasters either speed up or set in motion a pattern of decline that is marked by serious and ongoing instability. This instability may occur in one or all of the key spheres of these young people's lives: family, housing, school, friendships, extracurricular and recreational activities, and health and well-being. Of the three dynamic post-disaster trajectories that we identified in our research, the declining trajectory, as the term suggests, involves the children who are most susceptible to an array of negative outcomes.

In many instances, but not all, we found that children who struggled after Katrina were the same children who lived in precarious and unstable positions before the disaster. Their households had serious financial troubles, often involving at least one parent who was unemployed and unable to find a good job; their housing situations were insecure and their neighborhoods were unsafe; and their families had unreliable access to transportation, health care, or healthy food. Katrina essentially exacerbated a set of already highly difficult circumstances.

But these were not the only children who were at risk for decline after Katrina. We also observed children who had been in more stable situations before the disaster but whose post-disaster lives were marked by rapid increases in instability and vulnerability. These children experienced a similar accumulation of risk factors and lost many of the protective support systems that had provided a cushion before the storm. Some of these children experienced life-threatening evacuations, were displaced to faraway places, were forced into unfamiliar or even hostile new school and peer environments, or were exposed to new and negative peer influences. In many cases, their caregivers or other family members began to struggle physically, emotionally, financially, or otherwise after the storm. The children were left with few tools or resources to pick up the pieces after the disaster. What

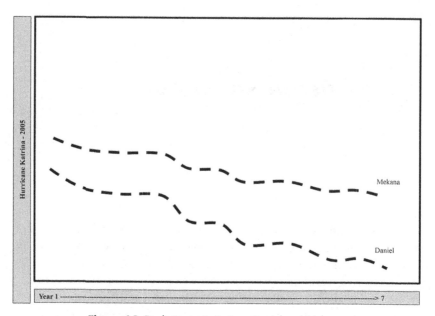

Figure I.1. Declining trajectories—Daniel and Mekana

happened to them during and after the storm acted to negate many of the advantages they had at their disposal before.

In this section of the book, we introduce Daniel and Mekana, whose post-Katrina experiences are examples of life trajectories in decline. Their stories follow the general patterns we discuss above, but they also bring to light important variations that can occur. Figure I.1 compares their pre-Katrina positions and their post-Katrina trajectories.

Of all the children in our study, Daniel was living in the most unstable situation before the storm, as you will see. Daniel's vulnerability was cumulative and his life was marked by a series of continuous shocks and setbacks both before and after the disaster.

Mekana was also vulnerable in many ways, like Daniel, but her pre-disaster situation was not nearly as dire. Rather, her story speaks to the mostly unrealized fragility in her life before Katrina and the distress related to how quickly things crumbled after the disaster. Indeed, Katrina altered nearly every aspect of her life and set her on a declining trajectory. Unlike Daniel, she did not appear to be in a constant state of crisis before the disaster. But the pieces and linkages that made Mekana's life work were more tenuous than anyone realized.

Daniel's and Mekana's stories illustrate how children and youth can slide down an unstable trajectory that both *stems from* and *creates* cumulative vulnerability. Their stories are different in many ways; what they share in common is an accumulation of disadvantage and a sharp downward decline in the disaster aftermath. It is crucial to remember that there are tens of thousands of children along the Gulf Coast who endured experiences similar to those of Daniel and Mekana. After Katrina, the unequal circumstances of their lives also very likely became more amplified and, in many ways, more cruel.

3

DANIEL
CUMULATIVE VULNERABILITY
AND CONTINUING CRISES

Daniel Taylor was 12 years old when Hurricane Katrina slammed into the Gulf Coast. We met him and his family soon after the storm and spent seven years tracing his post-disaster recovery.

To begin, a few words about this brave boy whom we watched grow into a young man. He is a heavy-set African American with a round face, large brown eyes, and a big and bright smile. His dark brown hair is often cropped short, although when it grows out and he cannot afford to get it cut, he likes to have his mother braid it into cornrows. His mom, Deirdre, describes him as a "well-mannered boy" who "respects everybody." We agree. From our first encounter, his thoughtfulness and maturity struck us as unusual for a child of his age. He is also quite sharp, loves to sing and play music, has a great sense of humor, reads a lot (a fan of Harry Potter), and dotes on his much younger sister. Daniel makes friends easily at school and in church, a skill he developed over the years as he moved from place to place. This talent for establishing friendships and finding supporters became essential after Katrina, as he and his family struggled through multiple displacements, economic instability, homelessness, and periods of separation.

THE CRISES BEFORE THE CATASTROPHE

Daniel lost his father, Leonard, in December 2003. He was only 11 years old when his dad died of cancer and related complications; his older brother, Caston, was 16 years old at the time, and his mother was seven months pregnant with Daniel's little sister. The family had long struggled financially, often just scraping by on Leonard's meager salary as a taxi driver and Deirdre's on-again and off-again work. They had experienced serious bouts of insecurity when Daniel was young. But Leonard's death pushed them deeper into a life of crisis and into what Laura Lein and her collaborators refer to as the "basement of extreme poverty."[1]

It was the loss of his father that marked the turning point in Daniel's young life. He went from a relatively stable existence to one where his mother often could not provide her family with the most basic and critical necessities: housing, food, health care, and support for their education. Hurricane Katrina would only serve to send him deeper into crisis and onto a downward trajectory.

Daniel's sister, Alexandria, was born in February 2004, just months after Leonard died. This was a time when Deirdre desperately needed help. She had some family living in New Orleans and surrounding areas in Louisiana and Mississippi, including two sisters and their families, but they were not close in an emotional sense and they often fought with one another. Without these connections, Deirdre tried to care for her children on her own. This differentiated her family from many other low-income African American households in New Orleans and elsewhere, which often depend heavily on such kin networks for assistance and care.[2] Without the material and emotional support that such networks can provide, Daniel's mother struggled on a daily basis with a number of serious issues.

Like many living at the margins, the Taylor family had trouble finding a good, safe home even before Katrina destroyed much of the affordable housing stock in New Orleans. Soon after Leonard's death, the family began moving in and out of a successive string of rundown rentals, often located in the most dangerous and crime-ridden neighborhoods in the city. They also spent time in homeless shelters, lining up early in the day in hopes of securing beds and a warm meal that night. Daniel explained that they had "been having it hard, even since before Katrina, going from pillar to post, from shelter to shelter, stuff like that."

Although creative and deeply committed to the well-being of her children, Deirdre had significant mental health issues. She would often become paranoid and angry. We would periodically receive long, rambling, profanity-laced handwritten letters and emails from her, where she would accuse everyone from a family member to a former neighbor to the governor of Louisiana of attempting to harm her and her children. She had been victim of a violent crime when she was younger and was perhaps suffering from some kind of traumatic disorder, although she was never diagnosed or treated by a mental health professional.

Deirdre had lost her own mother when she was only three years old and was mostly raised by what she described as an unkind aunt. Deirdre told us in person and in letters and emails that she had been abused by other family members as a child. She never finished elementary school and had no marketable credentials and few skills that could keep her gainfully employed. She also had no car and no driver's license to transport her to work, so when she did find employment, it had to be on a bus route or within walking distance of where they lived. That was itself a looming problem, because her family moved in and out of so many places in such a short period of time. Just before Katrina, Deirdre was employed as a cashier at McDonald's, but, as had happened so many times before, she lost the job after coming into conflict with her supervisor.

Deirdre's lack of stable employment meant no private health insurance and no regular annual checkups for Daniel or his siblings. Although they were, as Deirdre said, "blessed" to be mostly in good health, she and the children suffered from a lack of preventive care. For example, Deirdre had lost several teeth and would often experience debilitating toothaches, only going to see the dentist when she was in too much pain to function.[3]

The Taylor family also regularly did not have enough to eat, and when they did have food, it was often purchased prepackaged snacks from a nearby corner store or gas station. Daniel tended to go to school hungry, but he told us that he tried to keep his focus in class so he could keep his grades up and "do well." It was hard, though, as he was often worried about his mother's mental and physical well-being and other things like "where we were gonna sleep or how we were gonna eat." He also, on occasion, would miss school due to toothaches and other chronic health problems that went untreated.[4] Daniel was clearly living in crisis long before Katrina.

LEFT BEHIND

"There it is!" Deirdre shouts as we drive by a small, three-story apartment building located off a four-lane highway on the outskirts of New Orleans. Alice is driving our rental car and Deirdre is sitting in the front passenger seat, craning her neck to get a better view. Lori, Alexandria, and Daniel are squeezed into the backseat peering out the windows attentively.

On this day, nearly six years have passed since Katrina came ashore and the levees broke, stranding the Taylor family and tens of thousands of others who were unable to get away. They had told us the story of their dangerous and frightening evacuation many times before, a story that we recounted in chapter 2, but we had never seen the actual site where they were living when the waters started rising.

Daniel and Deirdre could still recall every detail of those traumatic days in 2005. The two of them and Alexandria were alone in their apartment the evening before Katrina made landfall (Daniel's older brother, Caston, had moved out and was living in California by that time). They hunkered down and prepared to ride out the storm in their one-bedroom apartment. The mayor of New Orleans at the time, Ray Nagin, had issued the first-ever mandatory evacuation order for the city earlier in the day, but many residents, the Taylors among them, had no car, no money, no real experience of life outside New Orleans, and no place to go.[5] As they listened to the wind pick up outside and the rain beat down on the windows, then, they prayed and waited.

Late that night and after listening to hours of ominous warnings on the radio, the family finally fell asleep together in the back room of their small apartment. Hurricane Katrina officially made landfall at 6:10 a.m. on Monday, August 29. The storm veered to the east of New Orleans, battering less populated coastal areas in southeast Louisiana and across the Mississippi Gulf Coast with vicious winds and a massive storm surge. New Orleans was missed by those winds and that surge, but as the flood control system circling the city began to fail, water gushed into neighborhoods, slamming into houses near the levees with the force of freight trains. The Taylor family was fortunate to live on the second level of their three-story apartment building, but as they watched the floodwaters begin to rise rapidly, they realized something was seriously wrong.

Deirdre was scared. They had lost power, they had not been able to afford to stockpile emergency supplies, and the water all around them was rising rapidly. It was Daniel, as we noted earlier, who devised a way to tie his toddler sister, who obviously could not swim, on to his mother so that they could evacuate safely. With Daniel in the lead, they descended their apartment steps into several feet of contaminated water, walked through the city, and made their way to a hospital, where they sought safe refuge. After five nights of sleeping on the floor of a hospital room, the three of them were finally evacuated by emergency responders. Crouched on the floor in the back of a large white panel van, Deirdre held Alexandria in her lap and Daniel leaned on his mother's shoulder. They stayed close together like that as the family was taken to a shelter in Baton Rouge.

As we sit in the car and Daniel and Deirdre continue to rapidly recount their evacuation story to us, Alexandria stares out the window. She is now seven years old, a "big girl," as she likes to call herself. But she was only a year and a half when they lived in that tiny apartment and evacuated as the floodwaters rose. She does not remember any of the details that her mom and brother share with us. But this is her story, too. She listens attentively and looks up at the building. She holds Lori's hand and squeezes it tight. She was too young to know how terrified Deirdre and Daniel were that morning, how frightened they were for her safety, but she understands now as the car falls silent.

PILLAR TO POST: POST-DISASTER MOVEMENT AND HOUSING INSTABILITY

Daniel had people who loved and supported him, but his post-Katrina story is one of continuing instability in all of the major spheres of his life. And these instabilities acted to exacerbate one another because they were part of a continuous web. A shock in one area of his life rippled across to the others. For example, when the family was forced to move out of one housing unit, Daniel and his sister had to change schools, make new friends, build new relationships with teachers, and learn to navigate new, sometimes hostile, neighborhoods.

Many of the issues that Daniel experienced after Katrina can be traced to housing. The Taylors had struggled with homelessness and unsafe housing conditions before the storm, and those challenges only worsened after Katrina. The fact that many families have unstable housing situations prior to disasters is one that has not been fully considered in the literature, which all too often assumes that for individuals and households to recover, "they must reestablish permanent housing."[6] For families that had no permanent housing before a disaster, what does "recovery" look like? What about when there is nothing to "reestablish" because there was no stability beforehand? Daniel and his family's struggle with housing underscores the importance of these questions.

In the seven years that we followed them, the Taylor family lived in disaster shelters, hotel and motel rooms, with extended family, in apartments and rental homes, in government-subsidized single-family housing, in homeless shelters, and on the streets. Figure 3.1 traces Daniel's and his family's movements across space, offering a summary of the number of moves that the family endured following Katrina.

After being evacuated from New Orleans by the federal government, Daniel and his family stayed for about two months at a shelter in Baton Rouge. They felt fortunate because, unlike many families, the three of them were able to stay together as they were transported out of the city and then relocated to a temporary disaster shelter. Soon after their arrival in Baton Rouge, they received their one-time $2,000 assistance check from FEMA.

These were emergency funds, meant to help evacuee households purchase basic necessities and, if necessary, secure transport to a different place.

The Taylor family used some of those initial funds to travel by bus to New York City. This was just a temporary diversion and was not intended as a permanent move. They then used their remaining funds to get the family, again by bus, back to Baton Rouge and the shelter. Then they left again for Los Angeles, where Daniel's older brother, Caston, was living. Deirdre "wasn't that close" to the rest of her family, and since they had no cell phone, they were not in communication with Daniel's aunts, uncles, and cousins during the weeks after the disaster as they were traveling from Louisiana to New York to Louisiana again and then to California. Little did they know that their family members along the Gulf Coast were frantically searching for them during this time, fearing that they had perished in the hurricane. When Daniel turned on the television one day and saw photographs of his and Alexandria's faces posted on CNN as "missing persons" from Katrina, he realized that "we had to call in and tell [my aunt] that we were all right." Daniel understood that his extended family had thought they were dead; this only further emphasized the horror of the evacuation from the flood-waters that they had so recently experienced.

The Taylor family stayed in California for about two months, moving from Caston's apartment to a shelter to a rundown long-term motel. They felt "stuck" and decided to leave. Deirdre, who was unable to find a job, was worried that if she stayed in California she would have to collect welfare, something she had done before and hoped to never do again. Also, the neighborhood where they were staying was, according to Daniel, "a very poor area" where there was "mostly drugs and stuff like that," so they "had to move from out of there."

During this time in California, Daniel was not in school because his mother worried that he would be killed in the nearly all-Hispanic school that he would have attended in the neighborhood where they were temporarily living. Deirdre had heard too many stories of African American evacuee children from New Orleans being beaten up and seriously harmed in the temporary schools they entered after the storm.[7] With all these worries in mind, the family returned to Louisiana in late December of 2005.

Although the Taylors never moved as far and wide again as they did in those months immediately after Katrina, they continued to move back and forth between Baton Rouge and New Orleans. During their initial return to Louisiana, they went back to the same church shelter in Baton Rouge that had been established for families dislocated by Katrina. Although persons of all races and ethnicities were welcome, the shelter ended up

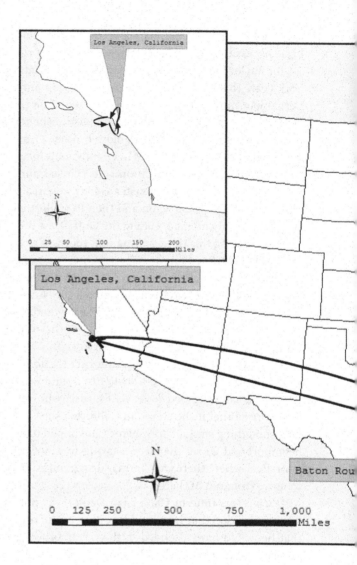

Figure 3.1. Daniel's multiple post-disaster moves by location

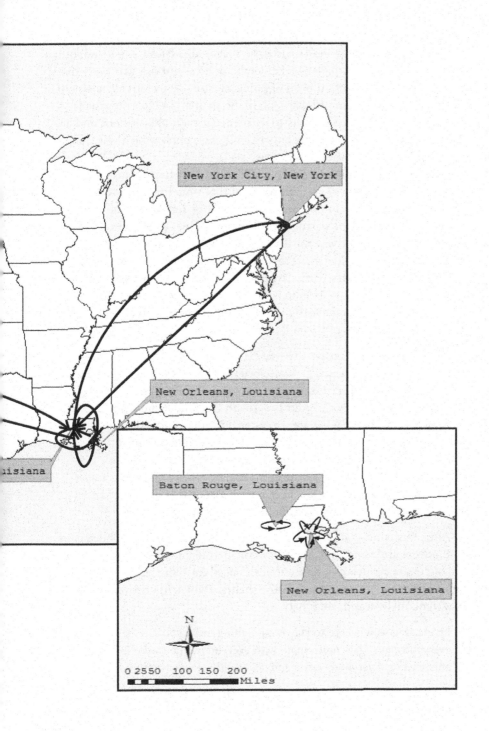

New York City, New York

New Orleans, Louisiana

uisiana

Baton Rouge, Louisiana

New Orleans, Louisiana

N

0 2550 100 150 200
Miles

serving all African American families (this was perhaps due to the fact that the church's leadership and congregation were all African American, but it also speaks to the broader racial demographics of those who were displaced after Katrina and in need of public shelter). The church leadership offered Deirdre a minimum-wage job in the shelter (an offer they made to all "guests" there), helped Daniel to enroll in a local middle school, and allowed Alexandria to attend the on-site childcare center, which was staffed primarily by Katrina evacuees, for free.

Daniel and his family were comfortable in the shelter because they felt protected and respected. They all spoke of that time fondly. Several other displaced families we interviewed in the shelter felt the same way and praised Mrs. Myers, the pastor's wife, who was chief of operations at the shelter, for the humane way she treated them and the work she did on their behalf. In the end, the Taylors were the last family to move out of the shelter. In fact, according to Mrs. Myers, whom we interviewed twice after Katrina, they almost had to "force them to leave." During one of our discussions, she recalled Deirdre's reluctance to move on from the shelter and into a FEMA trailer on the outskirts of Baton Rouge:

> Deirdre would not take one. She said she was going to stay here. Everybody else said, "We're going." We helped them move with our trucks and everything. And then she said, "I'm not going. I'm not going anywhere." So I said, "Oh, my gosh." And I met with the [leadership team at the church] and I said, "What are we gonna do?" They said, "She said she's not leaving," and I said, "We're closing our shelter." We wanted to close for lack of use, lack of demand. So I talked to [Deirdre] and I said, "You know, you're not taking this trailer for yourself, you're taking this trailer for your children. Think about how much better off they would be." I even [took her in the car] up to see the trailer.

After this conversation, Deirdre reluctantly agreed to leave the shelter and move with Daniel and Alexandria to an available trailer. Even though she understood the arguments about the need for more stable living conditions, her family had felt safe at the shelter. Daniel, in fact, remembered how thankful he was during that time:

> Just having somewhere to stay is something to be grateful for. We met everybody, got real comfortable with everybody. They were like family after a while. Everybody just blended in . . . there was a community feel.

Although the trailers were intended to be only temporary housing—18 months was the longest that the federal government expected evacuees to live in them—Daniel and his family were overjoyed once they actually made the move. He described the moment when they first entered their trailer:

> DANIEL: [My mother] let me open the door with the key. And when I got in, I was like, "Do we have to share a room with roommates or something like that?" She was like, "No." I said, "It can't be that all this is mine." I've never imagined having a big house like this under the circumstances, before Katrina and even after Katrina. So we came in, she let me unlock the door, and she let me choose which room I wanted . . . And then I chose that room, and then I went in, and I couldn't believe that I had my own room to myself. That was my first time ever having my own room to myself. There was just peace of mind, stuff like that.
>
> LORI: Just to have your own space?
>
> DANIEL: Yeah, just that space. It was, wow.
>
> LORI: Amazing?
>
> DANIEL: Yeah. At the same time weird, but at the same time, grateful, but at the same time a blessing. For me just to feel that way, it felt unimaginable, like it wasn't happening . . . And it was just a lesson just to have our own [place] and not worry about where we were gonna sleep at or how we were gonna eat, stuff like that.

The trailer itself was about 800 square feet, which meant that it was about three times larger than the 240-square-foot FEMA trailers that received so much negative attention in the local and national media.[8] Mrs. Myers fought long and hard for those particular trailers, as she wanted the evacuees who had stayed at her church to have the best possible temporary housing experience.[9]

Inside their mobile home, there was a bedroom in the back, where Deirdre and Alexandria slept on the floor on a double mattress. Daniel's bedroom was at the opposite end of the trailer, where he had a twin mattress, also on the floor.[10] Upon entering the trailer through a thin aluminum door, there was a small kitchen area and a living and dining area in the center of the home. Although the trailer was spatially well arranged for a family of three, the trailer itself had sewage leaks that the maintenance workers were slow to fix, and at one point the family had to deal with an infestation of mice.

The park in Baton Rouge where their mobile home was located, as well as most of the surrounding area, was overwhelmingly African American. The trailer park was located off a major interstate and included a mix of regular, full-time residents who owned their trailers, as well as a number of Katrina evacuee families, mostly from New Orleans, who had been placed in FEMA trailers.

With strangers all around, Deirdre was concerned about her family's safety, especially late at night.[11] She (as well as some of her neighbors whom we interviewed) expressed fears to us that there might be drug dealing or other criminal activities occurring. In light of this, Deirdre became especially protective of her children in this unfamiliar environment. Deirdre and her neighbors were not alone in their fears. One survey of Katrina evacuees in FEMA trailer parks found that 49 percent did not feel safe walking in their neighborhood at night and 45 percent were uncomfortable letting their children play in the trailer parks during the day.[12] Furthermore, some FEMA housing policies resulted in formerly homeless, drug-addicted adults suffering from mental illness living in trailers next to families with small children; and some of the trailer keys could open multiple trailer doors.[13]

Because the trailer park where the Taylor family ended up was spatially isolated and had no access to reliable public transportation, Deirdre was limited in the places where she could work. There was a Dollar General store less than a mile away (where she eventually did land a job), as well as a convenience store, a Piggly Wiggly grocery store, a couple of fast-food chain restaurants, a check-cashing business, a pawn shop, and several other stores targeted toward low-income and working-class individuals and families. To get to stores or to her job, Deirdre had to walk along the side of the four-lane highway that ran in front of the trailer park. At night this was especially dangerous.

The time in the trailer park was also difficult for Daniel. As we describe in greater detail below, he was out of school for almost a full two years when they lived in the trailer in Baton Rouge. During this time, Daniel spent most days inside the trailer caring for his little sister while his mom was at work. During the school year, when other children were away from the park, Deirdre only allowed her children to play outside after 3:00 p.m., when school let out. She also forbade Daniel and Alexandria to go outside at night without her.[14] This was a rule that Daniel did not dispute or bend, as he too was fearful of the "bad environment" surrounding the trailer park, where there were "lots and lots of drugs."

In the spring of 2008, Deirdre and her children faced eviction from the trailer because the 18-month period for free post-disaster housing had long since passed. So, they stuffed their one suitcase and several large black garbage bags with all of the belongings they could carry and returned to New Orleans via bus. Although it was difficult to leave the trailer and the temporary stability it offered, the family—and especially Deirdre—had longed to return home. They felt comfortable in New Orleans and knew how to get around. Daniel could have some independence there by walking and taking the bus on his own, and they hoped to return to their church, which was very important to Deirdre. Even before they were forced to leave the trailer, Deirdre had told us over the telephone and in letters that as soon as she could "scrape together the fare" for her family, they would be on the first bus back to New Orleans.

The family quickly realized upon their return that the city had changed drastically since the storm. For one thing, the population was much smaller, as tens of thousands of former residents had not yet made their way back. The four largest public housing projects in the city had been closed down and were later demolished by the federal government. Rental rates were now triple what they had been in 2005.[15] Entire neighborhoods were still mostly deserted. Charity Hospital, which provided medical services to the indigent, was now permanently closed (this was the hospital where Deirdre gave birth to all three of her children). The remaining health care infrastructure in New Orleans was badly damaged and/or disrupted and there were not enough health care professionals in the city to care for the sick.[16] Nearly 7,500 of the most experienced teachers had been fired and hundreds of schools had not yet reopened.[17] Grocery stores, police and fire stations, libraries, and other vital services were also slow to return, especially to low-income neighborhoods.

With no other option available, Daniel, his mother, and his sister moved into a motel. Under fire for "evicting" so many still-struggling evacuees from the trailers, FEMA agreed to pay for these motel stays for the thousands of remaining Katrina survivors who still, now years after Katrina, had not found a way to "reestablish" permanent housing.[18]

During a trip to New Orleans in June of 2008, Lori went to visit the family. Below we present a highly abbreviated portion of her fieldnotes from that afternoon.[19] They include a reference to the difficulties associated with finding the family, which was an issue with almost all the participants in our study since New Orleans residents, especially poor ones, moved so much after the storm.[20] The fieldnotes excerpt also provides a description of the family's living situation at the motel.

From Fieldnotes, June 22, 2008:

> *I arrived to the hotel in New Orleans, plugged in my laptop, and looked up the address that Deirdre had emailed me from the public library computer for their new place in New Orleans. Alice and I had no idea what sort of living situation they were in, since their address included a "room 312," but no mention of whether it was an apartment or a motel or what. We were*

worried that the family had ended up in another rundown place now that they were back in New Orleans.

I took a cab to the address Deirdre had sent. They were staying at an "America's Best Value Inn" in New Orleans.[21] The street was busy, two lanes on each side, with no nearby or easily accessible businesses. Charity Hospital was a couple of blocks away, but now it was all fenced off and is closed anyway.

The motel didn't look too rundown from the outside and the surrounding area had not received as much water as some other parts of the city. I walked into the front lobby and the man behind the front desk, an older African American gentleman, asked if he could help me. I said that I was looking for room 312. He told me that the elevator was broken but that I could go around the back to the stairs. As I walked around the place, I passed a gated swimming pool area. It was hot out that day, but no one was in the pool. I turned the corner and entered an unmarked yellowish door. The carpet was dirty and the air smelled of some mix of beer, cigarettes, urine, and just general lack of cleanliness.

Once I made it to the third floor, I knocked twice—loud and clear—on the white motel door. There was a peephole and Daniel opened the door and immediately said, "Miss Lori!" with the biggest smile I'd seen in a long time. I looked around him and saw Deirdre lying in the bed under the covers. The television was on. Daniel said, "It's Miss Lori." Alexandria said, "Miss Lori!" Then Deirdre said "Close the door."

I stood outside the door for about three or four minutes, trying to occupy myself by jotting notes. Once they got things settled inside, the family opened the door again, this time standing together. Deirdre had on a tight, white T-shirt dress with a collar. Daniel was wearing jean shorts and a green T-shirt with writing on the front. Alexandria had on little pedal-pusher pants and a Ben and Jerry's ice cream T-shirt. I was sure it was one that Alice had mailed them from Vermont when Deirdre had asked her for clothes, and I later confirmed that was correct.

Once they invited me in, I did a quick scan of the room. There were two double beds with heavily worn maroon bedspreads. A nightstand with a phone (the light was blinking and I wondered if they had intentionally not answered it?). There was a small table with one chair. There was also a microwave in the room, but no refrigerator. I wasn't able to see in the bathroom that well, but there was a shower and a toilet. Outside the bathroom there was a very small vanity with a sink. They had their toothbrushes and other belongings crammed along a small shelf above the vanity.

All of Daniel's clothes and belongings were in a large suitcase on the floor. Alexandria's clothes were in the drawers. Deirdre said she only had two outfits. She then told me that she "threw away" almost everything they had in Baton Rouge, but "they didn't have much anyway." I think it was because they had to ride the bus, and because they could only take the one suitcase and the black garbage bags.

Deirdre asked what I was doing there. I told her and then she expressed how happy she was to be back in New Orleans. She said, "I ain't never leaving this city again. Ain't no way I'm ever leaving for nothing." She told me that she spent $10 on bus fare to get them back from the FEMA trailer in Baton Rouge to the city. She also noted that FEMA was paying for one month's rent in the hotel. [Later Daniel said that he had been told by the FEMA staff member that "they had never even come and looked at this hotel before they decided to put the people from the trailer park in it."]

Then Deirdre dropped a bombshell: they were getting ready to be homeless in a week, so they were making preparations for the family to go to the Salvation Army shelter. Because he was over the age of 12, Daniel would have to be in separate quarters in the shelter, apart from his mom. He told me that he was scared because "there are scary people there," which Deirdre expanded on by saying that "there are a lot of mentally ill people there." They matter-of-factly discussed their impending homelessness, including asking me if I would "hold onto the children's photos" because Deirdre didn't have "anybody else" that she could "trust with the pictures" of her children. Holding back my own tears, I promised Deirdre I would mail her an envelope and a book of stamps so that she could send me whatever pictures she wanted me to put in safekeeping.

Deirdre said she was "putting in applications for jobs." She never indicated, however, where she was doing so. When pressed a bit, she offered a vague explanation of how she was trying to get Daniel enrolled in school for the fall 2008 term. She said they had tried five or six places, but "didn't have a good school yet."

After we visited and caught up for a while, Daniel and I left so that we could go get some food to eat. When I asked Alexandria if she wanted us to get her anything when we were out, she happily shouted, "Carrots!" with that adorable smile of hers. Her response prompted me to ask Deirdre how she handled food shopping and meal preparation given their living situation. She said that they don't cook because of the setup in the motel. Instead they walk every day to the gas station on the corner, "since there is nothing close by," and get some food. I said, "Oh, do you mean like canned raviolis and things like that?" and she said "Well yes, that is exactly it."

As Daniel and I walked down the stairs, I asked him what he thought *of the motel. He said there were a "lot of Mexican people" there, most of them working on the Katrina cleanup and recovery. He emphasized that he really liked the different cultures and that he was trying to learn a little Spanish. Then I asked if the other people from the trailer park in Baton Rouge were in the hotel. He said yes. Daniel shared that he was glad to be out of the trailer and was ready for something different. As we reached the bottom of the stairs and went to exit the building, two Latino laborers were walking in. Daniel said, "Hola, cómo estás?" The workers responded "Hola" back. I thought to myself, Daniel, always the one to make friends no matter what the situation.*

Soon after this visit in June of 2008, FEMA agreed to extend the number of months that they would pay for temporary hotel accommodations for the thousands of remaining Katrina survivors still without permanent housing. Fearful that the family would become homeless soon, we began to work with our networks of friends and colleagues in New Orleans to try to help the Taylor family secure more permanent accommodations.[22] Throughout the summer months we made calls to case workers from various aid organizations around the city. One of these professionals met with Deirdre and the family on several occasions. Deirdre also found lists of local churches that she thought might offer services to families like hers. She spent much of the summer calling these churches and walking in the heat with her children to different locations to find out if they could help with housing, food, or clothing.

Eventually, with the assistance of a FEMA transition coordinator, a housing caseworker from Catholic Charities, and a federally funded low-income subsidized housing program, the family was able to move into a two-bedroom apartment in Uptown New Orleans. This apartment was in a more unsafe neighborhood than where the motel was located or where they had lived before the storm, but it was still an improvement from the motel room because it had a full kitchen and a washer and dryer. Once the Taylor family was settled, they realized they still felt a little cramped in the apartment, but Deirdre put it all in perspective: "I don't need no big house. All I care about is that my children will still be with me."

Deirdre recognized the importance of getting out of the motel and into housing: "I just need adequate, stable housing. Then I can move on from Katrina." Rather than moving on, however, the family just continued to move. After the three-month temporary apartment subsidy ran out, they packed their belongings and transitioned to another rental unit in New

Orleans.[23] When that additional short-term housing subsidy ran out, Deirdre broke down and contacted her sister in Baton Rouge. Although their relationship remained strained, the sister agreed to take in the family for the summer. Deirdre managed to get a job in Baton Rouge at the Greyhound bus terminal and things seemed to be looking up. But then Deirdre's sister lost the lease on her apartment; soon after, as tensions rose in the household over finances and living arrangements, she asked them to leave.[24] Deirdre had saved some of the money from the two paychecks she managed to earn from the job at the bus station, and that was just enough to get her family back on a bus and back to New Orleans.

When they returned to the city, they had nowhere to go. Homeless, the family became divided for the first time since Katrina. Daniel, now 16 years old and thus too old to be with his mother in a shelter, had to move into a shelter for teens and young adults age 16 to 21. When we spoke to him on the phone while he was living there, he was managing the situation, but was also obviously sad and stressed. While Daniel was at the youth shelter, his mother and Alexandria went to a homeless shelter for families. The Taylors ended up spending an entire year separated. When we saw Daniel again in May 2011, we asked him during our interview about what this time was like:

DANIEL: It was so hard . . . You're living there with ex-convicts, some murderers, thieves, drug addicts.

ALICE: They were men, not just boys?

DANIEL: Sometimes it's boys, it's men and women, all 21 years old or below. But you don't live on the same floor as the women. They're separated. But you've got to take in the fact that they put you in the room with these people. I was there for a year, and I got accustomed to maybe three or four people. The only people I really got along with there was those three or four people who actually came in and out of my room, and the staff. The staff there is wonderful.

ALICE: That's good.

DANIEL: Not all of them. Some of them I don't agree with, but the staff there, there was some staff who really cared. It was just the fact that they let anybody in there. One day there was a floor lockdown. I had just came back from school, because I was going to school then, and they locked the floor down. I was like, "Why are we locked outside and we can't come in the building?" Everybody was like, "Somebody kicked a window on the third floor, and blamed it and said that [someone] tried to throw him out the window from the third floor." I was like, "Okay, whatever, I'm not even dealing with that." So I just went and sat in the park for the rest of the day, and it lasted until maybe

6:30, 7:00 o'clock that night and we were able to go back in because the police left around that time. They had to do fingerprints and all this other stuff, take pictures. And then they left.

ALICE: How did that make you feel?

DANIEL: Right then and there, I knew for a fact I had no stability. That let me know that I have to get to a point where I have to get a job and get out of there, because it's not working out. And then they [the counselors at the shelter] want you to save your money. And then another thing that really made me mad one day is, I would put my money in a [special] account. It's like an account that you put your money in. They keep it in a safe, and you save your money. It irked me, because one day I needed something, like I needed to pay my phone bill, and there were all these staff there, and nobody could help me out to get some money out of my account so I could pay my phone bill. The service manager, she came downstairs, and she said, "I'm real disappointed in you that you couldn't have waited until tomorrow." I'm like, "You don't understand. I have a mother who's four or five miles away from me who wants to call me every minute because she's a mother." And she was like, "Can't she leave a message here?" And I'm like, "If my mom can't talk to me face to face—on the phone—she's doesn't like that." And when they asked her to leave a message, she was like, "No, I want to talk to him now."

ALICE: Your mom would call you every day at the Covenant House?

DANIEL: Every day, just to see how I was doing. And I understand that, because she's a mother, and that's what she was going through.

ALICE: Would you see your Mom and Alexandria every day?

DANIEL: No. I was by myself most of the time. But it taught me how to fend for myself. It also taught me somewhat of how to be responsible. So some good things came out of [living at the] Covenant House. It taught me how to not depend on anybody else. They taught me, but in some instances I felt like I was put in situations where I had to either fend for myself or be without.

While Daniel stayed at the Covenant House, Deirdre and Alexandria spent most nights at the Salvation Army homeless shelter. It was free for Alexandria, but it cost $8 a night for Deirdre, which she could pay only if she asked strangers on the street for money. Other times, when she could not cobble together the funds for the shelter fee, the two of them slept on the streets or in public parks. Alexandria, now old enough to remember and recount vivid details from these nights, told us that "when it rained" she would "be crying." As difficult as this was, Deirdre at least had her daughter with her. The worst thing was not being with Daniel, "her baby," and not knowing how he was doing on his own. As Daniel mentioned, they did their best to call each other or see each other during this stressful time, but aside from the weekends they spent together "sitting in the park," he was on his own—a homeless child in the city.

After nearly a year had passed, a staff member at the Salvation Army noticed that Deirdre and Alexandria had been at the homeless shelter for too long and decided to help the family find new housing. With this assistance, they were able to move to another rental home that was paid for by a government-sponsored housing program. The Taylors were extremely happy to be reunited and to be in their own private space again. Their situation continued to be precarious, however, and they knew they could be forced to leave at any time and they would be homeless again.

During our visit in 2011, Daniel gave us a tour of the two-bedroom, single-story duplex where they had moved with the assistance of the Salvation Army staff. The family had a little food in the refrigerator, a sagging couch in the living room, a small table and three chairs in the kitchen, and newspapers taped to the windows for privacy. We observed three mattresses on the floor in two small back rooms for sleeping, stuffed animals on Alexandria's bed, and a small television in Daniel's room. Alexandria also had a small wooden school desk in her room and there was another desk in the front room where Daniel could do his homework—both of these pieces of furniture came from a kindly janitor at the school Daniel attended.[25] Beyond these items, there were very few personal belongings, and all the rooms were tidy. Pigeons nested above the front door, creating a mess on the front steps.

Time went on and many months passed as they lived in this temporary rental home. Deirdre still had no employment, and there was a heavy uncertainty about their future housing that weighed on the family at all times. Would they get their housing funding renewed or not? No one knew. This is a life of instability, of constant uncertainty. And while Daniel and his family had experienced housing insecurity before Katrina, their housing situation became more unstable and unpredictable following the hurricane, as evidenced by the post-disaster decline.[26]

DROPPING IN AND DROPPING OUT OF SCHOOL

As the family struggled after Katrina, Daniel's school attendance and performance suffered. He, like so many other displaced youth, attended numerous schools in the years following the disaster. He also missed almost two full academic years during his family's displacement and multiple moves in and around New Orleans after the storm. As alarming as this sounds, this was not an isolated incident. In the two months following Katrina, as many as 138,000 students were not in school. Somewhere between 30,000 and 50,000 K-12 students, most of them from Louisiana, missed virtually the entire 2005–2006 academic year following Katrina. In the following school year, 2006–2007, as many as 10,000 to 15,000 school-age children did not attend all or most days of school.[27] These numbers are staggering, and in most cases, it is unclear what happened to these children.

As shown in figure 3.2, Daniel's experience with schooling was exceptionally complicated, as he moved in and out of numerous educational contexts in the post-storm period. Daniel also faced many barriers in his education, including homelessness before Katrina, displacement afterward, bullying, years of missed classes, an inadequate foundation in math, and a lack of strong relationships with teachers and peers due to the frequent moves.

Bullying was among the most harmful issues that Daniel faced during the post-Katrina displacement. In Baton Rouge, he quickly became a target of older, hostile youth. As he rode the bus and walked through the hallways of the now overcrowded middle school he was enrolled in after the storm, he encountered rampant anti–New Orleans sentiments. Students at this school were angry about the "newcomers" from New Orleans and they judged him and the other evacuees based on what they "knew" about the city from media accounts and other sources. All people from New Orleans, but especially African Americans, had been widely portrayed in negative and highly stereotypical terms: dangerous, criminal, lazy, unintelligent, violent, gang members. This image followed many children during their displacement and when they enrolled in new schools around the country;[28] Daniel was no exception. He described the views of the other students in Baton Rouge:

> 'Cause for the simple fact [we are from New Orleans], some of them do not like us. Our reputation is the highest killer rate in Louisiana. That doesn't base anything on people you meet from New Orleans, you see what I'm saying? Because we're split up. Ninth Ward, parts of the Ninth Ward are real bad, but then there's other parts that are not real bad. And they based [their views on the bad] parts of the city, which, you can't really base your reputation off that.

Over time the hostility toward Daniel became dire. There were several incidents on the school bus where he was hit or otherwise physically hurt

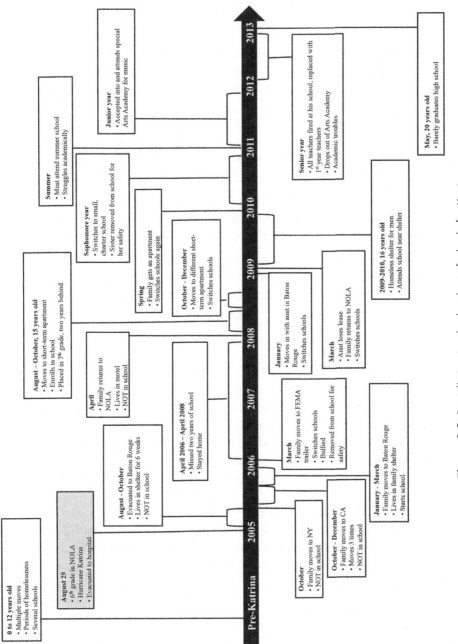

Figure 3.2. Daniel's time in school and out of school after Katrina

0 to 12 years old
- Multiple moves
- Periods of homelessness
- Several schools

August 29
- 6th grade in NOLA
- Hurricane Katrina
- Evacuated to hospital

October
- Family moves to NY
- NOT in school

October – December
- Family moves to CA
- Moves 3 times
- NOT in school

August – October
- Evacuated to Baton Rouge
- Lives in shelter for 6 weeks
- NOT in school

January – March
- Family moves to Baton Rouge
- Lives in family shelter
- Starts school

April 2006 – April 2008
- Missed two years of school
- Stayed home

March
- Family moves to FEMA trailer
- Switches schools
- Bullied
- Removed from school for safety

April
- Family returns to NOLA
- Lives in motel
- NOT in school

August – October, 15 years old
- Moves to short-term apartment
- Enrolls in school
- Placed in 7th grade, two years behind

January
- Moves in with aunt in Baton Rouge
- Switches schools

March
- Aunt loses lease
- Family returns to NOLA
- Switches schools

Spring
- Family gets an apartment
- Switches schools again

October – December
- Moves to different short-term apartment
- Switches schools

Sophomore year
- Switches to small, charter school
- Sister removed from school for her safety

Summer
- Must attend summer school
- Struggles academically

2009-2010, 16 years old
- Homeless shelter for men
- Attends school near shelter

Junior year
- Accepted into and attends special Arts Academy for music

Senior year
- All teachers fired at his school, replaced with 1st year teachers
- Drops out of Arts Academy
- Academic troubles

May, 20 years old
- Barely graduates high school

Pre-Katrina 2005 2006 2007 2008 2009 2010 2011 2012 2013

by other children. Deirdre described what happened one day after the bus picked Daniel up from the FEMA trailer park:

DEIRDRE: So after I saw [the bullying for] myself, when I brought him to the bus stop on the corner, about maybe 10 or 12 children on the bus, before he could even get on the bus—

ALICE: What were they doing?

DEIRDRE: Just trying to jump him. He said, "See, Mom? All I did was get on the bus." I'm standing there watching them! The bus driver ain't said nothin' about it. So when he got on the bus and she turned and he saw that they wasn't gonna stop and she kept driving, she didn't say nothing about it, I don't know her name, he got off the bus.

Deirdre believed this situation would escalate and become more violent, so she decided that Daniel had to stop going to school for his own safety:

He ain't goin'! I ain't gonna let nobody call me and say my child is dead on the floor in a pool of blood. No, indeed. He is not going [back to school] until I go back home to New Orleans. Other than that, everything else is obsolete.

Daniel also felt unsafe and wanted to stop attending school. He and his mother did not believe that the school administrators grasped the seriousness of the situation; it seemed that the institution was not as responsive as it needed to be. Daniel's experiences parallel those of many African American boys. Psychologists who studied bullying after Katrina found that displaced children reported high levels of both relational bullying, such as exclusion, spreading rumors, and mean facial expressions, and overt bullying, which includes being hit, kicked, or physically threatened; males and minority children reported higher levels of overt bullying than females and whites.[29]

Together, Deirdre and Daniel decided that he would stop attending school and would stay in the trailer to care for Alexandria. During this time, he woke each morning and helped dress and feed Alexandria. He read to and played with her during the day. He was exceptionally protective of and loving toward his younger sister.

Daniel eventually returned to school in the fall of 2008 after the family had moved back to New Orleans. By this point he was 15 years old and should have been in ninth grade. However, because he had missed two years of school, he was placed in a seventh-grade classroom. This was especially difficult for Daniel because not only was he a teenager, but he was also much taller and heavier than his classmates. His physical stature only made him stand out more. He was also more emotionally mature, but he realized that he needed to be in this class because of the extent of the educational curriculum he had missed since Katrina.

Daniel was not alone in feeling out of place. During our visits in 2009 to some of the New Orleans recovery schools serving kindergarten to eighth grades, we saw 17- and 18-year-olds who were walking the halls next to young children. When we asked one of the teachers what was going on, we learned that these youth had missed so much schooling and were so far behind academically that they were placed in a K-8 school. As one teacher flatly told us about the age and developmental differential, "It really doesn't work."

As Daniel continued to move into different housing and school settings, his academic performance suffered. By missing out on instruction time and important lessons, he did not have the foundation to move on to subsequent material. Many children, like Daniel, who missed schooling during displacement, could not catch back up to their grade level. For those who were underperforming academically before the disaster, they faced even greater risks and fell further behind. Daniel explained his struggles with mathematics, in particular, even before Katrina:

> I'm always messed up by math. I feel as though it's like I blame standardized tests, but I also blame the foundation that I had with math from early school, like first and second and third grade, because during those times, we were homeless. So I very seldom had a stable place where we could stay. We were always [moving around] and I was never in school. So that kind of threw me off in math, when I was goin' from this place to that place and should have been in the classroom learning, and it threw me off a bit. But I can't fault my mom for it or nobody else for it, it was just something that happened.

Daniel could clearly articulate how his early years of homelessness and lack of a steady school environment propelled him downward. After we met him, it was obvious to us how the numerous post-disaster displacements and continued school disruption accelerated a spiral already in motion. For instance, in the years following Katrina, Daniel failed the math portion of one of the required standardized tests for Louisiana. Even though he passed the English portion, he was still required to attend a summer school program.

Daniel knew full well how crucial school is for a child's future. He often drew on his own life path as a lesson for his little sister. This was painfully apparent as Daniel and Alice walked the aisles of Walmart in 2011. As they were shopping for food and supplies, he privately expressed his fears about his mother's plan to pull Alexandria out of school because one of the children threw a chair and hit Alexandria in the back. He said he "absolutely" understood why his mother wanted to keep Alexandria "safe from other children who are too rough." But Daniel also knew how it felt, every day, to walk into school as an 18-year-old sophomore, to lag far behind grade-level work in many subjects, and to stand out as an "oversized" student who needs extra help. "It hasn't been easy," he said quietly, out of earshot of his mother, who was shopping in a different part of the store with Lori and Alexandria.

Even for someone who makes friends easily and has determination, re-integration into a new school is exhausting and difficult. We found that Daniel always had a core group of friends when we would visit him—but they were always different friends. Because the family moved so often, and they only had intermittent phone service, it was difficult for Daniel to stay in touch with the friends he would make in each new school. It was the same story with his teachers and other adults in his life. Daniel could always name a teacher or a church pastor or some other person who was helping and supporting him. But those relationships were not enduring and thus they could not offer the stability and resources that he so desperately needed.

Post-Katrina studies reveal that displaced children who built a positive relationship with their schools, especially their teachers, what educational psychologists refer to as "school attachment," were doing better in terms of their academic grades and testing and also managing emotionally better than other displaced children.[30] So, Daniel and the thousands of other evacuee children who did not attend school during displacement lost out on not just the academic but also the emotional benefits of supportive adults in the school setting.

When we visited the Taylor family in the spring of 2011, Daniel was in a better high school situation. His mother had enrolled him in an international charter school that had recently opened in downtown New Orleans, and Daniel seemed to be thriving. The school had a small student body, with less than 150 students in the 9th–12th grades. All the teachers and staff knew him by name. He had a lot of supportive adults who were looking out for him, who would chide him if he even missed one class. They helped him buy a school uniform, but he had to work to "pay it off," as the vice principal of the school told us in no uncertain terms. He had many advocates at the school: the school secretary, whom he told us he "loved" and who also clearly cared deeply about him; the janitor, who told us that Daniel was "like his own son" and who taught him how to tie a necktie; the vice principal, who said she was tough on him because he "has a lot of potential." He was also involved in the school ambassadors program, sang in the choir, and was the stage manager for the school plays. He even started his own a capella singing group with three other boys from the school. In May of 2011, Daniel learned that he had been accepted to a prestigious performing arts program in New Orleans that would allow him to attend classes in the morning at his charter school and to participate in music training in the afternoons.

Even though things were looking up, his life was still precarious. His grades were better at the new school, but not "perfect." Because the school had transitioned to a different charter structure, all the teachers at Daniel's school had been fired the year before he started attending (so every one of the teachers we met was a first-year teacher at the school, many of whom had only just graduated from college). If the students did not keep their test scores up, the newly created school could lose its fragile charter status and close or experience another round of total layoffs. Daniel and the other students as well as the teachers were well aware of this, and it added anxiety to their lives.

Seven years after Katrina, as we were drawing our data collection to a close, Daniel was preparing for his final year in high school. Although he loved music and dreamed of going to "Juilliard, or somewhere like that," his grades in his math classes and on Louisiana standardized educational exams were so low that his prospects for attending university were seriously diminished. Moreover, even though he had received a scholarship to attend the performing arts high school in New Orleans, he left the program after only one semester due to the pressures associated with the classes and the schedule. Transportation from his home and to and from the two schools was also an ongoing challenge. Always a sweet child with a sincere interest in others and keen desire to make those around him smile, the years of pre- and post-Katrina instability had taken their toll, and Daniel was now frequently getting in trouble at his regular high school for missing class, acting out, and not following rules.

FAMILY INSTABILITY: FINANCIAL AND HEALTH CONCERNS

Daniel's family, although small, stuck together and supported one another. Both Daniel and Alexandria were well behaved and they told us they "mostly always" obeyed their mom. Deirdre fiercely protected her children, and her children loved her in return. Also notable was Daniel's care for his younger sister. Over the years we observed dozens of big and small acts of kindness and self-sacrifice on Daniel's part for Alexandria. Even when they spent the year apart when they were living in separate homeless shelters, Daniel was taking care of his little sister. During one of our visits, he explained how during that time he was able to get a part-time fast-food restaurant job and used the earnings to surprise his sister with Christmas presents:

> DANIEL: I was so worried about Alexandria not having Christmas that I made sure that she knew that she had toys for Christmas. It would have been her third or fourth Christmas [without gifts] . . . Because I remember days when I didn't have anything for Christmas or when I didn't get anything for my birthday. I wanted to make sure she has a good birthday experience, a good holiday experience.
>
> ALICE: You're a good brother.
>
> DANIEL: I had to make sure she had a good experience.
>
> ALICE: So you used your money from your job at Wendy's to get her things for Christmas?
>
> DANIEL: Yes. Other than that, a lot of her toys were donated from [staff at the] Covenant House. She's the only baby—they called her "the baby girl."
>
> ALICE: I hope that you got some things for Christmas, too?
>
> DANIEL: I didn't, actually. But I wasn't worried about me. I was more worried about her, because for a child, Christmas is everything. That's something you don't take away from them. They need to have it. So my Christmas present was making sure that she got the enjoyment that I had when I was her age. Once I could take pictures and see out of all the facial expressions the enjoyment that she gets from it, I was okay.

But even with all the sacrifices they made for each other, the family continuously struggled due to Deirdre's unstable employment. Deirdre's job challenges stemmed from many factors: her lack of schooling, her own personality, including the fact that she was sometimes quick to anger and difficult to work with, and her consistent but unacknowledged and untreated mental health problems.

Well beyond these personal issues, there were many other broader structural reasons why Deirdre struggled to find employment. First, there are few job openings for people without a high school degree, and the unemployment rate for this segment of the population was even more severe following Katrina. Second, New Orleans and Baton Rouge lack reliable or convenient public transportation, which low-income adults regularly rely on to access jobs, especially since poor families often cannot afford housing in urban areas that are growing and developing economically. Third, employers may have been biased against her social location and physical appearance. Due to inadequate prenatal care and significant vitamin deficiencies, Deirdre lost many of her teeth and was unable to afford any dental assistance. It is possible that her lack of health care and the subsequent dental issues affected her employability. As the sociologist C. Wright Mills observed long ago, it is often difficult to disentangle "personal troubles" from "public issues."

As a consequence of her unemployment, the family had a bleak financial existence and was forced into countless desperate situations. To supplement the food stamps and charitable donations, Deirdre sometimes sold her plasma for $50 a donation. In Baton Rouge, she regularly visited a plasma center that was within walking distance of their FEMA trailer; one time she went to have her blood drawn without having eaten anything for nearly two days. As the blood left her body, she passed out, and was helped by a stranger, a Louisiana State University college student named David who was also selling his plasma and sitting in the chair next to her. David, scared and shocked by what he saw, offered Deirdre a ride back to the FEMA trailer park after this incident since it would have been a two-mile walk for her to return home. David ended up befriending the family and helped them over the next few years, giving them money, food, and sometimes offering them rides in his car. He also took Daniel to the university so that he could "experience what it was like" to be on a college campus.

The Taylor family was able to cobble together an existence from these various sources. But they still faced persistent and serious food insecurity for years. During our first visit to their FEMA trailer in Baton Rouge, we saw that the cupboards and refrigerator were completely empty. It was near the end of the month and their food stamps had run out. When we asked Deirdre what she did during times like these, she said that she would either try to go to the church or the food bank to "get some supplies" or "they would just go hungry."

And they did go hungry. When we would visit, Daniel and Alexandria would often talk about food and ask for something to eat. Because of their food insecurity, we would bring food with us and build a trip to the grocery store into our field visits. As we would walk the aisles with the family, Alexandria would ask us politely if she could have vegetables and fruits, even turning down her mother's offers of ice cream or chips. It appeared her young body was craving nutrients.

Daniel also seemed to like healthy food, although he, like many low-income children in New Orleans, did not have much of an opportunity to eat it. During one visit, we took Daniel out to lunch. As we approached the salad bar, it was clear that he did not recognize many of the vegetables and he had a lot of questions. So we walked around the salad bar together, and we explained what things were. He ended up picking up some lettuce and cantaloupe, but then quickly noted that he "never really ate food like this."

In between our field visits to Louisiana, we would periodically receive emails from Deirdre that read like the following one:

> Hey Lori. Call me, it's urgent. We low on things such as food and I have no more stamps for milk. I know it's late to call you on Halloween and you all are busy. Call me after 9:00 p.m. tonight, Halloween, if you can. I'm gonna walk Alexandria to Palmer Park, the mayor's office is giving out candy for the kids. Gotta go. Call me [phone number]. Deirdre.

Daniel also emailed about the same subject:

> Hi Miss Alice. Mom wanted to know if you found a plug-in for the laptop that we could use. Oh, we also wanted to know if you can send some money 'cause we don't have any food for the baby [Alexandria]. And thank you for the jackets. Mom is looking for another job if you call she'll tell you the reason why. Daniel. P.S. Please and thank you.

And Deirdre left voicemail messages like this:

> Hi, it's Deirdre. I'm calling because I need to get some food for the children. We are wondering if you might call us back and use your credit card to order a pizza for us. David does this sometimes when we don't have any food in the house. Thanks, call us back at [phone number].

Receiving these types of calls and messages from the Taylor family was heart wrenching. In appendix B, we describe how we worked together to respond to these requests.

Even if Deirdre had the money, it would have been difficult to find places where she could purchase healthful food without access to a car. In many poorer neighborhoods there were no grocery stores at all and no place to buy fresh or healthy foods. Indeed, New Orleans is ranked the worst "urban food desert" in the United States; after Katrina the average grocery store in New Orleans served 16,000 people—twice the national average.[31]

An unhealthy diet can have many serious consequences for children. Daniel, for example, was dangerously overweight and had no regular exercise. Alexandria often seemed tired, possibly anemic. Decades of research have shown that nutrition affects school performance, behavior, and many other important aspects of children's development. Daniel and Alexandria also were behind on their vaccinations and did not have regular health care. Indeed, when Daniel and Alexandria got a toothache, they suffered as long as they could, and then went to the emergency clinic. When they were sick, they had to "ride it out" and "just hope" that it did not develop into something more serious. Access to doctors and clinics often requires health insurance, which in the U.S. is predicated on one's ability to pay either through employment or other sources. Following Katrina, the landscape became even more desolate: there were fewer grocery stores, less public transportation, fewer clinics and doctors, more crime, fewer parks and other public amenities (making it harder for children to play and get exercise outside), and fewer jobs.

Although young, Daniel had already led a difficult and precarious life. His family struggled before the disaster, but Katrina and all the disruption it caused put him on a downward trajectory. The instability that he experienced—economically, in housing and neighborhood context, schooling, with peers, and within his family—was simultaneous and enduring and led to greater cumulative vulnerability.

Even as these challenges mounted, Daniel remained a kind-hearted, likeable boy. He also kept an amazingly positive outlook, even in the face of so much uncertainty. As he told us once, reflecting on his own philosophy of life, "I don't have depression . . . I stand strong." His inner strength, charm, and charisma were always on full display when we would visit. And in part because of his personality, his genuine nature, and his humble demeanor, people seemed drawn to him. Daniel had the personal qualities one might expect to find in someone who succeeds in life. But that is not how the story ended. He was embedded in a family, a school system, a neighborhood context, a past—a habitat—that determined his fate, and that is as critical a lesson as we can learn from studying disasters. The social, not the personal, is what matters the most sometimes.

Daniel is not alone in this downward trajectory. He is like many children who lived in poverty and crisis before Katrina. We met many other young African American boys and girls who faced similar, and sometimes even more daunting, challenges including losing parents to homicide, watching gun violence unfold in their communities, and becoming caught up in the juvenile justice system and incarcerated. It is true that Daniel and these other children would have struggled and continued to face many serious disadvantages even if Katrina had never happened. But it did. And thus we cannot know what Daniel's life would have been like without the storm:

How hard things would have been for him, how much school he might have missed, whether his family would have struggled so tremendously with housing and food security. What we do know, for certain, is that Katrina and the disaster aftermath propelled even greater instability in all spheres of Daniel's and these other vulnerable children's lives. Like Daniel, tens of thousands of other children missed months and even years of school, struggled with bullying, endured homelessness, and suffered from a lack of food and health care as their parents sought to find secure employment and some modicum of economic stability after Katrina. In light of all of this, it seems to us that it is safe to say that Katrina made their circumstances even more dire, their experiences even more difficult. Indeed, for all the devastation that Katrina wrought in August of 2005, the most severe harm actually may have come in the years that followed, as the consequences of that disaster rippled across children's lives.

4

MEKANA
DISASTER AS CATALYST

Mekana Lambert, like Daniel Taylor, experienced a series of serious difficulties after Hurricane Katrina, including the loss of her home and permanent displacement to a faraway community, interruption of her schooling,
and the severing of family and friendship networks. What differentiates
Mekana's story from Daniel's, however, is that she was living in a less precarious situation prior to the catastrophe and displacement. She also had
comparatively more resources and a stronger social and economic support
system before and after the disaster. Yet, that stability was much more fragile than it seemed. Katrina, and all the disruption that followed, ultimately
served as a catalyst, placing Mekana on a declining trajectory in the years
after the disaster.

LIFE BEFORE THE STORM

Natalia Simmons, an attractive African American woman with sparkling
eyes and a sharp wit, was 20 years old when she gave birth to Mekana in New
Orleans in the fall of 1989. Mekana's biological father, Derrin Lambert, did
not provide much financial or emotional support during the pregnancy, and
he left soon after Mekana was born. Although a single mother, Natalia had
the help of a large extended family as she began raising her daughter in the
Seventh Ward neighborhood of New Orleans. She did not date much when
Mekana was young, but Natalia eventually met Shane, whom she described
to us as a "very nice man." After being in a relationship for a few years, Shane
and Natalia eventually married. Shane was good to Mekana and treated her
as a daughter, which was in part why Natalia fell in love with him.

Around Mekana's 10th birthday, Natalia and Shane bought a condo-
minium and moved the family to Slidell, Louisiana. Although part of the

greater New Orleans metropolitan area, their new community definitely had a suburban feel to it: compared to New Orleans, Slidell was less densely populated, was composed of a majority of white residents (80 percent), had a higher percentage of homeowners, offered access to higher performing schools, and had lower crime rates. Natalia and Shane decided to buy a house in Slidell for many of those aforementioned reasons, but also because they needed more space. Natalia was pregnant with her second child, and soon after their move, she gave birth to Kalisa, Mekana's younger sister. The family of four was happy in their new home. And, home ownership in a safer neighborhood was an especially important and hard-earned step as Natalia and Shane worked together to build a more economically secure future for Mekana and Kalisa.

Mekana, a pretty and bright girl, thrived in Slidell. Her mother enrolled her in what she felt was a "good elementary school" because it was racially diverse, academically comprehensive, and offered an array of activities and resources. Mekana made excellent grades—mostly A's—and over the next few years became an active member of several extracurricular and after-school programs. She also had many close friends, both from her old home in New Orleans and at her new school in Slidell.

Natalia and Shane were in a secure place economically. Natalia—who had had a difficult upbringing and had engaged in some low-level drug-dealing when she was a teen and young adult—was now earning "good money" as a certified medical transcriptionist. The job offered comprehensive health care and retirement benefits. Shane had ascended to a management position in the car dealership where he had worked for several years.

Natalia was careful to save her money as she was "preparing her daughters for college." Natalia had earned a high school degree and completed a few college courses, but she had loftier educational aspirations for both Mekana and Kalisa. She tucked away money each month to ensure that Mekana could achieve her dream of becoming "a pediatrician or a computer programmer," and that Kalisa could follow whatever path she might choose as well. Because Natalia became a mother at a young age and had a self-described "rough background," she wanted to make sure that she did everything in her power to push her girls to excel and achieve their dreams. Natalia was a fierce advocate for her daughters, always working on their behalf but also encouraging and expecting Mekana and Kalisa to be responsible and to follow through on their commitments at school and beyond.

Although things went well for the first few years after their move to Slidell, Natalia and Shane eventually began growing apart. They never fought much, but around Mekana's 14th birthday, her mom and Shane split up. Although Natalia and Shane were no longer a couple, Shane remained an important part of the girls' lives. He was always on time with his child support payments, often offering Natalia more money than the courts required. Importantly, he also continued to treat both his biological daughter, Kalisa, and his former stepdaughter, Mekana, with equal amounts of love and respect. Shane and Natalia remained on good terms, and after their divorce, Natalia continued to work hard to keep the family stable. For the most part, Mekana handled the divorce and the family changes well. Although she had a bit of temper and would occasionally get "sassy" with her mother, she seemed to be on a balanced path for her teenage years.

KATRINA STRIKES

Less than 48 hours before Katrina would lay waste to much of the Gulf Coast, Natalia was sitting in a mandatory training session for her job. She recalled the text message that she had received from a friend on that Saturday morning, August 27, 2005. It read: "Where are you?" Natalia responded, "In class." Her friend texted back, "The storm is coming!!" Natalia thought it would just blow over like hurricanes past, but then, more and more people started receiving increasingly frantic texts and phone calls. Finally the students told their instructor that they had to go.

After the class was dismissed, Natalia rushed out of the room and immediately dialed her elder daughter's cell phone. Mekana, a well-liked and active 15-year-old at the time, was busy doing what she did most Saturdays of late—hanging out with friends and her new boyfriend in New Orleans. Kalisa was with Shane in Arkansas that weekend, so Natalia was not worried about her safety.

Natalia reached Mekana and told her to get out of New Orleans and back to their home in Slidell as soon as she could. Mekana, who had been listening to the weather forecasts with her friends, did not have to be told twice. As Natalia drove back to their condo, she stopped off at a busy corner market and picked up water, canned tuna, and a few other supplies so that she and her daughter could ride out the storm together.

As soon as Natalia made it home and was reunited with Mekana, the phone started ringing off the hook as family members and friends called to encourage them to evacuate. Her uncle, who had worked for the New Orleans Police Department for over 30 years, sent two officers to the house to "encourage" them to get out of the area. Natalia hated to leave the home and belongings that she had worked so hard to acquire; they represented her investments in her daughters' futures. Like many American working-class families, she did not have any wealth beyond her limited savings and her home ownership,[1] and this made it even more difficult to leave everything behind and evacuate. This is a common situation reported by working-class families in other disasters.[2]

When Natalia witnessed the seriousness in her friends' and families' pleas, though, she decided it was time to heed their warnings. She and Mekana hurriedly packed two outfits apiece and some toiletries. They put food in a cooler and grabbed a few pillows, blankets, and other small things for the road. Natalia had a Ford Bronco that was in excellent repair and had a full tank of gas, so she and Mekana loaded up and drove a few blocks to pick up Natalia's best friend. By late afternoon on Saturday—about a day and a half before Katrina would actually make landfall—the three of them joined the stream of tens of thousands of evacuees making their way out of the most threatened areas.

They had hoped and planned to arrive by nightfall at the house of someone they described to us as a "friend of a friend" who lived in central Mississippi. However, the traffic was so congested heading out of New Orleans that they ended up sleeping in Natalia's vehicle on the side of the road that Saturday night. The storm was still far enough offshore that they were not worried about hurricane damage, but the night was a stressful and uncomfortable one. Finally, on Sunday, they reached their destination and soon after began watching the news coverage of the hurricane. They, like so many others, initially sighed with relief, thinking that the city had "dodged a bullet" when the storm passed and the city suffered minimal wind and rain damage. This relief soon turned to shock and then horror on Monday as New Orleans began to flood with water after the levee system failed.

After three days of little sleep and much pacing around the house where they were staying, Natalia and Mekana grew increasingly frantic with worry. They could not reach Kalisa and Shane because cell phones were not working properly, so they were unable to let them know that they had made it safely to Mississippi.

From the pictures flashing across the television screen, Natalia and Mekana were almost certain that their home in Slidell had been damaged in some way. The reality slowly sank in that the few possessions in the small overnight bags that they had taken with them to Mississippi might be all that they had left.

Natalia and Mekana wanted to get out of the unfamiliar house in Mississippi. More and more evacuees who were friends of the homeowner had started to arrive there, and it was getting crowded and tense. They still could not reach Shane or Kalisa, and they were growing increasingly anxious to learn the fate of their home in Slidell.

Natalia eventually decided it would be best to head back toward New Orleans and then on further west to Lafayette, where two of her brothers already lived and where two of her sisters had sought shelter before the storm. When she and Mekana arrived on her brother's doorstep, the family rejoiced because they had not been able to communicate since the storm struck and they had no idea if Natalia and her girls had made it out of the city alive.

Once in Lafayette, Natalia and Mekana took turns calling airlines and attempting to figure out how to get their "baby girl," Kalisa, back with them. Although Natalia knew that Kalisa was safe with her dad, she could not stand to be apart from her five-year-old daughter. She told us she "desperately needed" to have both Mekana and Kalisa with her. After hours on the phone during that chaotic period, an airline agreed to fly Kalisa to Lafayette for a reduced fare. Finally, a week after Katrina made landfall, Kalisa stepped off a small plane in the Lafayette airport and was greeted by tears of joy from Natalia and Mekana as the family was reunited.

LOOTING AND LOSS

As soon as the roads surrounding New Orleans began to reopen, Mekana, Natalia, and Kalisa returned to assess their home. As they approached the city, Mekana observed that it looked like "a bomb had been dropped" as trees were flattened for many miles around and debris was scattered everywhere. They found their home standing but severely water damaged and battered; the rain and floodwaters had poured in and soaked their rugs, clothes, and furniture. Mold was already growing up the walls, and rats were scurrying through the wreckage. The family was deeply upset at the sight of what had become of the condo, and they knew that it was now unlivable for health and safety reasons.

Yet, the gravest assault was not committed by the wind or water, but by human beings who came in and took their belongings. They stole jewelry and electronics and even, Mekana said, "wet clothes right out of the closets." The family was most disturbed by the theft of the girls' piggy banks. Natalia described the scene:

> They took whatever, my clothes, my kids' clothes, the DVD, movies—anything that wasn't nailed down, they took it . . . I thought, the clothes and the electronics, take that. But when they took my kids' banks—be-

cause I had a bank for my oldest for 15 years. So when they took the piggy banks, that's what bothered me the most.

Mekana had been saving money in her ceramic piggy bank since she was a very young child. Sometimes she and her mom dropped in loose change, and on special occasions like birthdays or holidays, they would tuck away 10- or 20-dollar bills. They estimated that they had saved over $1,000 in that piggy bank. Natalia planned to use this money to help pay for Mekana's college degree, while Mekana wanted to use it to buy her first car. It was crushing to lose the money to looters, as Mekana recalled:

> There was stuff that we were able to get, like I was able to get clothes and stuff, but a lot of our stuff was stolen. I had a gold necklace with my name on it, and they stole the necklace, but they left my name, they left the little nameplate. They stole my necklace. My little sister had a bracelet that has her name, and they stole that. I was like, "Why would you steal something with somebody else's name on it?" We had banks in our house, and those were stolen. Some of my clothes were stolen, my sister's clothes were stolen, my mama's clothes were stolen. Somebody had used my mama's toothbrush. I don't know what they were doing in my room, but they had, like, stuff all over my mirrors, a whole bunch of brown stuff all over my mirrors. You could tell somebody had been staying in our house and had took our groceries and put them by the front door. You could see where they was droppin' stuff at, like, they was comin' back to the house to get the rest of our stuff.

For decades, researchers have debated whether crime increases or decreases during and after a disaster.[3] Looting, which is generally understood as widespread theft of property in the context of a disaster,[4] is often at the center of the debate. According to sociologist Henry Fischer, looting is the most expected criminal response to a natural disaster.[5] Logically, opportunities for looting could increase following a disaster because private property is unprotected and police officers and other emergency responders are directing their focus toward search and rescue and other more immediate needs. Contrary to expectations, however, scholars find that incidences of looting in the aftermath of disaster in the United States are empirically rare, although certain circumstances such as delayed response efforts and high rates of pre-disaster inequality[6] may lead to more instances of opportunistic looting (when residents or outsiders take possessions for their own personal gain) and/or survival looting (when disaster victims steal items to survive, such as water, food, and diapers for babies).[7]

For those survivors unfortunate enough to have their property stolen after a disaster, looting represents a kind of double victimization. Mekana's family experienced exactly this type of harm after the event, when they first discovered their condo had been badly damaged in the hurricane and then realized that some of their treasured possessions had been stolen as well. Natalia described it as the "two strikes" that the family experienced immediately after Katrina.

After seeing their home and taking in all that they had lost, they realized how few options they actually had. So the family drove two hours west, back to Lafayette, where they decided to stay with Natalia's brother and his family. He did not have a large house, and it was even more cramped with Natalia and the girls there, but they tried their best to make it work.

This was an especially hard time for Mekana, who missed her friends and her boyfriend. She, her mother, and her sister cried a lot and watched news coverage of Katrina "almost non-stop" on television.[8] Natalia struggled during this period. She explained how hard it was when people would tell her, "It's gonna get better," and other such things that were meant to be comforting:

> I'm 36 years old now and I'm starting over with my girls. How can you tell someone it's "gonna get better?" They just make it seem like it's so easy. I'm like, "You don't understand the disaster. You do not. Families are separated, friends are separated. You cannot compare it."

As different parts of New Orleans, Slidell, and other surrounding areas continued to reopen after Katrina, the family returned to the city again. Natalia and the girls were talking more seriously about making a move back when Hurricane Rita, the fourth most intense Atlantic storm ever recorded, hit in late September of 2005. For many survivors, watching another huge hurricane churn in the waters off the Gulf Coast on the television news so soon after Katrina was an excruciating experience. Mass evacuations were ordered from Texas to Mississippi. Natalia, Mekana, and Kalisa rode out Rita with friends in Slidell, as forecasts predicted that Lafayette was going to be hit harder by this storm. After Rita passed, they assessed the latest harm to their deserted neighborhood and already badly damaged home. They asked one another how they could possibly make a go of it back in this place. None of their neighbors had returned. The family and friends who helped Natalia with childcare were scattered from Austin to Atlanta. Natalia was able to do her job from home as a medical transcriptionist, but she had lost her equipment in the storm and there was not much work to be had given the extensive disruption in the New Orleans health care infrastructure. Mekana's school had not reopened and her teachers were still evacuated. It was hard to imagine how they could resume any semblance of a "normal life" in post-Katrina New Orleans.

After much deliberation (and briefly considering a move to Arkansas or Georgia, where several members of their extended family had gone after Katrina), Natalia decided to keep her girls enrolled in school in Lafayette through the fall 2005 term. Natalia made this decision, at least in part, because she worried about further disrupting Mekana's education. Mekana, who was a sophomore in high school at the time of Katrina, experienced a decline in her grades after the storm; instead of A's, she was receiving some B's and even more C's. She told us that it was not that the schoolwork was that much harder in Lafayette. It was just that her mind and her heart "were not in it anymore."

Mekana longed to see her old friends. She created a MySpace page[9] after Katrina so she could find her boyfriend (whom she was unable to contact for nearly three months after the storm) as well as her friends from Slidell and New Orleans. She described the joy she experienced when she was able to reconnect with her peers, who were now scattered far and wide. She would often find them on the social networking site, share her cell phone number, and then they would reconnect:

> I'd find them online, and then people would just call. And I was like, "Oh, my God!" And I'd call up and they'd be like, "Remember me?" "Oh, my God, where you at?" "I'm in Louisiana, where you at, girl?" "I'm in Florida." "I'm in Atlanta." "I'm in Texas." It was crazy.

FROM THE GULF COAST TO THE ROCKY MOUNTAINS

Natalia's mother, her older brother, and one of her younger sisters had moved to Colorado several years before Katrina. But Natalia and the girls had never visited them, and Colorado was not a place they had ever imagined living. Louisiana was and always had been "home." Moreover, Natalia's relationship with her mother had long been strained; in fact, immediately after graduating from high school, Natalia moved out of the house so that she could put some distance between them. Her brother struggled with drug addiction issues and, according to Natalia, her mother "enabled" him. Natalia also felt that her mother "partied too much." Despite their struggles, Natalia was feeling desperate. She had a badly damaged house in Slidell to deal with, two children to care for, and a growing feeling that her family was overstaying their welcome at her brother's overcrowded home in Lafayette.

When the girls got out of school for winter break in December of 2005,

Natalia announced to them that they would be making the transition to Colorado to give life a try there. Natalia was hopeful that things might be different with her mother this time, having observed that after Katrina "families were mending." Kalisa was young and did not seem to mind the move, but it was difficult for Mekana to be uprooted yet again. She had just started to establish new friendships at her high school in Lafayette, and now that she had found her old boyfriend, she was hopeful that perhaps they would resume their relationship. But the decision had been made and there was no changing Natalia's mind. Natalia and the girls packed up their few remaining possessions and headed to Colorado, part of an enormous diaspora of over 1 million Katrina survivors who were displaced across the entire nation.[10] Within days of moving into her mother's Denver home, Natalia realized that she had made "a big mistake." The girls were "bawling every day" and Mekana, especially, hated Colorado. Natalia wryly compared the people in Colorado to the climate: both, she said with a sad laugh, were "dry and bitter." When Mekana's family was featured in a media story about Katrina, Mekana felt like the reporters got the story all wrong; it focused on them cooking gumbo and attempted to make them "look happy" in Denver, rather than telling the "real" story of their "trials and tribulations."

Mekana resumed classes at a new high school in Denver in January of 2006, and her grades slipped more; now she was receiving C's and D's and failing some of her assignments and classes. She associated her geographic moves with her declining grades: "My grades in New Orleans were good. When I moved to Lafayette, I had got C's in some of my classes. But up here [in Colorado], like, I kept getting F's." When we asked her about why her grades fell, she replied:

> Like, the pressure, the stress. The pressure because I am like, "Alright, I'm in [high school]. Senior year is right around the corner. I have to get on my stuff real quick." Then the stress because I couldn't get in touch with any of my friends at first. And I couldn't get in touch with my two sisters, my brother, and my three nephews [all from her biological dad's side of the family]. I couldn't get in touch with some others from my daddy's side of the family. And there was a lot of people I couldn't get in touch with. So it was the stress of that. It was just crazy. Stress from school, stress trying to find a job. Because I wanted a phone. Everything.

Mekana, similar to other children and youth in our study, found that anxiety from the displacement, the numerous moves, and the loss of kinship and peer networks interfered with her concentration and school performance. This anxiety was heightened by her age, as she was getting closer to the end of high school and was beginning to also worry about postgraduation plans and her future.

Mekana did not sign up for any extracurricular activities in her new school in Colorado, which made her feel even more isolated. The altitude, Mekana said, made running and playing sports "too difficult." But she also admitted that she was simply "not interested in getting involved." She longed for her old friends and spent most of her free time with other youth who had evacuated with their families from Louisiana to Colorado. These youth called themselves the "Katrina Krewe" and mostly kept to themselves. Mekana was "homesick" for New Orleans, which, she observed, was "really like no other place in the world. I mean, there's no other place like it. It's impossible to describe." It was hard when her old friends would call her up and say, "We're having a party, listen to the music!" They would then hold up the phone so she could hear the revelry, and Mekana would just "cry" and get "even more homesick, for real."

Mekana talked frequently about how she felt like getting in fights with teens at her new school in Denver who asked insensitive and hurtful questions. Likely due to the extensive media coverage that followed Katrina, her peers assumed that Mekana and her family did not evacuate before the flooding. They would ask her about the water and other terrible images of death and destruction associated with the hurricane. Mekana described her typical response to these types of questions:

> I'd be like, "That's a dumb question. Just because I'm from New Orleans, that don't mean that I was there during the hurricane." One person made me want to hit them so bad. They asked me, did I see people floating in the water . . . They asked me where I was from, and they was like, did I see people floating in the water. I was like—I just walked away. I didn't want to say anything. I knew my temper. Me and my mom are the same, like, when we get mad, we have the same temper. And we will snap like that. And to keep me from snapping and hurting that child . . . When that person asked me something like that, I would have hurt him. Really. And then I would have got kicked out of school and all that.

Despite the anger she felt and the difficulties experienced during her transition to Colorado, Mekana was quick to point out the small acts of kindness that really touched her. She received a new coat to keep her warm throughout the frigid winter months, and local firefighters donated money to Katrina survivors: $150 when they first arrived in Colorado, and then an additional $100 at the holidays. Mekana, who got hers all in one gift card because she arrived later, recalled how she spent this precious money:

It came from the firefighters and the church. I wrote them a thank-you letter. I just went shopping for my mom, I bought me some shoes, and I just went shopping for my little sister. I bought my mama so much stuff, she got mad. She was like, "That money is for you, why are you shopping for me? That's supposed to be for you!" I don't know why she always say that, because I still always give her stuff. She got mad, but I don't care.

Mekana, like many other young people we observed, thought of the needs of others in the disaster, and when given the chance, seized the opportunity to do something for them. Indeed, being able to assist others has been found to help disaster survivors emotionally recover;[11] for Mekana, it was satisfying to her to use her relief money for her mother and sister.

Some of Mekana's teachers went above and beyond to try to help her adjust. Because she was so depressed when she first arrived in Colorado, she started skipping classes. This led to a further decline in her academic performance. She attributed being able to finish her junior year of high school to one teacher, in particular:

Around the end of the school year, I wasn't going to class. I didn't want to do nothing. When I would go to school, I would see Mr. Piper in the hallway, and he would be like, "Don't talk to me! You weren't in my class today." But I knew he was always joking. So he brought me into his office and he got me to sign this little contract that I have to come to class every day until the end of the school year to pass his class. So he really helped me.

It also made a big difference to Mekana when teachers showed some awareness of—and respect for—New Orleans culture. It made her feel "special" when teachers would ask about Mardi Gras or other traditions associated with New Orleans, including the music and food. She noted: "Mr. Downy, he was sweet. He wanted to ask about food every time I would see him. 'You bring me some food? Where's the jambalaya at?'" Her teachers and fellow classmates also gave her a "Warmth of Colorado" blanket that was made for residents dislocated by Katrina. When we stopped by to see Mekana and some of the other youth who were displaced from New Orleans, they all wanted to show off their brightly colored blankets and posed proudly for photos. Even though the positive attention and gifts clearly meant a lot to Mekana, she continued to feel deeply unsettled in Colorado.

The family's living situation was perhaps the biggest contributor to their collective stress. Natalia and the girls were "miserable" living with her mother and brother. Soon after their move to Colorado, they began searching for another place to stay and eventually rented a two-bedroom apartment in a housing complex that was home to many senior citizens, almost all of them white. It was affordable and safe, and allowed easy access to Mekana's high school and Kalisa's elementary school and afterschool childcare center. But the other residents did not want them there. Their race—African American—made the family stand out, and their status as Katrina evacuees made them feel even more stigmatized. Natalia described the hostile treatment they received:

> NATALIA: The older people gave us hell. I think we were the youngest family, and we were the only blacks back there, and they didn't know what [race] we were because of our [light] complexion. They asked my landlord, "Where is she from?" He was like, "She's a Katrina evacuee." That was a slap right there.
>
> LORI: Because they didn't trust the evacuees?
>
> NATALIA: Because of what they've seen on TV and what they've heard. So immediately they didn't want me back there. I was having these old people literally toss trash on my lawn. At first I thought it was [due to stray animals]. But then they took out the light bulb in the front door. There was a lot of sabotage going on. I guess they wanted us to violate the lease so we would get fined or evicted. The final straw—they sent the police to my house and said I have a lot of traffic, that we were selling drugs and prostituting! That was the final straw. I had to get out of there. I was livid. I was livid. So of course, at this point I am hating Colorado. I'm like, "Oh, my God! These people are so mean!"

The family was on the brink of moving back to the Gulf Coast when Natalia met a man named Spencer. He was a native of Denver and a long-time employee of a local cable company. Spencer was very interested in Natalia, even though she resisted his advances at first because she wanted to "pack up her girls" and their possessions and leave Colorado. Eventually, though, she and Spencer started dating; a few months later they moved into his two-bedroom apartment in a three-story building on the outskirts of Denver. Although his apartment was a bit further from the girls' schools, they still had bus access, so Natalia felt certain that the move would not be "any more disruptive" than staying in the complex, where they were clearly not wanted.

Despite the new relationship with Spencer, Natalia was depressed and felt like she was still "grieving" all the losses caused by Katrina. She "hated life," was "disappointed in God" and stopped going to church, and was furious with FEMA and the way the post-disaster government assistance programs were being run. She applied for and received food stamps for five months after their move to Colorado—the first time in her life that she had accepted government aid. It was humiliating and she felt the social service employees treated her "like a criminal."[12] They infuriated her so much that she told us that "it was either walk out of there and not get it or choke [the welfare worker]." FEMA paid for three months' rent, but then she "couldn't take the fight" of dealing with their bureaucracy anymore. Natalia broke down and decided to use her savings; soon enough, her savings were gone.

In a matter of months after Katrina, the life they knew and the stability they had painstakingly created was shaken. Natalia and Mekana were stunned by their "fall from grace"[13] after the disaster, losing their economic footing and their dreams of upward mobility. Rapid downward mobility after disasters is a painful, and often irreversible, experience for many working- and middle-class families who have struggled to attain gains in financial security.[14] Single mothers and their children may experience even more substantial challenges in this regard.[15]

While Natalia had achieved a significant amount of intragenerational mobility—in other words, raising her family's economic and social status all within her generation, as opposed to the more common intergenerational mobility, which refers to the transfer of wealth from one generation to another—it was a very fragile transition. Natalia explained this turn of events:

> I was frustrated with the whole relocation because I had an awesome job and a great house. Everything was pretty much perfect and I had a good life and to start over, it's frustrating.

Natalia's losses included not only her home in Slidell and all of their possessions, but also a loss of momentum to a better life for her family. After all her hard work and planning, she and her girls lost everything and had to start over; this was financially and emotionally devastating for her. Moreover, while she tried to "hide" the stress and depression from her girls, she knew that it often "spilled over to them" even when she did not intend for it to be that way.

For Mekana, the crisis could not have happened at a more inopportune time. Katrina occurred during her teen years, which is a particularly difficult period to be uprooted and separated from friends and peers.[16] Mekana's age thus played a large role in her declining trajectory. Disasters disrupt critically important friendships, break up relationships, and make teenagers miss events like prom and senior trips and other rituals and ceremonies that, at the time, feel like (as one teenage Katrina survivor told us) "the most important moments" in their young lives.[17] Moreover, for teens, there is obviously less time to make up for lost schooling and a higher likelihood of dropping out altogether.

Mekana did end up completing the remainder of her high school years at a large, racially diverse Denver high school. But she never felt at home there. She continued to struggle with her grades; she developed few lasting connections with teachers or peers; and she became depressed after her friend Ryan was killed in a gang-related murder in Denver. She remembered flirting and joking with Ryan before his death, and how much she appreciated that he did not always focus on Katrina when talking with her:

> Ryan was from California, but he [lived] up here [in Denver]. Everybody that I met, people used to be like, "Were you in the hurricane?" When I first met him, he was like, "Where you from?" I was like, "New Orleans." He was like, "Man, I know they have some cute girls up there!" And I started laughing. And he was like, "I made you smile, I made you smile!" That's always something he used to do . . . We used to always joke around. Every time he used to see me, he'd give me a hug and pat me on my forehead.

Even at her young age, Mekana had already been scarred by acts of extreme violence. Prior to Katrina, the mother of one of her friends from New Orleans had been murdered. Then in Denver, she lost her friend Ryan in a shooting. And, later, when she was living in New Orleans several years after the storm, she helped her boyfriend, Darik, recover from the murder of his father. These traumatic situations amplified Mekana's vulnerability in many ways. She, like so many other African American youth, was forced to confront the death of a loved one at the same time she was attempting to recover from Katrina.[18]

As she struggled to deal with Ryan's death, Mekana became even more unhappy and increasingly unsettled in Colorado. It was a place that she never thought of as "home," and she was constantly devising plans to get back to New Orleans. Mekana told her mother on a daily basis that she wanted to "go back home" and Natalia would always respond: "Okay, how you gonna get there?" When Natalia returned to New Orleans on two occasions—once to deal with selling their badly damaged condo and once to see friends and family—Kalisa and Mekana could not go because school was in session. They stayed behind with their grandmother, and Mekana explained how hard that was for her:

> My mama, she left me twice to go back to New Orleans . . . I was so mad. I was like, "Why you just leave me?" She's like, "You got to go to school."

But, I said, "I want to go." I was with my grandma. And then [mom would] call me and say, "Oh, girl, I'm eating some crawfish." I know she was joking, but at the time, I was so mad. I said, "'Bye, Mama, I don't even want to talk to you no more." And I'd just hang up the phone . . . I'd be like, "Mama, stop doing this to me!" I'd just start to cry. I was just like, "Man, I want to go home!" I cried so hard. I did not unpack my stuff at all.

Another reason that Mekana had a difficult time in Colorado was that her relationship with her mother became more and more strained. Mekana would often grow upset when her mom would tease her, and they would fight over things like whether Mekana had her homework done on time or whether she was hanging out with friends Natalia did not like. Over time, their arguments increased and the level of emotional conflict escalated. Both mother and daughter were under enormous stress due to the displacement and grieving all their losses, and both acknowledged, separately, to us that they had trouble managing their tempers.

During Mekana's senior year of high school in Colorado, one of her friends from New Orleans who understood how homesick she was sent Mekana $82 so she could buy a Greyhound bus ticket and return to the city for a week-long visit. Mekana was so grateful that her friend did that for her. And, while it helped her to return to New Orleans, the visit only furthered her resistance to ever settling in Colorado.

COLLEGE BOUND

With her mother's encouragement, Mekana had long planned on attending college. After the move to Colorado, her desire to go to college only increased, as she saw this as her pathway back to New Orleans. Mekana was desperate to return to Louisiana and never considered staying in Colorado to work or to go to college. When it came time to fill out applications, she only applied to schools in Louisiana (even though her mother wanted her to apply to some universities in Colorado as well). Once the packets were sent off, she, like many other high school seniors across the nation, waited anxiously to receive admissions news.

In the end, Mekana was admitted to all three universities where she had applied. She remembered how it felt to get the news that she was accepted to Xavier, a historically black college in New Orleans:

That's the thing I really appreciated my mama for, because she was pushing me [to go to college]. She was like, "You need to get yourself together.

You know you need to do it." I applied for college, I applied to Xavier, I applied to SUNO [Southern University of New Orleans], and I applied for Dillard. I went—when I went to New Orleans for the summer with my [biological] dad, I called Xavier, checking up on my application status. They was like, "Oh, we already sent you an acceptance letter to your house." And I was like, "Oh, my goodness!" When I saw my dad, I was like, [singing] "I'm goin' to Xavier! I'm goin' to Xavier!" I was just so excited.

In mid-August of 2008, three years after Katrina, Mekana boarded a bus headed south. Soon enough, she would be attending classes at Xavier University. Xavier's facilities, which are located off Ponchartrain Expressway in New Orleans, were badly damaged in Katrina and the university had lost many of its best faculty members. Still, the university, like the city, was showing signs of recovery by the time Mekana arrived. She moved into a small two-person residence hall room and started her classes.

At first, everything was new and exciting. The freedom associated with starting college is exhilarating for most 18-year-olds; for Mekana, that feeling was intensified by her happiness to be back in a beloved place that was culturally familiar. Sadly, Mekana's excitement quickly gave way to the reality of making a life as a mostly independent young adult. Tuition was high for a private school like Xavier University—nearly $20,000 a year, and funding for her education was a major problem. Her biological father, whom she had never been very close to, had promised to pay for college. But as the hefty tuition bills started to arrive, he was unable to keep his word. Mekana worked every weekend at a minimum-wage job to help pay for the tuition and her living expenses, but she hated it. She liked going out with her friends but found the curfew for the residence halls to be too restraining. Mekana struggled to keep up with her classes, juggling school with her work schedule, and she lost interest in the curriculum. Her grades suffered as a consequence. In the end, Mekana lasted less than a semester in college.

Mekana, like many low-income and working-class, first-generation college students, faced challenges that are not as often encountered by higher-income, continuing-generation students. First-generation students, like Mekana, often have to work one or more jobs and typically have less time to spend on academic endeavors and extracurricular activities. Studies show they are more likely to have attended lower performing high schools, so they tend to need additional social support, mentoring, and even tutoring. They also face a "cultural mismatch" between the cultural norms of their upbringing and the norms of American universities.[19] Indeed, first-generation students are frequently raised with interdependent norms—including being tightly interwoven into familial and cultural communities that expect members to respond to the needs of others—while university cultural norms represent middle-class values of independence, working individually, "paving your own path," little adult guidance, and separation from parents. This cultural and class mismatch ends up undermining first-generation students' academic performance and contributes to the high dropout rate for low-income, first-generation college students. For Mekana and many other Katrina youth, dealing with the challenges of being the first in their families to go to college only added to the stress and challenges of the disaster displacement and disruption; it seemed, in fact, that perhaps they needed interdependence—and the guidance of adults—over independence at this point in their disaster recovery.

It is worth pausing for a moment to note that dropping out of college will have—and, as we describe below, already has had—serious repercussions for Mekana's future. For her, leaving college represents a critical moment in her declining trajectory. Indeed, in the United States, attending college is a game-changer, a door opener; the chances of economic stability and employment success are many times higher for those with a college degree.[20] Without a college education, Mekana faced more limited job opportunities and a much more unstable economic future.

For Mekana, perhaps the single biggest effect of Katrina was being thrown off her long-held plan for higher education. The looters had literally robbed her of her college savings. The destruction from the disaster had sent her and her family into a tailspin that involved unplanned moves and educational transitions that negatively affected her college experience. For one thing, Mekana admitted that she was not as prepared academically for college because her high school studies were disrupted by multiple relocations and anxiety about finishing classes on time. Mekana's decision to move back to New Orleans, although carefully calculated, was not well thought through in terms of the financial ramifications of taking out so many student loans. Moreover, once she actually started college, Mekana was without much adult supervision or support, as she was now many miles away from her mother, and in a university environment that, as noted, rewards middle-class values associated with individualism and independence.

Mekana's lack of success with college was further influenced by her discontent and disappointment about the conditions in New Orleans. After being so excited to return, she found that the city was "all messed up." She described it this way:

MEKANA: It's not even fun in New Orleans no more. That's my home and everything, but ever since the hurricane, it's like—I don't know. You'll be talking like [to your friends], "Man, what are you doing tonight?"

And they'll be like, "I don't know, probably staying in my dorm room."
It's not fun anymore.

LORI: So the city changed a lot, too?

MEKANA: Everybody's not back yet, and when you get to certain parts
of New Orleans, you still see the streets all messed up, you still see
trailers and everything all messed up. So nothing is the same anymore.

Indeed, nothing felt "normal" or "safe" or "stable" anymore. Mekana was
unmoored and unsure of where "home" was for her. Was home her mother's
apartment with Spencer in Colorado? Mekana didn't even have a bedroom
there (she slept on the couch or with Kalisa on her twin bed in her small
room). That was definitely not home. Was home her grandmother's house
in Denver? That was an even more uncomfortable and unfamiliar place,
especially because Mekana felt like she was betraying her mother every time
she went to see her grandmother because of their strained relationship. In
addition, she did not like being around her drug-addicted uncle any more
than her mother did. Was home the city of New Orleans? There was still so
much visible destruction and so much had changed. And, with the rising
rent prices and the lack of good jobs, Mekana could not afford the cost of
housing and she could not find employment that would allow her to support herself and pay off the debt that she had already incurred during that
failed semester in college.

Mekana was 18 years old and she was adrift. Her long-standing plan to
attend college and become a pediatrician or a computer programmer disappeared so quickly, and she had no backup plan. Her downward trajectory
was picking up speed.

BACK TO COLORADO

When the first semester of college ended in December, Mekana had to
move out of the dorm room she had been living in for the past four months
at Xavier. With the holidays fast approaching, Mekana became more and
more anxious to see her mother and little sister. So she scraped together the
funds, and she boarded another bus and returned to Colorado.

The winter chill had already set in, but this time the transition to the cold,
dry climate was less of a shock. Or perhaps Mekana was just less focused on
the weather because she was so relieved to be back with her family after a
rough semester in New Orleans. Mekana, Natalia, Kalisa, and Spencer celebrated Christmas together. Other than a major blow-up between Natalia
and her brother (who was using drugs again and causing family conflict),

it was a mostly peaceful holiday season. Mekana reconnected with the few close friends she had made at her Denver high school, and she was genuinely relieved and happy to be home.

As the new year approached, Natalia began to put more and more pressure on Mekana to find a job. Because the apartment that she and Spencer rented only had two bedrooms, a small kitchen, and a living/dining room, the space was quite tight. Sometimes, Mekana would sleep over at her girlfriends' houses just to get out of the cramped apartment and the increasingly tense atmosphere. Mekana observed that she and her mom were just "too much alike," and that "two people who are just alike cannot be in the same room." She continued: "I speak my mind, my mom speaks her mind. I don't bite my tongue; she don't bite her tongue. We just can't be in the same house."

With a high school diploma, Mekana was able to find some temporary work. One of her friends helped her land a position as a home health aide, although Mekana did not much care for the job. She also found part-time work as a sales associate at a department store and she spent some time helping out in her grandmother's home-based childcare center. The work with her grandmother only led to more tension with her mom, though, who did not like Mekana "hanging out" with her grandmother.

The main bright spot in Mekana's life was her little sister. She adored and doted on Kalisa, and often spent time helping her with her school activities and reading to her at night from their favorite book series, *Junie B. Jones*. Mekana loved spending time with Kalisa and took her role as a big sister seriously. She told us: "My little sister looks up to me and everything, and I love that she looks up to me. That's why I'm trying to get on the right track, so I can show her that once you get in a—once you get older and everything, you can see."

While Natalia genuinely appreciated the help that Mekana offered around the house and with Kalisa, the living situation quickly became untenable. By the summer of 2009, Natalia gave Mekana an ultimatum: "find a full-time, better paying job and get your own place." With a tight employment market in Colorado, and the Great Recession still unfolding, Mekana decided it would be better for her to return to New Orleans. Unlike Daniel, as described in the prior chapter, who worried about Alexandria's well-being when they lived apart, Mekana felt that her younger sister would be okay after she left because her mother was a "good mom" with a "good job" who loved her little sister. She would miss Kalisa deeply, but she needed to leave.

With the help of one of her older cousins in New Orleans, Mekana bought a ticket to return to the city. In August of 2009, she boarded yet another Greyhound bus with little more than a suitcase and a little cash that she had saved up during her time in Colorado. Mekana was met at the bus station in New Orleans by her cousin and aunt, who had offered her a place to stay while she found her footing. Mekana was grateful and she immediately began searching for work.

With "help wanted" signs in nearly every fast-food chain in the city, Mekana quickly was hired on at a burger place. But after two days she quit because she "could not stand the grease." Because she had a high school degree, Mekana felt that she could find something better and she did not want to get stuck in a dead-end job. She started looking for work again, but without a car and with little money to buy professional clothes for interviews, she felt stuck. At this time, the national economic situation was bleak; due to the recession, youth her age had a 30 percent unemployment rate, and the rate was even higher for youth of color.

The "drama" between Mekana and her family members started to escalate as well. Her aunt, who had never been overly kind to Mekana, became involved in a conflict Mekana was having with her cousin. Soon, the family was spreading terrible, hurtful rumors about Mekana and her personal life. She saw few options other than moving out of their house as soon as possible even though she did not want to be "run out" of New Orleans. Mekana explained why it was so important for her to stay:

> I wanted to go back [to Colorado] at that time, but I was like, "You know what? I'm not about to," because I'm not about to let nobody run me back and forth to Colorado. That's not setting a good example for my little sister, because she's looking up to me, and I don't want to leave Colorado one day and then be back in Colorado the next day, like, "Oh, I want to come out here and stay with you," trying to go stay with a friend or anything like that. I'm not about to let nobody run me away . . . So I was thinking about going back to Colorado, but I was like, "No, I'm gonna stay." I'm not about to let nobody run me away from home.

Thus, Mekana's extended family was helpful, but also problematic. Katherine Brown Rosier, in her ethnography of low-income mothers and their children in Indianapolis, found that extended family can be a source of support, but also stress. Sometimes, according to Rosier, close friends were a better option for assistance.[21]

Like the women in Rosier's study, Mekana turned to friends for assistance after things reached a breaking point with her aunt and cousin. Crying and distraught, Mekana called Aliyah, who was a friend from her former high school, to ask for help. Aliyah kindly offered to come get her and let her stay at her apartment. Aliyah, who had recently graduated from college and had given birth to a baby girl, was working nights at a full-time job. Because she was a single mom and her roommate was in the process of moving out of their apartment, Aliyah made an offer: if Mekana cared for the baby for some of the time while Aliyah went to work, she could live in the apartment rent-free. This actually worked quite well, as it saved Aliyah money on childcare, and it provided Mekana with her own bedroom in a nice apartment that was subsidized through a government housing assistance program. The only downside was that the apartment was located on the Westbank of New Orleans, away from the center of the city.[22] Many of the units in the complex were unoccupied, and the bus service surrounding the somewhat isolated area was sporadic at best.

A few months after Mekana moved in with Aliyah, we drove across the Mississippi River to visit her at the apartment. This section of the Westbank was predominantly African American. As we approached the complex, we noted that there were not many stores or other businesses. We saw no signs of public transport. There were few sidewalks and it was not a particularly pedestrian-friendly area; the transportation options and potential walkability were issues we were paying special attention to as we knew that Mekana did not have access to an automobile.

We eventually arrived at the apartment complex, parked our rental car, and went looking for Mekana. The complex consisted of several three-story beige buildings, with a parking lot along the outer perimeter. It was quiet and hot as we walked on the small path that weaved through the building grounds. There was a small pond in the center of the complex. We found her building, climbed up the outdoor cement stairs, and arrived at Aliyah's and Mekana's apartment. We knocked and were greeted by Mekana. She gave us both a hug and excitedly ushered us through the door so she could introduce us to her new boyfriend, Darik, a slender young African American man with a boyish smile. He was 20 years old and tall, but still had the face of a young teenager.

We greeted Darik and then Mekana showed us around the apartment. She explained her living arrangement with Aliyah, updated us on her family in Colorado, and showed off a new tattoo on her wrist. Darik listened intently. He had never been interviewed for a research study, and was intrigued that we had come so far to talk to both of them. After visiting with the couple together, we suggested interviewing them separately. Lori spoke with Darik in the small living room, while Alice asked Mekana questions in her adjoining bedroom. Aliyah and her daughter were out running errands.

Mekana and Darik faced particular challenges and risks after Katrina, shaped, in part by their age and stage of development. Research examining the impacts of disasters on adolescents has indicated that they may engage in risk-taking behaviors, may lose interest in school or social activities, and may rebel against rules and have other behavioral problems. Furthermore, teens may develop sleep and eating disorders, have trouble concentrating, experience feelings of confusion, and engage in less responsible behaviors. Finally, studies have found that they may be at increased risk for alcohol or drug misuse, have increased or decreased physical activity, and suffer from posttraumatic stress disorder (PTSD) after a disaster.[23] From our many conversations with Mekana, it appeared that she did indeed have some of these issues, including decreased physical activity, and she confided in us that she was unhappy about her weight gain. She was not having trouble with alcohol or drug use, but she did engage in other risk-taking behaviors, such as having sexual intercourse without any protection.

Mekana and Darik both became part of a broader trend in New Orleans: teens and other young adults who returned to the city without their parents. There are no firm estimates of how many youth fit this demographic, but we learned from many teachers whom we interviewed in the city that large numbers of adolescents came back to New Orleans and found shelter with friends and other family members and sometimes in FEMA trailers.[24] Some had no adult living with them at all. A school administrator, Joelle, whom we interviewed, described this phenomenon as "quite common." When students were absent from school or misbehaved in the classroom, she would try to reach a parent or guardian on the phone, only to learn that these young people had no adult living with them. Joelle, like others, found this pattern to be disturbing and dangerous, as the teens were often living in unsafe situations and engaging in "problem behaviors" stemming from the lack of adult supervision.

Sitting in the apartment that warm afternoon nearly four years after Katrina, talking with Mekana and Darik, we were struck by how they appeared and spoke as if they were simultaneously both older and younger than their chronological age. On the one hand, they seemed mature, worldly, and experienced. They had been through so much since Katrina, had lived in many different places, had been on their own for long stretches of time, and had made many decisions without any adult oversight. On the other hand, they also appeared young and vulnerable and in need of support, love, and guidance. It did not surprise us that they found each other and became emotionally attached so quickly. Darik expressed how being with Mekana might help him succeed:

> I like to be in the process of stuff. Like, she is trying to go to school, I do work. She is goin' to work, I be goin' to school. That's what I want to do with my life. I don't want to just be a nothing. People out here be killers, murderers. I don't like that. That's not me. Because I know I have a good heart. I have a beautiful heart. And my girl, Mekana, she has a beautiful heart. And that's why I love her and she loves me.

Darik also apparently craved the guidance and structure that being with Mekana provided. Despite their need for this relationship and their strong feelings for each other, it did not last. They were young, without roots, and basically penniless. After Aliyah decided to move out of her apartment, Mekana was once again without a home.

MOVING BACK TO DENVER

In the spring of 2012, Mekana decided return to Denver yet again. After she and Darik broke up and she moved out of Aliyah's apartment, she moved in with another cousin for a short time. But that was never meant to be a permanent place to stay, and she had to figure something out soon.

Mekana sensed that she was basically out of options in New Orleans, and thus felt her only alternative was to return to Colorado. Although she and her mom often had conflicts, they loved and missed each other. Mekana also wanted more regular contact with Kalisa, who was "growing like a weed" and was now taller than both her sister and her mom. Natalia invited Mekana to move back in with them "for a month or two" while she looked for work and found her own place to stay.

The economy had improved by 2012, and Mekana found a job in telemarketing and sales soon after she returned to Denver. She worked during the days and would "hang out" with her friends from high school at night. At a party one weekend, she met a young African American man, Simeon, who was 22 years old and a single father. She found him to be responsible and mature, perhaps as a result of being the primary caregiver for his young son. Mekana was drawn to Simeon, and they began dating. They moved in together after a few months. After a few more months, Mekana was pregnant. Although this was unplanned, she was excited about being a mother. She loved Simeon's son, and she was confident that she could take on this new role in life. Simeon and Mekana got engaged within a few weeks of learning that she was pregnant, and she felt that all was going well.

Mekana kept us up to date on all of these changes. She would often email or call with the latest news in her life. Sometimes she would text us photos of her with Simeon and his son or of her with her growing baby bump. During this period, she seemed genuinely happy and even "settled" for the first time since Katrina. It was interesting, though, as in many ways, Mekana did not choose Colorado as her permanent home; it was as if she grew tired of wandering and she finally allowed herself to stay in one place, even though she still did not know where she truly belonged. She never really planned her Colorado life, but it happened around her.

In early January of 2013, we woke up to an email from Mekana. The subject line announced: "She's here!" Mekana had big news to share. She was a mother. We opened the messages we had received eagerly, excited to see the photos that were attached of Mekana's new baby daughter. Mekana was beaming, holding her beautiful newborn baby in her arms.

Despite her joy about motherhood and the excitement of starting a family with her fiancée, Mekana was still vulnerable in many ways. She never returned to college. And while she was glad to have her telemarketing position, she did not find the work meaningful. She and Simeon now had two young children to raise, and while they were thankful to have each other, they knew the path ahead would be long and the struggles would likely continue.

Mekana's story shares many commonalities with Daniel's. Katrina was an exceptionally disruptive moment in both of their young lives, which led to varying degrees of instability across all the major spheres—housing, education, extracurricular involvement, family relationships, friendships, and health. But Mekana's downward decline after Katrina, in some ways, was even more precipitous than what Daniel experienced.

Mekana's life had balance and some degree of stability before Katrina. But the storm, as she captured perfectly in her own description, "truly changed everything." Before Katrina, she was in school, earning good grades, and on track for college. After Katrina, her grades declined substantially, she tried college, and ended up dropping out. Before Katrina, she had access to reliable transportation—her mother had a car and she had access to the public buses in New Orleans. After Katrina, Mekana had no car and there was no easy or accessible or affordable public transportation for her. Before Katrina, Mekana had health care and money through her mother's employment. But after, she had no health care and no access to her mother's income and health insurance. Before, she had safe and secure housing, but afterward, Mekana was nomadic and regularly had to rely on others for shelter. Before, she had consistent contact with her former step-father (whom she considered her "real" father) as well as her less-involved biological father; after, she had little connection to either. Before, she lived in comfortable and familiar surroundings with neighbors she trusted and relied on. After, she moved in and out of unfamiliar and unwelcoming, and even sometimes hostile, environments. Before Katrina, her working-class family was experiencing some degree of upward social mobility, with an eye on a better future. After, the economic and social gains they had made— especially their home ownership and college goals—were seriously dimin- ished. As with other working-class families after disasters, their recovery was more difficult for many reasons, including fewer savings, less wealth, little or no insurance, and struggles with the stigmatization and degradation of disaster assistance bureaucracies.

The number of displacements and the displacement location also mat- tered. As shown in figure 4.1, Mekana, like Daniel, experienced multiple moves in the aftermath of Katrina. Unlike Daniel, however, Mekana was permanently displaced a great distance from New Orleans and ended up finishing high school in a location well over a 1,000 miles from her former home. This distance for Mekana and many other evacuees proved to have a significant negative impact, as those who were "far from the familiar" were dealing with new climates, cultures, foods, politics, races, ethnicities, and styles of dress.[25] They were also more likely to find people with stereotypical views of people from New Orleans. But most important, the distance meant that they were less likely to be able to connect with their pre-disaster com- munities, visit and feel connected to their old homes, and to reconstruct their social and familial networks. For those who did decide to rebuild their homes, the longer distance made the process of rebuilding much more dif- ficult. Research has shown that lower income residents were displaced further and had fewer resources for travel back and forth, while wealthier evacuees were displaced closer to New Orleans. Overall, the number of moves and the more substantial distance contributed to Mekana's and to others' cumulative vulnerability, making it more likely that they would ex- perience a declining trajectory.

For Mekana, Colorado never really felt like "home," but neither did the "new New Orleans." She had to recover from a disaster at the same time that she was progressing through adolescence, which perhaps increased her risk for negative outcomes and vulnerability. She gave up her dream of

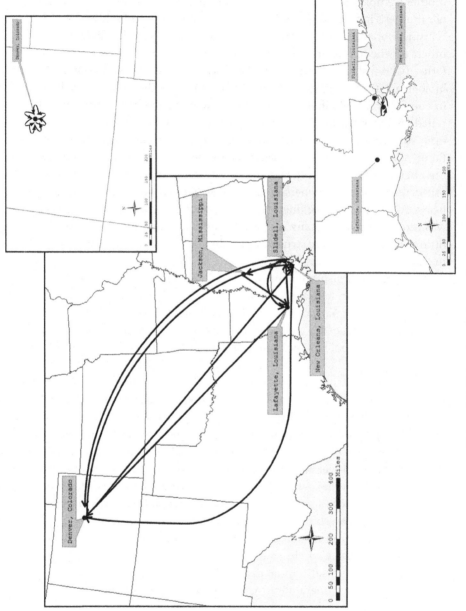

Figure 4.1. Mekana's multiple post-disaster moves by location

going to college and becoming a pediatrician or a computer programmer. The upward social mobility of her pre-disaster life disappeared. Her life as a young adult was taking shape in ways that were unexpected as Katrina laid bare the fragility of her pre-disaster social location. Mekana's story is a cautionary tale in some ways—a tale of what can happen even to those who are seemingly less vulnerable before disaster.

FINDING-EQUILIBRIUM TRAJECTORY

Disasters can exacerbate old problems, create new challenges, and contribute to substantial instability in children's lives, as was illustrated by Daniel's and Mekana's declining trajectories. Not all children and youth, however, suffer so much over the long term after catastrophe. Our study included some young people who endured evacuation, displacement, and disruption as Katrina's havoc unfolded, but who did not experience an ongoing downward spiral. We refer to this post-disaster pattern as the *finding-equilibrium trajectory*. It is characterized by a relatively brief decline in all of the major spheres of children's lives—their family and peer relationships, their housing situations, their schooling, their health, and so forth—followed by either a return to or a newfound type of stability.

It is important to emphasize, in no uncertain terms, that the children and youth who fit the finding-equilibrium trajectory endured many hardships as a consequence of Katrina. But their disaster experience did not ultimately diminish their overall life chances as it did for so many other children of Katrina. Why were the children and youth who fit the finding-equilibrium trajectory able to return to a familiar stable place or, in some cases, to experience new positive outcomes in the disaster aftermath? The answer to that question, which we discovered over time, was that pre- and/or post-disaster resource depth in many areas of the children's lives, access to helpful and supportive advocates, and the ability to mobilize resources from strong institutions made all the difference. To understand how these factors, among others, fostered resilience and kept children's trajectories from heading downward, we present the experiences of three children: Isabel, Zachary, and Cierra.

Isabel and Zachary are friends and neighbors, and their parents are part of a larger social network of families whose children attend the same elementary

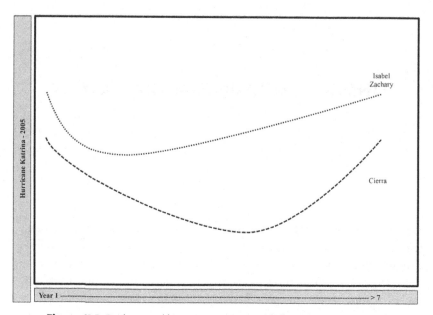

Figure II.1. Finding-equilibrium trajectories—Isabel, Zachary, and Cierra

school. Isabel and Zachary and their families illustrate the importance of resources and social networks. Because of their common backgrounds and the connections between their families, we include their stories together in chapter 5.

In chapter 6, we describe Cierra's life in the years before and after Katrina (you may recall that the book opened with an account of her and her mother's frightening evacuation from a flooded hospital in New Orleans). Cierra's life looked very different from that of Isabel or Zachary before the storm: Cierra certainly would have been considered "vulnerable" or "at risk," and she experienced hardships afterward, too. But Cierra rebounded from the stress and losses caused by the storm—which were more substantial in her life than in Isabel's or Zachary's—due to help she received from advocates, her peers, her mother, and various institutions. Cierra's story is one of recovery against the odds, and it sheds light on how, when the pieces come together, some children can have a brighter future after even the most traumatic disasters.

Figure II.1 compares the trajectories for Isabel, Zachary, and Cierra. Isabel and Zachary, even with their stronger support networks and more robust resource base, still experienced a decline after Katrina. With help, however, they found equilibrium. Cierra had fewer resources at the time of

Katrina and experienced a more substantial and longer term decline after the disaster, but like the other two focal children, was able to achieve equilibrium and recover in the disaster aftermath.

By carefully examining the stories of these three focal children, scholars and practitioners may be better suited to identify what can best help children and youth to cope and recover following even the most catastrophic of events. For example, preexisting financial stability was crucial for many children. In addition to Isabel and Zachary, we observed and met with dozens of children and families who were able to effectively use their families' education, wealth, and resource-rich networks to achieve stability, safety, and security in recovery. We also studied other children who, like Cierra, had extremely limited family financial or parental educational resources and were more at risk of becoming part of the declining trajectory. However, they were ultimately able to avoid it due to a combination of assistance and resolve—of their own and from others—and were able to achieve a steady state in the disaster aftermath. Chapters 5 and 6 document the finding-equilibrium trajectory.

5

ISABEL AND ZACHARY
RESOURCE DEPTH AND LONG-TERM STABILITY

It is almost 8:00 a.m. on a Friday morning in late May of 2007. We walk hurriedly down a beautiful tree-lined street in the heart of New Orleans, occasionally looking up to see strings of colorful Mardi Gras beads dangling from the branches. It is sunny and mild, and light drifts through the leafy canopy above us. We are headed to the daily "morning meeting" at Isabel's and Zachary's elementary school. This is a special tradition at their school, which is one of the few that reopened in the city in the 21 months since Hurricane Katrina.[1]

Two blocks away from the busy elementary school, we can hear the students and their families before we can see them. It is that unmistakable sound of excited children at the end of the school year, eager for the onset of the long, hot days of summer that mark life in New Orleans. We too are excited to be back, as several children in our study—including those from our core, secondary, and tertiary samples—attend this particular school and thus we had already spent a good deal of time there observing the children playing, conducting focus groups with students, and interviewing teachers.

We turn the corner and the school comes into full view. It is a modest two-story brick building surrounded by tall old, thick-trunk, oak trees and brightly colored flowers. It is easy to forget that not so long ago all of this beautiful foliage was turned a dull shade of brown by Katrina's floodwaters.

This is one of the city's few racially integrated schools, and there is a diverse crowd of schoolchildren in the yard. They are mostly black and white but some are Asian or Latino, ranging in age from about 5 to 11 years old, and enrolled in kindergarten through fifth grade. Beaming parents and grandparents stand chatting with one another, their eyes darting from their conversation partners to their rambunctious children at play in the schoolyard. Some of the adults are wearing casual clothes fit for the hot and humid day ahead; others are dressed in professional attire and clearly heading off to work after the morning meeting ends. There are also the younger siblings of the schoolchildren: toddlers on parents' shoulders, infants perched on their mothers' hips or sleeping in strollers, and preschool-age children sitting with their big brothers and sisters on the blacktop. Then there are the teachers, all of whom have that special look of simultaneous exhaustion and exhilaration that always seems to accompany the end of the school year.

We spot Zachary—one of our seven focal children in the study—first. He has grown a lot since we last saw him. He is taller and thinner, and his loose brown curls are longer and frame his tan face and brown eyes. Zachary's parents, Luke Baker and Amy Lacy, split up when he was very young. Never married, they remained committed to their son and coparenting. They live near each other and share equally in all aspects of raising their only child. We look around and see Luke standing under a tree joking with some friends. A writer and small-business owner who always exudes New Orleans cool, Luke is wearing his usual uniform: a pair of baggy shorts, a T-shirt, and a baseball cap covering up his blonde curly hair.

We approach Luke and say hello. As he is introducing us to his friends, one of the moms in our study, Beth Alphonse, walks up and teases her long-time friend: "Are you messing with these women, Luke?" We all laugh, as Beth smiles widely and then leads us over to the area where she had been standing in the schoolyard. We had been in Beth's home two days before when we interviewed her, her husband, and their children. Beth, a native of Louisiana, has a bright and easy smile, tan skin, and short red hair. She is standing beside her neighbor and best friend, Kate Banister. Kate, who like Beth has a special kind of youthful radiance about her, has shoulder-length brown hair and a smattering of freckles on her face and arms. Beth is holding her youngest son, Jacob, in her arms while Mason and Lily, her twin children, run around chasing each other. Kate also has three children, two girls named Tiffany and Isabel, and a boy, Wyatt.

We visit for a minute, but then the music begins and we, along with the rest of those standing in the schoolyard, give our full attention to the program beginning on the school's wide front steps, which serve as the stage. The music teacher takes the microphone, backed up by his "band" of fellow teachers and staff members from the school. They play their very own rocking rendition of "You Are My Sunshine." The youngest children, near the front, go wild as they shimmy and shake to the music. Zachary stands off to the left with a group of boys who appear to be about his age. They sway to the music, obviously enjoying the tune, but apparently resisting the urge to move about wildly like the "little kids" in their midst.

We then notice Isabel, one of our other focal children, who is doing a silly dance with her younger sister. After the song ends, the principal takes the microphone and announces that it is the last day of school. No one needs to be reminded of this fact, as evidenced by the giggles and cheers that erupt from the children and teachers. At the same time, some of the parents let out a laughing groan. After the announcements end, the teachers play two more songs, and we smile as we watch parents join right in as they dance with their children and sing along with the lyrics. It is a truly joyous occasion. On this morning, it seems that we, as well as others in our midst, have set aside all the ways that Katrina continues to unfold in the city and in the lives of children and youth, even if for just a fleeting moment.

In this chapter, we focus on Zachary's and Isabel's stories, which help elucidate the finding-equilibrium trajectory. Both children experienced a slight decline in the various spheres of their lives after Katrina, after which they rebounded quickly. We use the concept of *resource depth*, as defined and discussed in chapter 2, to help explain their post-disaster trajectory and to illuminate the various factors that kept them on an upward track rather than a downward spiral in the years after Katrina. As evidenced throughout this chapter, resources come in many forms—financial, social, cultural, educational, and personal—and, when available, they assist children and their families in a plethora of ways that are often hard to see but are critically important.

PACKING UP

On Saturday morning, August 27, 2005, Kate was roused out of bed by a 7:00 a.m. phone call. Kate's husband, Michael, was on the road with his band, so she reached across the bed and grabbed the phone on the second ring. Kate heard Beth say: "Are you awake?" Kate simply yawned in response. Beth, an early riser, had woken several hours ago. She brought Kate up to speed on the latest hurricane forecasts and warnings. She also said that she and her husband, Gavin, decided they needed to pack up the children and the dogs and get out of New Orleans before it was too late. These longtime neighbors had evacuated together before, including just a year prior, for Hurricane Ivan. But Kate, the more laid back of the two mothers, sensed a different sort of urgency in her friend's voice that morning. She immediately knew that a long and difficult day awaited her family, her neighbors, and her city.

Kate crawled out of her warm bed, went down and put on a pot of coffee, and then climbed back up the stairs to wake up Isabel. Kate asked Isabel, who was nine years old at the time, to get up and go wake Wyatt, who was six years old, and Tiffany, the baby of the family, who was three years old. She returned to the kitchen to pack a cooler full of sandwiches for the road. Then she gathered up her children's birth certificates and packed some toiletries and a change of clothes for herself. Fortunately, she had filled up the family car with gas just two days before, so she did not have to worry about dealing with the long lines at the filling station near their house.

Throughout the day, Kate and Beth were in constant communication. Isabel was their errand girl, running back and forth between the houses delivering messages and checking in on the progress of the packing. Kate told Isabel to put some clothes in her overnight duffel and asked her to help her younger siblings to do the same. Isabel, a thoughtful and sweet girl who is always eager to help, happily obliged. She also mobilized her younger brother, and together they carried containers of pictures and art supplies to the second floor of their house, "just in case" things got bad and the house flooded. Isabel often found herself in charge of helping the younger children. These requests were undoubtedly shaped by her gender and her position as the eldest child.[2]

Only a few blocks away, Zachary, who was seven years old, was sitting around at his mother's house tossing a baseball in the air and catching it in his favorite mitt. His mother, Amy, a tall pretty woman who worked at a nearby hospital, was on the phone with Luke, Zachary's father, who was at his home, a 10-minute drive away. Luke was noncommittal about whether he would evacuate. He had his business, after all, and he did not like leaving town. Amy was not particularly keen on evacuating, either—she had just bought a new house and was in the process of boxing up her things in preparation to move across the city. But they both agreed that given the size of the storm and the increasingly dire warnings, they had better get Zachary out of New Orleans.

Amy decided she would head toward Vicksburg, Mississippi, where they would ride out the storm in a local motel. Luke agreed this was a good idea, and he promised that he would call later in the day once he figured out whether he was going to stay or go. Looking back later, both Luke and Amy believed that they would have never been so proactive, and most likely "would not have evacuated at all," had they not been so concerned about keeping their son safe.[3]

THE EVACUATION

It was late Saturday afternoon by the time Kate and Beth had everything organized, packed, and loaded. The two moms buckled in their children, with dogs in the back, in their separate cars and then caravanned to a small town about two and a half hours northwest of New Orleans. They knew the route well, as they were driving toward the house of Beth's longtime friends, at whose home they had stayed at during their 2004 evacuation for Hurricane Ivan. This time, however, neither of their husbands traveled with them; while Michael was on the West Coast with his band, Gavin was in New York on a job assignment for his company.

Beth's friends, who were at their vacation home in another state, had a large house, a swimming pool, a hot tub, a big-screen television, friendly dogs, and an expansive yard. Beth and Kate and their families agreed that they were fortunate to have evacuated to such a "kid-friendly place." Michael later remarked that the families "evacuated up" to a "pretty idyllic situation" since they had none of these amenities in their own homes back in New Orleans.

When we asked the six children in the Alphonse and Banister families about their evacuation, they all commented on how much fun they had there; indeed, they all referred to their hurricane evacuation as a "hurrica-tion" since it felt like a vacation to them. Beth's older son, Mason, elaborated: "It was cool. There was a pool and a hot tub . . . and seven hundred billion dogs." Isabel corrected him and noted that there were actually "more like six dogs," but she still shared his enthusiasm for their evacuation destination.

Although the children in these two neighboring families were young at the time of the evacuation, it became an important milestone in all of their lives. Each time we would see them in the years after the storm, they would reference that time period. Isabel, the oldest of all the children, reflected on the experience nearly seven years after Katrina:

> I feel like I should think that it was really sad, but honestly, when I was there, I had a lot of fun in my evacuation. I didn't have to go to a new school and make new friends and be the, like, the "Katrina kid" or whatever . . . for me it was a little bit more like comfortable, I guess.

Like Isabel, the children of both families felt comfortable. Yet, like other parents, and especially the mothers in our study, Beth and Kate were feeling anxious about what was happening in New Orleans and wanted information. They were careful to shield the children from television broadcasts, so after they would go to bed at night, the two mothers would sit together on the couch and watch the round-the-clock coverage of the storm and the flooding of the city.

Meanwhile, in Mississippi, Zachary's family was having a more difficult evacuation. Amy and Zachary had arrived at the motel late on Saturday afternoon, after an exhausting bumper-to-bumper drive. Luke waited until the last minute before deciding that he was going to leave New Orleans, and ended up taking off in his unreliable green pickup truck during the early morning hours on Sunday, August 28. There was an ominous sense that something bad was coming, but the weather had not yet made a terrible turn. Knowing that Luke could break down on the side of the road just gave Amy one more thing to worry about, and admittedly, she felt "furious" at Luke for waiting so long and putting himself in harm's way.

Luke made it to the motel in Vicksburg, where the family rode out the storm. Soon after New Orleans started flooding, they began discussing what they were going to do next. Since Vicksburg had also lost power in the storm, Amy felt it was unsafe for her son to stay in the cramped, dark, hot motel room much longer. But Zachary's parents were not seeing eye to eye about where to go next. Amy wanted them to head to Mobile, Alabama, where she had lived before, had close friends, and had secured a place for the family to stay; Luke felt strongly that the three of them should drive to Atlanta, Georgia, where he had old friends and also had an offer of a place to stay.

Ultimately, Luke won out and the family evacuated to Atlanta to the home of his friends, a married couple with two young children, Joshua and Sophia, who were close to Zachary's age. Although Amy yielded to Luke's arguments regarding the importance of having a stable place for Zachary to stay, with children his same age, their initial conflict would be the beginning of months of tensions and fighting between them.

ADVANTAGES IN DISPLACEMENT

As information about the damage caused by Katrina began to emerge, and with the total mandatory evacuation of the city, Zachary's and Isabel's parents realized that their children's "hurrications" were going to be much longer than anyone expected. Indeed, the initial evacuation became a two-month dislocation. While this was challenging and inconvenient, they were better off than many others for several reasons.

First, Isabel's and Zachary's families had extensive social networks outside New Orleans.[4] These networks provided information, entrée to schools for the children, job opportunities for the adults, and access to teachers and doctors, as well as a substantial amount of emotional, material, and financial support. Importantly, it was also through these networks that the New Orleans families were able to procure free, secure, comfortable housing in safe neighborhoods during the displacement. In both cases, longtime friends who were members of their extensive social networks had extra resources to share. As Michael observed, they were "really lucky" that they were not "trying to find a hotel somewhere." He continued:

> It just goes to show that if you have social connections—I mean, there were people who lived in New Orleans who had never left Orleans Parish in their lives, so they just didn't have the networking that we had, or the skills to network. So we were fortunate just because we have so many relationships. I can't tell you how many people around the country said, "If you need a place to stay, you can come stay with us."

Michael was absolutely right in his observation. At the time of Katrina's landfall, over three-quarters (77.9 percent) of New Orleans residents had been born in Louisiana and most had spent their entire lives there.[5] Many of these individuals were deeply rooted in a geographic and cultural context and thus had strong connections within the city,[6] but not necessarily a breadth of networks, as Michael described in his family's case.

Many other children and families in our study also had social networks, and they attempted to mobilize them when they needed help. Yet, in the case of lower income respondents, their networks were financially disadvantaged; their connections had no extra houses, no extra beds or rooms, no spare savings, and no professionals with privileged knowledge. Few had residences outside of New Orleans. Moreover, if they were in New Orleans, they were likely now inundated by the disaster as well, and struggling to begin moving on their own path to recovery. Thus, while robust social networks are important, it is also crucial that the people within those networks have resource depth.

Second, Zachary and Isabel were enrolled in school in a matter of days following Katrina, so they did not experience the educational disruption that was common among so many children along the Gulf Coast.[7] As we describe in greater detail below, Zachary ended up in a highly regarded public elementary school in Atlanta, while Isabel and her siblings attended classes being taught by a former teacher from New Orleans who relocated to the same small town after Katrina. Both settings were safe and productive in terms of their learning environments, and they offered access to numerous supportive peer and adult influences. Moreover, reestablishing this sort of educational routine is critical to children's recovery after disaster.[8]

Third, the families soon discovered that although their neighborhoods back in New Orleans had some water and wind damage, their houses had not flooded, with the exception of a new home that Amy had purchased but had not yet moved into. The fact that they all had homes to return to was a tremendous relief to the parents and children alike. They knew when they eventually made their way back to New Orleans, they would have intact homes and possessions.

Fourth, the families were, in many ways, better off because they were able to evacuate in advance of the storm but also to stay nearby enough geographically that they could monitor the situation back home. Because they were only a few hours from New Orleans, and because of their social networks, they were able to receive regular updates on the status of their homes and neighborhoods. This was in sharp contrast to those in our study who were displaced much farther away and did not have access to the same knowledge.[9] Isabel emphasized how important this was for her and her family in terms of the comfort that came with just knowing what was unfolding at home:

> They had stuff on the news, but nobody knew whether their houses were okay or not. And I think that was part of the real scare of everything, that everybody was gone, and they didn't know until they came back if their house was okay or not . . . We were staying with a lot of journalists and stuff when we were evacuated, so we all had people who had passes to get back into the city [to check damage on the houses and report back]. I have a lot of friends who didn't know until they came back, like, months afterward and found their houses completely gone, back to places and their houses weren't even there anymore.

In this story the power of social networks is, again, especially apparent. Isabel's family's connection to professional journalists, who had special privileges to go into the closed city that allowed them to gather information, alleviated much anxiety for both the adults and the children.

This is not to say, however, that everything was "easy" for the families during the displacement. Luke's and Amy's fighting escalated in the months after Katrina. It was difficult for them to establish a workable parenting arrangement in the midst of all the upheaval the disaster caused. Although they tried to hide their arguing from Zachary, he knew that both of his parents were having a hard time. As he told us: "They were sad, like, once they thought about it, they would start crying and stuff." When we asked him how this made him feel, he simply responded, "Uncomfortable, you know?"

Isabel and her family were handling a different crisis in what they called their "blended household." Beth's elderly mother, who was in an assisted living facility before Katrina and was moved to a hospital unit just before the hurricane landfall, was literally "lost" during the evacuation. Beth and her older brother spent a number of tear-filled days after the storm on the telephone, frantically trying to find out about the whereabouts of their mother. Kate and Isabel provided as much support to her as they could during this time.

As the crisis with Beth's mother unfolded, Gavin was stuck on the East Coast and Michael on the West Coast due to their respective work commitments and the difficulty of getting flights back to Louisiana. This left Beth and Kate to parent together during the first week after Katrina. Although the phone lines were only working sporadically, Gavin and Michael called as often as they could to check in with their wives and children. Gavin recalled how challenging that period was, and how tense Beth became as the search for her mother unfolded:

> She's usually all loud and emotive. When she gets really calm and quiet, you know it's bad. I had some very bad times negotiating with the people I worked with on whether I was going to leave or not, and I got some threats about whether they could "depend on" me. Meanwhile, my mother-in-law is still lost. We don't know where she is. She was in the ICU [intensive care unit] at the hospital the last we knew, days before Katrina. We didn't even know where she was. I decided to stay for my job because we needed the cash and all that. It's one of a handful of decisions I regret, ever. It was too hard not being there. It's scary.

Beth and Kate also struggled being apart from their partners, but they knew they had to focus on the children. They organized the families and established a predictable, consistent routine—something that was critically important in beginning the recovery process for the children as well as the larger household.[10] They shopped for food, planned and prepared meals, supervised children playing, and arranged to meet other New Orleans friends who had evacuated to nearby communities. Gavin recalled how the mothers minimized the disruption during displacement:

> [The children] were in very familiar surroundings with lots of familiar people, and there was a routine, and they kept the routine. Beth and Kate were very strict about it. You get up, you pack lunch, you go to school,

it's real school, you come home in the afternoon, you do your homework. They were probably less disrupted [than other children] by design.

Kate and Beth were a "parenting machine," according to Gavin. Michael agreed:

From the very first days after the storm, just having people to go through this with was very comforting. Our family and the Alphonse family were under one roof together and we live on the same block and there's always been a very easy rapport between our families. The joke is, if Beth calls our house, I'll pass the phone to Kate and say, "It's your wife." [laughs] That's the relationship we have. And the kids are back and forth and in and out of each other's doors constantly.

Although the adults joked about the close relationship between Beth and Kate, the children also picked up on how tight-knit and special their bond really was. The children knew that these two women would take good care of them. As we saw with the other families in our study, and as has been reported in prior research, family labor in a disaster is gendered. Women are more likely to be the primary caregivers to children, spouses, grandparents, and often other members of extended families, especially if they are elderly or ill. Women are often the household managers and are expected to meet the emotional and physical needs of family as well as sometimes others in the community.[11] Furthermore, in a disaster, women are more likely to be in charge of securing various forms of disaster assistance for their families.[12]

Beth and Kate were "co-moms" to their children during the displacement. The children were enveloped in the warmth and familiarity of the two families. In fact, when we spent a day with the three Banister and three Alphonse children several years after the storm, we asked them to draw pictures of what helped them during the days after Katrina. Tiffany drew a picture of "my moms," Beth and Kate (see figure 5.1).

In addition to keeping things running smoothly around their temporary home, Beth and Kate also arranged to enroll their children in a local school. During the displacement, Isabel attended a small school with her younger brother and sister, Beth's twins, Mason and Lily, and several other displaced children whom she knew well. It also happened that one of Isabel's favorite teachers, Mr. James Fontenot, was displaced to the same town and ended up being hired on part-time by the school. Having a familiar and supportive face in the school made Isabel feel more "at home." Making the arrangements to keep all of the children together in the same school and getting Isabel into Mr. Fontenot's new classroom took a lot of diplomacy

Figure 5.1. *My Moms,*
by Tiffany, seven years old

and finesse on the part of Beth and Kate, but they made it happen. As a result, Isabel experienced a much higher level of security and continuity than many children of her age who were displaced by Katrina.

In Zachary's case, his parents' social networks and their resource depth connected him to Joshua and Sophia, whom he referred to as his "cousins" even though they were not related by blood. Both Joshua and Sophia accompanied Zachary to his new school in Atlanta, which eased his transition. With the influx of thousands of displaced children into the Atlanta school district, making sure Zachary was placed in Sophia and Joshua's school was only possible because of the lobbying of Amy, Luke, and Luke's friends. They went directly to the school administrators and emphatically argued for the importance of keeping the children together.

These middle-class parents were able to use their social capital to advocate for the classroom placements they wanted for their children. As other sociologists have long observed, middle-class parents, in general, have relationships with educational institutions that are distinct from those of working-class and poor families. Middle-class values and norms are often shared by the teachers and administrators and thus are rewarded in the school setting. As a result, the interactions between middle-class parents and teachers are smoother, and the parents are not intimidated by the authority figures and so feel more comfortable making requests on behalf of their children.[13] Recent research has shown that middle-class children are also much more proactive than their lower income counterparts in help-seeking, which grants them access to additional resources, individualized attention, and the support of teachers and other powerful institutional agents.[14]

While Isabel and Zachary missed their closest friends from home, they each had tremendous parental, peer, and sibling support during displacement. The fact that Isabel and Zachary knew that their friends had evacuated safely, albeit to many distant places throughout the United States, also made a difference, as did the fact that they could keep in touch via cell phones and email. Isabel drove this point home when she told us that she was "kind of" worried about her friends. But, she continued, "I knew they were all okay. Because I knew they all evacuated."

It is impossible to emphasize enough how central it was to Isabel's health and well-being to know that her friends were safe, rather than "maybe dead or drowned," like so many of the other children we interviewed thought had happened to their peers. Isabel's situation is in contrast to that of Daniel, who never reunited with his classmates and friends, and of Mekana, who was unable to locate her friends for weeks and even months after the storm, causing her great anxiety. Furthermore, Isabel was certain that being younger made her less focused on her friends; during an interview in 2011, she reflected back and told us that she was sure that had she been a teenager during Katrina, she would have been much more distressed.

When we interviewed Zachary six years after Katrina, he told us about his recent visit with Joshua and Sophia. It was clear how close he still felt to them, and he still referred to them as his "cousins." He remembered how much of a difference it made to have Sophia in the same classroom during the displacement, and to have the consistency of being able to stay in one place with her family, especially as his parents were forced to do the long, seven-hour drive between New Orleans and Atlanta every few days. Zachary's and Isabel's experiences with friends during this time highlight the often overlooked importance of friendship and positive peer relations for children.[15]

Luke and Amy took turns being with Zachary at the Atlanta apartment; he was settling in, but they were not. Amy looked back and agreed that displacement was an "amazing adventure" for Zachary and that he "loved the whole thing." She believed his relationship with Joshua and Sophia was the most important factor in making displacement a positive time for Zachary: "He gained a huge experience and meaning being with Joshua and Sophia. I think those two relationships are gonna be with him for the rest of his life and I think that's really important."

DECIDING TO RETURN

A month after Katrina, the Alphonse and Banister families began discussing their return to New Orleans in earnest. Although there was still standing water throughout the city, an increasing number of neighborhoods were beginning to reopen to residents. The families in our study were anxious to return and assess the damage to their homes and begin making the necessary repairs to permanently move back to New Orleans. On a Saturday morning in late September of 2005, Beth and Kate made the two-hour drive home. Michael and Gavin, who had returned for a short time from their work trips, stayed behind with the six children. Later, Beth and Kate recalled, through laughter and tears, the overpowering odor emanating from their refrigerators in their homes in New Orleans, which had been without power for weeks and were full of spoiled food and mold. After donning masks and hospital gloves, they managed to drag the appliances out into the street, only to leave them on the curb to be picked up by the sporadic garbage collection service.[16]

Beth and Kate returned to their temporary housing that night and informed their husbands that although their homes had sustained some minor wind and water damage, the structures were sound and could be moved back into at any time. Yet, neither woman was sure yet that she *wanted* to be back in the city. The streetlights were not working on their block. Mail service had not yet resumed. Most of the neighborhoods were still totally deserted. There were armed personnel patrolling certain areas in the city and many other unfamiliar outsiders who had descended as part of the Katrina emergency response. Almost no schools or hospitals had been reopened. The parks were all awash in mud, and both of the moms were deeply concerned about soil and water contamination.[17]

Zachary's mother had similar fears about returning to New Orleans, a city that seemed so badly damaged that she wondered if it would ever recover. Amy disclosed to us that she "wished" that Luke would relent and agree to move to Mobile, permanently. But he was unwilling to leave New Orleans, a city that had an almost magnetic pull for him and that was home to his successful business. Amy, who had long struggled with depression, had a difficult time after Katrina when she learned that the new home she purchased had been badly flooded. She had already moved some of her possessions, including Zachary's baby pictures, into the new house and they had been left sitting in murky floodwaters for days. (During our first visit to Luke's house, less than a month after Katrina, we observed several of the badly damaged pictures lying out on his table. He was attempting to dry them for his ex-partner. Even though he was frustrated with all the fighting since the storm, he obviously cared deeply for Amy and wanted to help replace a small part of what she had lost to the floodwaters.)

Although the loss of the pictures and possessions was heartbreaking for Amy, she had not sold her old home, which meant that she and Zachary had

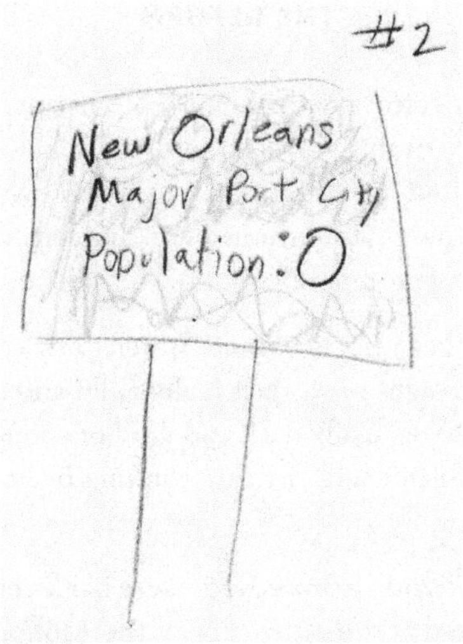

Figure 5.2. Drawing of "what Katrina did to New Orleans," by Zachary, 11 years old

a familiar place where they could return. Moreover, Luke's house had not flooded at all, so Zachary's old bedroom, including his toys, clothes, baseball cards, and other favorite things were all safe. Luke's house and Amy's old home are situated in areas of the city that are at slightly higher elevations than many other areas of New Orleans, so they were both less vulnerable to the flooding.[18]

Luke and Amy had already been making the seven-hour commute back and forth from Atlanta to New Orleans, so their big dilemma was when they would return with their child. Although Zachary was young, he influenced this decision as well, as he loved New Orleans as deeply as his dad and wanted to go back home as soon as possible.[19] When we asked Zachary to draw a picture of what had been most difficult since Katrina, he paused for a long period of time. He then picked up a few crayons and proceeded to draw a box in the middle of the white page. He sat there for a minute and then wrote, "New Orleans, Major Port City, Population: 0" in the center of the sign (see figure 5.2).

When we asked Zachary to describe his drawing, he responded:

So, it's like, Katrina made everybody leave. And it's a big city . . . so it's kind of odd to see, like, a population of that [size gone] . . . During Katrina I lived in Atlanta. It was all right. It was good to see something new. But I still wanted to be back in New Orleans . . . There [are] some things about New Orleans, you just want to stay here for.

Isabel and her family returned to their New Orleans home at the end of October 2005, just two months after the storm. They were happy to be back. Isabel was "really excited" to go home and was relieved when she got back to New Orleans and saw that her house was, indeed, still standing. Yet, the city was not the same. Her neighborhood, she said, did not feel right:

> Yeah, it was weird, because, like, there weren't any cars out, and all the trees were dead. At night it was just really quiet and none of the street-lights were on, so it was really dark and kind of spooky. And you didn't hear all the noise outside and the cars running by. It was just kind of a weird feeling.

Though none of her friends from school were back yet, Isabel was grateful that her family returned at the same time as the Alphonse family. She could play with her siblings and the Alphonse children down the block. Her parents also had support for all the challenges of being back in a devastated and only marginally functioning city.

Isabel's family, once again, was able to draw on their resources, often in the form of social networks, to settle into life back in New Orleans. Kate and Michael were able to enroll their children in a temporary school, organized by parents and advertised by word of mouth, until the public schools reopened. A local parent secured space for classrooms from her employer. Families were asked to pay the teachers out of pocket if they could, and Isabel's family contributed as much as they were financially able. When they needed answers about health risks, they used the Internet on their home computer to research Environmental Protection Agency (EPA) websites and contacted friends who were doctors to get reliable information.

Even on Halloween night, their social networks and financial and transportation resources helped them. As nightfall approached and their children put on costumes, Isabel's parents realized that trick-or-treating door to door, as they had done in all the years past, was not going to work. No one was home. Most houses in the surrounding area were dark. The electrical grid was still a mess, and there were still no working streetlights in their neighborhood or any of the surrounding neighborhoods. When the sun went down, they were standing with their kids and the Alphonse family, in costumes, in a "ghost town." Gavin remembered how "the whole city was deserted" that night. Kate added that it was "depressing." Tiffany was dressed like a "little princess" but could not even walk on the streets because there was "still so much debris." In order to save Halloween for their kids, they called some friends and found out about an event in town for the few residents who had returned; they drove their children to a local hospital for the festivities. Admittedly, "it wasn't as good" as their usual trick-or-treating ritual, but there were costumes and candy, and the kids made the most of it.

Zachary's family returned early to New Orleans as well, also just before Halloween. Amy hated Atlanta and felt like she had been there forever. Luke realized that they all needed to come back. When they found out from Kate and Beth that there was a local, community-organized school opening in October, the one Isabel had just started attending, they packed up and headed home. Daniel and Mekana, as described in chapters 3 and 4, did not live in families or communities that had the resources to engage in such a grassroots, labor-intensive enterprise as building a school from the bottom up. The school was organized through word of mouth, and even though parents tried to recruit children from other neighborhoods with few resources, they were unsuccessful.

When we asked Zachary how it felt to come back to New Orleans, he stated straightforwardly: "It felt good, but it felt sad to leave Atlanta." He would miss his new "cousins" and riding the school bus, a novelty to him, and going to Braves baseball games. But he also was deeply connected to New Orleans. When we asked him what he loved so much about the city he said, "The food. The culture. You see, like, anything can happen in New Orleans. You can do anything."

Zachary's parents moved back into their old homes and reestablished Zachary's routine of going back and forth between their two houses. He explained the system to us:

> Here Wednesday, every other Friday, every other Friday, which means Saturday after every other Friday, and Sundays, I think. Mom's Tuesday, Thursday, every other Friday and Saturday and Sunday sometimes. It's the same thing except, like, they switch off Fridays, and once you get Friday, that means you get Saturday, and the person that doesn't get Friday and Saturday gets Sunday.

For Luke, getting back into this routine—which was complicated for us to understand, but by this time was second nature to them—and having Zachary enrolled in school were the most important things when they returned. Once that routine was set, they all settled in and started to reassemble their lives. Amy loved being home and recalled the first weeks in the city:

> There were just a few people back and it was—for the first six months after, people started getting back and it was really lovely here. Nothing worked, but it was so nice. Everyone was so nice. There was no crime hap-

pening here. We were just like, everyone was so happy to see each other. You would walk down the street and see someone and you'd go and hug.

Zachary was happy, too. He enjoyed the temporary school and especially liked the long recesses they had in a city park. Luke described what the first few months were like after they returned home to New Orleans: "So things were scaled down and it was different, but then all of a sudden it was November, and before you knew it, time went by and it was Christmas and then normal school in January." Zachary's public school reopened in January; it was one of the fastest to recover in the city after Katrina. In addition, it was back in its original building with many of the same students and teachers. Most New Orleans children and youth, however, were not back in their neighborhood schools at this point; Zachary's situation was not the norm.

Zachary told us that most of his friends, as well as the friends of his parents, were able to return to the city. Like Isabel's family, Zachary and his family utilized their resources to find equilibrium. Amy and Luke had done serious damage to their relationship during displacement (by the end of their time in Atlanta they were barely speaking to one another), and if they were going to continue to amicably coparent their son, they needed to pay for therapy sessions. They did, and it helped. They also, like the Banister and Alphonse families, paid out of pocket for the volunteer teachers at the temporary school. Luke's business was doing well and he was pleased that they could contribute to the teachers' salaries until the public schools opened.

In addition to the monetary resources, which are obviously important in disaster recovery, Zachary and his parents relied on their friends and networks for emotional and social support as well as for scarce, valuable information (Where can you buy fresh fruits and vegetables? Is there a pharmacy open nearby? What days are the garbage and other refuse from gutted homes being picked up? Is the dust coming in through open windows toxic with asbestos? When will public schools reopen?). Research shows that individuals and households that have these "networks of care" are critically important in disaster recovery, and conversely, those persons who are isolated—both physically and in terms of information networks—tend to suffer more severe consequences.[20]

DECIDING TO STAY

Isabel's and Zachary's families periodically considered leaving New Orleans in the years after Katrina. Life was difficult after the storm. There were fewer amenities of all kinds.[21] And, after a period of decline, the crime rate started to climb again. In fact, every time we met with Zachary, he discussed his worries about crime. Several mothers in our study told us how they had been mugged on their own streets or had their cars broken into.

The city had changed in other ways as well. The overall population was smaller and it had a new racial makeup: proportionately there were now far fewer blacks and more whites and Latinos.[22] There were also fewer children, as many families did not return because of the lack of childcare and schools. There were more men than women, as construction workers, almost all males, flooded the city to do recovery work, and the city fired thousands of teachers, mostly female, who did not return.[23] This gender imbalance was obvious, and for many created a feeling of a lack of safety. And the city just felt, in some ways, less cohesive, with an influx of newcomers and the absence of old residents and longtime small local businesses that did not survive. The feeling of community solidarity that marked the initial days of return, when everyone was "nice," as Amy recalled, largely dissipated as time went on.

Isabel and Zachary and their parents also knew that many children and families who had returned were struggling. Some had moved back to the city and tried to reestablish their lives only to realize that they needed to leave. When we conducted focus groups with teachers, we learned that large numbers of children were "upset" and "often cried," and many others were "bouncy" and "could not focus" in the classroom. Childcare providers told us that the young children in their care were "acting out" and seemed more "quick to anger." A guidance counselor at an elite private school revealed during an interview that there had been several suicides[24] and discussed other devastating mental health challenges that mounted after Katrina; many students were depressed and dealing with anxiety. She said: "I have never made so many [mental health] referrals in my life." For Isabel and her family these broader realities became painfully personal when a teenager they knew who had been suffering from depression died of a drug overdose after she returned to New Orleans; members of the community blamed the losses caused by Katrina, and especially the death of her beloved dog, for her death.[25]

As parents, Beth and Gavin, Kate and Michael, and Luke and Amy spent countless hours talking with one another and other family members and friends in their social networks about whether they were doing the right thing in keeping their children in "the city that care forgot."[26] When Isabel developed asthma two years after the hurricane, a new wave of concern hit her own parents as well as other moms and dads in her neighborhood and social network. Was it simply genetic? Or was her health problem caused by the toxic environment in which they were certain they were living?

The children had fewer places to play, teens had fewer safe spaces to "hang out," and the signs of destruction were constant reminders of the disaster. Isabel and Zachary did not want to see the destroyed houses in the Lower Ninth Ward, and their parents did not want to show them. The adults worried about the overall physical, educational, and emotional impact on their children. Indeed, when we interviewed and conducted focus groups with their children, the parents were often curious if we had learned of any stress or concern expressed by their sons and daughters that they had missed or their children had not told them about (we discuss how we dealt with these inquiries in appendix B).

But even with these challenges, the pull was strong, and Isabel and Zachary regularly asserted that New Orleans was the place that they wanted to be. Almost all of their friends were back. Their school, which became a charter school in the disaster aftermath, managed to hire back almost all of its pre-Katrina teachers. Isabel's and Zachary's teachers received training in how to help children after Katrina, and they creatively used music, writing, theater, and dance as ways to encourage children to express themselves during the disaster recovery. Isabel described one such school project which was designed to help students deal with Katrina:

> I remember that after we came back here, we all made journals that we wrote in and put stuff in. It was like a journal—like a "Dear Diary" kind of thing. We cut out pictures from magazines. I remember it was fun to make, because it was like, "Here, write down everything you feel." It was more like a creative expression of it.

In addition, Isabel could walk to see her friends and Zachary could bike across several blocks from his mom's to his dad's house. Life was not easy, but they were home.

FINDING EQUILIBRIUM

There are several lessons to be learned from Zachary's and Isabel's postdisaster trajectory. First, both material and non-material resources were crucial in the pre-disaster period. Zachary's and Isabel's families were better positioned financially than were those of most of the other children in our study. Their parents, as well as most of their parents' friends, had college degrees and steady jobs. They owned their own cars and homes. While they did not earn excessively high incomes, and Isabel's family sometimes only had access to minimal health insurance coverage, they all had the safety net and privilege afforded by their social class, dominant racial status, and high level of parental education.

Zachary's and Isabel's families also had extensive social networks. Their parents had lived and worked in different regions of the United States and, as a consequence, had developed strong and weak ties both inside and outside the city of New Orleans and state of Louisiana. These networks provided long-term housing during displacement, information about the status of their homes, connections to create a grassroots alternative school, and access to precious information. It was important that their social networks had resources to share; they had resource depth. Thus, social class affects social networks. Gender, too, affects networks. As scholars have shown in the past, women often build and maintain more extensive social networks than men do, and this can be helpful in a disaster.[27] In addition, the men's networks that they had developed through their employment, which required both of them to travel extensively across the U.S., made a tremendous difference in the Katrina aftermath.

In the summer of 2011, six years after Katrina, Zachary and Isabel told us that they "barely" thought about the disaster anymore. Isabel, who was 15 years old by that time, said she had learned from the experience and it made her appreciate her family more. For Zachary, Katrina just reminded him of the fragility of the city that he loved so much. But they had both moved on. Isabel was already thinking about college and was certain that she wanted to move to another city, "like New York or San Francisco," in the future, but that New Orleans would always be her home. Zachary was considering being an actor or otherwise staying involved in the arts. They knew that "other people had it a lot worse" than they had, and they were thankful that they had been home, truly home, since the storm.

Unlike Daniel and Mekana, Zachary and Isabel experienced a shorter and shallower decline in the disaster aftermath, and were able to recover more fully and more quickly. Isabel was displaced one time, and Zachary only two times. This level of displacement is lower than what is reported for other New Orleans children: studies showed that the average number of displacements in the six-month period after Katrina was 3.5, and that the average number of school moves in the three months after Katrina was three, but ranged from one to eleven.[28]

Past disaster research has found that for communities, a longer emergency period, which typically implies more catastrophic losses and disruptions, correlates with a longer recovery period.[29] For the families in our study, this also held true: the longer the emergency, the more displacements; and the more substantial the upheaval, the longer the recovery. Daniel and Mekana, with less resource depth, were on a declining trajectory, while Isabel and Zachary, with the help of valuable family resources and strong social networks, were able to find equilibrium.

6

CIERRA
MOBILIZING RESOURCES

THE SAGA

One bad thing, which seems to have split at the age of six.
Since then, pain invited itself into the life of the child, with its waters
and winds who removed the child from the love of her city into a new
one she knew exactly nothing about. Now three years have gone.
That city turned from her house to her home.

POEM WRITTEN BY CIERRA WASHINGTON, 14 YEARS OLD

Cierra shared this poem with us one spring evening while sitting at the kitchen table. We were visiting her and her mother at their modest two-bedroom house in Lafayette, Louisiana. It was 2008 and nearly three years had passed since Hurricane Katrina uprooted them from New Orleans, but the storm was never far from Cierra's mind. A creative child, she continued to write stories and poems about Katrina long after the floodwaters had receded and she and her mother had settled permanently in their new community.[1]

Cierra told us that when she expressed herself through art, it helped her to heal from all of the hurt in her life. "The Saga" captures the arc of Cierra's struggle for recovery, an arc which includes pain, anger, hope, and acceptance. The poem opens with a reference to her parents' divorce when she was only six years old, an event which left an aching emotional wound; when we asked her about this experience, she explained that it made her realize "how it hurts and how hurt feels" because she was "so happy, just with my mom, me, and my dad."

The poem then shifts to the hurt that Katrina caused ("pain invited itself into the life of the child"), and her displacement from New Orleans to Lafayette ("waters and winds who removed the child from the love of her city into a new one she knew exactly nothing about"). In the years after the disaster, most of the poems and songs that Cierra wrote centered on

Katrina and its aftermath. She told us that one of the reasons she has long loved expressing herself through music is "because when I sing, I get all the stress out of my chest, and it just feels good."

Cierra, whose evacuation story opened chapter 1 and who was 11 years old at the time of Katrina, had a traumatic, life-threatening experience in the storm. She and her mother endured a harrowing period at a New Orleans hospital that was battered by the hurricane. That experience left them both deeply shaken, with painful memories of the horror they witnessed and the fear they felt as they wondered whether their family members and friends had lived or died. After they were rescued by boat from the hospital, Cierra and her mother stayed at a temporary shelter in Lafayette for three months. They then moved on to a FEMA trailer located on the outskirts of Lafayette for about two years. They finally secured a Habitat for Humanity home in Lafayette, the city where they would permanently settle after Katrina.

The losses they sustained as well as the subsequent displacement to a completely unfamiliar place were scarring to both Cierra and her mother. As Cierra explained regarding the forced relocation, "I never knew that Lafayette existed," and "honestly, I didn't really want to go." She yearned for her old life, her close friends from New Orleans, and all of the members of her extended family. She described her emotions as she settled into life in Lafayette after Katrina:

> Sixth-grade year I was—I don't know, I was kind of angry, and I didn't want to, like, be in anything or do anything. I just was very angry and I was mad because I wasn't with family, and I was missing my aunt so much because I was living close to my aunt [before Katrina]. I was missing all my family and my friends and the people that were really close to me that loved me the most.

Yet, notably, despite all the anger and upset, in the final line of her poem, Cierra writes that her new city had now become "home." It took years, but Cierra was eventually able to recover. This chapter tells her story.

FINDING EQUILIBRIUM

Cierra's evacuation and displacement experiences were starkly different from those of Isabel and Zachary, whom we described in chapter 5 and whose experiences also fit the finding-equilibrium trajectory. Isabel and Zachary, along with their families and pets, left the city safely *before* the storm and in the comfort of their family cars. They evacuated to the homes of friends, all the while knowing that most of their loved ones were safe. Their houses and belongings were spared from the floodwaters, and thus they were able to return home less than two months after the storm. Moreover, their former school reopened only months after the storm, due in large part to the mobilization of parental networks and their associated resource depth. Both Isabel and Zachary subsequently returned to classrooms with their pre-storm peers and teachers.

Cierra and her mother, Debra, were unable to evacuate before Katrina made landfall. This was due to several structural factors: Debra was required to report to work, she did not have access to a vehicle, and they had no financial safety net. Their social safety net—which consisted of a large network of family members in New Orleans—was torn apart in Katrina, as aunts and uncles and cousins were scattered across many states following the disaster. When the floodwaters inundated her home in New Orleans East, Cierra lost nearly everything—her clothes, schoolbooks, posters, and journals. Cierra never called New Orleans home again after the storm.

Before Katrina, the social circumstances of the other focal children of the finding-equilibrium trajectory were also quite different. Isabel and Zachary, both white and middle-class, had what we refer to as "resource depth," including high-functioning schools, home and car ownership, safe neighborhoods, two involved parents with steady jobs making livable wages, and high levels of social capital. Cierra, an African American child, lived with her single mother, who was employed in a low-wage job with little potential for advancement. Although Cierra's father, who worked as a bellhop at a local hotel, continued to live in New Orleans even after he and Debra divorced, he was mostly uninvolved in Cierra's life and contributed very little financially to help raise her (Debra received $127 per month in child support payments before Katrina, and these payments became sporadic after the storm). Cierra attended an all-black public school. She and her mother rented a small apartment in a house that belonged to a family friend who allowed them to live there temporarily. In sum, prior to the disaster, Cierra was more vulnerable and her life was marked by many more insecurities than Isabel or Zachary experienced. Yet, even though she had fewer resources at the time of Katrina and the *depth* of the decline after the disaster and the *length* of the recovery time were greater for Cierra, her trajectory ultimately is similar to that of Isabel and Zachary in that she, too, had a positive, upward recovery process after the disaster.

How is this possible? How did Cierra, who had access to far fewer resources, had a more traumatic disaster experience, and lived in a more precarious condition both before and after Katrina, achieve stability and security over time after such disruptive disaster and displacement? We found that the support and assistance of *advocates* and *institutions*, with her *mother as the primary conduit* to these resources, was the reason that she was able to find equilibrium.

Based on our observations and interviews, we came to define *advocates* as nonfamilial outsiders—shelter volunteers, teachers, church staff, and others—who worked on behalf of displaced children and youth and remained in their lives for an extended period of time after Katrina. For Cierra and many other young people in our study, advocates played a central and essential role in the recovery process. Each advocate served as a supporter, backer, and defender of others less powerful than themselves; these were individuals who promoted the interests of children and youth and/or who intervened on their behalf. An advocate is someone who identified the needs of children and their families and then stepped up to meet those needs. More often than not, advocates had more status, power, social and cultural capital, and access to material and non-material resources than the children and families whom they served. Often, their advocacy represented an extension of their professional work within an institution (such as through a church or school); but it is important to emphasize that advocates usually went well above and beyond their "normal" institutional roles and began mobilizing vital resources in the face of unmet post-disaster needs.

In addition to the help of advocates, Cierra received support and assistance from institutions.[2] An *institution*, for our purposes, is an organization or agency—whether governmental or nongovernmental, nonprofit or for-profit—that provides assistance to individuals, families, communities, or certain populations of people. Institutions include, for example, educational, religious, employment, and housing organizations and programs. Unlike an advocate or advocates, an institutional body is not simply an individual or a group of individuals, but instead represents a structure larger than the people who work within it and has very real and important effects on individuals and families. Institutions can have an enduring presence in people's lives, even when specific employees leave or certain client-provider relationships change.

Institutions were critical for Cierra because these are the structures that were able to offer resources to assist in the recovery process. While *individuals* (like Cierra, Debra, and the advocates) could ask for and help mobilize the resources, it was the *institutions* (like Cierra's school, FEMA, and Habitat for Humanity) that provided the resource context that was critical for the post-disaster recovery to occur.

In this chapter, we detail how and why the dedication and contributions of advocates, such as determined disaster shelter workers, teachers, and church pastors, and the resources and commitment of various institutions, such as integrated schools and housing programs and policies that assist the working poor, can make a difference in disaster-affected children's lives. Throughout, we describe how Cierra's mother was an instrumental intermediary for locating and mobilizing resources for her daughter. Debra repeatedly spoke to us about the importance of "motivating" her daughter and "introducing her to positive things" to "keep her on the right track." Without Debra as the critical link between her child and available resources, the advocates and the institutions might not have been able to assist Cierra and help her find equilibrium. Moreover, Cierra herself actively sought out people, activities, and places that directly benefited her recovery.

Cierra's case is critical to understand because it illustrates the role and importance of (1) people who serve as supportive advocates; (2) strong existing and emergent institutions (e.g., well-funded schools, effective governmental post-disaster relief programs, helpful religious and nonprofit organizations) that can offer vital post-disaster interventions; (3) a parent or guardian who mobilizes resources, develops capacities, and fosters and oversees networks; and (4) a child who is willing and able to actively participate in the recovery process. Without all of these factors simultaneously in play, Cierra might have not found equilibrium following Katrina.

AFTER THE STORM

When we first met Cierra, she was literally jumping for joy. It was early October 2005, and she and her mother were staying in the Cajundome—a large, multipurpose arena located on the outskirts of Lafayette and designed for sporting events and music concerts. Immediately following the storm it was converted to a shelter for thousands of Katrina survivors. When we walked into the main office of the Cajundome, we saw Cierra and Debra, who had just received the news that they would soon be able to move into a FEMA trailer in a newly established mobile home park for people displaced by the disaster. The park was located a few miles outside of Lafayette, in an expansive field off a winding two-lane, paved country road.

After weeks of sleeping on narrow cots, of waiting in long lines to use the shared restrooms, of bathing without privacy in the shower stalls, and of eating meals off paper plates with strangers, Debra and Cierra could not have been more relieved. Seeking refuge in a mass shelter is not what most people want after a disaster. Past research has repeatedly shown that dis-aster survivors prefer to stay in the private homes of family members or friends, or in hotels or motels instead of in large shelters with many people they do not know.[3] Mass shelters are not only uncomfortable; they often feel unsafe for the residents, as they are surrounded by strangers, day and night.[4]

This was certainly true for Debra, who never felt entirely comfortable at the Cajundome, even though she was so grateful for the people who ran the shelter. She was especially nervous at night, as all the evacuees slept in the arena on cots lined into neat rows with militaristic precision. Debra was very worried something bad would happen to Cierra as they were "sleeping in the wide open" with "no walls." So, for three months, Debra only "cat-napped" because she wanted to "watch Cierra sleep." Debra used to tell her daughter, "If you get up, wake me up before you go to the bathroom." Their living conditions, combined with the trauma of the storm and her lack of restful sleep, caused so much stress for Debra that after a routine exam, one of the volunteer doctors at the Cajundome placed her on blood pressure medication to try to bring her newly developed hypertension under control.

Debra described their routine in the shelter as follows:

> We would have to get up at the Cajundome when the lights come on at 5 or 6 and get the children ready for school . . . So that means I would have to get up early in the morning, go on out to the shower, see other people in the showers with their children, go into the bathroom to brush their teeth, and get them ready just like that to then go right outside and catch the bus.

When they were living at the Cajundome, Cierra got her menstrual period for the first time, and it pained Debra that she could not better support her daughter during that critical developmental moment. She told us:

> I was just so sorry it had to happen there, and we had to go through that trauma there. She was confused about it, no privacy. She would say, "Mom, hurry, hurry." I just sat her down and talked and hugged her. It kind of helped a little bit. At the time there was so much excitement . . . and I didn't have the time enough to be right there and baby her because so much was going on at the Cajundome.

At its peak, the Cajundome provided temporary shelter for over 18,000 evacuees. The shelter was run primarily by the original paid staff mem-bers of the facility. Later, the American Red Cross and other volunteer organizations arrived and assumed some of the operational responsibili-ties. The Cajundome employees and the new volunteers offered many services to the Katrina survivors, or "guests" and "residents," as the staff insisted they be called as they felt those terms were more humanizing than "evacuees" or "refugees." In addition to providing shelter, these services included free water, food, clothing, childcare, medical care, play therapy for children, tutors for homework, volunteers to play board games and do puzzles, organized basketball games, and video games. There was a coloring area with a table, paper, and crayons for children to make pictures and then hang them on the surrounding walls. There was also a dedicated area for donated toys—both new and used—that arrived by the truckload to the Cajundome.

Despite the programming and the services, a local volunteer, Beverly, told us in an interview that it was still "madness" in the shelter, with many thousands of people under one roof for months, and it was "heartbreaking" for her. Another volunteer, April, found that the children did not really need the new toys as much as they needed attention; she was astounded by how many children approached her and asked, "Will you play a game with me?" As we saw during our visit, and as the volunteers described, "It was bed, bed, bed, rows and rows of beds, no room for kids to play."

Even in this crowded context, though, we also saw children and youth helping one another, often in gendered ways: older sisters playing board games and coloring pictures with their younger siblings; older boys leading younger boys in basketball games and other activities.[5] Cierra also took on several responsibilities in the shelter, including taking care of a baby so that the child's mother could rest and attend to various recovery needs.

In receiving a trailer, Cierra and her mother were getting a new home, a place that was private, quiet, and all theirs. In a hallway of the Cajundome offices, we witnessed their elation at the good news. They hugged Ms. Sue and Ms. Renee, the Cajundome staff members who had worked tirelessly to find them the trailer and had delivered the wonderful news. The happiness was contagious; everyone there, including both of us, was laughing and clapping and some onlookers cheered loudly. Debra raised her hands in the air and said, "Praise God, praise God," repeatedly as she smiled and shed tears of joy.

MOBILIZING RESOURCES: ADVOCATES AND INSTITUTIONS

In the sections that follow, we explain how Cierra rebounded from the tremendous disruption and stress caused by Katrina. In particular, we focus on the role that advocates and strong institutions played in this process.

Throughout, we also emphasize how Debra, a determined mother, and Cierra, a bright and engaged child, were centrally involved in the recovery.

THE DISASTER SHELTER TEAM

Although Cierra and her mother were excited to secure the rent-free FEMA trailer and move on from the shelter, they were sad to leave the people at the Cajundome. They had grown quite close to the staff members there who had helped them and become an integral part of their disrupted lives. Debra said repeatedly that they "took care of us like we were newborn babies."

At one point, less than two weeks after their arrival, as Hurricane Rita threatened the Gulf Coast in September 2005, the residents of the Cajundome had to leave and move to a poorly equipped shelter in Shreveport. The evacuees were badly mistreated and had guns pointed at them by overzealous security guards. Cierra, who was still reeling from the Katrina evacuation, described the experience in Shreveport to us: "I cried every night. It's hard to just stand there and let people point guns in your face and cuss you out and stuff like that."

Debra was sad, angry, and scared for herself and especially for her daughter. She called Mr. Nate, the director of the Cajundome, so that he could help to fix the situation and get the Katrina and Rita exiles back to Lafayette safely. She was confident that he would defend them and advocate for their rights once he found out what was going on. And he did. He was furious about how the evacuees had been treated, and he was especially angry about guns being drawn on the exhausted and now terribly frightened Katrina survivors. Later, Debra bought Mr. Nate a plaque to thank him for everything he and his staff had done for her, for Cierra, and for the other survivors. When she described Mr. Nate to us, Debra evoked a biblical prophet who led a forsaken people to safety: "I call Mr. Nate my Moses. I gave him a plaque, like he is my Moses."

When the time came to pack up their few belongings and move on from the Cajundome, Cierra described how she felt:

> I was happy because we were moving, and we had a little bit more free-
> dom. We had our own shower, and we don't have to wait, like, a bunch to
> get in the shower after other people. But it was sad because that was my
> home for, like, some months, and I was getting attached to a lot of people.
> I was getting attached to Mr. Nate and Ms. Sue and Ms. Grace.

The relationships Cierra and her mother formed with shelter workers became a critical piece of their recovery, as the assistance of the Cajundome staff did not end when Debra and Cierra moved out, but instead continued for years afterward.

We learned about how the Cajundome shelter workers, including Ms. Sue, Ms. Renee, Ms. Grace, Mr. Nate, and their colleagues, continued to advocate for Cierra and Debra after they transitioned to the FEMA trailer. One way the advocates helped after the move was assisting with Cierra's transportation to school. The trailer park was located outside the school district where Cierra had already enrolled in classes when she was in the Cajundome. But when Cierra said to her mother, "Mama, I don't want to change schools. I met new friends. Why are they taking my friends from me?" Debra moved into action on behalf of her daughter. She said to herself, "Some way, somehow, I'm not gonna let them take this from you. I was like, she cannot change schools."

Debra went to Cierra's school and the administrative staff told her, "She can still come here as long as you can get her here. We don't have a bus that will come way out there." So Debra talked to Ms. Sue, Mr. Nate, and Ms. Grace. The advocates wanted to see Cierra stay in a stable school situation where she was happy, so "they just took turns" driving Cierra to school. The advocates would be at the FEMA trailer, sometimes at "five, six in the morning, ready to pick Cierra up."

The advocates continued with this early morning routine for several months until they managed to secure a car for Debra. When Ms. Sue's aunt passed away, she left her brown, four-door Chevy to Sue. Sue promptly turned around and gave the car to Debra. Debra, who did not have an automobile in New Orleans, had to pass a driver's license exam, get insurance, and then learn to navigate the unfamiliar streets of Lafayette. But she did all of these things, with the help of the advocates, and eventually was able to drive her daughter to school herself.

Advocates from the Cajundome also helped with childcare, which was critical for a single mother like Debra who had no social support network in Lafayette. Debra explained how she would rely on the Cajundome staff to help out with Cierra, while also emphasizing that she thought of them as not just helpers, but "friends":

I have some excellent friends that I met since Katrina . . . The Cajundome is still open to us. If I really have to be away from [Cierra] in the daytime like that, I can just call Ms. Sue, Ms. Grace, and say it—and [they're] just like, "Oh, yeah, let her just stay and do some office work," or something like that. "Days off from school, she could be helping me in the office or something like that," so the Cajundome is still like, if we need to use the facility to help ourselves get better . . . Mr. Nate is still tremendously helpful in our lives. If we call and say something we need, they'll find any way necessary. Not just me, anybody, to see how they could help us out. So we have positive friends that I know would help her.

In addition to their assistance with housing, schooling, transportation, childcare, and emotional support, the Cajundome advocates also helped with finding other types of assistance for Cierra, Debra, and other Katrina survivors. They connected them to resources such as mental health counseling and massage therapy sessions, both of which Debra felt were extremely beneficial as she and Cierra worked through the stress they experienced as a result of Katrina.

The advocates used their local connections in Lafayette to link Debra to employment opportunities when she was in the Cajundome. Debra had worked as a custodian at a school and at a hospital back in New Orleans, and the Cajundome staff helped her to find similar employment at a health care facility in Lafayette. Finding a job—even one that initially paid minimum wage—so quickly after the storm not only helped Debra begin the economic process of recovery, but also increased her self-esteem in that she was able to regain a sense of normalcy and routine so soon after the storm. When Debra began looking for a new job five years later, the advocates were at her side again helping her carry out a successful search. The advocates even offered Debra temporary paid work at the Cajundome, so she had funds coming in as she searched for her next job. All the while, they continued to watch over Cierra when Debra needed childcare or other types of assistance.

Before Katrina, when they lived in New Orleans, Debra and Cierra would have used their extensive family and friendship networks for these critical forms of support, such as help with childcare, obtaining transportation, and finding employment. Debra described the situation in New Orleans: "We lived . . . everybody in the same city and around each other. Your cousin might be around this corner, your auntie around this way. Me and my sister lived next door, across the street from each other all our lives." This meant that when Cierra came home from school while Debra was still at work, she could go to her aunt's house and her aunt would take care of her until her mother got home. The advocates helped to fill some of the tremendous void left by the loss of dense kin and friendship networks that were shattered in the post-Katrina displacement.

The networks and resources provided by the advocates—or located and arranged by the advocates—were crucial to Cierra's recovery. The role of her parent in linking her to the advocates and their assistance was also invaluable. Indeed, Debra's relationship with the staff at the Cajundome was a key part of their advocacy for Cierra; Debra, in essence, made it easy for them to help her daughter. This is apparent in the case of employment: the advocates had the connection to a workplace, Debra worked hard at her place of employment, and the steady job directly and indirectly benefited Cierra. This job success, and the resultant economic stability for the family, was a clear reward of their advocacy. In other cases, Debra was able to articulate what she needed, such as help with Cierra's transportation to her old school, to those who could meet those needs.

Debra would often ask for assistance with mobilizing resources when she saw that her daughter needed something. For example, when Cierra was struggling emotionally after the storm and seemed "really depressed," Debra reached out. She was scared when Cierra would not allow her to hang up achievement ribbons and other things that Debra felt were important in her life. She wondered if Cierra had become so distressed after Katrina that nothing—not even a special award or recognition from her school or church—could make her feel better. From Cierra's perspective, it just was not worth it to hang up those awards, as she felt like another storm could happen any time:

> In sixth grade, I was thinking, like, it can happen any minute again, and I'm like, "Oh, I don't want to deal with this anymore." Because I was like, okay, hang [the medals and awards] up, and then if it happens again, they're just going be destroyed and I'll have to do this all over again. I was just tired of feeling as though something was going to happen. I was just tired of it. [I told my mom], "Just put them somewhere, but not in my room."

It was heartbreaking for Debra to hear her daughter express such a perspective, and she was right to be concerned. Cierra told us that she was "in a rage, throwing things" after Katrina because she just "couldn't take it" when she realized that she and her mother had lost everything. After their move to the FEMA trailer, she continued to feel "angry" and "mad" as she reflected on all the losses endured as a result of the terrible storm. She was also upset by some of her new classmates, who seemingly did not understand what she had been through:

> And, then, in the beginning, students [in Lafayette] would ask a lot of questions that I'd been asked over and over again, and it was kind of annoying, a little bit. Like, a lot of people were nice, but there were some

that would make jokes and stuff about Katrina and [being] under water, and stuff like that, and that would aggravate me a lot.

Debra saw how many things were hurting her daughter, and, as a consequence, how much she was struggling with the abrupt and wholly unexpected transition to Lafayette. Debra contacted the Cajundome staff and went to the school to figure out the best place to go for mental health counseling. Fortunately, after these interventions and with the persistent support of her mother, Cierra regained perspective and her health. She reflected, four years after Katrina, on what she had learned:

> The thing that keeps me going is to know that what doesn't kill you makes you stronger . . . I don't want to brag or anything, but to me, I feel like even though I went through a lot of stuff, I mean, I feel like I'm more prepared than a lot of people, because now I know what I can handle and what I can do in different situations. So it helped me a lot, even though it hurt me a lot, it helped me.

INSTITUTIONAL SHELTER AND HOUSING SUPPORT

One of the largest sources of support for Debra and Cierra came from institutions that responded to their shelter and housing needs in the wake of Katrina. According to disaster scholar E. L. Quarantelli, there are typically four stages of housing need after a disaster: emergency shelter, temporary shelter, temporary housing, and permanent housing.[6] In this classic post-disaster housing model, emergency shelter is brief, usually less than 24 hours, and disorganized. Temporary shelter is organized, with food, bathrooms, and sleeping areas; most survivors stay in this situation for less than a week, although the duration is sometimes longer in catastrophic events. Temporary housing refers to movement into other quarters, with an expected short or temporary stay of one to six months, but also with the reestablishment of some routines and normal activities. Finally, permanent housing involves survivors returning to their rebuilt homes or to new quarters; this usually happens within three to six months of the event.

Debra and Cierra moved through each of these four phases, although their time in emergency shelter, temporary shelter, and temporary housing lasted much longer than the average length of time that Quarantelli identified in his writing. During the emergency phase of Katrina, for example, they sheltered in place for five days at the hospital where Debra worked in New Orleans.

Upon their evacuation to Lafayette, Debra and Cierra received temporary shelter for about three months at the Cajundome, a for-profit enterprise that—with financial support from the state and federal government—completely changed its mission in the disaster aftermath and worked with groups such as the American Red Cross to provide disaster relief.[7]

After the Cajundome, Debra and Cierra moved into temporary housing provided by FEMA. These trailers were paid for by the federal government, and in Debra's and Cierra's case, their trailer was free to them for a period of 18 months, with the option to buy the trailer after the free rental period ended. This temporary transitional housing is essential for disaster survivors who have lost their homes and have nowhere to go and no resources to pay for housing when the emergency shelters begin to close. Like many of the people we interviewed and spent time with during the course of this study, Cierra and Debra were immensely grateful to have a FEMA trailer, and it allowed Debra to find a job and begin saving money for permanent housing.[8] With their limited financial resources, their lack of ability to turn to friends or family for economic support, their displacement to a totally unfamiliar place, and the exceptionally low rental vacancy rate in Lafayette, they had no other options aside from this government assistance.

Cierra made friends with a few other adolescents in the trailer park, and their next-door neighbor was a friendly grandmother who was always kind to Cierra. But some of the adults in the park got into fights and "were not so nice," so she and her mother tried to lay low in their trailer and avoid those situations. Initially the park was missing outdoor lights and was "pitch black" at night; Debra and several other Katrina survivors mobilized and were able to get lights installed.

Even with the challenges they faced in the park, Debra noted that it was safer than New Orleans. Cierra "began to see that you can live without having bullets flying [from guns], hurrying home, hurrying back, before the dark . . . [Now] we don't have to be rushing inside." Again, while the trailer park was not an ideal setting, it was in many ways safer and more secure than the neighborhood where Cierra and Debra had lived in rental housing before Katrina.

Perhaps the most beneficial and life-altering assistance from a housing institution came from Habitat for Humanity, a nonprofit, nongovernmental, ecumenical Christian housing organization that builds affordable housing in both disaster-affected and non-disaster-affected areas. Central to Habitat's mission is the belief that everyone should have a decent, safe, and affordable place to live. Through volunteer labor and donations of money and materials, Habitat builds modest houses with the new homeowners working with the volunteers. Indeed, homeowners must invest hundreds of hours of "sweat equity" in building their own home and those of others. To date, the organization has helped to construct over 500,000 houses nationwide. The families purchase their homes with affordable loans. Upon moving in, the family must pay a monthly mortgage payment as they invest in homeownership. Debra, for example, paid $316 per month for their house in Lafayette.

Debra learned of the Habitat program through the Cajundome advocates, applied to the local affiliate, and was chosen as a housing recipient. Habitat selects potential homeowners based on their level of need, their willingness to become partners in the program, and their ability to repay the loan. On all three indicators, Debra scored well. Again, it is notable that the advocates helped Debra find a job and provided her with information about the Habitat program, which directly affected her and Cierra's access to permanent housing.

Debra was not a homeowner in New Orleans, and it was unlikely that she would have become one had they stayed in the city. In becoming a homeowner in Lafayette, Debra not only secured stable housing but also increased her financial wealth and security for the future. Moreover, the impact on Debra's and Cierra's feelings of self-worth was also critical to the family's long-term recovery. Debra was so proud to show us the "princess room" that Cierra had dreamed of and that the two had painted a pretty lavender color and decorated together. Habitat for Humanity was crucial for their financial, physical, and emotional recovery.[9] More broadly, their experience illustrates how housing is central to the recovery of disaster survivors.

TEACHERS AND SCHOOLS

Teachers composed another group of advocates who helped Cierra find equilibrium, and the schools she entered represented important institutions in her recovery. When Cierra was displaced to Lafayette, she was forced to leave an elementary school in New Orleans that she was emotionally attached to, and a small circle of friends whom she adored and had been in school with since she was four years old. The loss of these friends was heartbreaking, and every time we visited, Cierra would pull out photos and identify her friends from New Orleans and would share special memories about each one.

During the first year after Katrina, when Cierra was deeply depressed, she struggled in her new school and did not want to become engaged in anything—academic work, extracurricular activities, or making new friends.

Her grades fell drastically from where they had been before Katrina (she had been on the honor roll consistently in New Orleans), her motivation plummeted, and her mother grew increasingly concerned.

With her depression and these difficult circumstances, how did Cierra end up rebounding educationally? What we observed was that Debra stayed completely involved in Cierra's educational experience and that several teachers in her new school were determined to see Cierra succeed. Cierra also began to recover and remember the importance of school, as her mother and her teachers supported and pushed her through the difficult months after Katrina. All of their actions, together and in concert with the emotional support and resources provided by the Cajundome advocates and others, contributed to her ability to find equilibrium. Beyond all this individual effort and personal support, Cierra landed in strong, racially integrated, academically comprehensive schools in Lafayette. Thus, as we describe below, it was the connection between the individual-level initiative and the institutional context that helped Cierra to succeed.

As soon as Debra recognized how badly her daughter was struggling in school, she said to her: "This is not you. I know that you study well and you do your homework." Debra went to the school, met with the teachers, and showed them her daughter's grades and merit awards from New Orleans. Debra said to the teachers, "This is her. She's having a rough time right now, and I know you explained to me that you all are understanding, but I know that you have a whole bunch of children [to attend to]. But bear with me, she's going to be all right."

Debra talked to her daughter on a daily basis about the importance of school. She told her, "I understand that you're going through a lot, but you can't use that, because we're both going through a lot. We have to take this and really move up, because if you keep dipping like this, we're going to have a harder time." Debra was not averse to using discipline as necessary, either: she threatened to take away Cierra's phone and television privileges in response to her academic decline. More than that, though, she continued to try to positively reinforce her daughter and to work with Cierra's teachers to ensure her success in school. She explained:

> So [her grades] dipped, but I kept coaching her. The teacher was like, "I don't know what you did, but it's working." I said, "Just keep talking to her . . ." She was always on the honor roll. She knew that [school] was her job, and I had my job. My job was to go to work, and her job was to go to school. I didn't miss work, and she didn't miss school. I said, "I had to work hard to provide, and you have to work hard to provide. Because

some day, you're going to provide for yourself." And that's still the motto here.

Prior research by Katherine Rosier and William Corsaro found poor and working-class mothers taking similar actions. Like Debra, the women in their study valued education and consequently set high expectations for their children's school achievement. They saw education, and rightfully so, as a path to economic security, and thus they actively pursued opportunities so that their children could achieve educational success.[10]

Debra also made a strong effort to get to know all of Cierra's friends, and she was deeply mindful of the importance of positive peer influences. For example, during Cierra's sophomore year, one of her friends unexpectedly became pregnant. Although Cierra was close to the girl, Debra refused to allow Cierra to spend time with this classmate outside of school. After the girl dropped out of school following the birth of her child, Debra insisted that Cierra cut all ties and sever the friendship. This was a difficult time, as the girl became very upset with Cierra and tried to "pick fights" with her. After some time passed, Cierra revealed to us that she knew her mom had made the right decision in asking her to no longer "hang out" with this particular friend.

The teachers and other parents at Cierra's school saw how hard Debra worked on behalf of her daughter and how carefully she "coached" her to ensure her academic success. In recognition of Debra's involvement, the parents at Cierra's middle school elected Debra president of their Parent Teacher Association (PTA). Debra humbly told us that she was selected for the PTA leadership role because she was "the only one who showed up with a notebook and was taking notes." But we were certain that the parents at Cierra's school saw in Debra what we repeatedly observed: a quiet, thoughtful, and dedicated mother who wanted what was best for her child, and who was determined to work hard for the benefit of the school and parent-teacher relationships. As the years passed, Debra even turned to us—both university professors—for advice about Cierra's education beyond high school. During one visit, when Cierra was beginning to think about applying for college, Debra sat with us at the table for over an hour asking us questions about succeeding in higher education. During another visit, Debra asked if we would help Cierra with her math homework, as she was "struggling" with a few of the problems.

Teachers at the schools she attended in Lafayette wanted to contribute to Cierra's success, and several became her advocates. Notably, Cierra was not alone; we observed many displaced students who were being helped by caring teachers. Mekana, the focal child featured in chapter 4, for example, had several teachers in Denver extend themselves to her, showing her unwavering kindness and acceptance; she was especially touched by the Colorado blankets they gave her and the phone calls they made to ensure she stayed on track and in school. Isabel, as described in chapter 5, was assisted by her teacher Mr. Fontenot. He actually went so far as to design an entire educational curriculum for students affected by Katrina, both during the displacement and when they returned to New Orleans. Displaced students in other locations were also helped by teachers, and this assistance was critical.[11] Indeed, research shows that children and youth displaced by Katrina were much more likely to be doing well if they had strong and meaningful connections with teachers in their new schools.[12]

One of Cierra's teachers, Mrs. O'Grady, became her advocate in several ways. First, the teacher (who helped several youth who had evacuated because of the storm) could tell that Cierra was struggling in the months after Katrina. Mrs. O'Grady responded to this and gave Cierra general support in the classroom, checking in with her, paying extra attention to her. She also communicated with Cierra's mother; they worked as a team to help Cierra get through this transition.

As Cierra began to respond and become more engaged, her teacher nominated her for a prestigious fellowship for student leaders to travel to Washington, DC, to participate in a week-long program with middle school students from around the country. This was a turning point for Cierra, as this nomination, her acceptance, and the eventual journey to the nation's capital made her view herself in a new light and helped her to rebuild some of her self-confidence and hope for the future. Cierra also recognized what life-changing opportunities Mrs. O'Grady and her other teachers had opened up for her: "In New Orleans they had, like, a lot of talented people, and we didn't get a lot of chances. Kids didn't get a lot of chances. They didn't have stuff like Washington, DC, trips. It was like a once-in-a-lifetime chance."

Cierra's teachers and her mother also encouraged her to join in other activities, such as cheerleading, participating in a beauty pageant, running track, and being a member of the local 4-H club. Cierra followed their advice, and she not only got involved but also succeeded in all these new adventures. During each of our visits, she would excitedly recount her experiences with these new endeavors. On one occasion she performed one of the cheers for her cheerleading team for us, and on another evening, she proudly showed us a dress she had sewed for a 4-H competition. All of these extracurricular activities helped Cierra to make new friends, to come into contact with supportive adults, and to focus on her recovery rather than her losses. Cierra also realized how much she was learning and gaining from these experiences and new networks, and she began to regularly seek out new opportunities for herself as well.

Schools—which play a crucial role in helping children and youth regain a sense of normalcy and routine after disaster—also contributed to Cierra's ability to find equilibrium after Katrina. Beyond the things that individual teachers did for Cierra, the school she attended after the evacuation helped place her on the path to recovery by doing things like waiving immunization record and transcript requirements and offering free uniforms for students who evacuated.[13] Given everything they had lost and the disruption caused by the displacement, these actions taken by the school were significant in helping Cierra make the transition. Other schools with displaced students were also attempting to make these sorts of accommodations with records and uniforms; some, too, lessened homework requirements in light of the chaotic and cramped living situations of displaced families.

In Lafayette, Cierra's middle school and high school were solid institutions; they had well-trained educators, highly involved parents, and a diverse student body. Cierra, who had attended a racially segregated elementary school in New Orleans, commented on the diversity of students in the schools she attended in Lafayette:

> I like it better that way, because you get to know everybody. And when you go out into the real world, it is not gonna just be white people or black people, it's gonna be all different kinds of people. When you go to businesses and college, there's gonna be all different kind of people, so you have to get used to everyone. You have to be able to deal with different people and reactions and stuff like that. I like it better that way.

Almost all of Cierra's friends in New Orleans were African American girls (owing largely to the fact that she grew up in a racially segregated neighborhood and attended a segregated public school within a majority-minority city). When we asked her about her friendships in Lafayette, Cierra responded thoughtfully:

> I have Chinese friends, I have black friends, I have . . . Hispanic friends, I have Spanish friends, Africans. It's everything. And I think that's really good, because I wouldn't want to go to, like, an all-black school or all-white school. I really like the mixture of it, because you get to understand more.

As Cierra astutely observed, integrated schools have many benefits for students and the community. Research has found that racial integration is valuable for all students, but especially for students of color and for girls, who are more likely to reap more resources and rewards from racially integrated schools.[14] During our 2009 visit, Cierra told us that her best friend at school was white. Cierra was well aware that she had few opportunities in her former New Orleans school for interracial friendships.[15] She is not alone. Few children have this opportunity, as the majority of children in the United States do not live in racially integrated neighborhoods or attend integrated schools.[16]

CHURCHES AND CHURCH LEADERS AND STAFF

The third advocate team for Cierra was her church pastor and his wife. It took Cierra and her mother some time to find the right church in their new city, and they tried many places of worship until they found the one that felt like a "church home" rather than "just another church." On our early trips to Lafayette, they told us about their ongoing search for a church.

It was not until we visited in 2008, though, that they took us to the one they had decided on, Hope Baptist Church. It was a large church located on the outskirts of Lafayette, with an almost entirely African American congregation (on the times when we attended, we only saw one other white person besides ourselves). Pastor Brad and his wife, Mrs. Denise, a middle-aged African American couple, helped integrate Debra and Cierra into the church community, providing personal support as well as spiritual guidance. The pastor and his wife would take the youth on retreats, show them new places, and introduce them to new activities. Cierra told us they helped her through "tough times," and Debra felt that the pastor and his wife were like "parents." She explained:

> They are always trying to instill wisdom, but they be dead on the money with our youth. They [are] always doing something to promote them, so they have a lot of functions. They have acting plays. They have youth month. They really turn it over to them and the children get a chance to express [themselves] in acting. And then they take them on retreats and stuff like that.

As a result of the advocates' welcome and warmth, Debra and Cierra began attending the church four times a week. The Sunday sermons were lively and full of messages that encouraged positive family relationships and success among adults and youth. For example, one Sunday we watched as Pastor Brad pointed out a young boy, about eight or nine years old, and recognized him for his academic achievement, finishing his praise by proclaiming, "He's the next Barack Obama!" which was met with a wave of laughter, shouts of agreement, and applause. The pastor emphasized that "leaders are readers" and encouraged the other youth in the congregation to follow this young boy's lead by also focusing on schoolwork and academic achievement.

When we attended church with the family, we would sit on either side of Cierra. She always paid careful attention during the sermons, sometimes even writing a few notes in her small notebook that she carried with her everywhere. When it was time for the "meet and greet" portion of the service, Cierra and Debra introduced us to their church friends.

In addition to attending weekly services, Cierra joined the youth choir, a "praise and worship" group, and the church's acting troupe, which allowed her to sing and develop her dramatic talents. Cierra made new friends through the church, and would also bring along her school friends who did not belong to a congregation. On one occasion we rode along with Debra and Cierra so that they could pick up Cierra's friend, Destiny. Destiny was in a "bad home situation," according to Debra, and they were trying to exert a positive influence on her through exposing her to the church.

Cierra benefited greatly from the peer relationships that she developed within the church as well as from the positive adult role models that she encountered along the way. Once again, the actions of committed and thoughtful advocates contributed to Cierra's ability to find equilibrium.

These advocates were working within—and using the resources of—the institution of the church. Cierra's and Debra's church in Lafayette became a sort of second home for them, a place with resources for adolescents and families. Debra knew that the church setting was a positive one for Cierra and took her and her friends as often as she could. Historically, black churches in the U.S. have been bedrocks in neighborhoods, providing services and resources that their members were denied as individuals due to overtly discriminatory policies.[17]

In the Katrina aftermath, there is evidence of churches playing an enormous role in the recovery of survivors.[18] Some New Orleans churches set up satellite churches in new towns and cities where many of their members had been displaced. Churches also worked to locate their members and help them return to Louisiana if they needed funds for bus or plane fare.

NONPROFIT ORGANIZATIONS AND MENTORS

Nonprofit organizations like Habitat for Humanity played a substantial role in the recovery process, especially in terms of housing needs. Many national groups, like the American Red Cross, had more access to funds from out-side the Gulf Coast, while small, community-based nonprofits were more reliant on local resources in the aftermath. What they had in common, however, is that they played important roles in the disaster response and recovery for many families. The work of nonprofits is crucial because they help to meet basic needs related to shelter, clothing, health, and food.[19] Debra and Cierra, for example, relied on nonprofit food banks when they needed a little extra food assistance near the end of the month. A local non-profit program helped them pay their utility bills when they were not able to do so.

Other nonprofits addressed emotional and developmental needs. For Cierra, one of the most helpful organizations for her recovery was a national organization called "Big Brothers Big Sisters." This nonprofit organization matches adult mentors with youth who need some guidance or support. It is not designed exclusively for periods of disaster, but the organization became crucial in Cierra's recovery. When Cierra was struggling to settle in Lafayette, Debra began looking for people and organizations that could help her daughter. She was told by advocates at the school and at the Cajun-dome that Big Brothers Big Sisters might be a good fit. Debra explained to us why it was so critical that she make this connection for her daughter:

And then when she got to the Big Sister, she talked to them. We asked them to start that, because they had a lot for adults, but we was trying to figure out, "What did you-all have for teens, or the children?" Because a lot of the children—especially when we heard that the children were going through a state of depression, and sometimes children would be going through a state of depression like she was and you don't even know because we're not really paying attention and figuring out something so they can get through it. They might seem like they're getting through it, but later on in life it might crash. We had a lot of kids around here, you could tell they were crashing.

This worry about Cierra "crashing" led Debra and the Cajundome and school advocates to Big Brothers Big Sisters. After Cierra was matched with Lydia, the two of them would spend time together on their own. Lydia be-came Cierra's role model, mentor, and confidante, and they often saw each other every week, sometimes several times a week. Occasionally, the orga-nization would have events for all the "bigs" and "littles" to attend together. One event was a gospel concert. Cierra, who had never attended a large music concert before, excitedly relayed to us that she "loved it!" Debra did not approve of all music concerts for youth, but she liked the organization's choice for the children, trusted the mentor, and felt good about the experience for her daughter.

As time went on, Cierra did not need her "big" as much, but Debra pointed out that Cierra always knew Lydia was there and could call her at any time. The relationship, supported by the organization, lasted through Cierra's high school graduation and contributed to her ability to find equilibrium.

This chapter has emphasized how advocates and institutions, working together, played an important role in Cierra's post-disaster experiences and ability to find and maintain equilibrium after Katrina. In addition, as discussed earlier, Cierra's mother also was crucial in her role as the primary conduit to resources that could be mobilized when Cierra was struggling and needed assistance. Sociologist Frank Furstenberg has characterized parents like Debra as "exceptionally competent" in that they find ways to help their children avoid the negative outcomes of poverty, like teen pregnancy, and secure the necessary community support that helps them succeed in school and life.[20]

It is clear from our work that advocates, institutions, and parents and guardians are pivotal in the process of mobilizing resources for children and youth in a disaster. Furthermore, in addition to mobilizing resources, advocates are also building relationships with children and youth and their families, connecting them to services that will assist them long after the advocates' own actions, and helping to combat the social isolation that often occurs when families are displaced in disaster.

The individual-level actions of adults were critical in Cierra's and other children's recovery after Katrina. So too were the programs, initiatives, and resources that were provided by strong institutions. Our research revealed that no matter how hard working, caring, or charismatic the adults were in children's lives, they could not have helped in the ways that they did without these institutions and the many opportunities that the institutions were able to open up for individuals, families, and communities as a whole.

What about children and youth themselves? What role did Cierra play in her recovery? How was she able to identify resources, articulate her needs, and take actions to find stability and equilibrium? We found that the way that Cierra sought out resources was sometimes less obvious, but important nonetheless. With the advocates, even though Cierra was shy and often reserved in her interactions, she still worked to maintain the relationships and spent time seeking them out for support. She shared with us how it helped her to talk with Mr. Nate, Ms. Sue, and the others. Her participation in those conversations was not passive; she was actively drawing on their strengths and resources, looking to these key adults for support and guidance.

With schooling, Cierra was the one who asked her mother, pleaded with her, to stay in her first school since she was already adjusted and comfortable there. In addition, Cierra was responsive to her teacher's encouragement to go to Washington, DC, and to join in extracurricular activities while also putting in the effort to keep her grades high. She deserves the credit for the hard work that it took to take advantage of those opportunities and the bravery of stepping outside her comfort zone. To end this chapter, we include one more of Cierra's poems, which underscores her strength and healing.

Hey, you, yeah, you, the one in the corner
Who teased me for being so quiet
Well, listen up
I've got somethin' to say
I found the courage to stand up for myself
I found the words to show who I am
I found the voice to speak my thoughts, my fears, my dreams, myself

So you, yeah, you, the one that scared me so quiet
Pick up a pen
Find who you are
Let yourself be free
through poetry

POEM WRITTEN BY CIERRA WASHINGTON, 13 YEARS OLD

III

FLUCTUATING TRAJECTORY

Some of the children and youth we interviewed and observed, like Daniel and Mekana, featured in chapters 3 and 4, experienced a consistent decline after Katrina. Their lives were marked by mounting day-to-day troubles, serious disadvantages, and cumulative vulnerability. Others, such as Isabel, Zachary, and Cierra, whose stories are recounted in chapters 5 and 6, regained and sustained equilibrium in all the major spheres. Our research also revealed another distinct pattern in children's disaster-affected lives: what we call the *fluctuating trajectory*. This third section of the book examines this particular post-disaster process.

Over the years following Katrina, we found that children and youth in the fluctuating trajectory were not rendered as vulnerable as the children in the declining trajectory, nor did they attain as much security and stability as the children in the finding-equilibrium trajectory. The children who fit this third trajectory sometimes were doing well in one critical sphere (like housing) while struggling in another (such as family relationships). This lack of positive alignment across spheres—meaning that the spheres of children's lives were not in a similar place all at the same time—kept these children from achieving complete recovery in the disaster aftermath. Other children who experienced the fluctuating trajectory were in an even more constant and rapid state of flux, shifting from decline to equilibrium in all spheres, in a wave-like motion.

In the next two chapters, we introduce two focal children whose experiences illustrate these variations in the fluctuating trajectory: Jerron in chapter 7 and Clinton in chapter 8. Although these children's stories are similar in that they each experienced moments of emotional, familial, educational, financial, and social stability and instability following Katrina, different

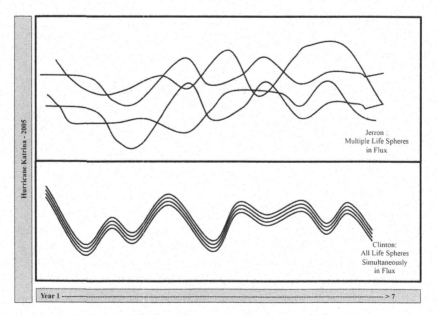

Figure III.1. Fluctuating trajectories—Jerron and Clinton

characteristics and life experiences drove their patterns of fluctuation. The spheres of Jerron's life were misaligned, which diminished his prospects for recovery. Clinton was in an even more constant state of flux, as the spheres of his life moved up and down rapidly. Figure III.1 illustrates these variations captured within the fluctuating trajectory.

Jerron, an African American boy from New Orleans who was six years old at the time of Katrina, struggled in the disaster aftermath because of the dislocation of his family, which was composed of an extremely close-knit, multigenerational network. Simultaneously, his life was stabilized in many ways following Katrina when his mom found a promising job and enrolled Jerron in a better school than what he had attended before the disaster. For Jerron and the other children and youth we observed whose lives followed a similar trajectory after the hurricane, we found that stability in some spheres can occur simultaneously with instability and uncertainty in other spheres. Moreover, Jerron's story helps show how complicated and interdependent the spheres of children's lives are. Indeed, when one critical sphere is unstable—in terms of being in flux or in a negative state—it is difficult to maintain a sense of equilibrium across all other spheres.

In chapter 8, we introduce Clinton, an African American boy who was only four years old when Katrina hit the Gulf Coast. At that time he was living with a family friend due to his mother's absence and was mostly in the care of his 18-year-old sister Brandi. Clinton's post-disaster experience—marked by his family's hardships and successes and his multiple moves—shows how rapidly children and youth can move in and out of stable circumstances in post-disaster settings and thus underscores how complex, dynamic, and difficult recovery can be. We watched Clinton's up-and-down pattern unfold over a seven-year period, with Clinton never moving into a steady and consistent decline, but also not able to attain equilibrium.

What kept Jerron and Clinton and the many other children and youth who fit this trajectory from moving into a more sustained decline that would have more closely resembled the children and youth we discussed in chapters 3 and 4? There are many answers to this question, but perhaps most importantly, the children represented by the fluctuating trajectory had a consistent supportive or stabilizing force or set of forces in their lives. As we detail in the next two chapters, these stabilizers served as anchors through the highs and lows that followed Katrina.

With that said, however, the children who fit the fluctuating trajectory undoubtedly were and likely will remain more vulnerable than the children and youth in the finding-equilibrium trajectory, who were more likely to have more resources, more advocates, and more stability. The children of the fluctuating trajectory had some support but not as much and not in every sphere of their lives. This, as we will show in chapters 7 and 8, delayed or diminished the children's recovery progress.

7

JERRON
MISALIGNED SPHERES

Every time we see Jerron, he says that he wants to move back to New Orleans. It is true, he tells us, that he has new friends in Lafayette, Louisiana, the city where he was permanently displaced after Katrina. And yes, his mom has a good job and they have a nice house in a safe neighborhood. He is always careful to express how thankful he is for his new friends and how glad he is that his mom seems happy in Lafayette. But Jerron's heart is in New Orleans. This sense of longing for the place where he was born and where he lived until he was six years old has everything to do with the fact that his father, grandmother, great-grandmother, and best friend are there, and he wants to be with them.

As a consequence of his longing for his family and friends, for his former life, Jerron had not yet fully settled, even years after Katrina. In 2009, his grandmother, Lila, sensed that Jerron was not content in his new surroundings. She explained her hopes for her grandson and expressed her willingness to help under any circumstance:

> I just want . . . I'd like for him to have a stable life, which he seems to be on the road to having, to have a home. Shaundra's [Jerron's mom] buying a house now, as opposed to, she was renting before. I see those things as advantages for her, and for him also, that eventually they'll be homeowners. Just the distance [is difficult], even though I'm two hours away from them now, and I tell her, "If anything happens to him, you give me a call, and I don't care what time it is, I can leave New Orleans and I can be there." So they know it's not a problem for Mama to come out.

Lila could identify both the positive and the negative outcomes for Jerron. Jerron's mother had the opportunity to become a homeowner, which introduced a new source of financial stability for the family. Yet, integral components of Jerron's familial and extrafamilial support network were separated from him now. This resulted in an almost continual sense of un-certainty in his life, and Lila knew that it was impeding his recovery in the disaster aftermath.

Jerron struggled with the post-Katrina displacement and the separation from his loved ones. He confided in us that he had a temper and often felt angry; one day, for example, he threatened to punch his school bus driver after he told Jerron to "shut up." His father, Eddie, expressed concern that Jerron was "acting out" and getting into trouble at school. Shaundra re-sorted to restricting Jerron's activities when his grades dropped to D's and F's rather than the A's and B's that she knew he was capable of earning.

Many of Jerron's troubles were influenced by how much he missed his family and his own preoccupation with having everyone together again. When we asked him, nearly six years after Katrina, what he missed the most, without hesitation, he replied:

> Family. In New Orleans, I used to have all my family. I used to go to every-body's house almost every single day. But not since I'm living in Lafayette. Really, I don't have any kind of relatives out here. I only have the family that lives with me right now. So I always look at my friends and I'll be like, "Oh, man, I can't wait until I get back to New Orleans."

Jerron's immediate and extended family loved him and cared about him; they were strong stabilizing forces who were all committed to helping him through the pain that Katrina caused. They worked out mutually agreeable visitation schedules. They made sure that Jerron saw all of his family mem-bers on important holidays. They expressed love through spending as much time together as possible. When Jerron moved into sixth grade, his mother enrolled him in a "school of choice" for environmental sciences; he had his first girlfriend, to whom he would often send playful text messages; and he loved playing baseball and football with his classmates and the boys on his street. But when his mother briefly considered returning to New Orleans six years after Katrina, he was ready to drop it all and go. "Adios, Lafayette," he said to us, grinning ear to ear.

Jerron and the other displaced children and youth who fit the fluctuating trajectory exemplify what happens when the major spheres of children's lives—family relationships, parental employment, housing, schooling, extracurricular activities, and friendships—are misaligned, despite the efforts of those around them. When we speak of *misalignment*, we mean that the spheres of children's lives were not in a similar place all at the same time. So, for example, these children were often doing well in one sphere of life (like housing) while struggling in another sphere (like family or peer relationships). This misalignment across spheres kept these children and youth from recovering fully—or reaching a place of consistent and ongoing stability—following Katrina. At the same time, because they had some source of stability in at least one critical sphere of their lives, they were not in a precipitous decline, either. This is what separated this group of children and youth from those we observed who were on the declining trajectory. We chose Jerron, who had just entered the first grade when Katrina devastated the Gulf Coast, as a focal child because he represents those children and youth who were not declining completely in their recovery, but who could not quite find equilibrium either.

In this chapter, we discuss several major spheres of Jerron's life in order to underscore the interconnection across spheres. Difficulty in even one major sphere of life—like family or friendships—influences all other spheres. In this case, Jerron's parents had stable employment, reliable transportation, health care, and housing, but this was not enough to drive his recovery, as his family situation remained uncertain and his friendship networks were disrupted for years after Katrina.

FAMILY: SUPPORT AND SEPARATION

The temporary and permanent separation from family members was devastating to many displaced children who experienced Hurricane Katrina.[1] Jerron's case helps explain why so many children who were dislocated from loved ones faced so many challenges in the disaster aftermath.

Jerron had an exceptionally strong multigenerational family, both before and after Katrina. For his first five years of life, he lived with his mother and father in the first floor of his great-grandmother's brick home in New Orleans. His grandmother and great-grandmother lived upstairs and the family members saw each other every day. On our first visit to their house, Jerron's grandmother, Lila, gave us a tour. She laughed when she pointed out her small "knick knack" room, which held dolls, stuffed animals, and various porcelain and china collectibles. The room was reportedly "off limits" to her energetic grandson. "Too much chance of him breaking something!" Lila exclaimed with a warm smile.

Lila was Jerron's kindergarten teacher. Once he entered school, they would leave the house together, holding hands, and would walk the few blocks to their school building. At night, they would often have large family dinners and, if it was not too hot, they would sit together on the screened-in porch and visit for hours. They spent most weekends doing things together, like going to local parks or just "hanging out" and watching television or movies.

About a year before Katrina, however, Jerron's mother and father split up, and he and his mother moved to a rental apartment. This was incredibly difficult for Jerron, who had just begun kindergarten and was an only child and the first grandchild on both his mother's and his father's sides of the family. Even with his parents going through a divorce, though, his mom still made sure that he was able to see his father and grandmother at least three to four times a week, which was very important to him. Shaundra also maintained an amicable relationship with Eddie, and she remained "like a daughter" to Lila. Eddie, for his part, paid $400 in child support every month, without fail. So, as far as divorces go, this one was disruptive and heartbreaking, but the family did everything they could to protect Jerron and to remain close through the ordeal.

Then Katrina came and scattered Jerron's loved ones far and wide. His family had the resources—including working automobiles, credit cards, and some savings—to self-evacuate in advance of the hurricane. His father left New Orleans in a caravan with his "lady friend" (whom he had started seeing soon after the divorce) and over a dozen members of her family. They headed north to a rural town in northern Louisiana. Jerron's paternal great-grandmother, his grandmother, and her best friend drove to Missouri to stay with old friends. Beloved aunts, uncles, and cousins were, as Jerron stated, "all over the place," finding shelter throughout Louisiana, Alabama, Florida, Tennessee, Texas, and elsewhere.

Jerron evacuated with his mother, her boyfriend, his maternal grandmother, and her sister. The group of five traveled in Shaundra's Ford Explorer from Louisiana to Mississippi, back to Louisiana, then to Georgia and Alabama, and finally to Lafayette, Louisiana. They moved multiple times over a three-month period, staying in motels, hotels, and the family homes of friends. Upon their arrival in Lafayette, the family began renting a two-bedroom apartment. Finally, well over a year after Katrina, they settled into permanent housing. Shaundra had a baby in 2007, but soon thereafter her boyfriend left and moved to Texas, effectively ending their relationship. Shaundra's aunt moved in so that she could help with the care of Jerron and his new baby brother.

During the initial displacement, Jerron had no physical contact with his father for months. The multiple moves to many different cities and states were disruptive in terms of his schooling and every other routine aspect of life. And those negative effects were only amplified because of the separation of the family members. Eddie was desperate to see his son, and Jerron was also distraught to be apart in this way. Eddie and Jerron had never gone more than a day or two without spending time together, even after the divorce, so the dislocation that followed Katrina was particularly traumatic for them.

When father and son were finally reunited at Thanksgiving in 2005, almost three full months had passed since the storm. They had spoken on the phone frequently during that period of separation, expressing their love for each other. Eddie recalled that "the fact that I couldn't see him was really killing me." He had been "trying to hold up" but the emotions were "spilling up" and after hearing his son's voice on the phone one day, Eddie told us that he "definitely lost it." As we listened to Eddie—an exceptionally gentle, but also quite tall, large, and muscular man—tell his story, we thought he might break down crying in front of us. Finally, when Eddie and Jerron and the rest of the family came together at the Thanksgiving holiday, Eddie was able to find some comfort. "Thanksgiving was good," he said quietly, as if he had been holding his breath for all those months.

Jerron's family was the bedrock of his life in New Orleans. They loved each other deeply. Lila adored her only grandchild, was proud of her son, and spoke of Shaundra with nothing but warmth. Their family relationships were healthy. Even Eddie and Shaundra, who had gone through a breakup and then a divorce, had a positive, supportive relationship. Eddie told us that during the first years of displacement they were "very good friends." And these were clearly not just empty words. We repeatedly witnessed their mutual kindness and cooperative approach to parenting during our visits, such as when they would negotiate whether Jerron could have a soda or a snack after athletic practice or when they would discuss who would help tutor Jerron that week with his schoolwork. Even with the divorce, we saw how warmly Eddie and Shaundra would greet each other, often with a long hug, and how Eddie would hold the door for his ex-wife and take her hand when she had to walk down steps. Although perhaps no longer "in love" in a romantic way, Shaundra and Eddie displayed much kindness and mutual respect.

The dislocation of Jerron's family in the Katrina aftermath disrupted a highly stable and critically important sphere of Jerron's life. Shaundra spoke to us about how this family separation affected her son:

SHAUNDRA: He talks about Katrina a lot. Just Saturday he told my aunt that he miss New Orleans. He was in tears and he told my aunt that he wanted to go back to New Orleans. And that's kind of hard for me,

Figure 7.1. *Mom*, by Jerron, 11 years old

because I don't want to go back. But it's hard to see him go through that. I just thought he wouldn't express those types of feelings because he was in New Orleans for such a short period of his life.

LORI: What do you think that was about?

SHAUNDRA: It's probably family, missing family. Him and his grand-mother, from this age all the way up until five, we lived [in the ground-level apartment] underneath Lila's house. She lived at the top, and me, Eddie, and him [Jerron], we lived at the bottom. He saw his grand-mother every day, and then he went to school with her every day. So I believe it's family. That's what he really misses.

It was understandable why Jerron missed his father and the rest of his family so much. When we asked Shaundra how much Jerron saw Eddie after Katrina, she said: "I want to say probably every other month. Not as much as a father and son should." The impact of going from seeing his father basically every day to "every other month" was profound.

Because of his separation from his father and his father's side of the family, Jerron depended on his mother and her family for much support in his recovery. Jerron told us that "sometimes I be cryin' over my dad." In order to understand how he dealt with those emotions, we asked him to draw a picture of what or who helped him the most after Katrina. He sat quietly for a few minutes as he drew a picture of his mother (see figure 7.1). Jerron described the picture and the encouragement his mom had provided: "She was teaching me how to erase all the bad memories. She would see me, like, with my head down, and she would say, 'Keep your head up, don't look down about it.'"

It is important to emphasize how important both sides of Jerron's family were to him. His mom and his maternal grandmother provided daily support and stability in his life, and he was obviously grateful for both of them. He also idolized his father and he missed his paternal grandmother deeply. Jerron recognized—as did his parents—how fortunate he was to have two sides of the family so involved and so dedicated to his health and well-being. At the same time, and as we describe in greater depth below, Jerron never fully adjusted to being physically separated from half of his family.

After living in a two-bedroom apartment for over a year after Katrina, Shaundra signed a mortgage for a new house and committed to establishing a new life for her family in Lafayette. When this happened, the realization sank in for both Jerron and Eddie that they would now confront a permanent separation. This was emotionally complicated for Eddie. When he was a child his father left him and his mother and never again involved himself much in Eddie's upbringing. That absence made an enormous impression, and he did not want his son to experience the same feelings of absence and confusion that he had. Even if he and Shaundra were not together, he wanted to be a substantial presence in Jerron's life. In retrospect, Eddie questioned whether he and Shaundra should have divorced because of the impact on his time with Jerron: "I probably never would have left if I would have known I can't see him every day."

Many children endured separation from their fathers in evacuation and displacement. Some of these children were in two-parent households before Katrina, and others lived with their mothers, but they were connected in important ways with their fathers and their fathers' families. Anthropologist Katherine Newman examines the issue of "absent" (or nonresident) fathers in her work on poor families and finds that while they may seem absent on the surface (the U.S. Census, for instance, may count the children as living with a "single mother"), they are still involved in their children's lives.[2] Fathers who fit Newman's description may not live with the children and their mothers, but they may visit, provide support, or otherwise be involved. This is important, as nonresident fathers who remain active tend to help raise more well adjusted children and adolescents than fathers who are totally uninvolved.[3]

Moreover, children of single mothers are often well integrated into their father's everyday family lives, and forge relationships with paternal grandparents, aunts, uncles, and cousins which help solidify their attachment to their fathers. A high proportion of the children we studied lived in a single-parent home before Katrina; but many of these children, like Jerron, were close to their fathers. The children benefited from that relationship as well as their relationship with the paternal side of the family. Thus, while some "single-parent families" are truly composed of mothers who are parenting on their own, this conceptualization of single parenthood is distinct from single-parent families where fathers are involved but not sharing a residence. We found that for some children and youth, displacement was the first time that they were truly separated from their fathers and their fathers' families, and being raised solely or primarily by their mothers.[4]

For Jerron's family, one alternative would have been for Eddie to move to Lafayette. Yet, this was not a simple proposition. Because Eddie continued to reside in his mother's and grandmother's house in New Orleans after Katrina, he was able to live rent-free, save some money from his two jobs at two local restaurants, and continue to pay full child support for Jerron. If he moved to Lafayette, that money for Jerron would then go to Eddie's rent. As someone working in the restaurant industry, Eddie needed to be in New Orleans, which is tourism dependent and has a service-based economy. It was also the place where he felt most at home, as he emphasized to us: "I love my city [and] I really love my jobs." Eddie also helped care for his ailing elderly grandmother when Lila would go to her job as a teacher. He would then leave for his first shift of the day, and a paid caregiver would come in to help until Lila could make it home after her classes. The family's ties were deep and they extended in many different directions, as we discussed time and again with all the members of the family.

On a warm May evening in Lafayette we yet again witnessed these kinship ties in action. Jerron had a baseball game that night, and his father, grandmother Lila, and Lila's best friend, Victoria, decided to surprise him by coming to the game. Eddie, Lila, and Victoria rearranged their work schedules so that they could drive the two-hour stretch to Lafayette, be there in time to watch his 6:00 p.m. game, and then drive two hours back late that night. It was not convenient, but it was important to all of them because they wanted to be a more regular part of Jerron's school and sporting events.

We arrived at the ball field before the New Orleans family got there. Jerron and his teammates, all dressed in stark white baseball pants and bright purple jerseys, were warming up as they ran around the field and threw baseballs back and forth. Shaundra was trying her best not to look too excited, or she would spoil the surprise. Just as the boys finished posing for a team photograph, Lila's car pulled into the parking lot and the family emerged. Jerron's face lit up and he was clearly thrilled. He threw his baseball glove in the air and then sprinted across the ball field and embraced his family in a long hug. For the rest of the evening, and all through the game, he was smiling. He would often look over into the bleachers to see his cheering fans, and it was clear that Jerron felt proud and loved. At one point, while running for home plate in the seventh inning, Jerron turned to his family in the stands and smiled widely and waved. His family laughed and clapped even louder.

While the dislocation from his father was perhaps the most difficult for Jerron, his physical separation from Lila, her mother, and all the rest of their extended network of family and fictive kin[5] was critical in explaining why Jerron himself, as well as his parents, did not think he was fully "recovered" from Katrina. We heard this repeatedly from different members of the family whom we interviewed, and this remained the case for years after the disaster. Even though he loved his maternal grandmother deeply, and she spoiled him, Jerron had an especially close and special bond with Lila. Lila, a no-nonsense type of person with a loving heart, was strict with him and held high expectations that he always tried to meet. He loved being with her. He told us that he especially enjoyed going to her New Orleans church, where he received special attention because he was known to everyone in the congregation as "Lila's grandson."

In addition to the love that his family so freely shared, they also provided a financial and social safety net for Jerron and for one another. Because his paternal great-grandmother owned the house in New Orleans, they had housing stability and a future source of wealth. His grandmother had a college degree and had spent her entire adult life as a teacher. This, again, brought financial stability along with a strong emphasis on the importance of education in the family. Jerron was not just raised by a "nuclear" family in the traditional sense—he had a whole web of people around him to care for him, to offer him love, to watch over him in daily life, and to provide important material and instrumental resources.

During one of our visits, when Jerron was eight years old, he put down his favorite *Frog and Toad* book and told us sadly that his family was "all over the place" and that things were "more harder than easy" for him. As the years went by, Jerron continued to struggle with the loss of this tight web of familial support.

SCHOOL: "BETTER" EDUCATION, STRUGGLING STUDENT

In the spring of 2011, we had the chance to visit Jerron's new middle school. We had heard from Shaundra, Eddie, and Lila that they were all very pleased with the school system in Lafayette; they were convinced that Jerron was getting a "better" education. Eddie, who along with Shaundra had attended one of the many failing high schools[6] in New Orleans, put it plainly: "The schools are better in Lafayette." After asking Jerron's permission to visit him at his school (and getting the okay from his mother), we drove across town to see him.

The old limestone building where Jerron attended middle school was a beautiful landmark in the sprawling city of Lafayette. We walked through the front door to be greeted by a friendly receptionist and treated to signs and murals, all extolling the virtues of peace, trust, kindness, and environmental sustainability. On our walk to the cafeteria, we saw black and white children, all in uniform, walking in pairs and small groups on outdoor walkways between buildings. At Jerron's lunchtime, we observed the children eating their school lunches and talking at their tables. Unlike some of the other schools we had visited over the duration of our research, the lunch staff was comfortable with the children socializing and did not scold the students or punish them for talking too much or too loudly during the lunch hour. After lunch, the children walked outside and headed to some tall shade trees next to a large grassy field. It was a warm spring day, so some students stayed in the shade and talked, while others played a game of football. The school had a large outdoor area with space to run around in.

This was a good school, and by almost any objective measure, the public schools in Lafayette are, as Eddie and the rest of the family believed, "better" than the public schools in New Orleans. In Lafayette, the average test scores are higher,[7] the classes are more racially integrated,[8] and a larger percentage of students graduate than from the schools in New Orleans.[9] Many other families displaced from Katrina to cities like Houston, Atlanta, Denver, and San Antonio also found the schools to have more resources and the teachers and school employees to be more highly qualified and responsive to their children's needs.[10] For many of these families, this was the first time their child had attended a higher quality school. Several parents in our study described this experience with better education systems as an awakening, and the schools became a large part of their decision to stay in their new locations and not return to New Orleans.[11]

If Jerron had stayed in—or returned to—the New Orleans system, he would have attended a public elementary school named Powell, where Lila is a teacher. Powell is classified as a "Recovery School," meaning that it was absorbed by the Louisiana Department of Education's Recovery School District (RSD) because it was "underperforming," even before Katrina. Being placed in the RSD was seen as a last attempt for the state to save the school because it was deemed "failing" and beyond what the local school district could manage. Powell obviously had tremendous problems before Katrina, and those only increased after the storm.

During our visits to Powell Elementary School post-Katrina, we observed crowded classrooms and the wide range of ages of children in the hallways. There were teenagers in the fourth grade, for example; these youth had missed so much schooling during years of displacement that they had no choice but to enroll in grades much beneath what their age would suggest (also see chapter 3 for a discussion of this phenomenon). Students were required to pass through a metal detector when entering the school, and a team of two armed security guards searched their backpacks. The vice principal explained to us that they "need these measures more for the parents" who visit and less for the young students. Regardless of why the measures were implemented, it was still startling to us, at the time, to encounter so much security upon entering an elementary school.[12]

In the classrooms, the older students were getting into fights and younger children were biting and otherwise acting out. Absenteeism rates were high at the school, and for several years after Katrina, administrators struggled to establish a consistent roster of students because children were being bussed from all over the city to Powell and the students' families were still in transition and attempting to settle after Katrina. There was little parental involvement in the school due to many of the structural factors that often impede low-income or working-class parents from taking a more active role in their children's schooling experiences.[13]

The building where Powell was located was old and rundown, with some graffiti on the side of the two-story brick structure and missing windows that had been boarded over. Teachers told us that the school's neighborhood was so dangerous that they could not safely walk to the corner store two blocks away on their lunch breaks—in fact, during one of our visits to the school, a teacher we met pointed to the corner store and noted that a young man had been shot to death at that location just a week prior.

Powell's outdoor space was a large blacktop surrounded by a chain-link fence. Prior to Katrina, the school had no playground equipment of any kind. This led to an array of problems during recess, even as a security guard watched over the setting, because the children and adolescents had nothing constructive to do. Several years after Katrina, the school was given a new playground structure from a nonprofit engaged in Katrina recovery work.[14] This was especially important since the only neighborhood park had been filled with temporary FEMA trailers, so there was nowhere else for the children to play.

Teachers informed us of the many issues that children at the school faced after Katrina. They included living in New Orleans without their parents; fearing for their safety on the way to and from school, and while at home; and experiencing tremendous food insecurity (at lunchtime, children would sometimes ask if they could have the food left on other children's plates at the end of the meal so that they could take it home). Many of the children and youth at the school were struggling with such traumatic Katrina experiences that they were not able to properly function in the school setting. Despite this, the school did not have the funds to employ a social worker or counselor to help the students, a fact lamented by the vice principal in our interview with her.

It is no surprise, given this context, that the school administrators and teachers were deeply challenged by many of the children in their charge. We interviewed a seventh-grade teacher from the school who had been assaulted by two boys in her class. She was transferred to another school and a new administrative position; she told us she would "never, ever" return to classroom teaching after that incident.

Lila had taught at Powell for nearly 40 years. She was aware that the school had been in decline before Katrina and that the educational conditions had plummeted sharply since the storm. Thus, when Jerron expressed his strong desire to return to his "old life" in New Orleans, Lila was certain that he did not understand exactly how much things had changed in the city—and how much of a disadvantage he would be at if he left his "better" school in Lafayette:

> Jerron was born here [in New Orleans]. He was here for the first [six] years of his life, so it's like a foundation for him, and he had to be uprooted and moved from this. So it's comfortable for him. See, he doesn't realize that a lot of changes have taken place here since he was here . . . But he thinks things were the same prior to him leaving here.

Jerron missed nearly two months of his first-grade year, when he and his mom were displaced to Baton Rouge. He re-entered school when they moved to Atlanta for a brief period, and then he switched schools again when they transitioned to Lafayette. By the time Jerron started second grade in Lafayette, he scored "below grade level" on a reading assessment. Shaundra said that after some time in the Lafayette schools, "his reading ability got higher. He's reading on grade level now."

But while Jerron was now attending a "better" school in Lafayette, from his perspective, he was not having a "better" experience. He struggled with his behavior and his grades at the new school. On one of our visits, Shaundra claimed that his teacher was great and that she liked having Jerron in her class; Jerron said this was not true and he told us that he and his teacher did not "get along." When we asked why they did not get along, Jerron responded:

Because I don't be turnin' in my homework when it is supposed to be done. Because I be goin' places . . . Sometimes my teacher is razzin' me. That's why I don't want to go to school every day.

Jerron also often got into fights with his classmates. He told us that during his first day of school in Lafayette, when he was only in the first grade, he got into a fight:

I just went up and [the teacher] wanted everybody to talk about themselves. I told them, "I'm from New Orleans and I moved here for Hurricane Katrina." And this little boy stood up and said, "New Orleans sucks." So I got mad and I just—I don't know, it's a whole other story. I just started fighting.

Jerron continued to get into fights throughout his elementary school years, as he struggled to deal with the anger and ups and downs he felt after Katrina. He claimed that students would often "get all over my face." And then, "I push 'em or I would hit 'em, and the principal would be right there and say, 'Jerron, why'd you hit them?' I only got in trouble once for that." In response to his fighting, Jerron often got "referrals" to the principal's office, write-ups in class, and he was suspended for three days of school at one point.

When Jerron transitioned to his new middle school, it looked like he might continue with his string of fighting. However, as he explained to us, this school was different. The school had defined "peace" and "no fighting" as two of its core values, and the principal made it clear to Jerron that his lashing out and other "bad behavior" would not be tolerated:

At the beginning of the year, they [the other adolescent boys] was ready to fight everybody from New Orleans. The first day of school, I got into a fight, but I didn't get the write-up, somebody else did. So when they got the write-up, they made me go in the office and they said, "Jerron, one thing you need to learn about this school: Do not ever, ever, ever try to fight with somebody at this school." So I had to talk with the principal, and that is what she told me.

Jerron did poorly in terms of his grades for the first few years that he was in Lafayette. He had little focus and did not care much at all about school. Jerron received low marks on his report cards and barely passed the required standardized tests. Shaundra was extremely frustrated about this and Eddie also felt irritated: "He got two D's. What's goin' on? So we buckled down." Shaundra would not allow Jerron to participate in team sports, and she also did not let him go outside and play with his friends until his homework was complete. Eddie also tried to intervene, but he could only do so from a distance and over the telephone, for the most part, given their physical separation. Shaundra would call Eddie to tell him about Jerron's academic performance, and then Eddie would talk to him. Eddie described a typical "grade intervention" as follows:

> Shaundra will call me: "He got a report card. He's got in trouble at school again." "Put him on the phone and let me yell at him some." Then Jerron says, "Hey, Daddy." And I say, "Haven't been doin' right, have you?" "No. This happened, this happened, this happened." It's a work in progress. I try not to stress. I'm very stress free, carefree. But I feel some stress about it.

Over time, it became obvious to us exactly how much stress Jerron's school performance was causing for him and for the adults in his life. Lila told us she was "holding her breath" until Jerron's test scores came in. Shaundra texted Lila on her cell phone to give her the good news when he passed his year-end standardized tests. Jerron often steered the conversation away from school and toward sports or other more "fun" activities when we would interview him. However, as he grew older and moved into middle school, we saw him begin to put more effort into his studies. And he did like his new middle school classes in Lafayette more than the elementary school that he attended in the city. With the environmental education focus at the middle school, Jerron had all kinds of new opportunities for learning. In fact, and as his mother proudly showed us, his picture was featured on the front page of the local newspaper after an ecology class field trip to the wetlands in Louisiana.

Even with the improved educational circumstances, Jerron's emotional attachment to his old school in New Orleans was still strong, and this affected his post-disaster trajectory. Five years after Katrina, when we asked Jerron to describe what he was most sad to have lost in the storm, he said it was his pre-kindergarten certificate that he received at Powell Elementary School in New Orleans. He drew us a picture of the certificate, which was damaged in the storm (see figure 7.2).

Jerron's educational *opportunities* increased in his displacement. But his personal educational *experience* was not better; he struggled much of the time and this sphere of his life was down more than it was up in the post-Katrina recovery period.

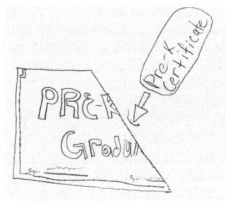

Figure 7.2. Drawing of tattered pre-K
certificate, by Jerron, 11 years old

HOUSING: MOVEMENT, THEN "HOME"

Four years after Katrina, we parked our rental car in the driveway of a white house with a small cement-floor front porch with white wooden pillars and lined with white plastic outdoor chairs. Shaundra, sitting on the porch and wearing a bright pink-and-orange floral top and cut-off jean shorts, looked up and saw us, and waved happily. Jerron was playing football in the grassy area that separated their house from their next-door neighbor. He stopped long enough to come over, to give us both a quick hug, and to touch the tops of our heads to show us that he was now nearly as tall as we were. We all laughed, and then he ran back and rejoined the game with several other boys from the neighborhood who all appeared to be around Jerron's age.

Shaundra invited us in. She introduced us to their family dog, Ace, a small "mutt" that they had adopted from the local shelter after they moved into their new home. We looked around and noted that she had purchased a new couch and recliner set and an end table since our last visit. We complimented her on the nice furniture, which she proudly noted she was able to "save up" for and buy after being promoted at her job. We congratulated her, and then she showed us around the redecorated house that had now become familiar to us. Jerron's grandmother was standing at the stove cooking chicken and mashed potatoes in preparation for an early dinner. The food smelled delicious and we were reminded of what a wonderful cook Jerron's grandmother was. As we walked around the home, we noticed that most of the rooms were tidy, as usual, although Jerron's room was messy and full of video games, books, and clothes spilling out of the two tall dressers.

Even though Jerron's small room was cramped, he later informed us that the "best thing" about the house was that he had his own bedroom. For his mother, the "best thing" was that she had become a homeowner for the first time in her life.

At the time of Katrina, Shaundra was renting a house in the New Orleans neighborhood of Gentilly, which was home to many working- and middle-class African Americans before the hurricane.[15] In the rush of the evacuation, Jerron remembered: "We had to pack all the things. We had to hurry up. I had to keep runnin' in and out, in and out, because I wanted to take all my toys. I was sneakin' 'em in my pants." When Jerron's mom saw that he had his favorite fire truck and motorcycles and other toys, she insisted that he put them back because their automobile was already too crowded. This was a decision Shaundra would later regret, as their house flooded and they lost everything. There were of course the irreplaceable items from Jerron's childhood, but even the things that could be replaced were not because, as was the case for many renters, Shaundra had no insurance on their belongings. She also received no aid for housing, as many disaster assistance programs are designed for homeowners, not renters, which helps explain why renters are often among the slowest to return and to recover after a disaster.[16]

As noted earlier, after Shaundra, Jerron, and their family members fled New Orleans in the wake of Katrina, they were displaced to multiple locations in four different states. Shaundra recognized how difficult this was for Jerron: "He was very stressed when we first went through the transition of living somewhere, going from state to state." But she also saw Lafayette as a chance for a new lease on life. She calmly told us: "I always wanted to get out of New Orleans, and I felt that Katrina was my way out." Shaundra had a cousin who was displaced to Lafayette, which is one of the reasons why she chose to relocate her family there after Katrina. Its proximity to New Orleans, and Jerron's father's side of the family, was also a deciding factor.

Shaundra, who had a high school degree and a few advanced professional training classes, managed to secure an excellent job soon after the storm. She worked for the housing authority, a public agency, helping people to find housing. Her job provided steady pay and health care for her and her children. With Eddie's reliable child support and her salary, she could afford summer camp for Jerron and childcare for Reggie, Jerron's younger brother, when the family needed it. She also qualified for a mortgage. She told us many times that she felt "blessed" to get the house.

Even though the new home may have been a blessing, it initially meant yet another move and another layer of disruption in Jerron's life. He had settled into the apartment across town and had made several new friends there. Even though both Eddie and Shaundra realized that moving again would cause more turmoil in Jerron's life, at least in the short term, they also recognized the long-term importance of becoming a homeowner. In fact, Eddie told Shaundra, "If you got the house, you should stay," because he knew that it was a good opportunity, and she might never have the same chance to own a home in New Orleans. Shaundra agreed:

> I really think we have been blessed. I mean, we have accomplished so much [more] here than what we did when we were living in New Orleans. We were renting a house in New Orleans. Now we own a house here.

She confided that owning her own home was what she "always wanted" but it could not happen in New Orleans because of her unpredictable, low-paying employment with no benefits and her inability to save enough money to make a down payment. Having a larger, three-bedroom home also allowed Shaundra to offer space to her own mother and Jerron's aunt, both of whom played a large role in Jerron's and his little brother's afterschool care while Shaundra was still at work.

The new housing provided a firm sense of stability for Jerron. Even as his family remained apart, and his school was up and down in terms of his grades and his behavior, Jerron was in permanent housing a year and a half after Katrina. This was a heavy "anchor" in his life, leading to a certain sense of security and comfort that had been missing as his entire family remained in transition for a long period after Katrina. Yet, at the same time, for displaced children and youth like Jerron, a new home offered stability for the family, but it did not remove the longing for their old homes and neighborhoods, as was so clear in Jerron's case.

Jerron's house in Lafayette was in a quiet, safe neighborhood. As a child in New Orleans, Jerron was exposed to a great deal of violence. Even at a young age, he would tell us about the bad things police had done to African Americans in the city; about the shootings, stabbings, and drug-dealing he learned about through the news and through the experiences of African American friends and family members. These incidents made Jerron realize, even as he longed for the city, that it might not have been the safest place. Eddie even noted that, when considering many factors, such as the violence, "When you think of New Orleans, you don't think kids. New Orleans definitely isn't a place to raise kids." Shaundra also stressed that point:

> And that's another reason why I didn't want to go back to New Orleans. It's safe here [in Lafayette]. You don't have to really worry about crime

like New Orleans had. And, you know, crime has gotten worse now since Katrina.

Lila agreed, and also sadly described the destruction of child-friendly spaces. The rebuilding of parks and playgrounds and other such places seemed to be low on the city's priority list, and she thought this was further delaying the recovery of the youngest survivors of the storm. Thus, even as the adults struggled with whether they had made the right decisions as far as where they were all living post-Katrina, they wanted to see Jerron succeed. For the time being, at least, this meant remaining in stable housing and a safe neighborhood, which also meant staying in Lafayette.

FRIENDS: OLD AND NEW

Jerron was sad after Katrina for many reasons, but especially because of the separation from his family, his city, and his closest friends in New Orleans.[17] He told us: "I really do miss my friends that used to be with me in New Orleans. Amanda. Jordan. My best friend, Samuel."

Most of Jerron's friends were displaced after Katrina and then eventually returned to New Orleans, while Jerron remained in Lafayette. Every time we visited, Jerron would speak of how much he missed Samuel, and Samuel's name always came up in interviews with Eddie, Shaundra, and Lila, as well. Samuel's mother was a friend of Shaundra's, so the two boys had met when they were very young and they played together frequently before the storm. After Katrina, Jerron tried to visit Samuel every time he had the chance to go to New Orleans, and sometimes he worried about him because of the city's crime rate. Jerron told us: "He's living in New Orleans. I want them to get out [of] New Orleans. Because they're like, if you're livin' alone, they're [criminals] gonna try to get you."

Jerron obviously cared about Samuel, and thought of him more like a cousin or even a brother. When Shaundra drove Jerron to New Orleans to see the rest of his family, he and Samuel would go to the park, play video games, or otherwise just hang out. It was painful to leave and say good-bye each time Jerron had to return to Lafayette. For Jerron, pre-Katrina friendships remained important even years after displacement. Our work suggests that this separation from friends and classmates was profoundly disruptive for young people. Jerron simply could not "commit" to a new life in Lafayette, and one of the many reasons for that was the distance from his old friends, especially Samuel.

As the years passed following the evacuation, Jerron's friendship with Samuel continued to grow and the boys remained close. Sociologists Patti Adler and Peter Adler would refer to Jerron and Samuel's friendship after Katrina as a "deep, compartmentalized friendship."[18] The Adlers found that children's and pre-adolescents' "long-distance friends," such as peers they met at summer camp or whose families moved away, offer a special relationship, giving them a "safe haven" outside of their regular environments and their everyday friendships, which typically stem from school environments. Indeed, these long-distance friendships, because they are not everyday and because they are outside of the school peer group, can be more intimate.

Given the scale of the disaster, most children and youth displaced by Katrina had friends who ended up far away. In our sample, we found that many were not able to develop compartmentalized long-distance friendships because the families were not able to arrange for visits or other ways to keep the relationships going. Jerron and Samuel were thus fortunate that they lived nearby enough that their families remained connected. When Samuel and his family returned to New Orleans, Jerron could see him when he visited his father and other family members.

At the same time, Jerron was able to make friends during his displacement. His mother made a point to reassure him that new friendships would develop: "You [are] gonna make new friends in different places, so don't keep on crying about going back to New Orleans." She was right, but that did not ease the desire to return to New Orleans. He made friends in Baton Rouge and Atlanta, and then again when he moved into an apartment in Lafayette, and again when he moved into the new house. He was close to Rashad, the boy who lived next door, and he had many friends at school and on his sports teams. We witnessed him joking with his friends on his baseball team, riding bikes around his neighborhood with other boys his age, and playing games at recess with his friends at school. Because Jerron had so many more opportunities for extracurricular activities in Lafayette, he also had more chances to meet new groups of children who shared his interests. He ultimately formed many new friendships that emerged from his participation in sports, church, and other activities. He was thus not limited to school, neighborhood, and family friends as the sites for finding and connecting with his peers.

Making friends did not appear to be a struggle for Jerron, and he seemed to enjoy his new friendships. When we visited him soon after he turned 12 years old, he even had a "girlfriend" from his middle school. Shaundra laughed and told us she was not ready for him to have that type of relationship just yet, but she also recognized that her son was growing up.

Friendships such as the ones that Jerron developed are some of the most important primary group attachments, affecting pre-adolescents' and adolescents' sense of belonging, identity formation, and social learning. For pre-adolescent and adolescent boys like Jerron, these friendship groups teach gender ideology, masculinity norms, and attitudes about violence.[19] In some ways, these friendships are as important to socialization as families.[20]

Interestingly, while Jerron had made new friends in Lafayette, those he characterized as his "best friends" were all still in New Orleans. Several years after Katrina, there was a period when his parents began dating again and it seemed like they might even remarry. Jerron wanted his parents back together for many reasons, and perhaps most importantly, because he "hoped and prayed" it would result in a move back to New Orleans. Jerron did not appear upset or concerned that this would mean leaving his new Lafayette friends behind. Instead, he was much more excited to return to his family and to Samuel and his other best friends in New Orleans. This was similar to Mekana's experience with friendships and displacement, as described in chapter 4. She, too, was pulled back to New Orleans because of her longtime friends who had returned to the city, which affected her own recovery.

In many ways, Jerron's new friendships helped him settle into his new life. They provided much-needed peer support and social acceptance. Yet, at the same time, the sphere of friendship, like schooling, was not straightforward, and in many ways was more down than up in terms of his trajectory. Jerron's unwillingness to commit to and truly embrace his new friendships contributed to the fluctuating nature of his recovery.

For Jerron, the spheres of his life did not fully align in the Katrina aftermath and, as such, he was not able to find or maintain equilibrium. In some ways, this is surprising, because so many things went right for him and his family, even after they suffered such tremendous loss in Katrina. His mother was quickly able to regain full-time employment with health care benefits. She had access to a well-maintained automobile and became a first-time homeowner in a good neighborhood. Jerron began attending a school that was, by almost any measure used to assess schools, "better" than the one he attended in New Orleans. And yet, Jerron never fully settled in Lafayette.

Jerron's case illuminates what happened to some of the children and youth we studied who ended up in new places—even places with good schools, safe neighborhoods, and positive extracurricular opportunities for children—but who never felt that they were "home." In every interview, formal and informal, we heard from Jerron himself, as well as all of his family members, about how badly he wanted to move back to New Orleans. This is significant. Many parents described to us the painful conversations with their children when they had to tell them that their family was never moving back to New Orleans. Some of those children clearly experienced a cultural loss and a lack of rootedness. The decisions also led to added stress within families, when the parents and children did not agree on where the family should settle.[21]

Jerron felt most at home in New Orleans because that was where he was born and raised before Katrina. He missed the city because that is where his father, his grandmother and great-grandmother, many of his other family members, and his closest friends had returned after Katrina. Jerron wanted his family and friends to be reunited and to live near one another as they had before the storm. So even as his family members were so loving, and so supportive—his anchors—they were not back together. That lack of stability in a core sphere of his life caused many fluctuations in other aspects of Jerron's well-being. This situation was compounded by the fact that at the time of Katrina he was dealing with another crisis—his parents' divorce—and had not adjusted to that disruption at the time of his displacement. One crisis on top of another contributed to the fluctuations that he experienced after Katrina.

In the end, Jerron had trouble fully accepting Lafayette as "home." He identified strongly with New Orleans and longed to live there again. His grades suffered and his behavioral issues got worse for a period after Katrina. Jerron never fully declined after the disaster, but he continued to shift up and down in the different spheres in his life. Never fully settling, never quite on a smooth path to recovery.

CLINTON
RAPID MOVEMENT

This chapter focuses on the experiences of Clinton Evans, an African American boy who was four years old when Katrina made landfall. Of all of the focal children and youth featured in this book, Clinton's life was in the most continual and rapid state of flux in the years following Katrina. He and his siblings—including his sister, Brandi, who was 18 years old and had just started her first semester of college, and his older brother, Aaron, who was 20 years old at the time of Katrina—were all living "lives in limbo."[1] Despite their own personal upheavals, however, the two older siblings were Clinton's most consistent and stable sources of support both before and after the storm. They were his anchors, even in extremely turbulent times.

We chose Clinton as a focal child and highlight his story here for two reasons. First, his experience aptly illustrates the fluctuating trajectory, emphasizing the ways that children's lives can shift from decline to equilibrium in all spheres, in a wave-like pattern. Second, Clinton's story underscores the important ways that siblings may protect one another in pre- and post-disaster settings. The role of siblings in supporting and caring for one another is a topic that remains relatively unexamined in the disaster literature.[2]

As the years passed, we watched Clinton—as well as Brandi and Aaron—move back and forth between moments of total familial crisis and breakdown to conditions that were rapidly improving and stabilizing. At one moment, things appeared to be going fairly well in terms of their relationships, schooling, housing, and so forth; at another, they were on a precipitous spiral downward.

We would often worry aloud to each other about their circumstances, and we came to feel a familiar sense of apprehension when we called to check in with the members of the Evans family. When we visited where they were living at the time, we were always concerned about what we might find. Would they be okay? Would their neighborhood and the surrounding areas be safe? Would they have enough food to eat? Would Karen, their mother, be using drugs again? Would Aaron have a job and a secure source of income? Would Clinton's school have good teachers and enough resources? Would Brandi be taking college classes? Would her car be broken down?

Because their living situations changed often, we traveled from Baton Rouge to New Orleans to Slidell in Louisiana and to Dallas, Texas, to trace the experiences of Clinton and his other family members. All along, we attempted to understand the social forces and factors, the resource availability and resource needs, and the family dynamics that shaped the movement of Clinton's post-disaster trajectory. With this in mind, we organize this chapter around a number of key markers that demonstrate the post-Katrina ups and downs in his life and during the disaster recovery. Specifically, we highlight 11 points in time, stretching from the period before Katrina's landfall in August of 2005, to just over seven years later, in October of 2012. The beginning waves in Clinton's trajectory happened in a short, compressed period of time; indeed, the first four points rapidly unfolded within a five-week period in 2005. However, as the years went on, the waves lasted for longer periods, so the later points in Clinton's trajectory cover more time.

Focusing on these recovery turning points clarifies how Clinton's life fit the fluctuating trajectory. Similar to Jerron, who was featured in chapter 7, Clinton regularly shifted between stability and instability; but unlike Jerron's trajectory, Clinton's fluctuation had an up-and-down, "rollercoaster" pattern.[3] Jerron often had one or more spheres of his life going well while other areas were misaligned, whereas Clinton experienced a pattern in which all spheres were simultaneously down, and then all spheres would stabilize, and then all spheres would shift downward again, and so forth.

BACKGROUND: ABSENT MOTHER

Even before Katrina, Clinton, as well as Brandi and Aaron, had already endured incredibly difficult circumstances. Their mother, Karen, had developed a serious drug addiction when Brandi and Aaron were around the ages of 10 and 12, respectively (this was several years before Clinton was born).[4]

When on drugs, Karen would often disappear for months at a time, leaving Brandi and Aaron to fend for themselves. Out of work and on the streets, Karen would not pay the rent or the utilities for their house in the Lower Ninth Ward neighborhood in New Orleans. This left young Brandi and Aaron living without electricity or running water at various times throughout their childhood. Brandi remembered this period of her life with sadness:

> It was plenty of days where we had to sleep in the dark. No lights, no water. It was like, "Are we alive?" You're staying in a house with no lights or water, no food. Just impossible.

Not knowing where their next meal would come from, Brandi and Aaron would survive on flour, sugar, or bread, hoarding whatever additional food they could find while at school or church functions. Were it not for the kindness of others—such as the landlord who let them remain in the house rent free or the women from their church who would bring over food—Brandi and Aaron would have experienced even worse conditions than they were already forced to bear.

Brandi and Aaron became accustomed to life without their mother, although they coped differently with her absence. Aaron grew increasingly angry and resentful, "just hanging out and partying" with his friends and disengaging from his studies. Brandi reacted in the opposite way, becoming more responsible and attentive in all aspects of her life.

All the while, Aaron and Brandi were confronted with the reality that they might never see their mother again. At one time, Karen was missing for so long that Brandi, who was by then 12 years old, thought that her mother had likely died. Then, one day, the police contacted them, as Brandi recalled:

> When we did find her, after all of that time, I done got prepared that she was dead. It was like, "Okay, she's gone. She didn't call. They don't know where she is." She was just dead. I lived with it . . . I was like, okay. So we got a call, and they were like, "Hey, we found your mom. She was somewhere in the street."

Soon after Karen was reunited with her two children, she became pregnant with Clinton. Clinton's father was also addicted to drugs; he did not help Karen during the pregnancy and he and his family played only a limited role in Clinton's early childhood. According to Brandi, when Karen found out she was pregnant, she quit using drugs, found a job, and rejoined her children in their household. She was clean for about a year after Clinton was born, but then succumbed to using cocaine again and returned to living on the streets.

As a consequence, when Clinton was one year old, Brandi, who was 15 years old at the time, became his primary caregiver. Aaron, who was 17 years old, was in and out of the house, angrier than ever at his mother and dealing with his own issues. As such, he was mostly unavailable to help his sister raise their baby brother, even though Brandi pleaded with him to support her. She told us how she would beg Aaron to just "stay together." She would tell him that "if we don't stay together, it's not gonna work." But ultimately, almost all of the responsibility for caring for Clinton during his youngest years fell to Brandi, still a child herself, albeit a highly responsible one. In many respects, their experience was gendered in ways that have long been identified in sociological literature. Specifically, Brandi took on the caregiving role, one often relegated to females, while her older brother felt less of an obligation to help with childcare, perhaps because there are fewer societal expectations for males to perform that type of labor.

To say that it was difficult for Brandi to raise a young sibling while attempting to finish high school would be a dramatic understatement. But with help, she did it. And later, reflecting back on the experience, she told us that when it came to caring for Clinton, she felt "good about that" and "the time that I had with him, it means so much to me now, it was worth it."

To care for Clinton, Brandi was especially reliant on the support of her grandmother, her high school teachers, and many different women from her church who often stepped in to assist. These women were stabilizing influences in Brandi's life—they were her anchors. By extension, they provided a stabilizing force in young Clinton's life as well. Brandi described how the process worked:

> I always had a lot of help. We even got Clinton in our preschool at my church. It was a hassle trying to get a ride there, but it was like, "Can you all come pick him up, bring him to school?" I always had a lot of help with that. A lot of my teachers at school who I was really kind of close with, I talked to them about the whole situation, and I was like: "Look, if I come to school in the morning and I'm looking dead to the world, this is why. I'm up with a baby, up in the middle of the night, getting a bottle."

This nonfamilial support was especially important since Brandi received limited assistance from family other than her grandmother. Although Brandi had an aunt, uncle, and cousins in New Orleans, she received less help with raising Clinton from kin than the actual size of the family might suggest. Like Karen, Brandi's aunt and uncle had both become addicted to drugs and were not available to contribute to the family in a meaningful way. This lack of tangible familial support rendered the Evans children even more vulnerable.

After Karen descended back into serious drug use, she lost her custodial job at a local public school and could no longer pay the rent. The landlord who had so long offered free shelter to the Evans children could no longer do this. Facing homelessness, Aaron decided to pursue a work opportunity in Chicago while Miss Shirley, who was a member of Brandi's church and had long known the Evans family, took in Brandi and Clinton.

POINT 1: DOWN

During Brandi's senior year of high school, she was accepted into a university located about an hour's drive from New Orleans. In the late summer of 2005, she packed her things and made arrangements for Miss Shirley to keep Clinton full time. Karen was still on the streets and mostly out of the picture, although in the past when she would re-emerge, Miss Shirley would let her stay in the house until she started using drugs again.

This was an exceptionally difficult time for both Clinton and Brandi. Clinton had turned four years old in March of 2005, and in May of 2005, Brandi graduated high school and prepared to go to college. Clinton loved his sister immensely, as she loved him. The thought of being separated from her little brother broke Brandi's heart, but she also knew that if she was going to make a better life for herself—and by extension, for Clinton—she had to further her education. Moreover, Brandi chose to major in child development, undoubtedly a decision shaped by her own turbulent childhood and her commitment to making Clinton's life as stable and secure as possible.

As Brandi prepared to depart, she remembered telling Miss Shirley: "Please, if you can just keep him for a little while, let me get up on my feet, and we'll see what happens after that . . . I'm like, 'I really need you to help me.'" It was no surprise that Brandi reached out to Miss Shirley in this way, as she trusted her completely with Clinton. In fact, when Clinton was a toddler, Brandi had tried to convince her mother to allow Miss Shirley to legally adopt Clinton. In the end, though, Karen would not give up her son, and so Miss Shirley continued to care for Clinton and serve as his informal guardian when Brandi left for college.

Miss Shirley's love and stability allowed Brandi to pursue her own dreams, but by all accounts, this was definitely a "down" period in Clinton's young life. He was already living in a fragile state, and the physical separation from his sister only added to the uncertainty in his environment. Brandi would no longer be there on a daily basis to advocate for Clinton, to ensure that he was fed, clothed, and brought to his preschool. She trusted Miss Shirley to take care of these things, but she was torn because she wanted to be there herself. In addition, it was an economically precarious time for Brandi and

Clinton. Brandi had to take out student loans to attend college and she was no longer able to contribute to any household expenses related to raising Clinton. Although she knew that college represented a long-term investment, she also realized that it diminished her opportunity to work and pay for things that she wanted Clinton to have in life.

POINT 2: UPWARD

As Katrina bore down on the Gulf Coast, Brandi realized how serious the storm was going to be. She packed up an overnight bag and locked up her college dormitory room. She gassed up her rundown two-door silver Chrysler and then drove east toward New Orleans. Later, she described matter-of-factly how she moved into action in order to be reunited with Clinton at Miss Shirley's: "So once Hurricane Katrina was coming, I was like, 'I need to go get my little brother.'"

Brandi made it to New Orleans and joined Miss Shirley and Clinton less than 48 hours before Katrina made landfall. This was tremendously helpful to Clinton, to have his sister, his anchor, back by his side. Brandi and Miss Shirley packed Clinton's things and then the three of them loaded up together and headed still further east to Miss Shirley's mother's home in Mississippi. Because Aaron was still in Chicago, Brandi and Clinton could rest assured that their older brother was out of harm's way as Katrina churned ominously toward the Gulf Coast.

Clinton was fortunate to be under the watchful care of his sister and Miss Shirley. Their very presence represented one of the many protective factors that kept Clinton from experiencing a decline at this point. Long after the storm, as we were tracing Clinton's trajectory with Brandi, she emphasized that the evacuation was definitely an "up" period for Clinton because they were back together and she could "comfort and reassure him."

Clinton's trajectory also moved in an upward direction during this point for several other reasons, especially when compared to the fate of many other children who were left behind in New Orleans to ride out the storm. Clinton was able to leave the city before Katrina made landfall, in contrast to other young people we interviewed who were in the city at the time of the storm and flooding, some of whom told us highly traumatic stories of fearing for their own lives, of waiting for days with no food and water, and of seeing dead bodies. Clinton was with two adults who both had access to working vehicles. This allowed Miss Shirley and Brandi to safely transport him out of the city and to protect him from the horrors that other children witnessed.

Clinton also was with adults who had networks of kin and friends outside of New Orleans so that they had places they could go and stay safely for long periods of time. Many New Orleanians had dense social networks concentrated within New Orleans, meaning that they did not know people outside of the city and therefore had nowhere to go when members of their entire support network lost their homes and evacuated. Clinton, Brandi, and Miss Shirley made it safely to the home of Miss Shirley's mother, knowing they could remain there as long as they needed to.

POINT 3: DOWNWARD IN DISPLACEMENT

The third point in Clinton's fluctuating trajectory was another downward movement, as the losses and disruptions from Katrina unfolded. The most traumatic issue that all of the Evans children dealt with during this period was the fact that their mother was missing after the storm. No one—not Clinton, Brandi, Aaron, or Miss Shirley—knew the whereabouts of Karen as Katrina crashed ashore. Brandi and Miss Shirley watched the television from Mississippi as New Orleans flooded, not knowing whether Karen was amidst the tens of thousands of people seeking refuge in the Superdome or on highway overpasses, or, even worse, if she was among the growing number of the dead.

It was a terrifying period for everyone in the family. All that they were sure of was that Karen had no car, no reliable friends or networks of support, and no cash given that she was unemployed and using drugs. For nearly a month, the Evans children moved through the days, not knowing whether their mother had perished in the catastrophe. Aaron described it as a "devastating, life-changing experience."

Clinton was less traumatized by the storm than his brother and sister, perhaps due to his younger age. But he did understand the destruction the storm caused and remembered that the storm was "big" and that "the water was high." We asked him to draw a picture of Katrina, which is shown in figure 8.1.

Here is how Clinton described the image he created:

Okay, well, it was black clouds. I think it looked like this, like black clouds everywhere. You couldn't see the sun. Like a big tornado, houses flying everywhere. Cars were up in the air, dropping on the ground. Windows broken, buildings down on the ground, crushed . . . So buildings would be broken down, houses flying up in the air, cars . . . Most people would be out, but they don't even know that the storm is there because most people can't hear, but they can see.

Figure 8.1. Drawing of "what Katrina looked like," by Clinton, eight years old

Once cell phone service was restored in the weeks after Katrina, Aaron and Brandi were in regular contact, trying to figure out what to do about their missing mother and also about how to care for Clinton. Aaron was stuck in Chicago and Brandi was uncertain about whether she would be able to return to her university classes that semester. Although Brandi tried to shield her younger sibling from the stress, it permeated every aspect of their lives. Clinton was forced to deal with being "in flux" as the life and routine he had grown accustomed to were gone, as was perhaps his mother.

POINT 4: DOWNWARD AGAIN

The fourth point in Clinton's trajectory was another down moment, in late September of 2005. In this downward motion all of the spheres in his life moved together; again, Clinton's spheres were not misaligned, they were simultaneously in decline.

Clinton was eventually reunited with his mother due to Miss Shirley's tenacity. For weeks after Katrina, she regularly searched an online registry that was established for family members and friends to find their displaced loved ones.[5] Brandi described how the process worked:

> So if [families] couldn't find somebody, they was putting them online and you could actually locate them from there. So Miss Shirley, she was always

on the computer trying to find other people, [including] my mama. She called me and she was like, "I know where you mama is." "What? Where is she at?" "She's in Baton Rouge." "Do you know a number or something?" "Yeah. Call her."

Brandi, shocked that her mother was alive, wrote down the telephone number as Miss Shirley recited it. Then, taking a deep breath, she picked up the phone and called a church in Baton Rouge that had become a temporary shelter to hundreds of displaced persons after Katrina. After a conversation with a volunteer, Brandi confirmed that her mother was actually at the shelter. The next day, she apprehensively drove Clinton to the shelter so that they could see Karen.

After they found Karen at the shelter, Brandi had to establish two things so that she could feel comfortable enough to return to college. First, she asked for her mother's word that she would no longer use drugs. Second, she talked to the church staff to ensure that her mother and Clinton would be cared for and receive the assistance that they needed. Although worried, Brandi felt confident enough, especially because she would be nearby, that she could return to her classes.

With Brandi back at school and Miss Shirley still displaced with relatives, Clinton had to stay at the shelter, where he had no connections to anyone except his mother. Even though the shelter was run well, it was still an overwhelming transition for a four-year-old child who missed his big sister and Miss Shirley, and who had never really lived consistently with his mother. Perhaps not surprisingly, Clinton regularly expressed that he wanted to go back to New Orleans. Karen described how difficult this was when we first interviewed her in the shelter:

> With my son, and him being four, it's hard to explain to him, or to get him to understand that you're not going to be where you were before. You're not going back to your old school. You're not going back to your old house. So now you have to deal with the fact that every day you have to tell him the same thing over and over. And he's saying the same thing: "When am I goin' back to my school? When am I goin' back home?" Or, "I'm ready to go back home. Call my sister. Call my brother. Where's my aunt?" . . . But when it's not a possibility, you have to let him know, "Hey, baby, we can't go back. There is no more home." And for a four-year-old, you can't explain it.

It is true that young children experience and process disasters in distinct ways. To a certain extent, the youngest survivors can be shielded from some things that older children and youth cannot; but at the same time, younger children have fewer or less developed life coping skills and fewer verbal skills which would allow them to put events in a larger context and to express their feelings about what is happening.[6]

Clinton desperately missed his family members and friends from his pre-school and his church in New Orleans. Karen noted that when the storm hit, Clinton, always a "people person," watched "it all go away" in terms of his family connections and friendships. She said that Clinton would constantly ask her: "Where everybody at?"

In addition to his other immediate and extended family members, Clinton also missed his father. Clinton had minimal contact with his father in the years before the storm, mostly because of his father's drug addiction, but he still had an important connection with him. Karen elaborated on Clinton's longing for family while in the shelter:

> He knows he wants to see his family, his dad. He calls their names. He may cry once in a while and say, "Oh, I want to see my sister." Or his brother, or dad, or aunt, or cousins. It varies. He will think about something and he'll say, "I wanna go." And that's how it is. Kids, they have to learn to adjust to it and figure it out. But with a four-year-old, you can't.

POINT 5: MOVING UPWARD

Clinton was coping with the simultaneous loss of familiar family and friends, housing, neighborhood, schools, church, and daily routines. But as the weeks passed, both he and his mother began to settle into a new normal. The church shelter where they were staying, and the people whom they met there, ended up serving as powerful forces in pushing Clinton's recovery process upward.

The church, which we visited on two occasions after Katrina, ran a well-organized shelter operation after the storm. The church pastor and his wife, Mr. and Mrs. Myers, who were the leaders behind the shelter they opened, were both strong advocates for Katrina survivors. As described in previous chapters, we found that advocates—those persons who protected, supported, and otherwise fought for the recovery needs for children and youth—often made the difference between a child declining in disaster recovery or finding some stability. Mr. and Mrs. Myers worked tirelessly, often putting in 16- to 18-hour days, to make the shelter as comfortable for children and families as possible, giving private rooms[7] to mothers with small children, establishing regular mealtimes, and creating paid jobs for the shelter residents so that they could work and, in their words, "reclaim a sense of self-worth."

It was within this safe, structured, and warm environment that Clinton's trajectory turned upward. With the support of the pastor's wife, Mrs. Myers, and the many other women in the shelter, Karen began to take her first steps toward getting off drugs.

Not only did Mrs. Myers provide support and respect; she also had a no-nonsense demeanor and held high expectations of her "guests" at the shelter. She required that each adult shelter resident, including Karen, take on a job helping with shelter or church operations. One of the mothers whom we interviewed at the church shelter explained how Mrs. Myers made the process work:

> Anybody who wanted to work, she gave you a job doing something. She just made up jobs. She said the state would only allow her to pay us $9.75 an hour. But whoever wanted to work, she just found jobs. Whatever you liked doing, you know. And I worked in the nursery.

Another mother whom we interviewed during a focus group in the shelter described how she felt about the job requirement:

> It's a blessing, yes it is. It gives everybody a chance to get on their feet. Because if we was to go individually to find a job here in Baton Rouge, a lot of us probably wouldn't have been able to obtain employment. But here they worked out a system where everybody's doing something while their kids are taken care of.

Mrs. Myers required the Katrina survivors to work because she wanted them to earn money and feel that they were making a contribution to the shelter. She also told us, though, that she did not want them sitting idle and watching television coverage of the disaster all day long. Mrs. Myers feared this would only heighten the anxiety of the adults in the shelter, which would then have negative effects on the children.[8] In addition, all young children, including Clinton, received a placement in the church preschool upon their arrival at the shelter. Older children and youth received assistance with getting enrolled in local public schools.

Mrs. Myers was described by the women we interviewed as a "mother hen" who wanted to protect them. Valerie, a Head Start teacher and the guardian of her two young grand-nephews, recounted how Mrs. Myers tried to shield the evacuees from the stigma of being displaced:

> Sister Myers, the pastor's wife, said, "They have nowhere to go. They have nothing. I don't want anybody saying anything rude. I don't want anybody accusing them of anything. I don't want anybody looking at them any kind of way." We all had to wear these [identification] bracelets. One

day she said, "Take them off, or when you go places everybody gonna know you're from my shelter. Take them off." We were her babies, everybody in that shelter. One of the ladies who serviced the candy machines or whatever, it was an outside agency, and she left the machine open or something and one little boy found it open and he told somebody it was left open, and the lady came and accused him, and she [Mrs. Myers] said, "Take the machine out. Because if you didn't see anybody take anything, I'm not gonna let you accuse them of doing anything." She was the mother hen! [laughter] She protected everybody.

In addition to Mrs. Myers, Clinton and his mother also had the support of the church's congregation. The church members treated them warmly and respectfully. They tutored Clinton and the other children and helped them with homework, drove them to the doctor when they were sick or on other errands, and planned fun activities and excursions. On some Saturdays, the local church members took the children from the shelter roller-skating or to a local park so the parents had time to themselves to "regroup." The displaced residents, many of whom were African American single mothers with children, did not know each other before the shelter, but they bonded over their shared situation and circumstances. Clinton became friends with some of the other children. Many of these women and their children ended up as neighbors when they were moved to a mobile home park, in the next point in the trajectory.

POINT 6: MOVING FURTHER UPWARD

The sixth point in Clinton's trajectory is when he and his mother moved into a FEMA trailer in November of 2005. During this time, his recovery process continued to move in a positive, upward direction. Several factors contributed to the upward movement that lifted all spheres of his life and continued to push him toward recovery.

Perhaps most importantly, it was during this period living in the FEMA trailer, which lasted from November 2005 through about July 2007, that his mother completely discontinued using drugs. To the absolute delight of Brandi, Karen put on some weight, one sign that she had stopped using the drugs that she had been addicted to for so long. Brandi had an honest relationship with her mother—likely as a result of years of being forced to confront her about her behavior. Thus, Brandi would directly ask her mother if she was using drugs, and would check on her on a daily basis. As a consequence of this open and regular communication, and of her own observations of her mother's physical appearance, Brandi was certain that her mother really had stopped using.

With the assistance of Mrs. Myers and the other advocates from the church shelter, Karen was able to secure employment at a nearby convenience store following her and Clinton's relocation to the trailer. The trailer park was in close proximity to Karen's work, which allowed her to walk (her 1990s model Pontiac was often broken down and generally unreliable).

This job provided a steady source of income for the family and renewed a sense of self-confidence within Karen as she was able to begin providing for Clinton and herself for the first time in his young life. When we visited them in the trailer, the home was furnished, the cell phone was working, and there was plenty of food. On one occasion, Karen made a celebration feast of jambalaya and shared it with us and with her neighbors in the trailer park; on another, she had enough disposable income to host a birthday party, complete with cake and gifts, for Clinton and his friends.

As Karen regained her health and achieved more stability and confidence in her own life, she was able to focus on her youngest son and his well-being. Although she struggled with her own issues and "adjusting" after Katrina, she tried to keep the focus on her faith and on Clinton:

> I'm more concerned about Clinton and trying to get him settled. You already know you are upset and trying to put yourself together, but you also have that little one that you need to get together. So once I got him settled, I know he's looking at me, so if he can see that I'm not totally relaxed, then that's gonna make it uneasy for him. So I have to keep my frame of mind in order to get his mind back on the right track. And praying, I think it helps a whole lot. I know it helps. I don't only think, I know it helps a whole lot.

As Clinton continued to adjust, Karen noted that it was good for her as well, because he would tell her: "Mommy, it's gonna be alright, okay? It's gonna be alright." Karen continued: "And I'm looking at him like, 'You telling me it's gonna be alright?' I know it's got to be alright."

Another factor contributing to the upward movement was that Clinton and his mom moved out of the evacuee shelter and into temporary housing. Although the shelter was a positive place in many regards, Mrs. Myers was the first to emphasize the importance of secure, individual family housing for establishing stable routines as well as fostering self-esteem. This sentiment was echoed by a FEMA long-term recovery case manager whom we met and briefly interviewed during one of our visits to the trailer park. At least initially, Karen was able to work closely with a case manager and receive many different forms of health and social services for both herself and Clinton. The trailer park offered a play area and access to young children his age. Clinton knew some of the children and their families from the church shelter, which Karen thought helped with his transition:

> Yes, he was happy. He was happy . . . It was also good because some of the people that was in the church shelter moved into the trailer park with us. So whoever was in the shelter, we had kids that came along with us.

Karen kept the trailer neat and tidy and would put up decorations for the holidays, birthdays, and other special occasions. Clinton had his own room in their trailer, which was larger than the small mobile trailers that were so often pictured in the news media to show their cramped space and unsafe environmental conditions.[9] Their trailer and the trailer park were not perfect (rain was thunderous on the roof, and Karen expressed some concerns about the overall safety of the trailer park). Nevertheless, it was a stable housing situation for Clinton.

Clinton's school situation remained steady during this time. Because of the proximity of the FEMA trailer park to the church shelter (about a mile apart), Karen was able to keep Clinton enrolled in kindergarten at the same school he had started while in the shelter after Katrina. Even when Karen's car broke down, a school bus would come pick him up, and the school was within walking distance as well.

The school Clinton attended in Baton Rouge enrolled an almost entirely African American student population. Like many racially segregated schools in urban areas, it was underfunded, lacked some critical resources, and was in disrepair. For example, when we visited, we observed broken windows, nonworking toilets in the girls' bathrooms, unmaintained dirt patches on the front lawn, and a boarded-up window in the principal's office. Despite these issues, it was at the school that Clinton began to come into contact with even more supportive adults on a more consistent basis, such as his kindergarten teacher. He also attended school with several of his friends from the trailer park and met many new friends as well.

Karen and Clinton continued to attend the Baptist church for several months after they moved out of the shelter. This meant that Karen had regular contact with Mrs. Myers and the other positive influences at the church, while Clinton maintained stability in that area of his life.

Clinton regained connections with both of his beloved siblings during this time. Brandi was nearby enough (only about one and a half hours away) and her car was still working, so she could visit regularly and check in on her brother and mother. After returning from Chicago to Louisiana, Aaron also lived in the trailer for several months. This was a special time, as Clinton loved having his big brother there with him to "hang out" and play games together.

Thus, for nearly two years after Katrina, Clinton was living in a much more secure state. Things seemed to be looking up, with his housing, education, and family situation all on an upward trend. On one of our visits to the FEMA trailer, Clinton had a kindergarten graduation ceremony at his school, and we were able to attend with his family: Karen, Brandi, a babysitter from the FEMA park, and an aunt and cousin from New Orleans. Dressed in a white dress shirt, a bright blue necktie, and black pants, Clinton proudly showed us around his school and posed for photos. In one picture, Clinton stands smiling shyly in the middle, holding his kindergarten certificate, sandwiched between Karen and Brandi, both beaming with pride.

POINT 7: ABRUPT DECLINE

At the seventh turning point in Clinton's Fluctuating Trajectory, approximately two and a half years after Katrina, all the spheres in his life declined abruptly and precipitously. The time in their FEMA trailer came to end after they had lived there rent free for nearly two years. Karen soon thereafter lost her job at the convenience store. Her car was no longer working, and without transportation, they were unable to regularly attend church. The course of Clinton's multiple spheres—housing, family, school, involvement with his religious community, parental employment, and transportation— moved in a downward direction, with no clear path to stability. Returning to New Orleans was problematic, so Clinton and his mother entered a period of uncertainty and more change.

During the spring and summer months of 2007, FEMA sent workers into trailer parks throughout the Gulf Coast region to inform Katrina survivors that they would need to begin making plans to leave the trailers. The Stafford Act allows for 18 months of federally sponsored housing in a post-disaster context.[10] Although many observers agreed that this was simply not long enough for people in the aftermath of a catastrophic disaster to regain stability,[11] FEMA still began its movement toward reclaiming the trailers, which were always intended as a temporary solution to the housing shortage. Initially, Katrina survivors were told they would be on their own to find their way into permanent housing.[12] Later FEMA offered additional housing support to displaced persons, and the agency put some individuals and families up in hotels for several months after their trailer time expired to avoid causing a jump in homelessness. As all this was unfolding, Karen was one of thousands of Katrina survivors who received word that the trailer would no longer be hers, and that she would need to make arrangements to move elsewhere.

As word came that she and Clinton would be losing their housing, Karen also lost her job. Although Karen was always more than willing to share the news with us when things were going well with her family, ever offering the positive outlook, she was much more evasive when it came to sharing bad news (see appendix B for more of a discussion of this issue and how we handled it methodologically). Thus, we never quite learned why it was that Karen lost her job—she was vague and said it had something to do with "cutbacks on the hours." What was clear was that her steady source of income was gone.

As all this was unfolding, Karen had a very difficult decision to make. Should she try to return to New Orleans? The recovery continued to progress there: more schools were open, and more jobs and housing were available than at any point since 2005. The public transportation was also getting up and running, which was important given that she no longer had access to a working automobile. Perhaps she and Clinton could return and make a new life there?

But that was not what Brandi or Aaron wanted for their mother or for their little brother. Both of the older siblings argued strongly that they did not want their mother back in New Orleans. She had been off drugs for nearly two years, and they feared if she moved back to the city, she would re-engage her old network and fall back into her habits of using drugs and living on the streets. Brandi expressed this concern:

> I don't want her to come back down [to New Orleans] and get trapped into anything else. Because she's fresh being off of drugs, and it's easy to tap back into it when you're so fresh getting out of it. It's not so good for me, because I want to be around my family, because I don't really have anybody here. But I want what is best for her. If it's the best to be away, that's fine. I can take a trip here and there to come see them. That's awesome for her.

Having been raised by a drug-addicted mother, Brandi was especially fearful for Clinton's future prospects were Karen to return to New Orleans. She explained:

> I would have cared if it had just been her, but I wouldn't have been so stressed if it was just her, because you're old enough to know right and

wrong, and you're old enough to take care of yourself. That's all on you. But when you have my little brother, it's a whole different ball game. It's not easy. I'm calling every minute, every second, every hour: "What are you doing? Why you-all outside? What you just sitting outside for? Why don't you just go in and close the door and stay inside and watch TV?" I have to ask questions.

Even if it were not for Karen's prior drug use, the family still would have been hesitant to see Clinton return to New Orleans. Though the city was beginning to recover, Karen had no job prospects, no leads on housing, and crime was a concern. Many of the schools in New Orleans were still failing, and children from all over the city were being bused long distances to get to their classes. This situation was not optimal for Clinton, especially since his schooling experience in Baton Rouge had gone smoothly. Moreover, Aaron, who had now been living in Dallas for nearly a year, had seen firsthand what he perceived as a difference between the children in Dallas compared to the children in New Orleans:

> I was meeting kids because I went to this church and I was running into kids and I was like, "Man, these kids are really smart." They are really smart and I'm thinking . . . they was just going to regular public schools you know . . . I was impressed with how smart the kids were out here . . . and I was just really impressed with how they conduct themselves.

During this tumultuous time, Karen moved with Clinton into an apartment in Baton Rouge that was for the homeless. She was without work, and barely getting by. Clinton began a decline in all areas of his life at this time, as his mother struggled to make ends meet and to keep the family afloat. Clinton, only six years old, had little agency to change the circumstances around him, and thus as his mother's economic and housing circumstances plummeted, so did his. As with other young children in crisis situations, Clinton was particularly vulnerable because of his young age and complete dependence on the adults in his life for his safety and well-being.[13]

POINT 8: BRIEF UPWARD MOVEMENT

After Clinton finished his first-grade year, Karen began making plans for what was next. In order to pay for their subsidized apartment, she had cleaned houses and done other odd jobs for a period of time in Baton Rouge. This was not a place where she wanted to stay long term, but it was the best option. Then, that summer, Hurricane Gustav barreled toward the Gulf

Coast. It was another huge storm, aimed directly for New Orleans on a day close to the three-year anniversary of Katrina. Gustav did damage along the Gulf Coast, knocking out the power in Baton Rouge for several days. This was the final straw for Karen. She had been somewhat ambivalent about moving to Dallas to be with Aaron and his family, but the storm was just one last insult on top of all the other challenges.

Aaron agreed to come and pick up Karen and Clinton since she still had no access to private transportation. So Karen packed up their few remaining possessions and moved her young son to Dallas. This was a city that she had never visited, so everything felt unfamiliar at first other than being with Aaron, his wife, Tanesa, and their baby, Noah. (Aaron and Tanesa, who met as children when Karen was the janitor at Tanesa's elementary school, found each other in Dallas through the social networking site MySpace, began dating, and had married about a year prior.) Yet, despite the unfamiliarity, moving to Dallas proved to be a positive transition because Clinton was reunited with his brother and Aaron's young family. This reestablished connection with extended family helped Clinton move upward on his post-disaster trajectory.

Once in Dallas, Karen and Clinton moved into Aaron and Tanesa's small, one-bedroom apartment. It was crowded in the apartment with the five people and the two families; Tanesa, Aaron, and the baby had the bedroom, while Clinton and Karen slept in the living room. It was not ideal, but the family made it work.

After missing his siblings for several years, Clinton was happy to be with his brother full time. Clinton adored Aaron, and Aaron was protective of his little brother. For both of them, being reunited was important emotionally and in other ways as well. In general, Katrina-affected children, including Clinton, who relied on several key sources of support to stabilize their recovery, did better and made more progress when they were near their anchors; conversely, being far from anchors often meant more challenges and less support for those children. Clinton's trajectory often moved upward when he was with his anchors—his siblings.

POINT 9: DOWNWARD AGAIN

After the initial happiness at being reunited with his brother, the reality of being displaced set in again for Clinton. The ninth point in Clinton's fluctuating trajectory was downward, as he dealt with starting over.

Clinton had left all of his friends behind, and, most notably, would now be separated from his sister. In addition to the cramped living conditions, the family was dealing with the stress of having a new baby with significant health issues. Noah had been born three months prematurely, requiring an extended hospital stay followed by oxygen and other necessary medical attention in the home. When we interviewed Aaron and Tanesa, they both asserted that when they had asked Karen to move to Dallas, she had agreed to help take care of her new grandson. Tanesa disclosed, though, that Karen did not end up assisting that much because she quickly found a job at Walmart and ended up working long hours there. Nevertheless, Aaron, Tanesa, and Brandi were pleased that they had achieved their goal of keeping Karen and Clinton from moving back to New Orleans.

The move to Dallas was a difficult transition for Clinton in many ways. He had left an environment in Baton Rouge at the FEMA trailer park that had become comfortable and familiar: his home, school, friends, church, advocates, neighbors, and everyday routine. His life was "in limbo," yet again. As with many children displaced by Katrina, the unsettledness and moving continued not just for a matter of months, but for many years. Other children in our study also found themselves at a crossroads two, three, four, or more years after Katrina. Research has found that thousands of children moved multiple times after Katrina, and that more frequent transitions led to more social, emotional, and educational difficulties for them.[14]

Clinton's move also forced him to adjust to living with his much older brother. Although he loved Aaron, he was not as close to him as he was to Brandi, and his relationship to each of them was quite different. Aaron and Brandi, in fact, had highly divergent views on childrearing and as a consequence had several major arguments regarding how to raise Clinton. Aaron felt that he needed to practice "tough love" and to "toughen Clinton up," while Brandi was more nurturing and felt that modeling good behavior, respect, and talking through challenges and issues was the best way to teach a child.[15] Brandi argued that there was "another route" for raising their little brother:

> Aaron kind of talked to [Clinton] to toughen him up. I'm like, "That's not how you do it." But you can't tell him [Aaron] anything, because he knows everything. "You gotta beat him up to make him rough." No. You can go another route . . . The same way you treat kids, they're gonna treat you, or even anybody on the street.

Clinton found himself surrounded by older family members sorting out their differences and finding a way to live in a small space together, and all of them dealing with Noah's special health care needs. In addition, Clinton had to confront other challenges. It was at this point that he realized that his contact with his father seemed to be severed permanently. While the father and son had had limited interaction before Katrina, it was enough to satisfy Clinton's needs. In the aftermath of the storm the family was never able to find out information about the whereabouts of Clinton's father or any other relatives on his side of the family. Unlike Jerron's father, Eddie, who went to great lengths to be reunited with his son, as discussed in chapter 7, Clinton's father never made any effort to locate or contact his youngest child.

In addition, Clinton had to start over at a new school, meet new friends and teachers, and learn new social norms. But most of all, he did not have his sister, his most consistent and positive source of emotional and intellectual support, with him.

POINT 10: MOVING UPWARD

Over time, Clinton got settled in Dallas and his trajectory began moving in an upward motion. His mother found success in her work, he was in a good school where he met many new friends, his family members were getting along and Brandi was able to visit more regularly, and Aaron and Tanesa were able to find the family a larger apartment. Overall, things were going well.

Several things contributed to Clinton's upward movement in all spheres of his life, which lasted for several years. All of the adults in Clinton's household had steady, full-time work. His brother actually had three jobs: one at a restaurant, another part-time position at a radio station, and a third position at an electronics store. Tanesa had secured full-time employment as a receptionist. And Karen was ascending the ranks at Walmart. She began as a cashier and was promoted to customer service, which meant she received better hours and more pay. She also, for the first time, was able to secure health insurance for herself and for Clinton.

As the economic circumstances of the adults improved, they moved into a larger apartment in a safer neighborhood with more amenities. They found a place a few miles from Clinton's school that was in a fairly well kept complex with a park and a swimming pool, both good for Clinton, who was often "bursting with energy." Importantly, this apartment had two bedrooms. Aaron and Tanesa slept in the large master bedroom with Noah in his crib. Clinton had his own room, which was neatly kept and even had a little desk for him to study. On one wall he had carefully hung up a poster of the New Orleans Saints, his favorite team, and on another he had taped up a birthday card that we had mailed him. Karen slept on the futon in the living room. There was a small fenced-in cement patio for the family members to step outside for fresh air or to smoke a cigarette.

The location of the apartment was convenient for Karen. She still had no access to reliable transportation, but she could walk to work. Aaron and Tanesa both had vehicles, so they could drive Clinton to school and then pick him up from the childcare center he attended afterward. This was important in terms of Clinton's trajectory, as their access to reliable transportation, and their willingness to drive him to school on a regular basis, allowed him to stay in his school and also avoided forcing one more major transition and associated disruptions in his life.

Everyone in the family agreed that the school he was attending was quite good. We had seen his school in Baton Rouge, and when we visited his school building in Dallas, we, too, were impressed. It was a newly built, brightly lit building with a beautiful entryway, a large library stocked with books, and modern classrooms and cafeteria facilities. The school was much more racially integrated than his Baton Rouge elementary school, with an equal proportion of white, black, and Latino students in each class. The educational environment was strong, and the teachers and administrators were professional and engaged. Clinton had exercise and recreation opportunities every day at school, and he also had the chance to get involved in chess club and flag football, two activities he loved. His afterschool program at a childcare center was near his elementary school and provided a free shuttle service between the school and center. Aaron said his brother was doing "really well" in Dallas and said he felt the "school system was much better" and offered many more opportunities for Clinton.

Clinton made many new friends during this period. We watched him clown around with the boys and girls in his class, and were so pleased when we realized how well adjusted and well liked he was among his peers. One day when we visited his school over the lunch hour, his friends crowded in and asked us to take their photo with Clinton. He also regularly had sleepovers at the apartment, where Karen would allow the children to stay up late watching movies and playing.

During this time, Karen became very involved in a church in the community. She would go on Friday evenings to a women's empowerment and prayer group (Clinton would go to the children's play group at the church while Karen worshipped). She also spent much of her Sunday at church, and attended on Wednesday evening as well. We attended services with Karen and Clinton there, and we watched as she laughed and cried during the service and were heartened as women gathered around to hug her as she left the church that evening. Karen loved her work and her church, and she felt safe in Dallas.

Clinton continued to maintain a close relationship with his older sister during this time in his recovery. Brandi was living in New Orleans (mostly staying on the couches of friends), but they enjoyed almost daily phone calls. When she spoke to Clinton on the phone, she would always ask him: "Did you pray today?" She also expected a progress report on school assignments, homework activities, and grades; she regularly stressed to her brother how important school performance was for his future. She also began to teach Clinton how to advocate for himself through these calls, as she described to us during one interview:

> I also ask about things he is not doing really good in. "What's going on with science?" "I'm having a really hard time. I don't understand it the way I do with the other stuff. It's really difficult." I'm like, "If you're having problems with that, you have to let your teacher know. They have tutors there. You have to let them know so they're able to help you."

One day when we were in Dallas, we were driving in our rental car with Karen and Clinton. Brandi called, and initially we just heard Clinton respond repeatedly with the word "fine" to what were obviously a series of questions coming from Brandi. Eventually, though, he started to open up and share about his school day and time at aftercare, as Brandi was clearly pressing him to elaborate on what he had been up to that day. Both Brandi and Tanesa described Clinton as "not very expressive," and it was apparent that Brandi was trying to coach Clinton to be more verbal and articulate.

Brandi tried to visit Clinton when she could, but she was still periodically taking college courses and holding down several part-time jobs, so it was not always possible for her to travel. Karen and Clinton made a few visits back to New Orleans during this time. One May Brandi surprised her mother in Dallas for Mother's Day. When we saw her a few weeks later, she showed us several pictures and excitedly recounted the arrival and how she showed up with a dozen roses. On another occasion, Karen and Clinton traveled to New Orleans when Brandi had surgery and was recuperating. When Brandi gave her first sermon at the church she had long attended, Karen and Clinton called to get all the details and then shared the story with everyone who was willing to listen. For Clinton, keeping this tie with his sister was one important piece of the upward wave in the trajectory.

POINT 11: A PRECIPITOUS DECLINE

In the final point of our tracing Clinton's recovery, seven years after Katrina, his fluctuating trajectory, once again, made a sharp turn downward. His mother was using drugs again, and she subsequently lost her job at Walmart. Aaron's wife, Tanesa, left Dallas and returned to New Orleans, leaving Aaron with Noah and their new infant son, Davian. Aaron, overwhelmed and angry, was barely able to care for his two young children, and was certainly not able to take on sole responsibility for Clinton. Clinton was eventually taken in and cared for by another woman, this one from Dallas, but also someone they had met at their church, much like Miss Shirley back in New Orleans. Within a matter of months, Clinton's enduring stable period was replaced by the breakup of his family, separation from his mother, loss of family income, declining performance at school, and uncertainty about the future.

Brandi recounted the events of this downward trajectory for us with an utter sense of sadness that we too shared. Karen may have approached someone for drugs (there were drugs and some drug-dealing at their apartment complex), or as Karen herself had feared, those with drugs would find her in a low moment and tempt her with an offer, intentionally getting her addicted again. Brandi was not sure which scenario occurred, but she pointed out that it did not matter. The end result was the same: they had lost their mother to drugs yet again.

Brandi was now 25 years old and living in New Orleans with a woman named Dana and Dana's husband and two young children. Brandi met Dana at church and referred to her as her "spiritual mother." She depended on Dana for emotional and material support. When Brandi received the news about her mother's drug use, she considered going to Dallas and bringing Clinton back to New Orleans. She decided, however, that that was not the best decision for Clinton or for her.

At this point in her life, Brandi felt that she might have a bright future. She was enrolled in college, taking classes to become a psychologist, and she had a steady full-time job at a home improvement store. If she brought Clinton back to New Orleans, she would either have to leave him alone frequently since she was gone in the days and evenings, or she would need to quit her job or drop out of college to care for him. She also knew the woman, Jackee, with whom he was staying in Dallas, and she liked her. Brandi was confident that Jackee was taking good care of Clinton.

This was an exceptionally difficult decision for Brandi. She knew, through Aaron and through her own visits to Dallas, that her mother was in and out of the apartment and was bringing in drug-addicted strangers. This terrified and retraumatized Brandi, reminding her of her own unstable childhood and of the "loss" of her mother to drug dependence. She remembered being a scared young girl, waking up to find men she did not know in her home doing drugs with her mother.

Brandi also noted that Clinton, always a quiet child, was beginning to withdraw. When she would ask him how school was going, he would not want to talk about it. Without the support of multiple adults in his life—and now relying totally on the kindness of one woman from church—he had fewer opportunities to participate in activities at his school. Not only was he living apart from his older brother, but he was also separated from his two younger nephews, whom he loved caring for and doting on. Clinton's trajectory at this point was clearly downward.

We observed Clinton's post-Katrina trajectory over a seven-year period. From the age of 4 to 11, we witnessed his life spheres move downward and upward, and then downward and upward again, like a roller-coaster. The trauma of the disaster and displacement was most compounded by his mother's drug use, a key factor in the wave-like movement in his process. Karen's addiction was exceptionally damaging to her own well-being, her relationships with her entire family, and her ability to provide a safe and healthy home for her young son. Her addiction also had ramifications for every sphere of Clinton's life, which helps explain why his fluctuating trajectory looked different from Jerron's, as described in the previous chapter.

Clinton might seem to fit a declining trajectory. Yet, as we learned over the course of this study, Clinton's older siblings were consistent anchors of support that the children of the declining trajectory did not have in their lives. This was an important difference and one that we might not have fully understood in just a year or two, but that was clear to us by the end of our research. Aaron and Brandi were not especially financially well off, but they both had maintained steady work for many years. Even as they confronted their own struggles in recovery, they regularly provided financial and material assistance to their younger brother. They felt responsible for him and made sure that he did not fall through the cracks. For example, even when the family faced the most dire circumstances, Clinton never ended up in a homeless shelter by himself, like Daniel did; this was because his siblings, at the most challenging moments, were either able to give him shelter or to find a caring person through church or another connection. Aaron and especially Brandi also tried to guide him to do well in school and focus on his studies. In part because of their life decisions and their advocacy, Clinton had the opportunity to attend a higher performing school in Texas, and most signs pointed to his continued matriculation there; this relative educational stability is another contrast to the experience of children of the declining trajectory.

And yet, Clinton is not likely to find himself in a situation like Cierra, with stability in family, housing, peers, school, and extracurricular involvement. For example, both his brother and sister have always lived in rental units or stayed with friends, and have never been homeowners. This contributes to their and Clinton's vulnerability and some level of uncertainty for all of them. In light of this and the path of his recovery thus far, it is entirely possible that Clinton will continue to fluctuate in the coming years, never finding sustained equilibrium, yet not completely declining.

CONCLUSION

For seven years after Katrina, from 2005 through 2012, we researched the experiences of children and youth who were affected by the disaster. We observed and interviewed their family members, friends, neighbors, teachers, and other caregivers. In addition to the larger sample of children and youth whom we studied, we followed a select group to explore more intensely how Katrina—the most disruptive and destructive disaster in modern U.S. history—unfolded in their lives. It was our goal to understand their experiences, to identify how others assisted in their recovery, and to document how they helped themselves and other children recover after Katrina.

While children are often depicted in monolithic ways—as little rubber balls that will "bounce back" after disaster, or, conversely, as vulnerable victims who are helpless in the face of extreme adversity—our research revealed the complexity of their lived experiences. As scholars working in this area have long argued, disasters are *not* equal opportunity events.[1] Children and youth, like adults, are positioned differently based on their race, social class, age, and gender *before* disasters strike, and these events subsequently influence their lives in varied and complex ways.

After Katrina we watched, often with a sense of helplessness, as some children, like Daniel and Mekana, slid on a downward trajectory. They were already disadvantaged in many ways, and the disaster and subsequent disruption led to a piling up of added vulnerability, even as these young people fought and struggled to recover. We also observed other children, such as Zachary, Isabel, and Cierra, who, with resources and support from their families, from advocates, and from strong institutions, were able to find equilibrium. And then there were the other children, like Jerron and Clinton, who were neither on a steady decline nor were they able to achieve complete and consistent stability in all of the spheres of their lives in the disaster aftermath. Their post-Katrina trajectories resembled the path of a rollercoaster in many ways. But with the ongoing help from anchors—both from inside and outside their families—they were able to avoid a downward spiral.

In this concluding chapter, we take a final and pointed look at the social forces and factors that contributed to each post-disaster pattern presented in this book: the declining trajectory, the finding-equilibrium trajectory, and the fluctuating trajectory. We then consider the capacities of young people and describe the many ways that they contributed to their own and to others' recovery.

THREE POST-DISASTER TRAJECTORIES

As noted above and as elaborated on throughout this book, we identified three distinct trajectories based on our research with children and adults in the aftermath of Katrina (see figure 9.1). In the prior chapters we focused on seven focal children to illustrate those patterns that typified the post-disaster processes among the children and youth in the much larger sample. Over the course of the entire project, and as described in chapter 1, we studied well over 650 children between the ages of 3 and 18 years and interviewed approximately 100 adults. Thus, while the book focuses mostly on the life worlds of the focal children, the broader patterns that we present are a reflection of what we learned from the entire sample and from our many research trips to the Gulf Coast.

As described in chapter 1 and discussed in greater detail in appendix B, we had varying levels of contact with the children in the focal, core, secondary, and tertiary groups as well as with the adults in the study. Some we interviewed at numerous moments in time after Katrina; others we interviewed or observed at one or two points. Thus, our methodological design does not allow us to say exactly how many children and youth fit each pattern. Population-based studies that draw on random, representative samples would be more appropriate for providing such a statistical silhouette. What we can offer, however, is a theoretical and empirical description of these patterns and of the social forces and factors that influenced them.

The children's post-disaster trajectories were shaped, in part, by their pre-disaster circumstances. But they were also influenced by their experiences in Katrina and in the post-disaster aftermath. When we concluded our formal data collection efforts in the fall of 2012, the focal children and youth whom we studied most extensively were in very different places in their lives and had experienced recovery in wholly different ways. Below, we revisit each trajectory and elaborate on the factors external to the children

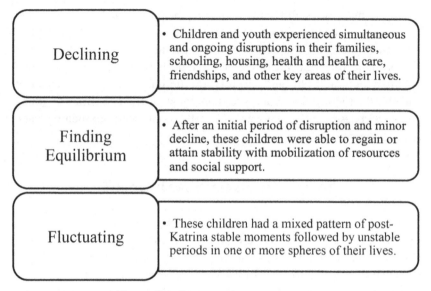

Declining	• Children and youth experienced simultaneous and ongoing disruptions in their families, schooling, housing, health and health care, friendships, and other key areas of their lives.
Finding Equilibrium	• After an initial period of disruption and minor decline, these children were able to regain or attain stability with mobilization of resources and social support.
Fluctuating	• These children had a mixed pattern of post-Katrina stable moments followed by unstable periods in one or more spheres of their lives.

Figure 9.1. Three post-Katrina trajectories

that played the most substantial roles in shaping the post-disaster patterns that we observed. In appendix C, we offer a number of recommendations for assisting with and enhancing disaster preparedness, response, and recovery efforts aimed at children and youth.

DECLINING TRAJECTORY

Daniel's recovery process, described in chapter 3, illustrates how the pre-disaster circumstances of the most vulnerable children were exacerbated by Katrina. In New Orleans, over 38 percent of children were living in poverty *before* the disaster. These young people, like Daniel, were situated in families with few of the resources needed to prepare for or evacuate from the hurricane and flooding. For example, between one-quarter and one-third of New Orleans households had no access to a car, and these households were disproportionately poor and black. Over half (56 percent) of New Orleans families with children under the age of 18 were headed by single mothers, many of whom were already struggling to find resources for their children before Katrina.[2] A large proportion of these low-income single mothers were African American, reflecting a national trend of disproportionately more women and people of color living in poverty.[3]

The case of Daniel illustrates how preexisting disadvantage—the crisis before the crisis—and the profound disruption caused by disaster can send children on a downward spiral. Children in the most precarious positions before disaster are at special risk for these downward trajectories; those who are already living at the margins are even more susceptible to experiencing extreme cumulative vulnerability after a disaster.[4] Moreover, while the children were vulnerable prior to Katrina, the disaster interacted with those vulnerabilities to make their situations worse. Put simply, the disaster intensified and accelerated their downward path.

Not only were the children and youth who fit the declining trajectory more likely to live in families with fewer financial resources, they also tended to have much less social and cultural capital than the other children whom we studied. The children of the declining trajectory more frequently lived in single-parent, predominantly female-headed, households, and were more likely to have relied extensively on kin who, like their parent or parents, lacked resources to help in the pre- or post-storm period.

We found that the children who fit this trajectory often had life-threatening and frightening evacuations from New Orleans. These negative experiences were mostly due to the fact that they were living in families with limited or no access to transportation, few or no savings and no credit cards, and limited or no strong social connections outside of the city. Some were trapped in the city during the storm and suffered greatly. Memories of what they witnessed and endured continue to scar the children and youth who experienced the horror of Katrina firsthand. And even those who were able to get out of New Orleans before the storm came ashore were more likely to be separated from family and friends for long periods of time.

We studied other children, like Mekana, who were less disadvantaged pre-disaster, but who became much more vulnerable after Katrina and experienced a similar precipitous post-disaster decline. Mekana's story shows how disasters, and especially the most catastrophic events like Katrina, can push some children into downward trajectories and positions of cumulative vulnerability.

Prior to Katrina, Mekana's mother was employed and had some savings and a reliable automobile. She was working hard to achieve middle-class status for herself and her girls. Yet, Mekana and her family found that the fragile but determined upward mobility of their pre-disaster circumstances was crushed in the disaster aftermath. Although Daniel's and Mekana's situations prior to the disaster differed in many ways, their post-storm experiences shared many common features—including frequent moves and disruptions, a loss of protective support systems, and an accumulation of vulnerability.

After the storm, these children and the others who fit this trajectory experienced many hardships. They were displaced multiple times, having to move to unfamiliar places and sometimes hostile and dangerous communities. Each physical transition meant adjusting to new surroundings, adapting to new cultural and geographic conditions, starting in a new school, trying to make new friends, and attempting to find new support systems, such as teachers and religious or community groups. The children of the declining trajectory, whose social networks were already resource poor prior to Katrina, often were displaced far from the limited support systems their home communities and families provided.

In the years following the storm, many of these children of the declining trajectory lived in precarious housing, resided in racially segregated neighborhoods with high concentrations of poverty and high rates of unemployment and violence, attended lower performing schools, lacked access to regular health care, and had a more difficult time re-establishing connections due to their ongoing mobility after the storm. Many children also dealt with hostility and bullying in their new schools either because of their race or because they were from New Orleans, making the already difficult transitions even more trying.[5]

Parents had trouble finding employment after the storm, leading to financial instability for the family and an uncertainty about the future. Parents also experienced barriers and felt frustration in trying to acquire aid. Mekana's mother, for example, felt stigmatized and that she was being treated "like a criminal" when she sought limited aid after Katrina.

We want to underscore that in no way are we finding fault with or blaming the children or their families for their decline in the recovery process. Most of the factors that contributed to their downward trajectory were not due to their decision making, their attitude, their work ethic, or a lack of resilience—although it is undeniable that these personal factors do matter in particular ways and we have tried to highlight these attributes throughout the book as well. What our work revealed, however, was that these children's trajectories were most powerfully influenced by economic, social, and structural factors that disadvantaged these children and their families both before and after Katrina. These forces affected their ability to find equilibrium, even though we found evidence that the children and youth of the declining trajectory were strong, hardworking, proactive, and used many creative problem-solving skills to cope and find solutions for themselves and their families. Moreover, the parents loved and cared for their children, no less than parents of children from the other trajectories. Thus, we found that *structural disadvantages*—not individual or personal factors—were what mattered most in determining a child's downward trajectory.

Even though there were differences across the declining trajectory, what all the children and youth who fit this pattern shared was the following: they experienced loss and significant and ongoing uncertainty across all major spheres of their lives. As a result of the disruptions and multiple moves, these children were less likely to establish stable connections and did not have access to advocates or anchors in the same way that the children who fit the other patterns did. These children and youth experienced enduring troubles for years after Katrina. Of all the children and youth we studied, they were the most vulnerable, and will likely suffer the longest term negative consequences from Katrina.

FINDING-EQUILIBRIUM TRAJECTORY

Cierra, whose recovery was typified by the finding-equilibrium trajectory, had reached a much greater level of stability and predictability than Daniel or Mekana seven years after Katrina. Like Daniel, she came from an African American family with a single mother and extremely limited financial resources, but her post-Katrina life was one of finding and then staying in a stable place. We attended her high school graduation and watched tears roll down her mother's face as Cierra triumphantly walked across the stage and accepted her diploma. She had been admitted to both a community college in Louisiana and a four-year university in Texas. Her future looked bright.

Similarly, Isabel and Zachary had regained equilibrium and maintained a positive upward trajectory after Katrina. Isabel talked to us frequently about her hopes and aspirations for her future education and career. Seven years after the storm, Zachary was playing sports and participating in drama club, and he had recently celebrated the return of his best friend to the city. Isabel and Zachary were happy, had predictable daily routines, were making plans for the future, and "rarely thought about Katrina" anymore.

The focal children and others who fit this trajectory were able to find equilibrium, even after experiencing an initial major disruption and decline after Katrina. Those children and youth with the greatest resource depth—personal, financial, cultural, educational, political, and social—were the most likely to find equilibrium. Yet for some children, like Cierra, with fewer resources pre-disaster, we observed that they were able to find equilibrium with assistance from at least one of their parents, adult advocates from outside the home, and strong institutions. Many of these children and youth also were able and willing to vocalize their needs and regularly asked for help. Their recovery process usually took longer, but it was possible nonetheless when they had access to strong networks of social support.[6]

In the seven years after Katrina, resource depth aided children, youth, and their families in numerous and varied ways. Sometimes it was easy to see how these resources mattered in shaping the finding-equilibrium trajectory, while other forms of capital were more hidden but significant nonetheless. In our work, we used the concept of *resources* in a broad sense, including the notions of social and cultural capital, concepts developed by social theorist Pierre Bourdieu. Social capital incorporates the idea of strong social networks, interpersonal connections, friendships, and acquaintance relationships that are often possessed by those with wealth and privileged social positions. These networks greatly helped families during evacuation and displacement by providing needed shelter. Both Isabel and Zachary, for example, evacuated to the homes of family friends who had large houses with spare rooms, local knowledge, and extra food and clothing. Moreover, families with preexisting financial resources were more likely to own a working vehicle and have money for gas and an extended stay somewhere outside the affected area—all things which were necessary to evacuate. Children and youth who had the resources to leave New Orleans before the storm made landfall and the flooding started were spared terrifying and life-threatening experiences.

In addition to aiding in the timely evacuation and finding safe shelter, resources assisted during displacement. Parents who were employed before the storm were often more successful in resuming their work or finding new employment; this was especially true for middle-class parents working in white-collar jobs. Furthermore, children of this trajectory were more likely to be back in school quickly, with a predictable daily routine, than the children and youth of the other trajectories.

Experiences in school were affected by the families' and children's cultural capital, in that their habits, skills, and knowledge influenced their interactions and relationships with schoolteachers and administrators. As during nondisaster times, those parents with more cultural capital had an easier time negotiating with new schools. This, for the most part, allowed them to acquire what they needed for their children through their interactions with authority figures who were embedded in better-resourced schools.[7] Zachary's parents, for example, were able to advocate on his behalf so they could enroll him in the same classroom as his close family friends, his "cousins."

Cultural capital was also useful when parents were dealing with authority figures or bureaucratic officials in other important institutions, such as in housing agencies, employment offices, and disaster recovery centers. Cierra's mother, Debra, used her skills to secure necessities for her and Cierra, including mental health counseling, assistance with schooling, disaster aid, employment assistance, and access to housing programs. While not possessing the resource depth and social capital of Zachary's and Isabel's families, Debra was able to interact with those in positions of authority, including employers, school administrators, and service providers, in ways that the institutions expected, demanded, and wanted. In turn, she and Cierra were evaluated and perceived more favorably. In addition, and it is important to not lose sight of this, Cierra and her mother ended up in a *social context* that allowed her the opportunity to attend a more highly resourced, academically comprehensive, and racially integrated school. They also relocated to a community that offered access to a housing market that Debra could afford and a job market where she could find work. So, again, while her personal characteristics and approach to her daughter's recovery mattered, so too did this broader social context.

Children and youth, like Cierra, who had less pre-disaster resource depth but still fit the finding-equilibrium trajectory, actually had their situations improve after the storm. This was due to extremely effective resource mobilization, which often occurred as a result of a highly involved parent (or set of parents) and with the support of advocates and strong institutions. Advocates such as the shelter workers, teachers, religious leaders, and youth mentors who assisted Cierra came into the lives of the children following the disaster. These individuals helped provide for basic needs in the immediate disaster aftermath, to establish child-friendly spaces in shelters, to link families to services during the early stages of recovery, and to make a family less isolated in a new and unfamiliar place.

Advocates, who were either employed by or closely connected to strong institutions, were able to identify needs in the lives of children and youth, and they had the power and networks to help parents to mobilize resources for young people. In addition, and importantly, advocates were able to see the linkages between a child's recovery and the recovery of the family and broader community. They understood that adults needed jobs and steady housing and childcare, and they subsequently helped parents achieve those things, knowing that this assistance would also help the child. They worked with the broader community to encourage recovery across multiple dimensions, and that made all the difference in children's lives. Thus, while advocates were strong, dedicated individuals, it is again important to emphasize that they could not have as successfully helped children in the Katrina aftermath without access to institutional support as well as policies and programs that were designed with the express intent of helping to build capacity and resilience among children and families.

FLUCTUATING TRAJECTORY

Clinton was the youngest focal child we intensively followed after Katrina. He was also the one who experienced the most rapid ups and downs after the disaster as his fluctuating trajectory unfolded. His recovery process illustrates how children's lives can shift in a fairly continuous wave-like pattern from decline to equilibrium and back to decline and then back to equilibrium in all spheres. Seven years after the storm, Clinton's mother, the most unstable person in his life, was using drugs again. But his sister Brandi and his brother Aaron, his most stalwart supporters, his anchors, remained. Aaron worked multiple jobs to keep Clinton fed and housed. He also stayed connected to their local church and to a neighbor in their apartments, which allowed Clinton a "safe refuge" when his mother sank back into the depths of depression and drug use. Brandi, although hundreds of miles away in New Orleans, continued to call every day to check on Clinton, to talk with Aaron about their younger brother's well-being, and to send small amounts of financial support when she could. These actions on the part of his siblings kept Clinton from moving into a steady decline after Katrina.

Jerron, another focal child, also experienced many serious ups and downs after Katrina, especially in the realm of his family situation and his schooling. His family was more stable than Clinton's, as both of Jerron's parents and his grandmothers were in his life and supported him wholly. But because Katrina led to his relocation, he was permanently separated from many of those who had been among his most consistent and steady supporters. His mother, however, was able to secure housing, a job, and health care. She also encouraged Jerron to participate in various extracurricular activities through his school, church, and neighborhood, which connected Jerron to positive adult and peer influences and kept him from moving into a decline. Jerron's recovery process shows how children and youth could experience sphere misalignment in their recovery. When one or several spheres of their lives were down—such as family and schooling—others were up—such as housing and friendships.

Clinton's and Jerron's experiences illustrate the fluctuating trajectory. These youth were more at risk of descending into decline during the post-disaster period, like the most vulnerable children in our study. For example, the children and youth in the fluctuating trajectory, like those of the declining trajectory, often experienced some or a great deal of social disadvantage and resultant instability before Katrina. They and their families often had fewer pre-event resources and thus were less likely to be able to effectively prepare for, respond to, and recover from the disaster. They tended to have more dangerous evacuations and more disruptive and longer term displacements. They did not always live in stable family circumstances, nor did they have access to the kinds of economic and social buffers that the children and youth of the finding-equilibrium trajectory often did.

So what, then, kept these children of the fluctuating trajectory from moving into complete decline? One factor that we identified was that these displaced children became involved—often at the urging of family members—in extracurricular activities such as athletics and church groups in their new communities. In addition, and perhaps most importantly, these children had one or more anchors in their lives. These were the individuals, typically family members such as grandmothers, older siblings, aunts, or others, who provided resources, support, and consistency. What differentiated anchors from the advocates is that anchors were part of the lives of the children and youth before the storm and they remained an active presence after the disaster, often increasing the levels of support and resources provided in response to the disruption caused by the storm. Thus, they acted as an important stabilizing force, even as the child experienced ups and downs in some or all life spheres.

This consistency and assistance translated into both tangible and more intangible resources after the storm. For example, the anchors were able to help provide housing, additional income through working one or more jobs, or access to health care. They also tended to be positive, steady figures who regularly offered guidance and emotional support to children and helped them cope with the effects of multiple displacements and family instability. These family members connected with the children and youth on a regular basis if they were living in a separate home, or they had daily, consistent contact when they were living together.

In many ways, the children and youth who fit the fluctuating trajectory continue to live lives where the preexisting disadvantages and the Katrina disaster are still unfolding and the "recovery process" goes on without end. For example, as we finished data collection in 2012, Jerron was in a much more stable place and, after seven years of struggling, had begun to thrive in his new community. Clinton, on the other hand, was at a dip in the rollercoaster, buoyed only by the ongoing support of his brother and sister and the other supportive adults whom they had enlisted to help him.

The focal children and youth clearly had very different experiences after Katrina. Above, we have attempted to offer explanations for the instability, stability, or ongoing fluctuations that they experienced. We also focus on characteristics that rendered children more vulnerable, or conversely, potentially more resilient, in the wake of the disaster.

"Resilience" is an increasingly popular term in which to frame the understanding of children and crisis, whether caused by disaster, divorce, death, parental incarceration, or poverty, among other disruptive experiences.[8] There is an extensive and growing literature on individual and community resilience, and researchers from different disciplines have studied the idea for decades. Yet, scholars continue to apply the concept in varied ways, and often there is disagreement over how to define and use the term.[9] That said, resilience is now regularly evoked to understand how children and adults respond to chronic adversity (e.g., poverty) as well as to more acute, sudden-onset events (e.g., natural disasters).[10]

As noted above, we acknowledge the importance of individual resilience traits that shaped the trajectories of the children we studied: the child's personality traits and other individual characteristics, including his or her optimism, intelligence, sense of humor, character, communication skills, tenacity, likability, and outlook on life all mattered. Many scholars use these traits to assess whether a child is resilient to adversity; an individually resilient child, some assert, will be able to deal with stressful situations. We do not dispute this robust body of literature, but instead choose to focus here on the idea that a child—regardless of individual traits—cannot recover from a disaster without the necessary *resources* and *social structural support*. Throughout this book and in our years of research, we focused on how the multiple systems in which children and youth are embedded shaped their post-Katrina outcomes.

In light of that, we pause here to consider a few social structural factors that differentiate children. First, it is important to realize that *age* mattered in a child's recovery, but that children and youth of all ages fit each trajectory. For the teenagers in our study, Katrina occurred at a time in their lives when finishing high school, making future plans, and being with friends mattered tremendously, and getting off track for a year or two had serious consequences for some in terms of their academic performance and interpersonal relationships. The younger children were sometimes less able to articulate the meaning of Katrina in their lives, but they, too, were aware of the mounting challenges caused by the loss, displacement, and disruption of routine.[11] No age group was immune from hardship or excluded from the possibility of a full recovery. Age, alone, did not determine the trajectory. Instead, the age of the child interacted with other key sociodemographic and social structural factors that ultimately influenced the recovery process.

Similarly, *gender* mattered in certain ways, although it alone did not predetermine recovery. For girls and boys, we observed that gender sometimes shaped a particular experience in recovery and the reactions to the experience. For example, boys and girls described different types of encounters with school, bullying, personal safety, friendship dynamics, risk of violence, and negative influences from peer groups. As sociologists have long shown, societal expectations are gendered; girls and boys are socialized to behave, express emotion, and move in social spaces in different ways. Consider the fact that parents often scold boys for crying or showing sadness, while the same behavior is supported for girls.[12] Boys are more likely to "externalize" emotions and act out while girls are more likely to "internalize" their emotions and experience depression and anxiety. In Katrina, research found that girls were more likely to show emotional distress than boys. [13] We, too, observed gendered differences in the ways that girls and boys responded to Katrina in terms of their caregiving activities, relationships, and willingness to ask for support and coping assistance. Even with these differences, girls and boys were distributed across all three trajectories.

Social class and *race* mattered as well in Katrina, just as these characteristics intersect and matter in profound ways during non-disaster times. Children of middle- and upper-class backgrounds, and white children, had resources and privileges that often helped them find equilibrium; poor children, especially poor children of color, were more likely to decline or fluctuate.[14] Yet, these were not absolutes by any means; significant and meaningful exceptions were found in each trajectory. Those exceptions, in fact, proved to be illuminating cases, and prompted us to ask more questions and dig deeper into what happened and why.

Another important aspect in understanding the three trajectories is to reflect on and recognize how each trajectory is a process meant to capture how Katrina affected many different aspects of children's lives, across space and across time. Indeed, even after our seven years of study, it was clear that the disaster continued to unfold in the lives of many children and youth. Disasters devastate, disrupt, and can ultimately seriously disadvantage children. This is not something that can be repaired in a matter of months or even years in the most catastrophic events. It is sobering to acknowledge that some children may suffer their entire lives due to the tremendous losses caused by Katrina; this suffering could ultimately result in generational effects.

As the number of studies of children and disasters has increased over the years, more scholars have called for closer attention to be paid to how young people contribute to disaster preparedness, response, and recovery efforts.[15] In response to these calls, a growing body of literature shows that children are not just "vulnerable victims." They have special talents, skills, and strengths, and more studies and programs have begun to document how they *can* and *do* contribute in positive and effective ways across the disaster life cycle.[16]

In light of these advancements, we worked to record children's strengths, as well as their vulnerabilities, as we researched their experiences after Katrina. We listened carefully as young people in our sample, their friends, and their family members and teachers talked about what the children and youth did for themselves and for others in the period leading up to and following Katrina. We, like many childhood scholars before us, tried to ensure that we viewed the children in our study as active social agents, not as passive.[17]

In this section, we describe what we learned in terms of how youth helped others before, during, and after the storm. Specifically, we discuss how children assisted adults and how they supported other children and youth as well as themselves. We close this section by reflecting, briefly, on how by helping others, children and youth also helped themselves in the recovery process (see figure 9.2).

CHILDREN HELPING ADULTS

In the days and hours before the storm, families were making plans and preparing for the imminent hurricane landfall. As described in the chapters in this book, children and youth played important roles in this preparation. Numerous children in our study helped their parents and other family members pack up belongings in order to evacuate. Isabel, for example, ran between her house and the neighbors to help her mother and her "second mother" (her mom's best friend) get organized to evacuate in two cars with six children and two dogs. Mekana worked alongside her mother so they could gather vital belongings and leave the city before the hurricane made landfall.

Sometimes the children's efforts were in response to the requests or demands of their parents or other adults. But we also learned of many instances where the children and youth took action on their own; some chil-

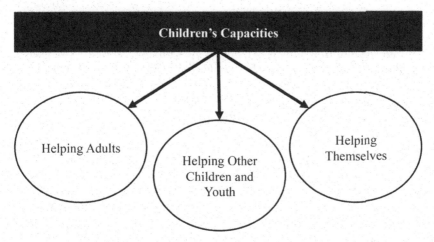

Figure 9.2. Children's capacities: helping others and helping themselves

dren even encouraged their parents to take additional precautions that they otherwise might not have. Now that many children in the United States learn about disaster preparedness in school, they bring information home and some children educate their families on how to prepare and motivate them to take action.[18] This can make a difference in all households, but is especially critical when children are the primary English speakers in their home, as was demonstrated by bilingual Vietnamese American youth after Katrina.[19]

The presence of children in the household was often a pivotal factor in evacuation among the families that we studied. Many parents explained to us that they likely would not have evacuated at all if they had not had children; they felt comfortable taking on the risk of staying themselves, but not comfortable with putting their children in such a situation.[20] Furthermore, some parents admitted that they would have returned to New Orleans soon after evacuation—likely too early given the scale of destruction—if they did not have children. Since schools were not open, they stayed away longer, which was perhaps better for the adults as well, considering the contamination, lack of services, and the stress of trying to function in such a heavily devastated area. One father explained that his children were the main factor in his decision not to return right away: "With having kids, we have definite parameters. We need a school. We need electricity. We need clean air. We need clean water. And if we don't have those, then we're staying put."

In some of the most dramatic stories we gathered after Katrina, we learned of instances where children behaved in exceptionally heroic ways during the actual storm itself. Their actions literally saved the lives of others. As we recounted in chapter 3, Daniel was the one who devised an escape plan for his family, and he also helped find a way for his mother to attach his baby sister to her chest so they could move through the flooded streets together.

Another middle school student who participated in one of our focus group interviews told us about his uncle, who was disabled and could not swim and was left stranded in his house in the city. This boy, who had evacuated to a safer part of the city, got a thick piece of foam, ventured out in the flooded streets, and took it to his uncle's home. When he got there, he handed the foam to his uncle and said, "You gonna have to hold on to this." He then carefully navigated the deep water, holding onto the foam and his uncle the entire way, until they arrived on dry ground at the Superdome.

Mekana's teenage boyfriend, Darik, saved his mother from the flood-waters that rushed into the city after the levees gave way. He explained: "I was already home when my mom turned on the news and they said it was going to be a Category 5 hurricane. And then when it started raining hard she knew we gotta leave. The water was up to my waist. I come back to put my mama on the boat, the water was then up to my neck. I had to hold my mom." These actions and others that we learned of took ingenuity and a great deal of courage.

During the initial evacuation, children "distracted" the adults. Many of the mothers and fathers whom we interviewed explained that they felt it "saved" them to have the children around. They kept the television sets turned off because they did not want the children to see the hurricane destruction and victims, and as a result they, too, were not as haunted by the images of devastation all along the Gulf Coast.[21] They also focused on the children's needs, which sometimes meant doing fun and meaningful things with their children like reading a book, watching a movie, or playing games. One father noted that he felt sympathy for a group of adults who evacuated to the home next door, as they had no children to focus on during the displacement. He said that having diapers to change and baby bottles to prepare actually helped the adults "because it gave us direction" and emphasized that they "didn't have time to wallow in it." Another mother agreed, saying, "You have to soldier on if you want your kids to be able to do the same."

Importantly, many young people gave their parents emotional support. When we interviewed the children and youth privately, they would tell us that they knew their parents were "under a lot of pressure" or "stressed." Sometimes they spoke of how much their parents had "cried since Katrina," even as they "tried to hide it." In response, children of all ages in our sample did many different things to comfort and reassure their parents. Even the youngest children regularly expressed their care and concern by offering "daily hugs," drawing pictures that said, "I love you" and telling silly jokes to make the adults smile. Jerron tried to cheer up his mother, who was pregnant at the time and exhausted, by kissing her belly and singing to the baby.

Others, especially the adolescents and teens in the sample, were more direct in sometimes asking their parents if they wanted or needed to talk. A teenager in our study who went away to college soon after Katrina comforted her mother and expressed concern for her well-being. Her mom explained how her teenage daughter helped her: "She was worried about me, she said, 'Mama, nobody's here with you.' I was like, 'I'm okay, I'm a big girl. I mind me. I can be here by myself.' I guess she wanted me to be with family."

While some children had seen the adults in their families in stressful situations before, others had never witnessed them struggling so much and even occasionally descending into tears. Clinton, as described in chapter 8, would observe his despondent mother and often tried to reassure her that everything would be okay; she told us that this reassurance from her young son meant a lot to her and helped her to see that he was going to be okay. Another father, who evacuated with his wife, children, and another family with young children, remarked:

> It's funny, because we kept thinking we had to protect the kids . . . But it was just the opposite. One of the worst days, one of the worst moments after Katrina, when all the adults were trying not to explode, our little girl walks up to the piano. She had never played a piano, but she crawled up and started playing "Happy Birthday" to [one of the mothers]. We were kind of rescued by them, a lot . . . They were the ones keeping us sane.

During the long recovery period, children and youth helped their parents and other adults in their families settle into new routines, into new homes and different neighborhoods, and even into new ways of living. Families who moved into Habitat for Humanity houses were required to put in a certain number of "sweat equity" hours, so that everyone would be a part of the building efforts. One mother noted how important it was to her young son to be given a job at the Habitat site, and how much he was able to contribute to the overall effort. Another mother, whom we met at the same Habitat for Humanity housing site, also said that it meant a lot to her that her adolescent daughter was able to "build the house" right alongside her. They were more invested in the home as they had contributed so much to actually constructing it. When her adolescent daughter gave us a tour of her room, she exclaimed, "I helped build this!" Her pride was apparent. In another instance, three teenage sisters who had been displaced with their family from Louisiana to Texas all worked sorting donated clothes for Katrina survivors in a large airplane hangar.

Isabel and her younger sibling wanted to go help after the storm, and so they asked their parents if they could volunteer at one of the mass shelters. Their parents, inspired by their children's generosity, agreed. When they arrived at the shelter, Isabel told us that one of the Red Cross volunteers said, "You're from New Orleans. You're supposed to relaxing." Isabel responded, "How are we supposed to relax?" Although the shelter workers were initially taken aback that such a young child wanted to help so badly, they eventually let Isabel, her sibling, and some other children "give things out" to other Katrina survivors. Although displaced themselves, it was clear that these children still wanted to assist others.

As the years went on, we observed many families continuing to have to make difficult decisions about housing, school, finances, jobs, relationships—all as a direct result of the ongoing displacement and a lingering uncertainty about further relocation. In many cases, children were part of the decision making, although it was more explicit in some families and less so in others. Children offered their opinions, sometimes solicited and sometimes not, but almost always clearly communicating their own needs. Young people would often let their parents know what they did and did not like about the new schools or new neighborhoods, and this had a powerful influence on parental decision making.

As the parents watched their children adapt to their new environments, they were often inspired by them and subsequently felt more connected to their new homes, neighborhoods, and the many new people who surrounded them. As one mother told us, after expressing her initial worry about how her son was "gonna get along in a new school, with all those new people," she saw how he adjusted, and said, "Hey, I can do it too!"

Children also contributed in other ways to the recovery of their families and their communities. In some of the most devastated neighborhoods, students worked together to raise funds for other affected areas. Several of the teenagers in our study got jobs after Katrina and then used part or all of the money they earned to contribute to bills that their families had to pay. Even when families did not need the teens to contribute their salaries to general household expenses, the youth in our sample still gave generously, buying surprise gifts for their parents just to "cheer them up" or to let them know they were "appreciated."

After seven years of research, we were quite taken by how much the adults were helped by children of all ages. It was not just mothers and fathers whom the children assisted, however. The beneficiaries also included other adult family members such as aunts and grandparents, some of whom did not live with the children, and adult neighbors, family friends, and others who worked at their childcare centers, schools, and churches. One of the teachers whom we interviewed noted how much it meant to her to simply see the children in her class each day. Several shelter workers described how encouraged they were by the children with whom they worked on a daily basis for weeks and sometimes months after the storm. Children also helped adults expand their social networks, increase their social capital, and reduce social isolation. This was especially apparent in childcare centers and schools, as children's participation in these institutions created daily opportunities for the adults—including parents, teachers, and other staff—to communicate, socialize, exchange valuable information, and share resources.

CHILDREN HELPING OTHER YOUNG PEOPLE

The children whom we studied not only helped the adults in their lives, but also did many things to contribute to the health and well-being of other young people. Before Katrina made landfall, the older children and youth often took responsibility for their younger siblings. Watching them and caring for them aided their parents and also made the children feel "responsible"; contributing something important to the family increased their feelings of self-worth and competence.

As the storm rapidly approached, some of the youth we interviewed played a central role in evacuating their younger siblings, cousins, and other children in their families. Just as they helped adults, they also moved their brothers and sisters to spaces where they felt they would be safe. As recounted in chapter 8, Brandi left college so she could help Clinton pack up his things and get out of New Orleans before Katrina made landfall.

The children who were not able to evacuate before the storm—typically because their parents did not have the means to do so—also played a role in helping to protect and even save the lives of other young people. One boy whom we interviewed, who was only 14 years old when Katrina happened, described how he rescued his younger family members:

> I'm holding my nephews and nieces up, I'm holding them above the water, my sister is on my back, by my neck. I'm holding them. I was trying to find a boat or a box or something so we could sit them on top of the box and push them. So we finally got a little boat. I put my nieces and my nephew and my sister in it. I was pushing it. And I was in the water, me and my brothers was in the water, my uncle, my mama, my auntie,

and my cousins, my nephews and nieces, they was in the boat. Finally got them on top of the thing for safety.

Another adolescent boy described how his older teenage brother saved both him and their infant sister from the rushing floodwaters after Katrina:

> We was walking from my house on the bridge, and I was holding my sister because she couldn't walk. She was only eight months. And you couldn't see the curb [because of the water]. Everybody else was big, my mom and my brother, and then just me and my little sister. We were walking, and I ain't see the curb. You can't see in that water. I ain't seen that curb, and I stepped down and my little sister almost died, and I don't know how to swim. My brother jumped in there and got me and got my little sister.

Young people who were trapped in New Orleans for days after Katrina often actively worked to keep their siblings calm. These children shared what food they had access to and their limited water supplies. They did their best to comfort those around them while shielding them from further trauma.

We spent many hours observing children who ended up in public shelters after Katrina. We saw these young people care for other children. They played games with their own siblings and other children they met in the shelter. One mother at a shelter explained the dynamic: "The older ones, they comfort the younger ones. They all play real well together." These children helped their peers with homework. They walked them to and from the school bus that would pick them up outside the shelter in the mornings. Cierra even became a babysitter in the shelter where she and her mother, Debra, had to stay for six weeks after Katrina. She cared for an infant on a regular basis, which allowed that child's mother to stand in long lines to get her disaster assistance, to talk to other parents, and to get some much-needed rest. Debra felt that it also helped Cierra to care for the baby: "She loves babies. And it made her feel as though she was doing something real great, by helping out and caring for them."

Notably, children's caretaking work was often gendered; girls and boys took on overlapping as well as distinct jobs within their families and communities. It was common to see girls assuming tasks that they modeled after their mothers, such as caring for babies, helping to prepare meals, and cleaning up spaces. All the while, boys modeled their tasks after fathers or other men around them, often asking to do "outside work" or engage in activities that are viewed as socially acceptable for males, such as playing sports with younger children.

Not only are boys and girls reflecting the gendered behavior of adults, they are also responding to social cues and expectations about "appropriate behaviors" for each gender. A Red Cross worker in a large mass shelter in Lafayette commented on this:

> Predominantly I see the girls—and I hate to say it, but—really being stereotypical in gender roles as far as caretaking, acting like mothers, making sure baby has the appropriate clothes on so they're not too hot or not too cold, feeding the baby for Mom, stuff like that. Whereas boys are more likely to just kind of—I mean, I notice older brothers, they appear to be siblings, I don't know if they are, but older brothers playing catch with the other kids, engaging them in some kind of active play. Whereas the girls are more like, they just sit down and color and stuff like that.

Research on other disasters has documented gender differences in adult caregiving work in disasters, but less attention has been paid to children and youth and gender differences.[22] In non-disaster times, parents often expect girls to take on the care of younger siblings and household tasks such as cleaning, and boys to assume traditionally male tasks at home such as lawn mowing. Over the past few decades, those expectations have changed for many families. Likewise, we observed some deviations from traditional gender patterns, such as Daniel taking on a primary caregiving role with his younger sister during their years of displacement.

We also documented in our fieldnotes how children, regardless of gender, "stuck together" after Katrina. For instance, at another evacuee shelter we observed, this one in Baton Rouge, the children went to the playground or walked home after school, always as a group. A single mother staying at the shelter described how the older children kept the younger ones with them: "They comin' home together as a group, as one." Another mother at the same shelter agreed, noting that she thought the children stayed together because they had all "been through the same situation," which "brought them together" and caused them to have a "special bond."

Some of the children in our study spoke of how they got help from peers. For example, when we asked Zachary what helped him most after Katrina, he responded: "I think meeting my friends and telling them my whole story kind of helped me." When we asked him to expand, he paused, reflectively, and then responded: "It helped me get all my feelings out and not just have it all bottled up. A lot of people say you should just say how you feel. I think my friends helped because they can understand better than family." During a focus group, a boy stated succinctly: "I don't talk to nobody but my friends . . . Because you come to rely on your friends." One of his classmates, a 13-year-old girl, chimed in and elaborated:

If something is really wrong, my friends at school would see there's something wrong with me and they would always be like, "What's wrong?" And then I'd be like, "Leave me alone." We all have that little problem, like, "What's wrong?" "Nothing, get away from me!" But still, when you tell your friends that, they still won't leave. They'll sit there and be like, "We're not leaving until you talk!" That really makes me feel like they really are my friends. They really try to make you laugh.

These examples of support are in line with other work that argues that children's peer cultures can be helpful and positive, and not always laden with bullying and peer pressure, as is often thought.[23]

Young people generously shared their time, communicating regularly with their siblings and friends. When Brandi had to return to college after Katrina, she called Clinton every day, often multiple times a day, just to "check in" and make sure he was doing okay. She would call and say, "Hey buddy, how is it going?" and then would proceed to help him with his homework over the phone. She coached him to make sure that he would talk to his teachers if he needed additional help outside the classroom. All the while, Brandi was busy herself attempting to recover from the shock and disruption from the storm. She admitted that time was "a little bit crazy," but it was most important to her to ensure that her little brother "got everything that he needed" in terms of his education. A New Orleans elementary school teacher described how she sometimes saw children "comforting each other when they would fall down and get hurt," and generally just "being more friendly" after Katrina.[24]

As teens took on extra jobs after Katrina, they also used the money they earned to support their siblings. Brandi and Aaron, for example, started working extra hours and even additional jobs so that they could help support Clinton and ensure that he had food, clothing, shelter, and health care. When Daniel turned 14 years old, he started working a number of odd jobs to help pay for things for his little sister. He was very attentive to her needs and wanted to make sure that she had a "birthday gift and at least one gift under the Christmas tree" every year.

Katrina-affected youth did many things to help other young people who had survived the storm. We also found that non-disaster-affected children who lived in the cities where Katrina survivors evacuated played an important role in fostering the adjustment of their peers. In Denver, where Mekana and her family relocated, students raised money to buy gift cards for the "Katrina kids," and they distributed the "Warmth of Colorado" blankets to evacuees. Mekana's friend gave her money for a bus ticket to New Orleans, knowing that Mekana was desperate to get back but had no funds to travel. In several communities throughout Louisiana, where most of the public schools require students to wear uniforms, we learned of children and teens who donated their old school uniforms to their new classmates or who raised money to purchase new uniforms for displaced children. At a church shelter in Baton Rouge, adolescents who were regular members of the congregation threw a birthday party for a boy who survived Katrina and was staying in the shelter. Other youth who were members of this church took children out to movies and set up a reading and afterschool program for the younger children.

We found that many schools in the communities that enrolled a large number of evacuated students set up "buddy programs" that matched long-time students with the new students from the Katrina-affected areas. These sorts of programs were quite useful in that they helped the children who were displaced and attending new schools adjust more quickly. It gave these young people a link to vital peer connections and sources of emotional support.

We interviewed several volunteers at shelters who spoke at length about the touching things children from across the United States and from other countries did for Katrina children. For example, one volunteer in Lafayette, Louisiana, described the "beautiful notes from children to children." She said that there were just "boxes and boxes of these letters" that had been sent from all over. Children also did things like donate their toys, collect money in their communities, and send goods to those children most affected along the Gulf Coast. One shelter volunteer confessed that she cried when she opened a box of donated goods and found a handwritten note from a young child taped to a toy, telling a Katrina child that the toy—a personal favorite—was now hers. Another shelter volunteer, who became emotional when she described to us the acts of kindness she witnessed, said, "It was so touching to see how involved other children were in trying to give these Katrina children just a little piece of pleasure." A childcare worker in Lafayette said that young children in her childcare center, all under the age of five years, were constantly thinking about the Katrina children who had lost their toys. They would ask their teacher, "Do you think they would like this one?" or "Would one of them like a transformer?" and hold up a toy from their classroom. These children also asked their teacher if they could visit the sick children who had been evacuated in Katrina to local hospitals.

Children who live along the Gulf Coast were dramatically affected by Katrina. And, in some cases, these young people mobilized in response to the disruption that they experienced as they took the lead in trying to return a semblance of normalcy to their lives. We observed many youth-led organizations in action in our years of research after Katrina. For example, the group Kids Rethink New Orleans Schools emerged after the storm and began organizing around issues related to getting public schools reopened, obtaining fresh food for cafeterias, and stopping unnecessary suspensions against youth.[25] Students of the Storm was another emergent grassroots group of youth (modeled after an adult organization, Women of the Storm)[26] that traveled to Washington, DC, to lobby elected officials on behalf of children and youth and to tell them how the disaster affected young people's lives. The Vietnamese American Young Leaders Association (VAYLA) is a youth-led organization that was formed in the Katrina aftermath; it focuses on organizing youth around the most pressing issues facing the Vietnamese American community in the New Orleans area.[27] The SHOREline program, which was founded in response to long-term research on Katrina and the BP Oil Spill that followed, engages high school youth in project-based learning, where they identify problems facing youth and their communities and then develop and implement their own solutions.[28]

These organizations, and many others, have made a tangible difference in communities along the Gulf Coast.[29] They have also changed young people's lives. One boy from New Orleans, a Rethinker (the moniker for members of Kids Rethink New Orleans Schools), told us that the first time he spoke in front of an audience as part of the work he was doing, he "realized what a difference" he could make in the world. After four years of being involved in Rethink, he had developed a number of skills and was heading off to college to major in mechanical engineering. For many of the children who became involved in these grassroots groups, this was the first time they had participated in community organizing or political activity; it gave them a new perspective on their ability to induce political and social change.[30]

Katrina-affected youth also took part in many other emergent activities to help children in the region and elsewhere recover. After all that they had witnessed and experienced, many of the young people in our study told us that they had developed more "empathy" and "understanding" for what children in disasters go through. Isabel described how her New Orleans school worked together to raise over $2,000 to send to families affected by another large disaster. She reflected on that work and said:

> I feel like we can relate to what they're going through. Maybe not exactly the same, but the feeling of having to start over. I think that here [in New Orleans] people can really sympathize or empathize with the people because they kind of know what they are going through. And I think we've all seen how much people can help, so we kind of want to go above and beyond in giving help.

The children and youth whom we studied helped adults and other young people after Katrina. They also engaged in many activities that ultimately helped themselves. These children were active agents in propelling others' as well as their own recovery forward.

Children and youth did many things to take some control of their own situations and circumstances during the evacuation. In many cases, they not only helped their parents to load vehicles with clothes, food, water, vital documents, and photo albums, but also, on their own initiative, packed up things that were most special and meaningful to them. For example, one of the youngest girls in our study took her favorite teddy bear. She told us it was important for her to grab it because she had had "that teddy bear for a long time and it was really comforting." She also brought a favorite stuffed horse; she slept with the bear and the horse each night of the evacuation, and saved those animals for many years after Katrina as reminders of all that she and her family had been through. One little boy made sure that he had a memento that his grandmother, who had passed away before the storm, had given him. Another girl collected all of her school yearbooks so she could take them with her. Mekana told us that the "first thing" she grabbed was her photo album because she did not want to "lose memories" in the disaster. Several teens prioritized gathering up their cell phones and other devices that would allow them to stay connected with their friends and family members.

The evacuation experience made some of the youth think more systematically about what they would take in future storms. Cierra noted that in Katrina she evacuated with "simple things," like her "music CDs and clothes." But a few years after Katrina, when she and her mother had to evacuate from another looming hurricane, she was more careful to bring "things that were close" to her heart, like her "journal, pictures, and stuff like that . . . phone books," just in case she was not able to "come back and get in touch with friends."

For those families that were able to get out of the city before Katrina, we learned of the things that children did for themselves during that evacuation period. For instance, younger children in the study played games as they and their families awaited Katrina's inevitable landfall. Indeed, children who evacuated from New Orleans invented a game they called "Evacuation" in their new temporary home. In this game, they ran around their house with bags and tried to throw as many things in the bag as quickly as possible, as if they were frantically leaving their home before the hurricane.[31]

After Katrina crashed ashore and the levees failed, the young people in our study watched and listened and learned about the devastation. They were interested in knowing more about what this would mean for their lives, their families, and their communities. Although parents often tried to shield their children from being overexposed to the news after the storm, we also found that the pre-teen and teenage youth were interested in understanding, on a deeper level, how this disaster would shape the future of their city and their coastline. When they were out of school during the evacuation, parents said their children would often "ask a lot of questions." They would then get on the Internet or otherwise engage in conversation with adults and other youth to try to learn more about the effects of the storm. In some ways, this seemed to restore a sense of control in their lives, as more information allowed them to better grasp the complexities of what was unfolding around them.

As the recovery process began, children engaged in a number of creative activities. Some of those whom we studied wrote songs, stories, or poems; chapter 6, for example, opens and closes with Cierra's poems. She found that expressing herself through poetry calmed her and helped her get through rough times. Others wrote diaries or letters, sang or played musical instruments, drew pictures, kept journals, or otherwise found creative mediums for expressing themselves.[32] While some of these activities were required as part of school assignments, and thus all children in the classroom completed them, others were more spontaneous and were initiated directly by children. Daniel began writing a book about his experience in the storm, while Mekana spent many hours after school making special digital photo collages that she could send to friends who had been displaced to many different places.

Like Mekana, many of the children in this research developed their own creative ways to find and reconnect with loved ones. Often it was the children in families who knew how to use social media—such as MySpace and Facebook—who set up accounts and began re-establishing vital peer-to-peer networks. In some cases, the children who did this then helped the adults in their lives to set up pages as well. This allowed the adults to also find their friends. In turn, the children and youth said they "felt good" they were able to help.

One of the things that many of the children we interviewed said to us was that after a while, they just "didn't want to talk about Katrina anymore." Yet, interestingly, these same young people often were the ones who reached out—when they were ready—to peers and adults for assistance with their recovery. The support they requested ranged from "just needing someone to talk to," to actually seeking formal mentorship or counseling. Some of these same children, especially teens, were also eager to talk with us or to draw pictures during our visits, which allowed them to reflect on their experience. Some shared their journals, artwork, and personalized photo albums. Others sang songs for us or showed us their dance routines. While some children spoke of being "over Katrina" or not wanting to talk about the hurricane, we sometimes found that they were referring to describing the day Katrina made landfall. The aftermath, or the many years of their life displaced and uprooted and in limbo, which they may not define as "Katrina," was something they were actively processing and coping with on a daily basis. This was not something they were "over."

As these young people talked about the disaster with us, they often noted that it made them feel good that they were helping themselves, and also potentially helping others through participating in our research project. As Cierra said, "If something was to happen, I know how it feels to feel like you've lost everything. I know how it feels to feel like your family is here and there. So I feel like . . . it's good . . . to share this story and to help others."

The youth in our study took on jobs after Katrina not only to support their families and younger siblings, as described above, but also to support themselves. Many of the adolescents and teens were faced with the harsh reality that any "safety net" their parents may have had in place for them—such as extra savings or a college fund—was gone after Katrina. Thus, they moved into action and began earning money so they could pay for things for themselves, and in some cases, begin saving for college or life after high school. Other teens returned to New Orleans without parents or guardians and were living on their own; in those precarious, unstable living conditions we found evidence that teens and youth were sharing material and emotional resources.

It is important to remember that children and youth do not experience a disaster in a vacuum. Some of the young people in our study were living in impoverished families and disadvantaged neighborhoods before the storm. Others watched, after Katrina, as their siblings or parents descended into depression or otherwise struggled emotionally or physically. These children were dealing with multiple crises before and/or after the storm. The coping skills they developed (or refined) as a result of Katrina helped them to manage and to move forward in the face of disaster.

HOW HELPING OTHERS—AND HELPING THEMSELVES—
HELPS CHILDREN RECOVER FROM DISASTER

Taken together, it is clear that children and youth contributed in many significant ways to their families, other adults, and other young people as they prepared for, experienced, and recovered from Katrina. They also took positive actions to help themselves. So what does this tell us about children and youth in disasters and how does this matter in young people's lives?

First and foremost, children and youth had a strong desire to help and be of assistance to others. Past research on adults has documented that the need to be involved in the communal recovery effort can be powerful in a disaster aftermath. This need can be felt by survivors, bystanders, and those who otherwise identify with the disaster. Early disaster researchers wrote of convergence behavior in disasters, where large numbers of "helpers" descend on the scene after an emergency or disaster.[33] Research on the 9/11 terrorist attacks found that volunteers felt that the need to help was "overpowering" as they needed to do something to transform such a negative experience into something positive.[34] Research on the 2008 Sichuan earthquake in China found that the disaster prompted elementary school children to share, have empathy, show altruism, donate, and think of others.[35]

There are, however, often barriers to providing assistance, such as the presence of more volunteers than tasks, logistical issues in a disaster aftermath, or exclusion of some groups from the spontaneous disaster volunteer efforts.[36] As described above, Isabel found that when she tried to volunteer, adults told her that Katrina survivors should be "relaxing." She was irritated by this remark. Even at her young age, Isabel wanted to volunteer; she recognized her own need to serve others and she wanted to act on that. For children, the barriers may be greater, as some adults may overlook their desire and capabilities, thus closing off the chance for children to meaningfully contribute.

Yet, helping in a disaster aftermath can take many forms. And opening up varied opportunities for children and youth to assist can make a tremendous difference to their own recovery. As illustrated throughout this book, children and youth helped before, during, and after Katrina in substantial and varied ways. They offered emotional, physical, and financial support to those around them. They provided assistance in private arenas, within their families and homes, and in more public spaces, such as in mass shelters and in schools. Thinking broadly about how children help in a disaster allows us to see the potential for them to play an active role and lets us acknowledge that they took the initiative in many instances; like adults, they needed to help.

Second, by helping others, children and youth were able to contribute to their own healing and recovery. Again, research on adults has shown that finding a way to assist survivors in a disaster situation has many positive outcomes, such as increasing feelings of solidarity and interconnection, promoting healing, and fostering empowerment. Indeed, helping other people after a disaster is one potential route for survivors to "transform feelings of helplessness to feelings of efficacy."[37] Children, too, need to regain a sense of control in the face of situations such as disasters, where they may feel powerless or helpless. Children and youth, who usually have fewer opportunities for publicly expressing their views and have limited political voice or power, may lack efficacy, or the ability to influence their surrounding environments.

With the proper support, though, children can and do positively influence those around them. By helping others, children and youth often told us that they felt "proud," "more in control," "powerful," and like they were "making a difference for others." And this made a difference in their own lives and in their own recovery. Contributing to the health and well-being of others through volunteering or just "helping out" in big and small ways was important to children and youth in this study, and it positively influenced their post-disaster trajectories.

CHILDREN, YOUTH, AND DISASTERS IN THE FUTURE

Disaster risk is on the rise in the United States and globally. With the increase in climate-related disasters, population growth, rising levels of social and economic inequality, and the movement of more people into more hazardous areas, more children are living at risk than ever before. Katrina, the most devastating disaster in modern U.S. history, was perhaps a harbinger of what is to come. This disaster, like all major events, revealed the vulnerability of those living at the margins of society, and it also shed light on some of their special strengths and capacities.

We hope that this book has helped to focus attention on the ways that disasters can exacerbate old problems, create new challenges, and contribute to significant instability in children's lives. At the same time, disasters can open up new opportunities for change and growth, revealing needs but also the special capacities of young people. Through carefully examining the spheres of children's lives and their post-disaster trajectories, our goal was to document their experience and to help others to think more carefully about how we can best support, encourage, and inspire youth while also understanding their contributions to disaster recovery.

Appendix A

WHO COUNTS AS A CHILD?

Given the focus of this book, it is important to define what we mean when we refer to "children" and "youth." While this may seem like a relatively straightforward task, the reality is that who counts as a "child" in various social, legal, and political contexts is a matter fraught with inconsistency.[1] Indeed, the very notion of "childhood" as a distinct, even special, phase in the life course is a relatively recent societal construction associated with dramatic shifts in family structure, schools, medical and behavioral science, and the labor market in developed and developing countries.[2]

The United Nations Convention on the Rights of the Child, which was first introduced in 1989, specifies that a child is anyone below the age of 18.[3] Similarly, the United States Census and many other federal and state-level agencies define children as persons age 18 and under. The United Nations defines "youth" as those aged 15–24, although their definition varies based on geographic context. Many youth studies scholars, however, argue that youth is a socially constructed phase between childhood and adulthood that cannot be tied to a specific age range. While difficult to define, "youth" is seen as a broader concept than adolescence and as a period of some independence.

There is obviously incredible difference between a newborn baby and an 18- or 24-year-old. Yet, there is also a clear rationale for including such a wide and varied swath of any given population under the age categories of "children" and "youth." Namely, children around the world are considered a social minority group because they are marginalized in terms of wealth, social status, and political power. Children are also a numerical minority in the United States—where girls and boys age 18 and under make up about 25 percent of the total population—and most other high-income countries. In developing countries, children often comprise closer to half or even a statistical majority of the population; nonetheless, children and youth typically remain disenfranchised from core social institutions.[4]

When studying and writing about children and youth, scholars tend to rely on more carefully age-disaggregated data. The most finely grained analyses highlight the considerable variation across the age continuum by distinguishing infants (0–1 year); young children, preschool-age children, and/or toddlers (2–4 years); children

(5–12 years); adolescents, and/or teens (13–17 years); and youth or young adults (18–24 years).[5] This terminology is by no means fixed, nor is there universal agreement on when each age category begins or ends.

Like scholars in other fields, disaster researchers most often use the more generic terms "children" or "children and youth" to refer to all persons age 18 and younger, while also differentiating between categories based on chronological age and stage of development. In disaster management, children, when they are considered, have been defined as an "at-risk," "special needs," or "vulnerable" population and subsequently grouped among the elderly, persons with disabilities, the medically dependent, persons with special transportation needs, and/or persons with limited English proficiency.[6]

As adults continue to debate and alter various age categories, few observers have stopped to ask "children" what they wish to be called. Barrie Thorne found that older elementary school students prefer to be called "kids" as they view the word "child" to be condescending.[7] Sociologist Valerie Moore argued that "children" is a top-down term, implying that they are beings still in development and not capable social actors.[8] Over the past two decades, however, the word "kids" has fallen out of favor with many researchers, child rights advocates, childcare providers, and even some children given the definitional association with "baby goats."

Throughout this book, we have chosen to use the broad terminology of "children" or "children and youth" to represent the experiences of our 3- to 18-year-old respondents. We recognize, however, the definitional complexity and social contestation that underlies this decision. Thus, where appropriate, we have attempted to use more specific age groupings and to maintain children's self-definitions. While we predominantly use the terms "children" and "youth" throughout, we draw on the words of those whom we interviewed for this book and thus also use "kids," "teens," "adolescents," and other descriptors.

Appendix B

STUDYING CHILDREN AND YOUTH IN DISASTER
A NOTE ON METHODS

In order to really communicate with the kids, we've got to practice deep knee bends. We've got to get down there so we're face-to-face with them. We've got to try to get into their world and stop telling them about ours. Listen to them. Ask them to tell us what they see and feel and hear, because, you may be surprised, they may teach you something.

LEO F. BUSCAGLIA

Our objectives are twofold for this appendix. First, we describe the study that serves as the foundation for this book, detailing our research design, time line, research sites, participant sampling, methods of data collection, and techniques of analysis. Second, we identify the key challenges we faced and reflect on the insights that we gained through completing this work. We organize the appendix around what we did and the decisions that we made in order to carry out this research. Throughout, we highlight issues and opportunities that arose as we conducted the study and wrote up the findings.

Our intent in sharing this information—including what worked and what did not work—is to help inform future studies on children, youth, and disasters. In particular, we want to assist scholars and practitioners who plan to conduct child-centered research, something that, at least until relatively recently, has been mostly lacking in the field of disaster studies. We also hope that researchers already doing research in this area will find the description of methodological innovations and improvisations useful, and that this will lead to additional conversations in this important subfield of disaster research. Finally, while the type of long-term, team-based ethnography that we completed for this book is becoming more common in the social sciences, this methodological approach is still rare in disaster research. Thus, we share these stories to assist researchers who are considering or are actually working individually, as well as collaboratively, on longitudinal projects.

Just weeks before Katrina made landfall along the U.S. Gulf Coast, we were sitting together at a meeting and ended up engaging in a long conversation about doing a collaborative project on children in disaster. We both had a long-standing interest in vulnerable populations and disasters, we had collaborated before on other studies, and we were interested in doing another project together. Recently we had both read the same journal article—one calling for additional social science research on children and disaster. We were inspired and we decided that we would like to heed that call together.[1]

At the close of our conversation in early August of 2005, we agreed to work together on a future project on the topic of children and disaster. We envisioned that this would likely be a few years down the road, given our other research, teaching, and service demands as university professors.[2] And then, two weeks later, on the first day of our fall semesters at our respective universities, Katrina struck.

After a flurry of phone calls and emails, we decided that this historic event was so important that we needed to start our project immediately. Three days after the levees broke in New Orleans, we started writing our research proposals for quick response grant funding and human subjects approval through our respective university Institutional Review Boards (IRBs).

From the outset, our goal with this work was to understand the experiences of children in the aftermath of Hurricane Katrina. Our early work asked the following questions: (1) What were the children's experiences in the disaster? (2) What did others do for the children to lessen their vulnerability? (3) What did children do for themselves and others to reduce disaster impacts? and (4) What were children's experiences with relocation, particularly with schooling, family, and friendships?[3]

We wanted to identify how adults helped children and how children themselves assisted in their own and others' recovery after Katrina. In order to accomplish this work, it was crucial that we commit to following children over the long term so that we could actually see these processes unfold in their lives. We hope that it will be obvious to readers what different stories we might have told if we had stopped after only one, two, or three years of data collection.

When we started this project, we did not identify a potential end date. Early on, we recognized that the profound disruption caused by Katrina and the resultant displacement of the families we were studying would likely warrant a much longer term examination than is typical in the field of disaster studies. We also soon started to see the divergent tracks that the children in our sample and their families seemed to be on in terms of their recovery. We thus knew that we would likely have to observe and interview the families for years after the event to provide a suitably nuanced portrait of children's post-disaster experiences and trajectories.

With each foray into the field, we learned more about the children's trajectories. At the end of each research trip, we would reassess where we were in the project as a whole and make a decision about what we needed to do in terms of next steps in the project. For example, at the beginning of the second year of our study, we realized that some of the children were in less stable situations and declining *more* than they had been in the immediate aftermath of the disaster. This observation alerted us to the danger of leaving the setting too early and possibly misrepresenting the complexity of children's experiences and the cumulative and enduring vulnerability of some.

With the perspective that time and distance allows, several things have become clear. First, it was critically important that we began our project so soon after Katrina, as some of the things we learned early on from families (e.g., the trauma of the evacuation, the early decision making regarding resettling in particular communities) helped us to understand why the trajectories unfolded as they did.

Second, by meeting with the children and families multiple times over the years of the study, we were able to trace their post-disaster trajectory. We saw the upward or downward movement in people's lives, which simply would not have been possible without collecting data at multiple points in time.

Third, the longitudinal design made a difference in the quality of data we were able to gather. We saw how individuals opened up to us. Children, sometimes hesitant at first, often began to share more of their stories as they matured and became more comfortable around us. As one mother told us about her son: "He's shy until he gets to know you. Then he'll talk." Our repeated visits also made a difference to adults; as one teacher told us, "You kept coming back, so we knew you cared." A child reflected on how the media focus on survivors had "died down," but we were still there:

> At first I was so excited about [your study], because you all came, like, right after the newspapers and the news channels. They came because we were from New Orleans, and we were getting these houses built. We did interviews and we were on the news and in the paper, and then you came right behind it, so it was like, "Okay, here we go again, I get to tell my story." [laughs] But after a while, everything died down and it was quiet, but, from then, we kept up with you both and Mom stayed in touch with you all. It's awesome.

Others also were curious about what we were doing with the data, where we were in the study, and what the study was really about. In the first years of the study, we found that participants had different ideas about our project, for example, introducing us as "writing a story" on children, or in town to "help children." In the later years, participants had a much clearer understanding of our research and their role within it; the idea of a "book" as the final product was clear and tangible.[4]

Many marveled at how many years we spent in the field, sometimes asking us when we would be done. On one visit, a mother joked about how long our study was taking, saying that by the time we had finished everything, her young son would "probably have facial hair!" We had concerns about participants getting tired and overwhelmed by being studied for so long, but we never found any evidence of that.

Indeed, one woman, when asked if she felt "overstudied," or "studied out," replied: "No, we haven't really talked to anybody in a long time."

GAINING ACCESS

Gaining permission to enter into and become part of the everyday lives of your research informants is vital to qualitative work. Yet, in research with children, acquiring access to their life worlds can be especially difficult. Most children's settings are monitored by vigilant gatekeepers—parents, childcare workers, teachers, and others—who are dedicated to protecting the children in their charge.

Parents, mostly mothers, were the ones who gave us permission to ask their children to participate in this study. There is absolutely no way we could have completed this research if the children's parents had not given us access to their homes and children. Not only was it required by our university IRBs, but it was also a prerequisite for us to see and speak with the children in the first place.

In addition to parents, other adults also helped us gain access to children. At a church shelter we visited soon after Katrina, for example, the pastor's wife was especially protective of her shelter residents and was wary of people taking advantage of them in any way. When we showed up to meet her, she allowed us in only because we came with the blessing of an interfaith minister whom we had interviewed previously, who in turn had only had us in her office for a meeting because a colleague she trusted had vouched for us.

Similarly, there were many instances where we needed to have institutional gatekeepers on board and often to pass through multiple layers of scrutiny before we were granted access. One of the most difficult places to gain entrée was the Cajundome, a mass shelter in Baton Rouge. We had been warned by a Cajundome volunteer that "they won't let you in," encouraging us instead to "just hang around outside." When we arrived, there were two groups trying to run the shelter: the American Red Cross, which had out-of-state administrators and volunteers, and the Cajundome staff who ran the facility on a regular basis. The conflicts between these two groups, and the confusion over which group was in charge, posed difficulties for us. We received permission from the Cajundome staff to enter the shelter and interview staff, volunteers, and residents, only to be told later by the Red Cross staff that we had to leave the premises immediately. The Red Cross staff explained that they had been "burned" by a journalist who posed as a researcher and then secretly recorded film footage inside the shelter. Later, the Cajundome staff overruled the Red Cross, but we were still forced to "sneak in" a side entrance, where we believed that people assumed we were volunteers arriving for our shifts.

Similar issues arose with gaining entrée to school settings. In the early stages of the research, we attempted to gain access to one school system by making phone calls and sending emails to school administrators. They in turn required that we send numerous forms, letters, and notices from our universities, over a period of many months, only to have them never respond to our requests to visit. That official route to access turned out to be a dead end. Later, numerous avenues into the schools emerged; all of these were due to more personal connections, such as a parent or a teacher introducing us to the principal, who would then invite us to visit a classroom or to speak with teachers.

In the end, and as the above stories illustrate, we gained access to various settings through both personal and professional connections. We contacted friends of friends of friends when necessary. Sometimes we made the most of circumstances related to our work, such as when we volunteered to deliver a student's master thesis to a charter school in New Orleans, allowing us the opportunity to meet teachers and students, get a tour of the school, and spend an afternoon on their campus.[5] We found that persistence, friendliness, and the willingness to let the informants set the terms of the visit or interview were the most helpful approaches.

In addition to the adult gatekeepers, we also had an ethical imperative to gain permission from the children themselves before we could observe or interview them. We focused on the adults initially, and we found that that upon entering the scene, children paid close attention to how their parents, teachers, and other trusted adults interacted with us, and how they reacted to being interviewed. The adults also influenced the children, as evidenced when we asked a young boy if we could interview him, and his mother encouraged him by saying, "Go on, go talk to the nice ladies." Other children who participated in the study were much more eager and excited to volunteer to be interviewed. Some teens passed on information on our study to their friends, who then also volunteered to participate.

Regardless of whether the children were quiet or gregarious, we made sure that every single child we approached was informed of the study and had the opportunity to ask questions and to offer assent before we began asking any questions. We did this not only because our IRBs required it, but also because we believed in the importance of the informed consent process. We prepared a simple script that we followed before each interview, and upon each return visit, we asked the children permission to be reinterviewed. No child ever turned us down, and no child (or adult) withdrew over the years of this study.

USING MULTIPLE METHODS TO STUDY CHILDREN

From the outset, it was clear to us that if we were going to learn about children's experiences after Katrina—their vulnerabilities, their strengths and capacities, and the short- and long-term effects of the disaster on their lives—we would have to rely on multiple, creative, and complementary methods to study young people in their daily environments. See figure B.1 for an overview of the methods we used to collect data for this seven-year project; in this section and the one that follows, we describe the methods depicted in the figure in greater detail.

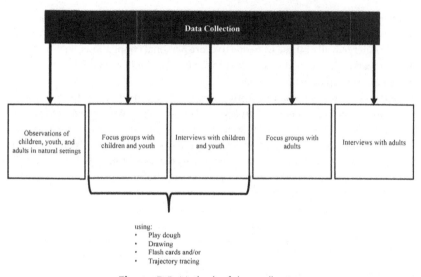

Figure B.1. Methods of data collection

OBSERVING CHILDREN IN MULTIPLE SETTINGS

We spent many hours observing children and the adults who care for those young people in various settings: in temporary shelters and in their homes and the homes of their extended family and friends, in childcare centers, in classrooms, at special events in auditoriums and elsewhere on school grounds, at parks and playgrounds, in church, and in many other places. Table B.1 summarizes (1) the multiple locations where we conducted observations as both active participants and more passive observers, depending on the context; (2) the people we observed within each context; and (3) what we observed in terms of physical space, resources and amenities, and personal interactions. In addition to the specific sites and groups listed in the table, we attempted to observe certain things at each site, such as the number of persons in the setting; demographic composition of all persons, with a focus on race, class, gender, age, and ability; age and quality of infrastructure; and so forth. So again, while we focused on observational moments specific to each context, we also attempted to gather particular things of sociological interest to us across the sites.

As we observed children and adults go about their lives, we were careful to record detailed and systematic fieldnotes.[6] In order to capture the things we saw and heard, we carried small notepads with us everywhere. Most often, we would jot down short notes about things we wanted to follow up on as well as what we actually observed. We would later develop these notebook jottings into full fieldnotes. It was admittedly quite difficult to do this. We were typically in the field and interacting with respondents for 10–14 hours each day, and sometimes for longer. We would then return during the late evening to the hotel or home of a friend where we were staying.

Although usually exhausted from a long day of traveling around and from listening actively to our participants, we would then need to write up those notes. Often Lori would type the notes on her laptop. As she was typing, we would discuss the organization of the notes. Alice would also be processing her own handwritten notes and helping Lori to add details from things that we had seen and heard that day. This was so helpful, as one of us would remember something, and then it would prompt a memory in the other, allowing us to continually expand and refine our notes.[7] Moreover, and we said this to each other many times, without "pushing" each other to "just write a little bit tonight," we likely, as individual researchers, might not have gotten as much written during the evenings as we actually did. But because we had each other, we were able to move forward with the fieldnotes, even after the long research days.

Even though we tried to move forward with the fieldnotes each night, we were often unable to complete our full fieldnotes at the end of the day. We know this violates recommended best practices, but writing up full fieldnotes takes an enormous amount of time.[8] Thus, we would do our best to get a solid enough outline down that we could then pick up the writing process after we returned from the field. This was the best balance we could achieve in the face of long days and not enough time for data collection, data processing, travel to different research sites, and sleep.

In light of the challenges we faced as researchers conducting a study in a location far away from our own homes, sometimes we would also weave our observations into our audio-recorded interviews. When we observed something we knew we would want to remember later, we would intentionally say things aloud during the recorded interview like: "I see that the refrigerator downstairs is unplugged and empty. How long has it been that way?" Or, we would spend time asking the child to describe, in his or her own words, the room where we were conducting the interview. This allowed us to learn more about a child's favorite book or toy or bedding set, for example, and to have the observation recorded, from the perspective of the respondent, for later transcription.

Occasionally, when we were particularly pressed for time and/or when we had just observed something that was quite vivid and important to the study, we would speak our notes into our audio recorders as we were driving or wrapping up things for the evening. For instance, one day we were in Baton Rouge at a kindergarten promotion ceremony, and then we had to leave soon after to drive to Lafayette to meet up with another family and to attend another event that evening. We had observed much at the school in Baton Rouge that we did not want to forget. So during the one-hour drive from Baton Rouge to Lafayette, we talked to each other about what we had observed, while keeping our audio recorder running. We later had those notes—and others where we did this—transcribed so we could have that data available for analysis as well.

We captured many things in our fieldnotes. We attempted to always "paint a picture" of the scene. What did it feel like? What did the place look like? Who was present? What were they wearing? What were they saying? We wrote about more

Table B.1. Observation sites and types of observations

Observation sites	Whom we observed	Examples of what we observed
Disaster temporary shelters	Shelter volunteers, aid workers, police and private security officers, building staff, adult and child disaster survivors	Building structure (e.g., sports arena, church, school, etc.), security lines, first-aid tables, counseling areas, basketball courts, cots and other sleeping areas, spaces turned into dormitories, childcare areas, homework areas, play areas, meal preparation, bathrooms, staff offices, interactions between different groups and survivors, aid workers' break rooms
Disaster relief centers	Aid workers, adult and child disaster survivors, volunteers	Emergency and long-term relief lines; interactions between aid workers and adults; interactions between caregivers, volunteers, and children; items being distributed to survivors
FEMA trailers and other temporary housing	FEMA aid workers, adult and child disaster survivors residing in the trailers, visitors to the trailers, mobile home park residents who lived there prior to Katrina	Mobile home space; living arrangements; household amenities; access to food; area surrounding mobile homes; surrounding neighborhoods; surrounding infrastructure, including highway systems, access to nearby amenities and resources (e.g., schools, stores, workplaces, banks); play areas; interactions between Katrina survivors, aid workers, and non-Katrina-affected residents
Permanent housing and surrounding neighborhoods	Adult and child disaster survivors who had transitioned to permanent housing, adult and child neighbors	Housing type (e.g., single-family home, apartment), housing quality, living quarters, household amenities, food and other necessities in the home, laundry availability, neighborhood type and design, neighborhood demographic composition, nearby amenities and resources
Public recreation sites	Children, parents, babysitters, and other caregivers	Playgrounds, park open space, sports areas, running/walking tracks, interactions between children, interactions between children and adults
Childcare centers	Childcare staff (center directors, teachers, receptionists, etc.), young children, parents	Reception area; classrooms; indoor and outdoor play areas; staff offices; interactions between staff, children, and parents; parent drop-off and pickup times

Observation sites	Whom we observed	Examples of what we observed
Schools	Front office staff; security guards; school administrators, teachers, janitorial and other support staff; elementary, middle, and high school students	Security area, where applicable; reception area; administrative offices; classrooms; playgrounds and school gardens; hallway art and other decorations; bathrooms; cafeterias; auditoriums; special events at schools (e.g., graduation ceremonies, plays, musicals); interactions between students and school staff; interactions between parents and school staff
Churches	Pastors, church staff, child and adult congregants	Services; reception areas; church childcare; musical performances and other special events; interactions before, during, and after services
Laundromats	Child and adult disaster survivors, local residents of receiving communities where displaced persons relocated	Laundry facilities, waiting area, coin operation, interactions between families, clothing types, amount of clothing, parking area, how customers traveled to the Laundromat
Shopping locations	Child and adult disaster survivors, other shoppers	Walmart, grocery stores, types of goods available, flyers on bulletin boards (such as for the Road Home Program or mold removal), items bought by the respondents themselves and by us for the participants in the study
Barbershops	Child and adult disaster survivors, barbers, residents of receiving communities	Barber facilities, interactions and conversations among clients and barbers, waiting area, general atmosphere
Restaurants	Child and adult disaster survivors, other diners, wait staff, restaurant managers	Menu options and food ordered; interactions between family members with each other when they were deciding where to eat and what to eat; interaction during mealtime itself; interactions between child and adult study participants with restaurant staff; fast-food restaurant children's play areas
Special events	Child and adult disaster survivors, residents of receiving communities	Second Lines, parades, and festivals; parties and other celebrations; food and drink, music, attire, mood

mundane moments, such as what it looked like when we watched families stand in long lines waiting to fill out forms for post-disaster aid, as well as more emotional times, such as when we observed parents cry as they saw their children walk across the stage at high school graduation.

As the research progressed, we continued to record interviews with the participants. But we also spent more and more hours with the families in the study in informal settings. We visited with parents and grandparents as they prepared meals and sat out on their front porches drinking iced tea. We walked with children to their favorite "snowball" (the Louisiana version of a snow cone or shaved ice) stands in New Orleans, often holding their hands as we walked across busy streets. We gave children piggyback rides through Walmart as we helped their mothers shop for school supplies. We sat for hours in church, listening to sermons and watching children and their families interact with friends and religious leaders on Sunday morning. We listened to youth sing us their favorite songs. We stood shoulder to shoulder to watch colorful parades and "second lines" (a New Orleans tradition of dance and revelry after a brass band parade). We attended sporting events, observing children interact with their peers and coaches when their parents were not around. In each case, we attempted to describe the situation in our fieldnotes in detailed terms.

We tried to be as unobtrusive as possible as we went about observing and writing jottings in the field. However, at times, we became a part of the scene. For instance, when we would sit in classrooms and watch children, sometimes the teachers would ask questions or play more interactive games, and we would be invited to join in. One Monday morning a teacher had the children in her class describe what they had done over the weekend, and she included us in the activity.

We took many photographs to augment our memories of settings and to help us complete our fieldnotes. In addition to photographing the participants themselves, we also took pictures of their homes, their school classrooms, and their neighborhoods. Taking pictures was especially useful to help us remember some aspect of the setting that might have been difficult to get into the fieldnotes—for example, a lengthy sign about guns and drugs mounted on a school exterior, a full-page poem written by a child and posted on a bedroom wall, or a teacher's message to students covering an entire blackboard. We always asked permission to use our cameras in someone's home or classroom, and we were almost always granted permission to take photos.[9] Even though our participants were almost always happy to smile for our cameras, we were careful to explain to respondents that because we had promised to protect their confidentiality, we would never use photographs that would identify them or their homes in published work or public presentations.[10]

THE POWER OF FOCUS GROUPS WITH CHILDREN

In addition to the observations, we gathered focus group data from the children. Over the course of this study, we conducted a total of 10 focus groups—a method which involves carefully planned discussions designed to obtain perceptions on a defined area of interest[11]—with children. Our groups ranged in size from two to six children.[12] All of the focus group discussions were audio-recorded and transcribed verbatim. Some of the focus groups were planned well in advance; others were spontaneous as we would arrive on a scene where there would be multiple children and we would attempt to draw on that opportunity to gather all of their voices during whatever time we had available.

Focus groups are not only advantageous in that they allow researchers to collect a great deal of information; they can also be beneficial and empowering to the children themselves. The arrangement allows them to outnumber the adult facilitator, which can help minimize the power differential between adult researchers and younger respondents.[13] This matters because adults can often be intimidating due to their physical size, age, and relative power, authority, and control compared to children.[14] Consequently, younger respondents may achieve a sense of strength in their numbers. Moreover, if the participants do not know the researcher well, the group setting can provide a more secure space for children, allowing them to be more talkative and playful than they might otherwise be. Focus groups allow children to engage with one another and to provide support for one another. The group setting seemed to take some of the pressure off, relieving children's nerves, at least in some cases, to speak into the audio recorder. By being with their peers, and sometimes friends or siblings, in these groups, they were able to encourage one another and to offer comfort if a member of the group became upset while telling a particular story. For example, one middle school student described how valuable it was to have her friend present as she shared her experience: "The first time it was kind of hard for me to explain the story of the hurricane. I kind of cried a little bit. I had one of my friends, she was there, she was supporting me, helping me or whatever, so she really talked for me or whatever." Thus, focus groups can have a social support function,[15] allowing the participants to share their stories and to develop some solidarity with others who are going through similar challenges.

ATTAINING DEPTH THROUGH INTERVIEWS WITH CHILDREN

We conducted dozens of one-on-one interviews with children. As described in chapter 2, some of the children were interviewed only once; others, including the focal children and their siblings, were interviewed multiple times over the years of research.

For these more formal, audio-recorded interviews, we followed an interview guide with a bulleted list of key topics. We developed a new interview guide each time we went into the field, constantly refining it based on what we had learned during our prior field visit, and what we hoped to learn during the present research trip. Before we would turn on the recorder, we would spend time explaining to the child participant what we would do in the interview,[16] leaving plenty of time for the children to ask us questions before we would proceed. We also conducted many more informal, conversational interviews that were not audio-recorded, but instead were captured in our fieldnotes.

Some of the children were reserved and cautious, at least initially, in the interview process. For example, one boy told us that he did not always like being interviewed "because sometimes it can be [an] uncomfortable situation where you might not want to say something." As time progressed, even the more quiet children in our study tended to open up and share more stories. As noted above in the discussion of the importance of the long-term nature of the study, perhaps this had to do with developmental change—they were obviously maturing over time and likely becoming more comfortable with the communication style that in-depth interviews require. But we think it was more than that: the children also became more comfortable with us over time. We could tell this because they would sometimes say things like, "I knew when you came back, I wanted to tell you about this." And they would often remember things they had told us in a prior interview and then would want to follow up on that to update us on what had happened since the last interview. We also changed and improved as interviewers. We too became more comfortable, more adept, and more creative in our interviewing techniques, as we describe below.

While the more formal interviews were almost always conducted in homes or schools, the informal interviews occurred in many other settings, such as at shelters, on school playgrounds, or at church. The various places where we conducted interviews allowed us to gather additional observational data and enriched the stories that we collected. During the course of interviews, children would sometimes stand up and offer to show us something that they had been referring to; we always kept the recorder running during those moments and treated that important information as additional data. Children were usually eager to show us around their rooms and homes, before, during, or after interviews. One girl said to us, as soon as we arrived: "I want to show you my new toys!" She promptly grabbed our hands and took us back to her room to show us her stuffed animals, organized neatly in a play baby crib in her room. If the moment allowed for it, we would almost always ask if we could go ahead and turn on the recorder so we could capture the narratives (and our questions) that were so often part of these "tours" around homes and schools. In this way, the children taught us the importance of not just diving into a formal interview, but instead starting where the children were and with what *they* wanted to share with *us*. That tended to make the interviews feel much more natural, and it helped us to collect richer data about the children's lived experiences and their surroundings.

ATTAINING DEPTH THROUGH INTERVIEWS WITH ADULTS

This study included many interviews with adults as well. Over our seven years of research, we interviewed well over 100 adults both individually and in pairs. We spoke with many of these adults on multiple occasions, as they were the parents, teachers, and childcare providers of the focal children whom we were following over time. In addition, we did one-time interviews with post-Katrina volunteers, shelter workers, aid providers, church pastors, and others in all of our field settings.

With each trip, we modified our interview guide for parents as well as other caregivers. This guide contained a number of open-ended questions that we both followed, loosely, as we interviewed the adults. Initially the questions were quite general and were more focused on the disaster story and evacuation experience. As the years passed, and as we refined our analysis, we began focusing more intently on the spheres of children's lives, the recovery process, and the trajectories that we saw unfolding. Thus, we made sure to ask all the family members of the children questions about housing, employment, schooling, friendships, extracurricular activities, and health and well-being. When we interviewed an adult from a specific institution (such as a schoolteacher or a disaster relief worker), we modified our interview guide to attain more information about that institution.

Some of the interviews felt like a conversation, especially with parents, but we always had specific questions to ask. At the end of interviews, we encouraged adult participants to add anything else they felt was relevant or to comment on anything that they thought was important but we did not ask about. Some of the adults in our study worried that they had talked too much or had "overshared." One mother, for example, remarked after a long interview: "It was really nice talking to you, and I feel like I'm blabbing off too much." We quickly reassured her, and others who expressed similar sentiments, that there was no such thing as talking too much; we were there to listen.

ADAPTING IN THE FIELD AND CONDUCTING FOCUS GROUPS WITH ADULTS

We conducted seven focus groups with the adults in our sample. These focus groups were all spontaneous. The groups ranged in size from three to four participants. When we entered a site, such as a temporary housing shelter, school, or childcare center, we occasionally were given the opportunity to talk to several adults at one time without any advance notice. At one emergency relief shelter we visited just a month after Katrina in Baton Rouge, for example, the shelter director assembled four women at a table to talk. At a few of the schools we visited in New Orleans, teachers offered to be interviewed together in their classrooms after school. We had to be flexible and open to whatever arrangement might present itself.

With these focus groups, we followed the same general interview script as when we interviewed adults individually. However, we allowed more time and space for collective discussion and for the adults to lead the way.

As we have written about elsewhere and discuss above in the section on children and focus groups, this method can provide a social support or empowerment function, especially with marginalized, stigmatized, or vulnerable individuals.[17] In these settings, participants are able to share their stories, develop a sense of solidarity, and put their experiences in a larger framework. Through the process of sharing stories collectively, individuals who previously believed they were alone in their experiences often come to realize that others are going through the same thing. Participants can transcend individualism and have their "Is it just me?" questions answered in focus groups.[18]

Indeed, focus groups can reframe personal troubles as public issues. In disaster situations, especially, the support and empathy generated in focus group settings can be therapeutic. In our groups, it was not uncommon for us to witness collective laughter, verbal cues of affirmation, and the sharing of sorrow. In one of our focus groups with teachers and guidance counselors at a private Catholic school in New Orleans, the women listened intently as they shared about what happened to them in Katrina, how their own children had fared, and how the children in their school were doing. When the school counselor told a story of a young girl who had committed suicide after the storm, the women listened to one another and comforted each other as they cried and lamented the loss of such a young child.

USING CREATIVE METHODS TO EVOKE RICHER NARRATIVES FROM CHILDREN

From the outset of this research we realized that if we wanted to attain the best data from children possible, we would need to be creative with our methods. Rather than relying solely on the open-ended interview or focus group format, we sought out resources and guidance (from books and articles as well as from colleagues who conduct research with children) to identify various best practices for engaging young people in the research process.[19] Below we summarize some of the approaches that we used to elicit richer narratives from the child participants.

USING PLAY-DOUGH IN FOCUS GROUPS AND INTERVIEWS

Before our data collection trip in the spring of 2007, we spoke with an education professor who specializes in research on refugee children who have recently resettled in the United States. She recommended that we bring play-dough with us, so the youngest respondents would have "something to do with their hands." We followed her advice, and we are glad we did.[20] It helped make the conversation easier to have the youngest respondents handling the play-dough, as it gave them a simple, creative, tactile task. (We open chapter 2 with an excerpt from one such interview, where the child was playing with play-dough as we interviewed him.) Working with the play-dough meant that the children could avoid making eye contact, and having something to work with seemed to put some of the youngest participants more at ease. Indeed, the use of the play-dough created an overall atmosphere that was quiet, relaxed, unrushed, and child centered. Sometimes the children made silly objects, so we could share a laugh. It also allowed us to make fun of ourselves, as we were unskilled at forming certain objects, and thus the children could see that their play-dough art was often much better than ours.

The play-dough allowed us to give the children breaks in telling their Katrina story, as we would pause the interview questions to ask about what they were making with the play-dough. This was especially important for the youngest respondents in our study. For example, one respondent who was only four years old when we first interviewed him became somewhat confused as he was telling his own Katrina story. He was not sure if he was still "in his mama's belly" when Katrina happened (he was not; he was two years old). As we gently clarified his age at the time of the storm, he played with the play-dough and then was able to continue speaking with us.

When the interview was complete, we would often take pictures of the play-dough creations. We would then help put the play-dough back in the container and let the child know that it was his or hers to keep. We were glad to be able to leave it behind as a small gift for the children, many of whom had very few toys at this time.

USING DRAWINGS IN FOCUS GROUPS AND INTERVIEWS

We also used art to evoke more in-depth narratives from the children we interviewed. During a third data collection trip to the Gulf Coast, we brought a stack of white paper and many boxes of crayons with us. At the beginning of that round of interviews, we would sit down with the focal children, as well as with their siblings and neighborhood friends when they were around, and would ask the children if they would be willing to do some drawings with us. In all cases, the children agreed, often enthusiastically. We did make sure, however, that we only asked those children in the study who were young enough (e.g., 12 years old or younger) that we thought drawing would be age appropriate.

As they readied themselves with the crayons and paper, we would then ask a series of questions, leaving the children time to draw a picture in response to each question (or multiple pictures, if they so desired). We always kept the audio recorder running during these sessions. The question prompts for the drawings included the following:

- What did Katrina look like?
- Who or what helped you after Katrina?
- What was something difficult or hard that happened because of Katrina?
- What was something good that came out of Katrina?

Interestingly, sometimes children would start off by asking for clarification, which we liked, as it showed us they were comfortable requesting more detail. For example, one child said: "Is it okay if we don't draw very well?" We immediately responded that of course that was fine, while noting that our own drawing skills were quite limited! In another instance, one of the child participants said to us: "Can we just draw anything? Or does it have to have to do with Katrina?" We responded to all questions and we emphasized repeatedly that there was no "right" answer and that we were not looking for any representation in particular. Instead we just wanted them to draw whatever came to their minds first and whatever images they wanted to put on the paper.

As we did this activity, it was important to us that we were not confused with teachers and that the children did not feel like we were giving them an "assignment," even as we were asking them to do certain things for us. The children seemed quite comfortable, and they would regularly ask us for certain colored crayons or for more time as they were drawing. Sometimes they even posed their own questions that they wanted to draw something in response to.

On the occasions when we had children draw in groups, it was interesting to see how the respondents would sometimes observe and reflect on one another's work. For example, as two neighbor boys sat side by side drawing pictures in response to our question about what Katrina looked like, one of the boys peered over at his friend's paper and then looked at his own and said to us: "But we didn't draw what [Katrina] looked like, we drew what it *did*."

Sometimes after we would give a drawing prompt, the children would say things like "I don't know" or "I don't think I remember that." But as they began drawing, they often did remember key details. They would speak out loud, exclaiming, "Oh yeah!" or "I remember that now" as they moved forward with their picture. In one instance, when we asked a boy to draw something good that came out of Katrina, he looked at us, thought about the question, and then asked us, poignantly: "Did anything good come out of Katrina?" We acknowledged that it was a good question, and then we asked if he would like to think about it for a few minutes; during this time, he came up with something positive that he wanted to draw about.

Once the children completed their drawings, we would ask them to hold them up and describe them for us. When we were done, we collected the drawings with the understanding that they might appear in the book. Interestingly, none of the children asked if they could keep them—if they had, we would have asked if we could take the drawing with us, scan it, then mail it back. Children did on occasion, however, ask, "What are you going to do with these drawings?" To which we always responded something along the lines of "We are going to take them all, look them over, then use what we learn in the book."

When we returned home, we scanned all of the drawings and then later matched the narratives from the audio recordings to the drawings for analysis. Through these drawings and the associated verbal descriptions we were able to learn more about the child's view of the disaster and experience during recovery. Sometimes children would draw something that they had not mentioned in interviews and thus the pictures provided new insights and perspectives. In response to the first question we asked, regarding what Katrina looked like, children often drew ominous clouds, threatening waves and/or winds, and treacherous water swirling around homes; the accompanying narrative might be that the disaster was "bad" or "scary." Often children would choose black or brown crayons from the crayon box to draw the murky floodwater or the ominous clouds. In addition to those images, children repeatedly drew representations of upended houses and cars, trees, and/or people affected in the storm.

While we asked the children the same question to encourage their drawing, age often determined the type of drawing that was created. For example, figure B.2 was made by an 11-year-old girl and shows more sophisticated abstract objects that

Figure B.2. Drawing of "what Katrina looked like,"
by Isabel, 11 years old

symbolize the event: the fleur de lis symbol of New Orleans, the waves of the water breaking through the levees, an eye crying showing the sadness, and the "X" hash mark that was drawn on houses after they had been checked by search-and-rescue groups. As an older child, she created a more complex visual representation than some of the younger children whom we had draw for us.

The drawings also provided us with insight into the children's feelings about the disaster and displacement. One boy in our study drew a picture of his beautiful purple house in New Orleans, and described to us his fears that it had flooded in the disaster (see figure B.3).

The children did not just draw bad or traumatic things that resulted from Katrina. They also drew "good things" that happened after the disaster and in response to our question about this area of their life. One young girl drew a picture of two girls, with the words "I made new frineds [friends]" (see figure B.4). It shows a child's positive attitude and the idea that displacement could sometimes open up opportunities for new relationships.

Because creative drawing, sometimes called "free draw" or "free art," where the artist can draw whatever he or she chooses, was something that many of the children had done in school, they were comfortable with this method, and would transition easily between talking to us about Katrina, sharing about their day-to-day lives, and describing their own drawings as they worked. We also sometimes had younger siblings draw pictures to help occupy them while we engaged their older siblings in the drawing and interview activity. The paper and crayons also came in handy in school settings, as at times we wanted to interview adults either before or after school, but

Figure B.3. Drawing of "something difficult that happened because of Katrina," by Chance, seven years old

Figure B.4. Drawing of "something good that came out of Katrina," by Tiffany, six years old

there was a child in the classroom. In those instances, one of us would go over and sit with the child and draw together, while the other conducted the formal interview with the adult. When we were done with the drawing activity, we would always leave some of the blank drawing paper and at least one box of crayons with the children in the study, as we had done with the play-dough.

USING FLASH CARDS IN INTERVIEWS

Just prior to our final data collection trip, we had read a recently published book on methods for studying children.[21] One of the things the author recommended was using visual prompts to put the control of the interview in the hands of the young respondents. Intrigued by the possibilities of using this interviewing tactic, we developed a set of flash cards for use during interviews with the focal children in our study. These cards represented the key spheres of children's lives that we had been learning about over the years of this research: immediate and extended family, friends and classmates, housing, schooling, fun and extracurricular activities, and religious involvement (see figure B.5).

We gave careful thought to which spheres would be represented and how each sphere was depicted on the cards. We settled on the six shown in figure B.5, but we also could have included a number of other key areas that obviously affect a child's post-disaster life, including parental and/or youth employment or health and health care, for instance. In the end, we settled on the six main topics shown in figure B.5.

In terms of how each sphere was represented on the cards, not all of the children lived in single-family homes, so we made two flash cards for "house"—one that looked like a single-family home and another that looked more like an apartment building. We also tried to make cards that showed peers and family members who were both black and white, and families that were not just traditional mother-father–two children structure. For those who were not religious, we either did not use the card or we let the children remove it from the pile on their own. For the "fun" card, we opted against images that showed activities that not all children had access to, such as biking, traveling, or boating. It was important that each child, of any age, could examine the drawing on the card and have the image conjure up thoughts about his or her own life.

As we were conducting the interviews, we laid out the flash cards on the table, bed, or floor, and then asked: "Which of these would you like to talk about first?" We wanted the child respondents to choose and hold the cards themselves, so they had control over the activity. After we laid the cards out, we did not touch them.

Once the child picked up a card, we would then say something along the lines of "Okay, you chose the 'school' card. Will you tell us about that?" We asked these open-ended questions because we wanted to see where the child would go with the conversation. Sometimes children began discussing why they selected a particular card (e.g., "My family is the most important thing to me, so I wanted to talk about

Figure B.5. Flash cards used as interview prompts

that first"). Other times they would explain that there was something they wanted to share about that topic (e.g., "I chose the 'friend' card because my best friend just moved back here, and I want to tell you about that"). As the child began talking, we would ask a series of follow-up questions to make sure we were attaining the information we needed about the child's recovery in that sphere of life and overall trajectory.

After the child had finished sharing about a topic, we would say: "Which one do you want to talk about next?" We proceeded in this way until the child had picked up all of the available cards. (As an aside, it was interesting to watch how the children worked with the cards. They would often pick them up and when finished talking about a topic, they would turn them over or stack them off to the right or the left, as if we were playing a game.)

We used these cards with all of the focal respondents and their siblings, and we found them to be highly effective in terms of allowing the children to set the tone and pace of the interview. The pictures on the cards helped the younger children, who could not yet read, while the adolescents and teens often held the cards and gave thought to which card they wanted to discuss first. As we examined these transcripts in relation to our earlier ones, where we were not using these visual prompts, we could see the difference in terms of how much the children shared and how much easier it was for us to probe and follow up on their responses with additional questions. Previous research has also found that having some type of prop, such as stickers with drawings on them, increases the communication between children and interviewers.[22]

During our closing interviews, we asked the children what they thought of using the cards, since we did not introduce this method until our final round of data collection. One of our seven-year-old respondents told us: "They were kind of helpful, because it gives you topics." Another boy in our study encouraged us to use the cards and picture drawing simultaneously with children. He said:

> You could let them choose a card . . . ask them "which one do you want to do first?" They say "cards." They grab one card, they choose any card they want, or they can draw a picture. So the same thing you did for me, but a little different. They choose . . . they can start out with whatever they want to.

Another child commented simply and enthusiastically: "The cards are so fun."

TRACING THE TRAJECTORIES

A final approach that we used with just a few of the teenage respondents in this study—and only during our final data collection trip seven years after Katrina—was to actually ask the youth to verify whether they thought we had correctly depicted their trajectory (or the trajectory of their siblings). We went about this in the following way: We would place a blank sheet of paper in front of us, and then we would draw the trajectory for the child. So, for example, if the child's recovery was captured by the fluctuating trajectory, we would draw the ups and downs in the line, pausing when there was an "up moment" (e.g., a parent found a job and secured housing) or a "down moment" (e.g., a child had to move schools due to an additional displacement and lost contact with friends and supportive adults) to describe why we thought this was the case. Once the full trajectory, with some associated notes, was sketched out on the paper, we would ask the teen to respond.

We decided to use this approach only with the older youth in our study because it required a great deal of verbal communication and concentration. We thus made the methodological decision to use this with the teens, but not with the younger adolescents and children. In retrospect, we think we could have likely used this approach with some of the younger children as well, but since we were trying out something new, we felt most comfortable carrying this out with the older youth.

After testing this method, we decided that it was, indeed, an interesting way to verify our data analysis and "member check" our presentation of the trajectories. Most of the time the youth agreed with what we had to say, but at some points in the trajectory, they would challenge or offer additional depth and explanation for what we had presented. For example, we did the trajectory-tracing exercise with one focal child's older sibling, who was a young adult by the time of this interview. We wrote up the process in our fieldnotes afterward:

From fieldnotes, October 18, 2012:

At the end of the dinner (after she had some chocolate cake), we got out a piece of white paper and a black Sharpie marker. We told her about the up-and-down fluctuating trajectory and asked for her help in thinking about her younger brother's life since Katrina. It did not appear that she was interested in drawing the figure herself, so we took care of that, but only moved the marker after consulting with her about the points and the direction we should move as we traced the trajectory on the paper. We placed the paper on the table, and the three of us leaned our heads in to work on it together.

For the most part, she was in agreement with our trajectory as we had drawn it. She appeared highly engaged and was talking throughout as she helped us to connect the dots and the lines on the model. There was only one point in the trajectory that she disagreed with, so we discussed it and figured out how to draw that point. It was good that she challenged and corrected us, as it seemed to show that she really was in agreement with the other points, and also that she felt comfortable expressing a perspective different from our own. When we finished the activity, we took a moment to look at the whole trajectory together. It helped us acknowledge what a long and up-and-down journey it had been for her little brother, and for the family as a whole.

In this example, we were able to gain more data from this trajectory activity, as the young woman described above offered new insights and shared stories we had not yet heard. This was somewhat surprising as we had now known her and her family for nearly seven years. We integrated all the new material that we learned from this approach, as well as the other creative methods, into our broader analysis.

The process of gaining trust and developing rapport are of vital importance in ethnographic research. In our work, we purposely engaged in various actions and activities in order to establish more meaningful connections between ourselves and our respondents.

First, we used small-group interviews and respondent-centered, conversational interviewing methods, where we privileged and respected the voices of the participants.[23] We asked open-ended questions and allowed the children and adults to largely direct the pace and content of the interview. We worked to connect first and foremost as human beings, finding common ground as parents or dog lovers or women or as people who care about children, for instance, and then letting that humanness serve as the core of our interactions.

Second, we kept in touch with respondents through telephone calls, letters, email, and text messages between field research visits. Participants almost always called us back when we left messages and regularly responded to our emails. A few of the participants were letter writers, so when we would send cards or letters, we would on occasion receive mail in return from them. Because letter writing is more uncommon these days, we found that some participants, especially mothers, felt that we were particularly "nice" for sending handwritten notes and cards. It also meant a lot to us when we would go into a child's room and see a gift displayed or a card tacked to a bulletin board or taped to the wall.

Third, during our field visits, we often volunteered to take families out to lunch or dinner before or after conducting interviews. We ran errands to the grocery store, laundromat, and Walmart. As described in greater detail below, the families that we took on errands often did not own a car and were struggling financially. We knew this and would often offer to pay the check or the bill.

Fourth, and perhaps most important in terms of establishing trust, we demonstrated a long-term commitment to the people in the study through our ongoing efforts to stay in touch and our return visits to the various research sites. Over time, a number of the participants started introducing us as "our friends from Vermont and Colorado" or as "the people who came here to help us after Katrina." The children in our study sometimes even told us what a difference it made to them as they got to know us over time. For example, one girl who was only eight years old when we first met her, but whom we interviewed many times over the subsequent seven years, said: "I mean, it [being interviewed] brings back memories, but sometimes that's what people need to get it out. I don't mind. In the beginning, it was kind of scary, but now, I feel better about it. It's like a release."

Part of the commitment was also demonstrated by the physical distance we traveled to see participants. It was clear that those in this study were intrigued that we had come such a long way to learn from them, and this showed that we really did care about their stories.[24] One teenager told us: "I'm glad that you all had the time to come down here to interview us. I'm glad of this. That's because I can get my point across to people." Another teen enthusiastically said to Lori: "I'm glad you all did come from way away in Colorado to see us. [I said] 'Hey, my friends comin' from Colorado! I want to meet them.' Colorado, that's far from here!"

A fifth way that we attempted to establish rapport was through sending gifts to the participants that we believed would be meaningful or useful. As described in prior chapters in the book, we understood the suffering caused by a loss of a lifetime of photographs, for example. Therefore, we took pictures of the children and their families and mailed them along with a thank-you note after each one of our data-gathering trips. The children, in particular, tended to enjoy having their photos taken and they would often pose playfully for the camera. After we asked one young girl if we could take her photo while she was coloring on a piece of paper, she turned and said to us: "You gonna take a picture of me? I'm glad. I'm gonna be so cute!"

The children sometimes asked us to take additional photos of them. Because we had digital cameras, and we liked having as many shots to choose from as possible, we always obliged. We showed the children their photos in the digital camera screen after we took them. This exchange captures how things often went with the children in these situations:

YOUNG GIRL: Cheese! Where's the picture? Cheese. Where's the picture? [laughs]
LORI: You're so cute.
YOUNG GIRL: Take another picture. Cheese!
LORI: Okay! Ready? [laughs]
YOUNG GIRL: When the picture's gonna come out?
LORI: Miss Alice and I are going to mail them to you and your family. Come here and look at the screen. You are so cute!
YOUNG GIRL: Take another one!

Although we tried to always be purposeful and genuine about developing and fostering relationships with our participants, we also encountered various barriers along the way. One of the first challenges we encountered occurred during our first forays into the field. This issue was related to the lengthy informed consent form required by our university IRBs. The form was long, dense, and contained complex legal language. We had several situations early in the research where we sensed that the participants were suspicious of or intimidated by the daunting document which we placed in front of them and then would have to ask them to sign on the spot. Several low-income African American women whom we met in shelters in Louisiana initially seemed eager to tell their stories, but then hesitated once we took out the forms. One woman, upon seeing the form, displayed a quick and profound shift in her posture and her facial expression. She had been leaning in, ready to tell us her story. As soon as we produced the sheets of paper, she pushed her chair back from the table, crossed her arms, and her expression became more distant.

It was after that interaction that we decided to apply to our IRBs for "verbal assent" instead of "written consent" for both the adults and the children. This was not meant as a shortcut, nor did it imply that we took the informed consent process any less seriously; instead, we genuinely sensed that the legalistic forms were compromising our ability to conduct the research. Even worse than that, though, we were worried that the forms were somehow doing harm to our participants because they were so lengthy and unwieldy. After speaking about this challenge with representatives from our university IRBs, they actually encouraged us to pursue verbal assent. In response, we modified our existing IRB protocols, and ultimately received permission to ask for verbal assent from the adults and the children in our study. We continued this practice for the duration of the research.

Interestingly, we discovered that verbally explaining the risks and benefits and having a conversation about all the points that were previously covered as part of the form, such as confidentiality, had many advantages. The verbal explanation was easier to understand, allowed us to more completely articulate the issues, and seemed to leave our participants much more at ease. By having a full conversation (instead of handing them a form and briefly going over the points), we increased the trust between us.

Another challenge to keeping trust and rapport emerged as the research progressed. As we got to know the participants better, sometimes they would invite us to events and we were simply unavailable to go. For instance, we were asked to attend a baby shower for one of the young women in our study but neither of us could be there. We were sad about this, and we admittedly worried aloud to one another that our lack of availability might damage the relationship. We sent an apologetic note, and Lori asked her family member who made quilts to create a special blanket for us to send to the baby shower. The blanket integrated the colors of green, gold, and purple, which are so often associated with New Orleans and Mardi Gras. After the young woman received the gift from us, she sent us excited thank-you emails, and later, a photo of her child wrapped in the blanket.

As is probably evident, we genuinely liked the people in our study. We cared deeply about the recovery of the children and the families whom we followed over time. We felt empathy toward them. We believe this type of genuine concern contributes to feelings of trust and goes a long way in helping researchers develop rapport. Liking the participants of your study is not a requirement, of course, but respecting who they are and the lives they are leading creates a research climate of trust and can certainly help build rapport.

IDENTIFYING A DIVERSE SAMPLE

Because we were interested in commonalities as well as differences among children, we needed to include a diverse sample of individuals in our study. At the same time, within that sample we wanted to "dig deep" into each child's life world in order to better grasp the richness and nuance of the child's own individual experience. As described in chapters 1 and 2, we sought both *breadth* and *depth* in this research.

Because we wanted to include as many varied experiences as possible, we intentionally chose children from diverse racial and ethnic backgrounds, from a range of social classes, and an almost equal number of girls and boys. Our final sample included over 650 children and youth and over 100 adults, as discussed in chapter 1. The larger sample included children ranging in age from 3 to 18, as well as children's parents, grandparents, teachers, neighbors, principals, and school counselors. We also interviewed disaster relief workers and shelter volunteers, childcare center staff, church members and staff, and government and nonprofit representatives. As part of this larger data collection effort, we visited different types of schools (public, private, and charter) of varying sizes and with radically different sociodemographic compositions of the students and teachers. Moving into these different field sites exposed us to a diverse array of children and adults.

From the larger sample that we assembled in the first three years of the study, we carefully and intentionally chose seven focal children who represented the experiences of the larger sample in terms of race, age, social class, and family structure; we also sought out children with a range of disaster evacuation and displacement experiences, and with varying degrees of disaster loss. Through interviewing and observing many children and family members from diverse circumstances and in different social positions, we were able to attain the breadth of information about large numbers of children that we were looking for. After we chose the seven focal children, we continued to meet, observe, and talk to other children and adults, but again, as the research progressed, we also really focused in on the focal children and the people surrounding them most closely.

To obtain the depth we needed for our study, we examined the focal children from multiple perspectives. We interviewed and reinterviewed these children, observed them in multiple settings, and interviewed central persons in their lives—their parents, grandparents, siblings, teachers, caregivers, and friends—on many occasions as well. Bringing together many points of view helped us to create a much more vivid and holistic picture of the child's circumstances. Often we heard about situations or experiences from different people, all adding new details or information or opinions about what had happened.

Moreover, we found over time that we were able to gain certain parts of a story from some family members (such as past or present drug use, struggles with depression, etc.) that some members were not willing to share. This filled in gaps and helped us to understand children's situations much more fully. Sometimes respondents wanted to give "socially desirable" responses. One mother, for example, implied that she evacuated with her son and that she made sure he was safe in the disaster. Years later, however, we interviewed several other family members and found out that she was actually not with the family, but out with friends, and did not help her young son evacuate. We were shocked at this development, and thus we revisited several of our earlier transcripts as we were certain the mother had told us she had evacuated with her youngest child. Upon reexamining those transcripts, we realized she had not out-and-out lied to us, but she was clearly being evasive and somewhat

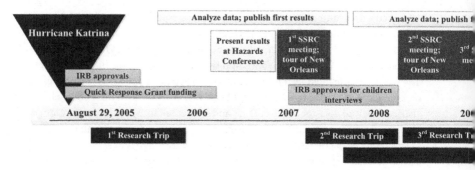

Figure B.6. Research time line

deceptive in her responses. Had we not cast a wide net and talked to many important figures in the child's life, we would have never uncovered this information.

In another circumstance, a teen whom we interviewed described her older brother as "mean" and "angry" and explained how often the siblings got into fights; this contrasted with the older brother's rosier account of their sibling relationship. We tried to take each respondent's narrative at face value, but we were reminded in these instances and others of the importance of attaining multiple perspectives so we could more fully understand the forces shaping children's post-disaster recovery.

TRACKING CHILDREN AND FAMILIES OVER TIME

Because we followed the focal children and families in this study over many years, we developed a number of different methods to ensure that we could stay in touch and also find the families as time passed. In the case of the most highly mobile families—and especially those families with few economic resources and limited social ties—this was no easy feat.

Fortunately, there is a long history in the social sciences of documenting best practices for how to "track and trace" residentially unstable or otherwise disadvantaged populations. This includes low-income families and other groups that are most likely to lack access to telephone services, email and computers, and so forth. In our study, we had families from a range of different socioeconomic backgrounds. Those of middle-class standing often had multiple phone lines (land lines, cell phones for the adults and youth in the family, etc.). Those working-class and especially low-income families in our study typically had fewer resources and lived in much more precarious and resource-scarce situations.

Over the years, we did a number of things to ensure that we could actually stay in touch with the families. These actions included the following:

• We set a schedule so that we would call on a regular basis to check in. We were especially careful to do this with families that we knew lacked access to the

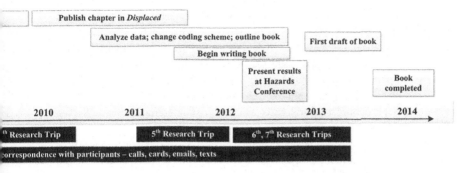

| 2010 | 2011 | 2012 | 2013 | 2014 |

Publish chapter in *Displaced*

Analyze data; change coding scheme; outline book

First draft of book

Begin writing book

Present results at Hazards Conference

Book completed

th Research Trip

5th Research Trip

6th, 7th Research Trips

orrespondence with participants – calls, cards, emails, texts

Internet and/or did not have email addresses. Sometimes it was hard for us to know when to call, as the families in our study kept quite different schedules and we lived in different time zones than our participants. We always asked respondents the best time to call, but on occasion we would call and wake someone up or we would catch someone at work. For the most part, though, the telephone calls worked well.

- We sent cards and letters through the mail. Borrowing an idea from sociologist Annette Lareau, who also followed children and families over time, we mailed birthday cards to the children each year and would enclose a $5 bill inside.[25] We tried to mail other things (small gifts, graduation cards, etc.) periodically as well.
- For those families that had email, we would often write messages to a parent or a child to check in, say hello, share a resource we had found, and so forth.
- We also texted periodically with those in our study who had access to cell phones and text message services.
- We used social networking sites, such as MySpace and later Facebook, to keep in touch with several of the families.[26]

These various methods of following the families, when combined together, helped us to keep in touch for many years (see figure B.6 for an overview of our research timeline). We did not lose any of the families in our study over time, but this took a lot of consistency in terms of scheduling to ensure that we would, indeed, be in regular contact with the families.

ANALYZING THE DATA AND WRITING AS A COLLABORATIVE AND EVOLVING PROCESS

As with all other aspects of this research, we shared responsibility for analyzing and writing up the findings. This meant that we sometimes worked side by side, sometimes divided tasks, and sometimes took turns with certain responsibilities.

We cannot imagine this happening any other way, as we accumulated a great deal of data that took an enormous amount of time to organize, process, analyze, and then write up. By the close of our formal data collection, we had well over 100 transcripts of the audio files we had collected, each ranging in length from 15 to 35 single-spaced pages;[27] copious handwritten and typed fieldnotes; stacks of drawings from children; hundreds of photographs of participants and observation sites; and many flyers, brochures, reports, and other secondary material that we collected while in the field.

Fortunately, because we published chapters and articles as this research was progressing, we were continually analyzing and working with this data. That is, we did not wait until the close of data collection (and the start of writing this book) to begin analyzing the data (see figure B.6). Instead, after each field research trip, we would return from the Gulf Coast and begin organizing the data we had collected. We would take the fieldnotes that we had started while in the field and begin passing those back and forth. We would add to those documents by typing up our remaining handwritten notes and jottings. We would download our audio files and send those off to the professional transcriptionist, who turned the audio recordings into full-text documents for us.[28] We would scan and upload the drawings and then make sure to share them with each other. In short, our first step when returning from the field was to get organized and to get the data in a usable form.[29]

Once we had done this, we uploaded the textual data to Atlas.ti, a qualitative software analysis program that we taught ourselves to use in anticipation of this project. We selected Atlas.ti in part because it was one of the few programs—at least at the time we began our analysis—that would allow us to share a file so that we could pass the data back and forth and share in the responsibility for coding it.

During our first stage of analysis when using Atlas.ti, we coded the empirical material contained in the interviews and fieldnotes at a very general level in order to condense and organize the data into analyzable units. We assigned codes to segments of interviews ranging from a phrase to several paragraphs. We based these codes on emergent or a priori themes (i.e., based on questions in the interview guide or the existing literature on topics such as children and disasters). In some instances, we assigned more than one code to the same text segment. This initial "open" coding[30] resulted in a list of themes, issues, and accounts of behaviors. Second, we began to examine the patterns between different a priori and emergent categories. Third, through the process of constantly comparing these categories with each other, we further condensed the different categories into broad themes associated with our areas of interest for the book. By completing all of our coding in Atlas.ti, we were able to access all the data we needed on any given topic or theme in a more systematic and thorough way.

After this first pass of coding all of the interview and focus group transcripts and fieldnotes, we realized we wanted to shift the conceptual organization of the book. So we went back into Atlas.ti, where we had already coded all of the data, and reread and recoded all of the transcripts associated with the focal children. It was a time-consuming process that added several additional months to our project time line, but it needed to be done in order to access and analyze the data for our new model. While daunting at first, it was absolutely necessary and it allowed us to re-immerse ourselves in the data with a different angle of vision, which was important. We still used the first round of coding for certain things (as in chapter 9 where we report on the different strengths and capacities that we found across all interview transcripts); but the second round of coding ended up being most crucial in terms of the final presentation of data for this book.

We divided the responsibility for coding equally. We scheduled weekly calls and during this time we would decide who was going to code which set of transcripts. We would then "trade off" with the coding from day to day, so that we could read the transcripts that the other one had coded, and then begin coding a new transcript during our next work session.

DECIDING HOW AND WHEN TO ADDRESS DIFFERENCES AND COMMONALITIES: AGE, GENDER, RACE AND ETHNICITY, FAMILY STRUCTURE

There were social, cultural, and demographic differences between us and the participants. For us, one of the main issues was how age affected our research design and implementation. As adults studying children, we were cognizant of the power differential, not to mention size difference, which, as sociologist William Corsaro aptly points out, affects the nature of interactions between child participants and adult researchers.[31] And yet, although we are adults, when we started this research we were fairly young adults, which probably played a role in helping us to gain access to the children and families we wanted to study. Alice was the age of many of the parents in the study, while Lori was younger, which may have prompted some of the young children to see her as an aunt figure, while some of the teens may have felt more at ease because she was an age in between them and their parents.

Race and social class also played an integral role in our research, as it does in everyday life. We are both white, middle class, and have a high level of formal education. Some of our respondents were of the same racial and class backgrounds as us; many were not. Indeed, the largest demographic in our final sample was working-class and low-income African Americans. This was consistent with the pre-storm population of New Orleans.

We were cognizant of the race, class, and education differences between us and our respondents, and we always tried to be sensitive to this. Nonetheless, sometimes we stumbled. For example, one evening we stood outside a high school graduation for one of the girls in our study, soon after having met her uncle for the first time. While trying to make small talk, we asked him where he had gone to high school in New Orleans. It turned out that he had dropped out of school after the sixth grade. This was a sharp reminder to us not to make assumptions about our participants.

Those in our study, in turn, were aware of our differences and sometimes articulated them, and sometimes did not. Those differences sometimes emerged as we participated and observed in different settings. For instance, an all-black barbershop, filled with men and boys, fell dramatically silent when we entered (to bring a young boy in our study in for a haircut). The barbershop remained unnaturally hushed until our departure. The all-black churches we attended, by contrast, seemed unaltered by our presence. Pastors and their wives greeted us warmly and welcomed us to the church. Congregants shook our hands and smiled during the meet-and-greet portion of the service, but most took no notice of us during the rest of the service.

In our one-on-one interviews and conversations, we did not sense any widespread "holding back" because of our demographic characteristics. One black teen, when recounting a story about discrimination by whites that she faced, peppered her story with "no offense to you all" comments, but she still shared the story. Thus, difference was often present and even openly acknowledged, but how it played out in interactions and relationships varied.

We also come from different regions of the country than our research participants in the South, as well as from each other. Lori is originally from a very small farming community in Kansas, while Alice grew up in Washington, DC. Our backgrounds provided each of us with certain knowledge, sensibilities, and familiarity in the research setting, such as Lori's understanding of more rural, religious-oriented culture, and Alice's connections to urban schools and spaces.

Our experiences as members of families also informed how we related to our research participants. Alice is a mother of two young children. Lori does not have children of her own, but has a close connection to her nieces and nephews. We both like children and enjoy their company—something that compelled us to launch this project in the first place and that we believe was important to our ability to successfully access those whom we wanted to study. Lori, who has 10 nieces and nephews back home in Kansas, has the skills to engage and play with young children, while Alice used her experience as a parent to contemplate challenges that the children and families were facing (her own children were near in age to many of the children in the study, so she had a close reference point).

Gender also played a role in our researcher–research participant interactions and relationships. As women, our navigation of the research setting was undoubtedly different in certain ways than it would have been had two men set out to do the same study. Many of the children's primary parents were women, and often these women seemed comfortable speaking to us and allowing us into small, private family spaces to interview them or their children. Mothers allowed us to interview their female as well as male children in bedrooms or other private or semiprivate spaces without another adult present. We were quite aware of how easily we moved in and out of schools, often just signing in with little explanation of our reason for being there, and then being allowed to sit for long periods in school cafeterias or on playgrounds, watching, taking notes, and otherwise observing and interacting with children, all without question. We also walked in the back door of shelters—spaces that, mind you, were being guarded by armed personnel—after Katrina, and we were sure we were never stopped or questioned because we looked like the masses of other white women volunteers who worked in these spaces. We were cognizant of how our racial, class, age, and gender identities intersected, in many ways privileging us and helping us to gain access to areas of interest.

DISCLOSING INFORMATION AND MAINTAINING CONFIDENTIALITY

As with all social science research, what is disclosed in an interview must be treated with the utmost respect and careful discretion. As the majority of our participants were children, we felt an especially strong responsibility to ensure that we protect their identities and their confidentiality. We have never lost sight of the fact that the children and families who participated in this project trusted us with personal, sometimes truly heart-wrenching, information; we thus viewed it as our ethical responsibility to tell their stories without compromising the trust of those who told them in the first place.

The nature of our relationships with the children's parents was critical. Foremost, we had a shared interest: the well-being of their children. At times, though, some parents asked us questions that we could not, in good conscience, answer fully. We would ask them how their child was doing; they, in turn, would ask us how we thought their child was coping after Katrina. To honor the child's confidentiality, we would not divulge what a child had told us in the interview. This was often challenging for us, and we gave it a lot of thought. We recognized that when the parents asked us about their children it was coming from a genuine place of concern: they saw us as professionals who might be able to assess how their children were doing, especially in relation to the other children we were studying. They want to help their child, and they believed, understandably, that we might have information that could assist. Usually, we found a way to answer that was descriptive enough but did not reveal what the child had told us; we could take the issue at hand (e.g., homework, isolation, friendship, nightmares, etc.) and tell the parent, more generally, what we had seen work with other families or what the literature says on the topic. Most often, however, parents understood that they could not ask us questions about what a child said in an interview, so we fortunately were not frequently confronted with having to tell parents that we could not tell them what their child had said to us in confidence.

On a few occasions, parents asked us if they could "listen in" as we were interviewing the children. This is where having two of us, and the fact that our research design involved interviewing the parents and the children, was very helpful. Typically we would divide up and one of us would stay in one room interviewing the adult or adults in the family, while the other would interview the child or children in a separate room. There were a few instances where parents were in the same room (perhaps making lunch while we interviewed a child at the table), but we tried to avoid this if at all possible by going into separate rooms of the house. We always explained this was to respect their confidentiality, and if we encountered particularly persistent parents, sometimes we told them it was required by our university IRBs, which was indeed true.

We also realized that we needed to be careful to protect the adult's confidentiality as we interviewed children in their homes. While Alice was interviewing a 10-year-old boy in his bedroom, he paused and said to her: "Listen to Mama. She talking about me. Because one day I was crying because I wanted to stay in New Orleans." Alice responded, "You think that's what she's telling Miss Lori right now?" He said, "Yeah." As soon as Alice realized that the child could hear his mother so clearly, she tried to refocus his attention on their interview.

Because we were in regular contact with families as well as with children at schools, on playgrounds, and in other public places, occasionally adults or other children would ask us whether someone they knew was going to be featured in our work. We tried to be vague about the book and the participation of particular children or families in the study, again, to ensure that we protected the identities of those children and families we knew were going to appear more prominently in the book.[32]

To protect the identity of those in the study, we changed some of the descriptions of the children and their families. We wanted the reader to have enough information to get a strong sense of the children, the families, how they lived, and of their disaster recovery situations. At the same time, we strove to ensure that no one reading our work could ever identify any particular child or family member. We therefore tried to strike a balance between authenticity and confidentiality throughout the project. For example, we altered some physical descriptions and personal characteristics of children and adults (e.g., modifying someone's job or hobby or omitting reference to the braces on their teeth) and changed the names of some communities (e.g., describing Baton Rouge rather than Shreveport). We spent a lot of time talking about this, and we decided to only make these changes when they would not alter the essence of the experience, but would help protect a child's identity.

We were also careful when we referred to other participants in the study, especially when we were following up on a lead that someone had given us. Indeed, as the research progressed, we found that core participants were often eager to volunteer the names of potential respondents. We appreciated this a great deal (and took it as evidence that people enjoyed being in the study and truly wanted to help us to succeed). We did run into a challenge, though, in that we had to maintain confidentiality at the same time that we often needed to reference the personal contact who had given the name in order to continue the classic "snowball sample." In the end, we tried to strike that ever-difficult balance between using the name of the person who had referred us and not disclosing too much about his or her role in the actual study.

Both of us have interviewed many adults, for various different projects, using small digital audio recorders such as the ones we used in this study to capture the interview data.[33] Most of the adults we encounter in our research are relatively comfortable with these devices and have likely seen them at some point (this is especially true now that recording devices are ubiquitous on smart phones and other modern technology). We learned quickly, however, that children—and especially the youngest in our study sample—had often never seen an audio recorder before. For some, such as kindergarten and first-grade students whom we interviewed in schools, the recorders were a source of fascination. They tended to want to hold them and to say something funny into the recorder before the interview started.

Other children just seemed genuinely curious. One seventh grader asked us: "Why are you recording what we're saying, anyway?" Lori responded: "Miss Alice and I, we are writing a book about children after Katrina. So we have recorded people for the last four years. We have all these recordings and we are going to use them to write a book." The adolescent responded: "Oh!" And that was the end of it.

Not all children, however, were as intrigued by the devices or curious about what we were doing. Some teens, in particular, seemed quite self-conscious, at least initially, as they stared at the recorder sitting in front of them. There were times, especially during the initial interview, when some of the children in our study expressed that they were "nervous" or "shy" to speak into the recorder. We always, of course, asked permission before recording, and we also stopped the recorder on the rare occasion when a child became emotional and either asked us to stop recording or we offered to do so.

Children occasionally would tell us that they wanted to say something "off the record" for the study. We assured the child we would not use anything that he or she did not want us to, and we stuck to that promise. Rarely, a child would pause and say: "You aren't going to tell my mom that, are you?" In those cases, we were careful to underscore for the child that everything he or she said would be kept in confidence.

Once the interviews were recorded and transcribed, we had to make decisions about keeping an authentic voice in the research. The quotes from participants included in this book are exactly their words, as they said them. However, we often removed "um" and "ah" when it seemed that such pauses took away from the participant's ideas. We made sure, though, to never remove anything that would change the tone or intent of the quote. Sometimes, for flow, we would shorten phrases (always indicated in the text with ellipsis, ". . ."). At times we corrected grammatical mistakes in our presentation in the book, again for clarity, but often we left these utterances in.

Most of the children in this study were originally from the South, and thus had a distinctive regional accent and/or a New Orleans style of speaking. For example, children often told us when they had a birthday that they "made eight" or that their brother was "making 10" instead of "turning 10." Children would often say they were "staying" somewhere, such as in a certain neighborhood before Katrina, which, to us, sounded like a temporary arrangement, but for many New Orleanians "staying" somewhere was synonymous with "living" somewhere. The New Orleans vocabulary also included French and Creole words, and children often used words such as "beaucoup" instead of "many" when they spoke to us.

As is common throughout much of the South, the children in the study referred to us as "Miss Alice" and "Miss Lori," which is seen as a respectful way for children to address adults. The adults in the study often ended sentences to us by saying, "Yes, Ma'am," especially after we had asked a question or made a request. We noted that the adults also often referred to us as "ladies," "sweetie," "baby," and "honey," but almost never referred to us as "women." We never took these utterances as pejorative, and instead truly appreciated that respondents spoke to us as they spoke to their Southern relatives and friends.

RESPONDING TO UNMET NEEDS AND SHIFTING VULNERABILITY

What should researchers do when the participants in their study are fighting hunger? Or facing homelessness? Or struggling with posttraumatic stress disorder or other mental health issues? Studying children and families in crisis presents important methodological and ethical issues: when, if at all, is it appropriate to intervene in the lives of participants, and what should be done when study participants have needs that they cannot meet on their own?[34]

Because we were studying persons affected by disaster (many of whom were already living in precarious situations even before their lives were further disrupted by Katrina), we were confronted on multiple occasions with the question of what to do for families that either needed episodic or more long-term assistance. Before continuing here with what we did and how we made decisions about when and how to help, it is important to say a few words about our own philosophy. We viewed each participant in this study as helping us to further our own social science research agenda and goals. Thus, we saw them as giving of themselves—their time, their emotional energy, and their thoughts—for the project. They did not receive payment for completing the interviews, although we tried to give all the participants tokens of our appreciation such as toys, photos, and other small gifts. While we tried to "give equally" in certain ways, at the same time, we recognized that some children and families needed more help than others. We spent many hours discussing this issue, and we finally decided that it was fitting to help those who needed help, when we were able to. Thus, our assistance was not distributed evenly across all participants in the study but rather was given to those children and families who had the greatest unmet needs.

We tried to assist in various ways. As we always had a rental car while in town, and many families did not own or have access to a working vehicle, we drove them where they told us they needed to go. Many families were displaced to temporary housing in isolated areas, such as trailer parks, that were not connected to any public transportation, so getting rides became critical. We drove these families on errands or outings, such as to grocery stores, barber shops, churches, pharmacies, places of employment, laundromats, childcare centers, or car repair shops. In addition to our desire do something for them, we also treasured these moments. During these errands and outings, we learned so much as we spent longer periods of more informal time together. Indeed, while one of us was driving (usually Alice), the other (usually Lori) was sitting in the backseat, most of the time with a little notepad in hand, jotting down important things that the children or adults would say during the drive.

Another way that we assisted was to purchase meals or groceries for the families that were living in food-insecure environments. When we noticed empty cupboards and refrigerators, we communicated to each other that we would need to make a grocery store stop. We would shop with the family and let them choose what groceries they would like, or we would bring food with us to a family's house so we could all eat together while we talked.

As the project unfolded, we decided that eating lunch or dinner out with the family should be a regular part of our research visit. Since we were not paying the participants, we felt this was the least we could do to thank them for the time they were spending with us. Moreover, we found that we often learned as much, if not more, during the informal mealtime as we did during the formal interview time that often preceded those meals.[35] We always tried to let the family decide where they wanted to eat, so we would be at a place they felt comfortable and where they liked the food. During one visit, we took a teenager out to eat, which is described here in an excerpt from our fieldnotes.

Fieldnotes, June 22, 2008:

We sat down to eat at the restaurant he had chosen, and surprisingly, he didn't really like any of the food on the plate. We were a little worried about it, but then we turned over our cards (to indicate we were ready for the main course). Then two waiters started bringing out all of this meat. There were 18 different kinds of meat (this is why we went to this Brazilian restaurant, because he said he really liked that particular kind of food). We had the option to choose chicken wrapped in bacon, steak, ribs, ham, turkey, steak wrapped in bacon, chicken breasts, etc.

It was a LOT of food, and we didn't eat but about a bite of each kind of meat because it was so much. He LOVED it though, and said that it was "the best meal he [had] ever had." The meal cost $40 a piece. Although a bit pricier than what we typically paid, we wanted to do something special because he had revealed that he and his family were, yet again, on the brink of homelessness. It was a sad and overwhelming meal. We tried to ask him some questions as we ate, but at some point, we just stopped probing and focused on "lighter" conversation.

During the course of interviews and while visiting the homes of respondents, we would identify other things that families needed. For example, children from low-income families would mention that they did not have school supplies because their family could not afford them. In response to learning this, we would order a back-pack and supplies to be shipped to the family. When youth or their parents would notify us that they were getting ready to lose cell phone service because they did not have money to pay the bill, we would try to cover that expense for a month or two so we could ensure we could continue to keep in touch and that the family would have a way to communicate with each other. A teen in the study noted that this action "really helped me out. When I needed my bill paid for my cell phone, [you] paid my bill. It was something you didn't have to do, but you did."

If we observed that families did not have basic home items like sheets, blankets, or towels, we would return to our own respective homes and would mail gently used things from our closets to the families in need. When one girl in our study did not have appropriate clothes to wear to school, Alice sent her daughter's hand-me-down clothes. On another occasion, Lori mailed the extra purses in her closet to a mother who expressed a desire to have a "nice handbag" for job interviews.

At times we helped by providing advice or information when it was requested. Parents, or children themselves, would occasionally ask us to help with problem solving or other forms of guidance. Sometimes the questions or requests were directly related to the disaster recovery process, while at other moments families wanted to talk to us about other life or professional matters. One mother, for example, asked us to talk to her son about how to best prepare for a job interview.

We tried to mentor the young people in the study when it seemed appropriate. Some parents asked us to help their children with homework or to provide advice to their son or daughter regarding how they might address a teacher at school. We became a resource for some of the focal children in the study, and even agreed to serve as a reference on job or college applications. One teen in our study accompanied us on some of the interviews we conducted with her friends. She told us later that "it has been real nice. Because when I went on the interviews, I learned a lot of things about my friends, like how their life was during the hurricane. It kind of helped me have a more [positive] outlook on them."

Help also came in other forms. One family, for example, struggled for years with housing and health issues, so Lori made calls to housing advocates and dental clinics on their behalf. In another circumstance, a family's car broke down and Alice was able to use her AAA car service membership to have the car towed. Once we got it to a shop, Lori bought a new battery for the vehicle so that it would run again.

In retrospect, we believe our system of need-based giving worked pretty well. A few professional colleagues raised eyebrows, as some social scientists are not comfortable with "unequal giving" between study participants or even with compensation of any kind for research participation. But we found that confronting so many unmet needs was often overpowering. And since we were able, we could not imagine not helping when we were receiving so much in return. Children and families thanked us and appreciated what we were able to do. One mother said to us, "I was helped a lot by the church [after Katrina], and you all helped me a lot."

We do not believe that our assistance and gifts changed the data or significantly altered the interactions with our participants; we never felt that anyone stayed in the study because of the help that we gave. We worked hard to make sure that the children and their families were not uncomfortable with the assistance. We understood the stigma of charity,[36] and made efforts to frame our help as gratitude and compensation for their participation, not as a handout.

It was not a perfect system, however, and there were times when we had to discuss how to handle a particular need. Only one family actually made direct requests of us—for money, food, and other assistance—and we had to regularly be in contact with one another, as co-researchers, to decide on appropriate parameters when their requests became more frequent, and sometimes more expensive and elaborate. For example, the mother in this family asked us to send several hundred dollars to cover expenses related to her son's senior year in high school. We talked with each other, as we always did when we received such requests, and we decided this was just too much of an expense. We told the mom and her son, and although they were disappointed, they said they understood.

We gave and sent some items, such as clothes and sheets, to this same family that struggled so terribly with finances. But then we would notice when we visited that they did not have these items in their FEMA trailer or other temporary housing. We do not know what had happened to the items, and we did not ask because we did not want to make anyone uncomfortable or self-conscious. Since we gave them as gifts, clearly they were free to do with them as they wished. We were, however, always curious about whether they had sold the items, given them away when they moved, shared them with friends or family in need, or something else.

Perhaps the hardest issue was that we could not help more than a little here and there; many of the families had needs that were systemic and deeply complicated. Also, because almost all of this assistance came from our own funds, we had to figure out how to balance our own financial situations and what we could actually give. We often wrote personal checks or pulled cash out of the bank to pay for the family that most often requested things from us or when we were buying items for other families in need. We did not keep exact track of who was paying what; instead we just tried to find a balance and address the most pressing needs. On occasion, we sold textbooks and then took the money that we earned in that way and shared it with the families.[37]

WORKING AS A TEAM

Over the course of our study, each of us remarked many times: "I could not have done this alone." From the start of this project, in August 2005, we discussed every aspect of the research design, data collection, and data analysis in great detail. We made almost every decision together. Because we live in separate states, we scheduled regular phone calls and would talk for one hour, sometimes two, each week. Every day for years we emailed questions, logistical concerns, thoughts, and ideas for new coding schemes. On the best days, we contacted each other regarding potential conceptual breakthroughs. On more difficult days we wrote each other to lament our slow progress or our challenges with making sense of what we were seeing in the data. Our regular communication helped us to stay in touch and to stay on top of things to make sure the research would continue to progress, even as we juggled the many other demands in our lives.

When we were in the field, the importance of working as a team was apparent. It helped tremendously to have two of us because while one was driving, the other could be looking at a map, helping to navigate, calling the next respondent to confirm an appointment, or otherwise preparing for whatever was coming next in our busy schedule.

There was strength in our numbers, and we experienced an enhanced sense of safety. Although for the most part we felt secure when traveling around, there were a few times when we did not feel that way. For example, one night we had offered to return to a FEMA trailer park in Baton Rouge well after dark, when the mother of one of two of the children in our study was off work and agreed to allow us to come interview her and her son and daughter. As we drove into the park, we saw a large group of men who were out drinking and were yelling loudly at one another. Perhaps it was just innocent partying but it put us a bit on edge because of the alcohol, because it was late and dark outside, and because there were no women present. Alone, we might have been scared, and turned back. Together we decided to forge on. There were many other nights like this, as we traveled through unmarked, dark streets in New Orleans that were still missing signs even years after the storm. There were also times when we walked or drove through areas that were lined with abandoned buildings and had no streetlights. It made us feel much better to be together in those instances.

In terms of data collection, there were real advantages to us being together. As described earlier, we often split up when we arrived in a home, with one of us going off to interview the children, while the other would interview the adults. We rotated who did what, so we would each have a chance to speak with children and adults and so that all of our study participants would be familiar with us. Sometimes we would arrive at a setting and be unprepared for how many people would be there who might be willing to be interviewed. In those cases, we would quickly devise a strategy for us to divide and conduct separate interviews or focus groups. (When we later coded the transcripts that emerged from the recordings, we made sure that the one who had not conducted the interview read and analyzed that particular transcript on the first pass; that way, both were familiar with everything that was said, regardless of who conducted the interview.)

When we conducted an interview together, we would always establish who the "lead" interviewer would be, so we would not overwhelm the participant or be "talking over" each other. This worked well, as one of us could focus on the interview while the other was jotting down observational notes that were later developed into full fieldnotes.

We were also able to pool our collective financial resources to carry out this study. Over the course of the research, we continued to apply for and receive a number of small grants from various funding organizations. We managed to stretch $1,000 here or $3,500 there into enough funding to cover a week or so in the field and then to use any remaining funds to have the interviews professionally transcribed. While traveling, we always shared a rental car and a hotel room, which cut down on expenses. When we were paying out of pocket for things, like the dinners or groceries for families, we would just rotate who was paying, and we decided that it would all come out even in the end.

In addition to pooling financial resources, we were able to draw upon our distinct and overlapping social networks in the study region. After Katrina, we called on these generous individuals quite often. They helped us to find people to include in the study, offered us places to stay, recommended businesses or service agencies we should visit or refer our participants to, and so forth.

We made many difficult decisions together as we confronted challenges in the field. For example, one of the mothers in our study struggled with mental health issues and also had terrible financial problems. In anticipation of visiting this particular respondent, we would call each other to decide what to do, how to respond, and how we might be able to help with the situation. While actually in the field, we knew each other so well that we could just exchange glances or a few quick words, which would guide us with how to proceed in responding to difficult moments.

We also served as a source of emotional support for each other. We saw and heard many terribly difficult things over the course of this research. We recorded accounts of premature death, murder, suicide, drug addiction, rape, bullying, and many other forms of violence and trauma. We spent many hours with children attending dramatically underfunded schools, teachers who had "given up" after one too many challenges, teens who thought they might die during the flooding, and families who saw their loved ones descend into depression. We supported each other as we also experienced the emotional ups and downs as we watched the families go through difficult struggles.

In some cases, we also had to decide if we would intervene in difficult situations. At one point, one of the boys in the study was on the brink of becoming homeless, and we talked about whether we might be able to provide him with a place to stay. In another instance, a mother decided to keep her youngest child out of school after she was hurt in the classroom; the child wanted to return but the mother did not want her to go back. In yet another case, one of the mothers in our study resumed using drugs, years after Katrina. When her daughter revealed this to us—and told us that "strangers were coming and going" from the apartment at all hours of the day and night—we became very concerned about the youngest child in this family, who was still at home. These were exceptionally difficult circumstances for us to be privy to, and we would talk at length about how and when to intervene in these situations.

A final note on working together: we genuinely like and respect each other. We are more than just professional colleagues. We are also very close friends who hold similar values and share similar outlooks on the world. Our commonalities, and our genuine care for each other, made all the difference throughout this journey, as we went to great lengths to protect and support each other personally and professionally. Conducting seven years of research and then spending over two years working on the book took a considerable amount of time and energy on each of our parts. Completing this study was hard work and required a lot of sacrifices, and we were intentional about respecting each other's lives and other personal and professional commitments. This made the entire process joyful in many ways.

CLOSING RITUALS AND KEEPING IN TOUCH

Because we followed the participants in this study for so many years, we became quite invested in and attached to the children and their families. We watched the children change and grow over an extended period of time. In many cases, we shared important and even exceptional milestones with these young people. We attended their school graduations. We were part of their birthday and graduation parties. We watched them perform on stage and listened to them sing and recite poems as they shared their creative outputs with us. As some of the oldest youth in our study aged, we were invited to weddings and baby showers.

As we drew closer to the families, we found that we were invited more and more often to these occasions. We also found that we had a more and more difficult time saying good-bye, as evidenced by this exchange, after we had spent an afternoon and evening with a mother and her daughter:

ALICE: She's going to say her good-bye, because she has to—
LORI: But this is just a temporary good-bye.
ALICE: [The teenage girl] was wondering if we could come to her high school graduation next year, and I said we would love to, if we can make it.
LORI: If there's any part of us that can be down here, we would love to do that.
TEENAGE GIRL: You all can put it in your calendar.

The more we got to know the families, the more intimate things we shared. Sometimes the parents and even the children would refer to us as "family" or "extended family." On occasion they would tell us that they loved us. For instance, one of the grandmothers of one of the focal children in our study wrote us to notify us that her mother (the focal child's great-grandmother) had passed away. We expressed our sympathy through a card and flowers. Upon receipt, she wrote us and said: "Thank you all for the beautiful flowers. They surely helped to lift a bowed down head and spirit. Love you both!" One little girl, whom we had by this time known for years, exclaimed: "Miss Lori. We had fun today!" Lori responded: "Yes we did!" Then, when Lori got up to leave the room for minute, the little girl turned to her and said, "I love you, Miss Lori."

It was a struggle for us as researchers to figure out how we were going to bring this study to a close. We did not want to just "leave" the setting, but we also knew that it was time to end the data collection. At the same time, we realized that we would likely want to continue to trace the trajectories of these children, out of our own curiosity and because one day we may want to update this book. Thus, we tried to balance closing out the study with the need and desire to continue to keep in touch.

As the project started to wind down, we also considered what final questions we might like to ask the children and their families in the study. They had been under our microscope for seven years of their lives and we wondered how they felt about the attention and the project overall. We realized that our study was difficult for many of them to initially conceptualize, but by the end, they understood that their story, their experience, was going to be captured in a book that would be published. It would be something that they could hold in their hands and read. And others, too, would be reading it.

So, we decided to try a few questions on our last visits that we referred to as our "closing ritual." We wanted to create a space for all of the respondents to be able to reflect on their participation and be able to say how they felt about it. We wanted to know what they thought about being part of the study. This was for our own purpose as researchers, and we were also just genuinely curious.

After we asked the closing questions, many respondents took a selfless approach and used the time at the end to wish us well and tell us that they hoped the book would be successful. One mother remarked: "I'll be prayin' that you'll finish that book and it'll be a million-dollar seller. I already know it will."

One of the most frequent responses during these final sessions was to explain to us how their participating had helped them, as it had provided an opportunity for them to talk about what had happened to them and how they were feeling. One father explained how the interview process felt to him:

It's extremely interesting and probably very helpful, because I know the first time you interviewed, it was kind of like a weight thing, like lifting, just being able to talk about it and say everything. It was like a breath of fresh air, maybe almost like a flow-through of Katrina within me, to see what comes out of it. I can't wait to see the book to see everybody else's stories . . . [Being interviewed] is a relief, it's a breath of fresh air to be able to get it out, all the stuff that we went through during the time that this was goin' on, it's like a relief.

One teen (a young woman by the end of the study) felt that talking about Katrina, and having someone to listen, was helpful to her and would likely be to others as well:

I think it's good, because that gets a lot of people to open up, which—a lot of people don't talk about Katrina. That's one of the things that's still kind of buried, hid, and if somebody does talk about it, that'll give them that time to say how they felt. I really think it's good.

When asked if she minded talking about her family and her experience, she responded:

I'm comfortable now. Before you guys probably would have come and talked to me, I'd be like, "No, I don't want to talk about it." . . . So it's good, because you bring it out of people to see where they were and if they're still at that same position, if they have grown, if they haven't. So that kind of pulls them out . . . I would think it was a really smart idea that you guys did this. And I'm sure it probably was a little bit overwhelming, because it's like, "Oh, my God, these people with these issues and problems! What can we do? How can we help them?"

She continued:

But having this time and sitting down with them, knowing these families, that really means a lot. It really does. You're traveling far to come and spend hours or a few minutes, whatever. That touched them in their hearts. It's like, "Man, somebody really did care about me. People love me. They want to know where I am and how I'm doing." That means a lot to people. A lot of people don't say it, but it means a lot to them. They don't have a lot of people that's gonna sit down and talk with them about that, because the other people they're around are struggling with the same exact thing. So if you guys come and sit down and you're pulling it out of them, they're able to release it, and then being that same person, to go and do it to their friends or family members or strangers, whatever. To be that person, like, "Okay, tell me how you felt. Tell me what your ideas are. Tell me what was the struggle." To kind of open them up and build that confidence in them . . . You all are doing a really good job.

Several of the younger children in our study told us that they were happy to be a part of the project or even that they found it fun, as described by this young boy:

I thought it was pretty cool, being in a book is pretty cool, it's like being in a movie, except a little less, because you don't get an image. . . . It was not difficult. It was fun.

As we spoke, he acknowledged that it was different for him because he had not lost as much in the disaster and his recovery was not as difficult as some of the other children in his school. Another boy told us that he liked that we came and asked questions because it showed that "people care." One young boy told us he was happy about being in the book because he believed the book publicity would result in him "becoming famous" on the Internet.

Parents also expressed that participating in the study had been good for both them and their children. One mother reflected on how her son felt about being in our study:

I think he loves it. I think he loved the attention. Because when I told him last week that you all were coming, he was all excited. He was like, "When do I meet 'em? When do I see 'em again?"

Another father simply said: "I'm glad that you guys care to hear about this. I hope it all adds up and makes sense."

One woman, married to the older sibling of one of the children in our study, asked about potential royalties from *Children of Katrina*, believing that there might be a lot of money coming in from the sale of the books. She was the only one who asked about the issue of profit, and she seemed to be asking out of curiosity more than out of a desire for personal gain. We told her that if we made any substantial royalties off the book (which we thought was unlikely), we would talk to respondents about the possibility of donating them to nonprofit organizations that help children in disasters.

Young people told us often that they felt good about their participation in the project because they wanted to help other people. One girl, for example, explained why being in our study was "really nice":

If something was to happen [now], I know how it feels to feel like you've lost everything and I know how it feels to feel like your family is here and there. So I feel like it'll be good, it's a good—it's a advantage to use that book to help others.

In our final conversations with the children and adults in the study, we emphasized, as we had from the outset, that we would be using pseudonyms, or "fake names." Many of them requested that we use their real names. In response, we explained that we were not allowed to because of rules we had to follow that were set by our universities. One older teen preferred to use her own name; she said she was an "open person" but she understood our institutional and ethical constraints, stating, "It is what it is. It is not a problem."

We sometimes asked participants if they wanted to select their own pseudonym, with the understanding that we could not promise to use it. This often produced some funny potential names from the youngest children. The members of one focus group, in fact, laughed for some time as they each came up with a name they would like to use. The conversation proceeded like this:

ALICE: You all are going to be in our book. But you'll have different names. We won't use your real names, so you'll all have different names.
LORI: Do you have any names you might like us to use, if we can?
[laughter]
BOY PARTICIPANT 1: I want to be Gordon Sanchez!

BOY PARTICIPANT 2: I want to be Chico!

GIRL PARTICIPANT 1: I want to be Sarah!

BOY PARTICIPANT 3: I want to be Chuck Norris.

BOY PARTICIPANT 1: I'll be Chuck Wilson.

BOY PARTICIPANT 2: I'll be Chuck Woods.

BOY PARTICIPANT 3: Michael Jordan.

BOY PARTICIPANT 2: No, I want to be Bob.

[laughter]

BOY PARTICIPANT 1: I want to be Owy.

BOY PARTICIPANT 3: I want to be Sadam. How about Quadam?

[more laughter]

Some of the children were much more serious in the process. For example, when one boy quietly picked the name "Darren," we asked what significance it had to him. He replied, simply: "It's just what came to mind." Another boy, three years old, when asked for his name for the book, picked the name of his older brother, his hero, while a 10-year-old boy asked us to make his name "sound cool." One mother asked that we use her and her children's middle names, so when they opened the book they would be able to easily identify themselves. (We decided against this suggestion, or any suggestion to use any actual names, again, in response to our need and desire to protect our respondents' confidentiality.)

These final conversations were a time for the participants to think about and express any concerns about their stories being told publicly. It gave them a chance to tell us if a piece of their experience had to be changed or left out, and why. Overall, children and their parents seemed quite comfortable with the public nature of the study results. When we asked one father if he had any concerns about his son's and the entire extended family's story appearing in the book, he answered, "Not at all." A mother answered the same way, repeating it for emphasis: "Not at all. Not at all."

Having these closing conversations was important methodologically as it allowed us to better understand how children and adults thought about their own participation in the study. But it was also important emotionally, as it allowed us to connect with our participants on a deeper level. In the end, we hope to return to all of our participants and hand-deliver a copy of the published book. This will be just a small token meant to represent the immense gratitude we feel toward them and all that they shared with us over the many years of this study.

RECOMMENDATIONS FOR IMPROVED DISASTER PREPAREDNESS, RESPONSE, AND RECOVERY EFFORTS FOR CHILDREN AND YOUTH

This appendix describes some of the ways that children and youth may be assisted after disaster.[1] We draw on what we learned from our seven years of research in the aftermath of Katrina. We organize our recommendations below by the spheres of children's lives that we focused on: family, housing, school, peers/friendship, extra-curricular activities, and health and well-being. Over the course of our study, we identified a number of actions across each sphere of children's lives that would help inform better preparedness, response, or recovery for children and youth in disasters.

FAMILY SPHERE

Children and youth are embedded in families. Their families of origin are critical to their experiences before, during, and after a disaster.[2] Families with resource depth are in a better position to protect their children from disaster effects and to help them to recover. Conversely, when families have few resources and are not thriving, children tend to suffer various negative consequences. After a disaster, all families, and especially those at the margins, need to attain and/or regain several basic, but crucial, forms of information, support, and opportunities, including the following:

- knowledge of the whereabouts and safety of family
- connection and communication with family members
- reassurance that they will see family members again if separated
- recognition of all family members, including fathers (who may live separately from their children), grandparents, and siblings
- routine and predictability in post-disaster family life
- compassion, as they may be dealing with other crises (such as divorce, death of a grandparent, or parental drug use)

Parents, frequently mothers, take on enormous caregiving responsibilities in a disaster.[3] They need the following types of support:

- support from other family, friends, and advocates
- childcare services that they can trust and that are reliable and affordable
- resources and services that they can help mobilize and then pass on to their children
- assistance if they are too stressed, exhausted, or overwhelmed to cope on their own

SHELTER AND HOUSING SPHERE

Often, shelter and housing needs after disaster are conceptualized as a linear progression from emergency to temporary to permanent housing, with each new move along the way assumed to become more secure.[4] Our research shows that in some cases, especially for the people in the most vulnerable pre-disaster circumstances, housing may be much more uncertain and unstable for long periods of time, and this can have serious ramifications for children's health and well-being.

In regard to post-disaster housing, we advocate for the following:

- offering free childcare and creating child-friendly spaces for children to rest, play, interact, and study at all shelters after disaster
- making sure that those spaces also include key people who will protect, comfort, and otherwise support children recently affected by disaster
- ensuring that shelters have private spaces for girls and boys, men and women, and transgendered individuals, so that child disaster survivors and their families can have privacy and maintain a sense of dignity
- making temporary and transition-to-permanent-housing assistance a top policy priority and funding local, state, and federal government housing programs for families; this is especially vital for those with the least access to private recovery resources, such as low-income renters
- offering temporary housing options that are built using materials that are safe and healthy for occupants
- setting up temporary housing sites that include parks, playgrounds, and other safe spaces
- assisting families to move back into pre-storm homes if desired
- giving displaced residents as well as returnees (including children and youth) a voice in communicating and shaping post-disaster housing options
- being cognizant of potential class, race, and ability biases in housing aid and working to overcome resultant structural disadvantages
- ensuring that emergency shelter spaces and post-disaster temporary and permanent housing options meet Americans with Disabilities Act requirements and are accessible for children and adults with disabilities
- investing in rapidly repairing, rebuilding, and/or creating affordable housing options for families

SCHOOL SPHERE

The school sphere is fundamental to children's recovery. It is a special sphere in that it is unique to children and youth and it has specific time parameters: when the window for schooling is gone, children cannot get it back. Children who do not return to school after a disaster and/or who miss critical stages in their cognitive and social development due to the disruption caused by disaster may suffer irreparable harm in terms of their intellectual growth, development, and future educational goals.

The school sphere, as with the other spheres, is marked by inequality, with some students having access to greater advantages than others. Some school districts, often segregated by race and class, have more resources and support than others; some families have the ability to enroll children in private schools that require tuition or can arrange to be in a high-quality school district, while other families do not have those options. Many things can and should be done to support disaster-affected children and youth and their educational process, including the following:

- emergency preparedness training for childcare workers, teachers, and other professionals who care for children on a regular basis
- assistance with developing emergency response plans, provided by emergency managers and targeted to childcare professionals, school administrators, and others who are responsible for preparing children and the spaces where they play, receive care, and are educated
- reopening of schools (including childcare centers and preschools) as quickly as possible after a disaster; this means allocating proper resources to repair, rebuild, and/or revive schools in disaster zones
- support to schools in receiving communities that receive large numbers of displaced children and youth
- emotional support for students through optional peer-oriented and/or peer-led groups
- access to licensed professional counselors, social workers, and school therapists
- training of all school staff (including staff in receiving communities)—from upper-level administrators, to teachers, to custodians—on how to be supportive of children and youth who have been affected by disaster and how to recognize signs of distress
- provision of disaster preparedness, response, and recovery curricula within classrooms
- lesson plans and assignments designed to actively engage children in projects relevant to their lives and communities (e.g., risk-mapping activities allow children to identify and locate the threats in their communities; project-based learning programs allow children to design their own solutions to challenges they identify; art therapy projects can help children to process their disaster experience)

- opportunities for children to help their schools' and classmates' recovery; this could, for example, come in the form of service learning, fund-raising, mentoring programs, or community action activities
- immediate and long-term support for teachers, who are often recovering from disaster themselves (e.g., financial, professional, and emotional support)
- training of school staff regarding the possible bullying and stigmatizing of disaster survivors; staff should be reminded that such bullying may be exacerbated by perceptions about region of origin, gender, age, race, or other characteristics
- integration of displaced children in classrooms, with familiar faces from their home community if possible
- establishment of predictable routines within classrooms and schools
- funding for school programs in arts, music, drama, and creative writing to encourage expression and foster healing

PEERS/FRIENDSHIPS SPHERE

All of the children in our study, regardless of their personal characteristics or post-disaster trajectory, spoke of the importance of their friends and peers during the interviews. When they were separated from friends, they talked about the lengths they went to in order to find or reunite with them. Often locating, communicating with, and being able to see friends was dependent on a family's resources, such as access to computers and transportation. When children were fortunate enough to return to the same classroom or neighborhood with their pre-storm friends, they would articulate how much that meant to them.

Friends matter a lot. Limited research, however, has focused on the role of friends in children's lives in the disaster aftermath.[5] Yet, there are many things that could be done to help children and youth in the friendship/peer sphere during disaster recovery, such as the following:

- recognizing the importance of friendships and peer support and the way these dynamics affect a child's recovery
- having adults and other youth help displaced children to locate and reconnect with their friends
- facilitating children's communication with old friends—through calling, texting, emailing, social media, and other mediums—so that disaster-affected children can know they are safe
- helping children make new friends in new situations through "buddy programs" or other means
- supporting children as they cope with separation or loss of old friends, classmates, and/or boyfriends and girlfriends who are now far away

EXTRACURRICULAR ACTIVITIES SPHERE

The extracurricular sphere permeates many different contexts, such as religious institutions, athletic teams, or organizations like scouts or 4-H. This sphere encompasses the places where children and youth may find friends, connect to supportive adults outside their household, discover new strengths of their own, acquire new life skills, gain access to resources, and create new social networks outside of family and school. Once again, inequality marks this sphere, and attention must be paid to how to give children from low-income families the same access to these important activities. The following would help all children post-disaster:

- create age-appropriate extracurricular activities for children and youth of all ages
- integrate children into community- or faith-based groups, as appropriate
- encourage children to find an in-school and/or afterschool activity that interests them
- help children to take on leadership roles in extracurricular activities
- provide practical and financial assistance, such as transportation, fees, uniforms, paperwork, and various accommodations
- open up spaces for children and youth to share their experiences through various creative mediums, including writing, art, dance, and other forms of expression

HEALTH AND WELL-BEING SPHERE

The physical and emotional health and well-being of children and youth is a fundamental part of their recovery and is highly contingent on the status of the other spheres of their lives. When children lack stable housing, when their schools remain closed, when their parents are struggling, when they are separated from their friends, and when they are unable to participate in meaningful extracurricular activities, children are likely to suffer physically and emotionally. Health and well-being is not distributed equally. Low-income children and children of color face more health challenges, such as asthma and food insecurity, and have less access to high-quality, affordable health care. Focusing on the health and well-being of all children—across all stages of disaster—is essential. Our recommendations for promoting health and well-being include the following:

- recognizing the importance and interconnectedness of physical and emotional health
- increasing preparedness efforts in order to diminish children's exposure to disaster
- assisting in evacuation so that children are not exposed to life-threatening, traumatizing experiences

- supporting children in the disaster aftermath by providing immediate as well as long-term access to affordable and quality mental and physical health care
- teaching children about fundamental health issues and how to make healthy choices for their bodies (e.g., food, tobacco, drugs, alcohol, sex)
- providing safe places for children to get fresh air and exercise
- recognizing that environmental destruction can affect children more than adults, as their bodies are growing and toxins can do more damage
- restricting children's access to areas where there are environmental risks such as spilled oil, sewage, asbestos, contaminated soils, etc.
- lowering the risks to children from the effects of disaster damage to buildings and other structures (black mold, mildew, hazards in disaster demolition and abandoned structures, etc.)
- decreasing exposure to toxic or hazardous materials in the rebuilding process (carpet glues, paint, cleaning solvents, etc.) and limiting time spent in construction sites (home, school, religious institution, library, community center, etc.)
- planning for and providing long-term emotional assistance, such as counseling, as disaster effects are enduring[6]

The aforementioned recommendations for encouraging better preparedness and more rapid recovery among children and youth are not mutually exclusive, nor are they exhaustive. They are meant to promote thinking about how individuals and institutions can come together to support children and youth in the disaster aftermath. This is not meant to be a "final statement" on what children and youth need. Instead, we hope to take what we learned from children in Katrina and use that to focus attention and to promote discussion of how to support the youngest survivors during times of distress and ultimately reduce suffering in future disasters.

NOTES

FOREWORD

1. Garmezy, Norman. 1971. "Vulnerability Research and the Issue of Primary Prevention." *American Journal of Orthopsychiatry* 41(1): 101–116.

2. Rolf, Jon E. 1999. "Resilience: An Interview with Norman Garmezy." Pp. 5–14 in *Resilience and Development: Positive Life Adaptations*, edited by M. D. Glantz and J. L. Johnson. New York: Kluwer Academic/Plenum.

3. Abramson, David M., Irwin Redlener, Tasha Stehling, and Elizabeth Fuller. 2007. "The Legacy of Katrina's Children: Estimating the Numbers of At-Risk Children in the Gulf Coast States of Louisiana and Mississippi." National Center for Disaster Preparedness. Research Brief 12. New York: Mailman School of Public Health, Columbia University. http://hdl.handle.net/10022/AC:P:8845. Accessed on August 25, 2014.

4. U.S. House of Representatives. 2006. "A Failure of Initiative: The Final Report of the Select Bipartisan Committee to Investigate the Preparation for and Response to Hurricane Katrina." Washington, DC: U.S. House of Representatives. http://www.katrina.house.gov/. Accessed on November 7, 2014.

5. Masten, Ann S. 2014. *Ordinary Magic: Resilience in Development*. New York: Guilford Press.

6. O'Dougherty Wright, Margaret, Ann S. Masten, and Angela J. Narayan. 2013. "Resilience Processes in Development: Four Waves of Research on Positive Adaptation in the Context of Adversity." Pp. 15–38 in *The Handbook of Resilience in Children*, 2nd ed., edited by S. Goldstein and R. Brooks. New York: Springer.

7. Anderson, William A. 2005. "Bringing Children into Focus on the Social Science Disaster Research Agenda." *International Journal of Mass Emergencies and Disasters* 23(3): 159–175.

CHAPTER 1

1. Camfield, Laura, Natalia Streuli, and Martin Woodhead. 2008. "Children's Well-Being in Contexts of Poverty: Approaches to Research, Monitoring, and Participation." Young Lives Technical Note no. 12. Oxford: Department of International Development, University of Oxford, p. 9.

2. Irwin, Jude, Fran Waugh, and Michelle Bonner. 2006. "The Inclusion of Children and Young People in Research on Domestic Violence." *Communities, Children, and Families Australia* 1(1): 17–23, p. 17.

3. Boocock, Sarane Spence, and Kimberly Ann Scott. 2005. *Kids in Context: The Sociological Study of Children and Childhoods*. New York: Rowman and Littlefield.

4. Lloyd-Smith, Mel, and Jane Tarr. 2000. "Researching Children's Perspectives: A Sociological Dimension." Pp. 59–70 in *Researching Children's Perspectives*, edited by A. Lewis and G. Lindsay. Philadelphia: Open University Press.

5. Peek, Lori. 2008. "Children and Disasters: Understanding Vulnerability, Developing Capacities, and Promoting Resilience." *Children, Youth and Environments* 18(1): 1–29.

6. Handel, Gerald, Spencer E. Cahill, and Frederick Elkin. 2007. *Children and Society: The Sociology of Children and Childhood Socialization*. Los Angeles: Roxbury.

7. Ibid., p. 28.

8. Babugura, Agnes A. 2008. "Vulnerability of Children and Youth in Drought Disasters: A Case Study of Botswana." *Children, Youth and Environments* 18(1): 126–157; McFarlane, Alexander C. 1987. "Family Functioning and Overprotection following a Natural Disaster: The Longitudinal Effects of Post-Traumatic Morbidity." *Australian and New Zealand Journal of Psychiatry* 21: 210–218.

9. Boocock and Scott, 2005, p. 33.

10. Children in a Changing Climate. 2009. "A Right to Participate: Securing Children's Role in Climate Change Adaptation." Brighton: IDS/Children in a Changing Climate, p. 6.

11. Fleer, Marilyn, and Gloria Quiñones. 2009. "A Cultural-Historical Reading of 'Children as Researchers.'" Pp. 86–107 in *Childhood Studies and the Impact of Globalization: Policies and Practices at Global and Local Levels*, edited by M. Fleer, M. Hedegaard, and J. Tudge. New York: Routledge, p. 104.

12. For information on the many reasons why individuals did not or could not evacuate in advance of Hurricane Katrina, see Brodie, Mollyann, Erin Weltzien, Drew Altman, Robert J. Blendon, and John M. Benson. 2006. "Experiences of Hurricane Katrina Evacuees in Houston Shelters: Implications for Future Planning." *American Journal of Public Health* 96(8): 1402–1408.

13. Katrina resulted in disproportionate death rates among the elderly and African Americans. Studies show that among persons who perished in New Orleans in the hurricane, 67 percent were at least 65 years old; prior to the storm, this group represented just 12 percent of the population. Moreover, in Orleans Parish, the mortality rate among black adults was 1.7 to 4 times higher than among white adults. For more information on the missing and deceased, see Brunkard, Joan, Gonza Namulanda, and Raoult Ratard. 2008. "Hurricane Katrina Deaths, Louisiana, 2005." *Disaster Medicine and Public Health Preparedness* 2(4): 215–223; Sharkey, Patrick. 2007. "Survival and Death in New Orleans: An Empirical Look at the Human Impact of Katrina." *Journal of Black Studies* 37(4): 482–501.

14. Plyer, Allison. 2014. "Facts for Features: Katrina Impact." New Orleans: The Data Center. http://www.datacenterresearch.org/data-resources/katrina/facts-for-impact/. Accessed on November 11, 2014.

15. Peek, Lori, and Kai Erikson. 2008. "Hurricane Katrina." *Blackwell Encyclopedia of Sociology*, edited by G. Ritzer. Oxford: Blackwell.

16. Louisiana Department of Health and Hospitals. 2006. "Hurricane Katrina: Deceased Reports." http://www.dhh.louisiana.gov/offices/page.asp?ID=192&Detail =5248. Accessed on September 30, 2011.

17. The last child to be brought back together with her family after Hurricane Katrina was reunited in April 2006—nearly eight months after the storm. For a full accounting of the scope of the separations that children and their families endured, see National Center for Missing and Exploited Children. 2006. "Final Report: Katrina/Rita Missing Persons Hotline." http://www.missingkids.com/en_US /documents/KatrinaHotlineUpdate.pdf. Accessed on September 30, 2011.

18. Davis, Mary Ann, and Lee M. Miller. 2014. "The Impact of Hurricane Katrina on the U.S. Foster-Care System." *Children, Youth and Environments* 24(1): 82–107.

19. Casserly, Michael. 2006. "Double Jeopardy: Public Education in New Orleans before and after the Storm." Pp. 197–214 in *There Is No Such Thing as a Natural Disaster: Race, Class, and Hurricane Katrina*, edited by C. Hartman and G. D. Squires. New York: Routledge.

20. Abramson, David, Irwin Redlener, Tasha Stehling-Ariza, and Elizabeth Fuller. 2007. "The Legacy of Katrina's Children: Estimating the Numbers of Hurricane-Related At-Risk Children in the Gulf Coast States of Louisiana and Mississippi." Research brief prepared by the National Center for Disaster Preparedness in collaboration with the Children's Health Fund. New York: Mailman School of Public Health, Columbia University.

21. The Scott S. Cowen Institute for Public Education Initiatives. 2010. "The State of Public Education in New Orleans: Five Years after Hurricane Katrina." New Orleans: Tulane University.

22. McLaughlin, Katie A., John A. Fairbank, Michael J. Gruber, Russell T. Jones, Matthew D. Lakoma, Betty J. Pfefferbaum, Nancy A. Sampson, and Ronald C. Kessler. 2009. "Serious Emotional Disturbance among Youths Exposed to Hurricane Katrina Two Years Postdisaster." *Journal of the American Academy of Child and Adolescent Psychiatry* 48(11): 1069–1078.

23. D'Antonio, Heather. 2009. "The State of Mental Health Care in Post-Katrina New Orleans." *Louisiana Law Review* 69: 661–689.

24. Save the Children. 2006. "Katrina Response: Protecting the Children of the Storm." Westport, CT: Save the Children.

25. Lauten, Anne Westbrook, and Kimberly Lietz. 2008. "A Look at the Standards Gap: Comparing Child Protection Responses in the Aftermath of Hurricane Katrina and the Indian Ocean Tsunami." *Children, Youth and Environments* 18(1): 158–201.

26. Casserly, 2006.

27. For a statement on ethical issues in researching Katrina survivors, see Browne, Katherine E., and Lori Peek. 2014. "Beyond the IRB: An Ethical Toolkit for Long-Term Disaster Research." *International Journal of Mass Emergencies and Disasters* 32(1): 82–120.

28. Phillips, Brenda. 2002. "Qualitative Methods and Disaster Research." Pp.

194–211 in *Methods of Disaster Research*, edited by R. A. Stallings. Philadelphia: Xlibris.

29. Miller, Lee M. 2012. "The Receiving Communities: Section Introduction." Pp. 25–30 in *Displaced: Life in the Katrina Diaspora*, edited by L. Weber and L. Peek. Austin: University of Texas Press.

30. For studies on shifting contexts of reception in communities where Katrina evacuees landed, see Miller, Lee M. 2012. "Katrina Evacuee Reception in Rural East Texas: Rethinking Disaster 'Recovery'." Pp. 104–118 in *Displaced: Life in the Katrina Diaspora*, edited by L. Weber and L. Peek. Austin: University of Texas Press; Peek, Lori. 2012. "They Call it 'Katrina Fatigue': Displaced Families and Discrimination in Colorado." Pp. 31–46 in *Displaced: Life in the Katrina Diaspora*, edited by L. Weber and L. Peek. Austin: University of Texas Press.

31. Lareau, Annette. 2003. *Unequal Childhoods: Class, Race, and Family Life.* Berkeley: University of California Press.

32. Class status can be and is regularly defined many different ways. In our research, we brought together three indicators to identify a family's social class: education, employment, and wealth. We have operationalized those indicators using the following parameters: *Middle-class children* belong to families where at least one parent has a college degree or some other higher education credential and/or is stably employed in a highly skilled professional or managerial position. Middle-class families also own homes and working automobiles. *Working-class children* are members of families where at least one parent has steady but not high-paying employment. These families may own modest homes, but they tend to have accumulated only limited or no net wealth. *Low-income children* and their families are just getting by; their parents have not earned a college or technical school degree. They are employed inconsistently, often in temporary, low-skilled, dead-end positions. They do not own homes and, if they own a car, it is usually an unreliable one. *Poor children* and their families struggle financially in every way—precarious or no permanent housing, no automobile, no parental employment, and no wealth. For a discussion of the complexities of defining social class, see Lareau, Annette, and Dalton Conley, eds. 2008. *Social Class: How Does It Work?* New York: Russell Sage Foundation; Wright, Erik Olin, ed. 2005. *Approaches to Class Analysis.* Cambridge: Cambridge University Press.

CHAPTER 2

1. For overviews of the sociological study of childhood and discussion of the importance of researching children and youth in social and historical context, see Corsaro, William. 2014. *The Sociology of Childhood*, 4th ed. Los Angeles: Sage; Pugh, Allison, J. 2014. "The Theoretical Costs of Ignoring Childhood: Rethinking Independence, Insecurity, and Inequality." *Theory and Society* 43: 71–89.

2. Abramson, David M., Yoon Soo Park, Tasha Stehling-Ariza, and Irwin Red-

lener. 2010. "Children as Bellwethers of Recovery: Dysfunctional Systems and the Effects of Parents, Households, and Neighborhoods on Serious Emotional Disturbance in Children after Hurricane Katrina." *Disaster Medicine and Public Health Preparedness* 4: S17–S27.

3. Masten, Ann S., and Jelena Obradovic. 2008. "Disaster Preparation and Recovery: Lessons from Research on Resilience in Human Development." *Ecology and Society* 13(1): 9.

4. Weems, Carl F., and Stacy Overstreet. 2008. "Child and Adolescent Mental Health Research in the Context of Hurricane Katrina: An Ecological Needs-Based Perspective and Introduction to the Special Section." *Journal of Clinical Child and Adolescent Psychology* 37(3): 487–494, p. 489.

5. Jabry, Amer. 2005. "After the Cameras Have Gone: Children in Disasters." London: Plan International. In this report, Jabry argues that the media has long used children's suffering as a device to garner readers, but journalists and reporters rarely are able to stay in the setting long enough to understand the magnitude of children's loss.

6. For a comprehensive overview of how social stratification and inequality influence disaster outcomes, see Reid, Megan. 2013. "Disasters and Social Inequalities." *Sociology Compass* 7(11): 984–997.

7. Phillips, Brenda D., Deborah S. K. Thomas, Alice Fothergill, and Lynn Blinn-Pike, eds. 2010. *Social Vulnerability to Disasters*. Boca Raton, FL: CRC Press.

8. Fothergill, Alice, Enrique Maestas, and Joanne Derouen Darlington. 1999. "Race, Ethnicity, and Disasters in the United States: A Review of the Literature." *Disasters* 23(2): 156–173.

9. For summaries of research on income, poverty, and disasters see McCoy, Brenda, and Nicole Dash. 2013. "Class." Pp. 83–112 in *Social Vulnerability to Disasters*, 2nd ed., edited by D. S. K. Thomas, B. D. Phillips, W. E. Lovekamp, and A. Fothergill. Boca Raton, FL: CRC Press; Fothergill, Alice, and Lori Peek. 2004. "Poverty and Disasters in the United States: A Review of the Sociological Literature." *Natural Hazards* 32: 89–110.

10. Enarson, Elaine. 2010. "Gender." Pp. 123–154 in *Social Vulnerability to Disasters*, edited by B. D. Phillips, D. S. K. Thomas, A. Fothergill, and L. Blinn-Pike. Boca Raton, FL: CRC Press.

11. Peek, Lori. 2010. "Age." Pp. 155–185 in *Social Vulnerability to Disasters*, edited by B. D. Phillips, D. S. K. Thomas, A. Fothergill, and L. Blinn-Pike. Boca Raton, FL: CRC Press.

12. Save the Children. 2007. "Legacy of Disasters: The Impact of Climate Change on Children." London: Save the Children.

13. Ibid.

14. Lindsay, Bruce R., and Francis X. McCarthy. 2012. "Stafford Act Declarations, 1953–2011: Trends and Analyses, and Implications for Congress." Congressional Research Service (CRS) Report for Congress. http://www.fas.org/sgp/crs/homesec/R42702.pdf. Accessed on March 4, 2013.

15. Peek, Lori. 2008. "Children and Disasters: Understanding Vulnerability, Developing Capacities, and Promoting Resilience: An Introduction." *Children, Youth and Environments* 18(1): 1–29.

16. Norris, Fran H., Matthew J. Friedman, Patricia J. Watson, Christopher M. Byrne, Eolia Diaz, and Krzysztof Kaniasty. 2002. "60,000 Disaster Victims Speak: Part I. An Empirical Review of the Empirical Literature, 1981–2001." *Psychiatry* 65(3): 207–239.

17. Wang, Cong-Wen, Cecilia L. W. Chan, and Rainbow T. H. Ho. 2013. "Prevalence and Trajectory of Psychopathology among Child and Adolescent Survivors of Disasters: A Systematic Review of Epidemiological Studies across 1987–2011." 2013. *Social Psychiatry and Psychiatric Epidemiology* 48: 1697–1720.

18. Temple, Jeff R., Patricia van den Berg, John F. Thomas, James Northcutt, Christopher Thomas, and Daniel H. Freeman. 2011. "Teen Dating Violence and Substance Use following a Natural Disaster: Does Evacuation Status Matter?" *American Journal of Disaster Medicine* 6(4): 201–206.

19. Weissbecker, Inka, Sandra E. Sephton, Meagan B. Martin, and David M. Simpson. 2008. "Psychological and Physiological Correlates of Stress in Children Exposed to Disaster: Review of Current Research and Recommendations for Intervention." *Children, Youth and Environments* 18(1): 30–70.

20. Zahran, Sammy, Lori Peek, and Samuel D. Brody. 2008. "Youth Mortality by Forces of Nature." *Children, Youth and Environments* 18(1): 371–388.

21. For evidence of the increased incidence of child abuse following disasters see Curtis, Thom, Brent C. Miller, and E. Helen Berry. 2000. "Changes in Reports and Incidence of Child Abuse following Natural Disasters." *Child Abuse and Neglect* 24(9): 1151–1162; Keenan, Heather T., Stephen W. Marshall, Mary Alice Nocera, and Desmond K. Runyan. 2004. "Increased Incidence of Inflicted Traumatic Brain Injury in Children after a Natural Disaster." *American Journal of Preventive Medicine* 26(3): 189–193.

22. For an assessment of the role natural disasters and other crises play in heightening children's vulnerability to trafficking see Maalla M'jid, Najat. 2011. "Report of the Special Rapporteur on the Sale of Children, Child Prostitution and Child Pornography, 19th Session of Human Rights Council." New York: United Nations Office on Drugs and Crime (UNODC). 2008. "An Introduction to Human Trafficking: Vulnerability, Impact, and Action." Vienna: UNODC; United States Agency for International Development (USAID). 2006. "Literature Review: Trafficking in Humanitarian Emergencies." Washington, DC: USAID.

23. Research from across the United States shows that residential mobility and changing schools increases the chances for dropout. For example, Silver and colleagues (2008) found in a study of Los Angeles high school students that those youth who changed schools at least once were twice as likely to not graduate as students who did not change schools during high school. Reynolds and coauthors' (2009) review of 13 relevant studies found that students who changed residences three or more times in their lifetimes were three times more likely to drop out than youth

who never moved. High residential mobility also has long-term consequences for very young children. A longitudinal study by Ensminger et al. (2003) found that children who moved three or more times between birth and first grade had 70 percent higher odds of dropout than non-movers. For more information see Ensminger, Margaret E., Shannon G. Hanson, Anne W. Riley, and Hee-Soon Juon. 2003. "Maternal Psychological Distress: Adult Sons' and Daughters' Mental Health and Educational Attainment." *Journal of the American Academy of Child and Adolescent Psychiatry* 42(9): 1108–1115; Gasper, Joseph, Stefanie DeLuca, and Angela Estacion. 2012. "Switching Schools: Revisiting the Relationship between School Mobility and High School Dropout." *American Educational Research Journal* 49(3): 487–519; Reynolds, Arthur J., Chin-Chih Chen, and Janette E. Herbers. 2009. "School Mobility and Educational Success: A Research Synthesis and Evidence on Prevention." Presented at the Workshop on the Impact of Mobility and Change on the Lives of Young Children, Schools, and Neighborhoods. June 29–30. Washington, DC: National Academies Press; Rumberger, Russell W. 2011. *Dropping Out: Why Students Drop out of High School and What Can Be Done about It.* Cambridge, MA: Harvard University Press; Rumberger, Russell W., and Katherine A. Larson. 1998. "Student Mobility and the Increased Risk of High School Dropout." *American Journal of Education* 107: 1–35; Silver, David, Marisa Saunders, and Estela Zarate. 2008. "What Factors Predict High School Graduation in the Los Angeles Unified School District." Policy Brief. California Dropout Research Project. Santa Barbara: University of California.

24. Students who fail courses in middle school or early high school are less likely to graduate than their peers who pass all their courses. For example, Silver et al. (2008) found that students who passed ninth-grade algebra were twice as likely to graduate as students who failed it. Grade-point average in middle school has also been shown to be more predictive of dropout than scores on eighth-grade academic performance tests. See Kurlaender, Michal, Sean F. Reardon, and Jacob Jackson. 2008. "Middle School Predictors of High School Achievement in Three California School Districts." California Dropout Research Project. Santa Barbara: University of California; Rumberger, 2011; Saunders, Marisa, David Silver, and Estela Zarate. 2008. "The Impact of High Schools on Student Achievement within the Los Angeles Unified School District." Latino Scorecard Education Action Team. Los Angeles: Institute for Democracy, Education, and Access; Silver et al., 2008.

25. Peek, 2010.

26. Lonigan, Christopher J., Mitsuko P. Shannon, Charlotte M. Taylor, A. J. Finch, Jr., and Floyd R. Sallee. 1994. "Children Exposed to Disaster: II. Risk Factors for the Development of Post-Traumatic Symptomatology." *Journal of the American Academy of Child and Adolescent Psychiatry* 33(1): 94–105; Shannon, Mitsuko P., Christopher J. Lonigan, A. J. Finch, Jr., and Charlotte M. Taylor. 1994. "Children Exposed to Disaster: I. Epidemiology of Post-Traumatic Symptoms and Symptom Profiles." *Journal of the American Academy of Child and Adolescent Psychiatry* 33(1): 80–93; Vogel, Juliet M., and Eric M. Vernberg. 1993. "Part 1: Children's Psychological Responses to Disasters." *Journal of Clinical Child Psychology* 22(4): 464–484.

27. Young, Helen, and Susanne Jaspars. 1995. "Nutrition, Disease, and Death in Times of Famine." *Disasters* 19(2): 94–109.

28. Ibid.

29. Peek, 2008.

30. Bourdieu, Pierre. 1986. "The Forms of Capital." Pp. 241–258 in *The Handbook of Theory and Research for the Sociology of Education*, edited by J. Richardson. New York: Greenwood Press, p. 248.

31. Barnshaw, John, and Joseph Trainor. 2007. "Race, Class, and Capital amidst the Hurricane Katrina Diaspora." Pp. 91–105 in *The Sociology of Katrina: Perspectives on a Modern Catastrophe*, edited by D. L. Brunsma, D. Overfelt, and J. S. Picou. Lanham, MD: Rowman and Littlefield.

32. Lareau, Annette. 2003. *Unequal Childhoods: Class, Race and Family Life.* Berkeley: University of California Press.

33. Lareau, Annette, and Elliot B. Weininger. 2003. "Cultural Capital in Educational Research: A Critical Assessment." *Theory and Society* 32: 567–606.

34. For an account of how race, class, and cultural capital condition interactions with disaster recovery officials, see Browne, Katherine E. 2015. *Standing in the Need: Culture, Comfort, and Coming Home after Katrina.* Austin: University of Texas Press.

35. Calarco, Jessica McCrory. 2011. "'I Need Help!' Social Class and Children's Help-Seeking in Elementary School." *American Sociological Review* 76: 862–882.

36. Barnshaw and Trainor, 2007.

37. Fothergill and Peek, 2004.

38. For a discussion of the contributions of childhood scholars in identifying children's roles as active social agents, see Pugh, 2014.

39. Corsaro, 2014.

40. Rosier, Katherine Brown. 2000. *Mothering Inner-City Children: The Early School Years.* New Brunswick, NJ: Rutgers University Press.

41. Anderson, William A. 2005. "Bringing Children into Focus on the Social Science Disaster Research Agenda." *International Journal of Mass Emergencies and Disasters* 23(3): 159–175.

42. Plan International with World Vision International. 2009. "Children on the Frontline: Children and Young People in Disaster Risk Reduction." London: Plan International UK; Save the Children. 2011. "Children's Charter: An Action Plan for Disaster Risk Reduction for Children by Children." London: Save the Children UK.

43. United Nations International Strategy for Disaster Reduction. 2011. "Children and Young People are Partners for Disaster Risk Reduction: Step Up for Disaster Risk Reduction!" New York: UNISDR. http://www.unisdr.org/2011/iddr/. Accessed on January 12, 2012.

44. Owen, James. 2005. "Tsunami Family Saved by Schoolgirl's Geography Lesson." *National Geographic News*, January 18.

45. United Nations International Strategy for Disaster Reduction. 2011. "Chil-

dren's Charter: How Empowering Children Saves Lives." http://www.unisdr.org/archive/22601. Accessed on January 15, 2012.

46. Ibid.

47. Nikku, BalaRaju, Nepali Sah, and Ravi Karkara, with Sibghatullah Ahmed. 2006. "Child Rights Perspective in Response to Natural Disasters in South Asia: A Retrospective Study." Kathmandu, Nepal: Save the Children.

48. Mitchell, Tom, Katharine Haynes, Nick Hall, Wei Choong, and Katie Oven 2008. "The Role of Children and Youth in Communicating Disaster Risk." *Children, Youth and Environments* 18(1): 254–279.

49. Sontag, Deborah. 2010. "Haitian Orphans Have Little but One Another." *New York Times*, July 5.

50. Although more than one-quarter of New Orleans residents had no access to a private automobile, there was no plan implemented for transporting these residents safely out of the city. See Bullard, Robert D., Glenn S. Johnson, and Angel O. Torres. 2009. "Transportation Matters: Stranded on the Side of the Road before and after Disasters Strike." Pp. 100–152 in *Race, Place, and Environmental Justice after Hurricane Katrina: Struggles to Reclaim, Rebuild, and Revitalize New Orleans and the Gulf Coast*, edited by R. Bullard and B. Wright. Boulder, CO: Westview Press.

51. Hurricane Cindy made landfall on July 5, 2005. It was the third named storm of the 2005 Atlantic hurricane season and the first to reach hurricane strength. Cindy killed three people and led to heavy rainfall in several states and an electrical blackout and flooding in New Orleans. This may have prompted some residents to evacuate before Hurricane Katrina in August.

52. Daniel is an example of a child who, as the unfolding disaster placed him and his loved ones in grave danger, drew on his personal courage and wherewithal to avoid tragedy. There are also examples of children making important contributions to efforts to mitigate disaster impacts before they occur. Many children now receive hazards education training in their classrooms. The value of such training can be seen in several examples, including a 2010 student-led drill in a Colorado high school where youth trained in disaster management took on various roles such as incident commanders and safety officers, evacuating their entire school safely in minutes. Colorado Office of Emergency Management. 2010. "Student-Led Evacuation Drill Using the Incident Command System—April 28, 2010." http://www.coemergency.com/2010/04/student-led-evacuation-drill-using.html. Accessed on January 20, 2012.

53. Phillips, Brenda A. 2009. *Disaster Recovery*. New York: CRC Press, p. 22. Phillips's definition builds on the work of Mileti, Dennis S. 1999. *Disasters by Design: A Reassessment of Natural Hazards in the United States*. Washington, DC: Joseph Henry Press.

54. FEMA IS-1, Toolkit, p. 1. No date. As cited in Phillips, Brenda A. 2009. "Independent Study 1: Emergency Program Manager." Federal Emergency Management Agency. http://training.fema.gov/IS/crslist.asp. Accessed on August 20, 2014.

55. Aldrich, Daniel P. *Building Resilience: Social Capital in Post-Disaster Recovery*. Chicago: University of Chicago Press, p. 5.

56. Franks, Bridget A. 2011. "Moving Targets: A Developmental Framework for Understanding Children's Changes following Disasters." *Journal of Applied Developmental Psychology* 32(2): 58–69.

CHAPTER 3

1. Lein, Laura, Ronald Angel, Julie Beausoleil, and Holly Bell. 2012. "The Basement of Extreme Poverty: Katrina Survivors and Poverty Programs." Pp. 47–62 in *Displaced: Life in the Katrina Diaspora*, edited by L. Weber and L. Peek. Austin: University of Texas Press.

2. Stack, Carol B. 1974. *All Our Kin: Strategies for Survival in a Black Community*. New York: Harper and Row; Litt, Jacqueline. 2008. "Getting Out or Staying Put: An African American Women's Network in Evacuation from Katrina." *National Women's Studies Association Journal* 20(3): 32–48; Litt, Jacquelyn. 2012. "'We Need to Get Together with Each Other': Women's Narratives of Help in Katrina's Displacement." Pp. 167–182 in *Displaced: Life in the Katrina Diaspora*, edited by L. Weber and L. Peek. Austin: University of Texas Press.

3. In instances where we saw participants in our study suffering physically or emotionally, we reached out through our own networks to try to identify help. For instance, when Deirdre emailed Lori repeatedly to tell her about her terrible toothache, Lori contacted colleagues at the Children's Health Fund—a national organization that runs a free health care clinic in New Orleans—to see if they or one of their partners could provide dental care for Deirdre. The contacts at the Children's Health Fund identified a local dental school that would provide care at a reduced cost. We then passed that information on to Deirdre. We discuss this issue of locating and providing resources for our study participants in much greater depth in appendix B.

4. For a description of how food insecurity as well as chronic and acute health issues affect children's ability to learn and be educated, see Gracy, Delaney, Roy Grant, Grifin Goldsmith, Anupa Fabian, Lori Peek, and Irwin E. Redlener. 2014. "Health Barriers to Learning: A Survey of New York City Public School Leadership." *SAGE Open* 4. DOI: 10.1177/2158244013520613.

5. In the aftermath of Katrina, many pointed out how flawed the evacuation plans were for the poorest residents of New Orleans. It was well known, for example, that New Orleans had one of the lowest rates of car ownership in the nation. Yet, when the mayor ordered a mandatory evacuation, there were no buses or trains or other options to help tens of thousands of carless residents leave the city. It was a situation that was anticipated, and yet no plans were in place to help some of the most vulnerable residents, including the elderly, children, people with disabilities, and the caregivers of all of these groups of people. For a much more in-depth discussion of these and other issues, see Bullard, Robert D., and Beverly Wright, eds.

2009. *Race, Place, and Environmental Justice after Hurricane Katrina: Struggles to Reclaim, Rebuild, and Revitalize New Orleans and the Gulf Coast.* Boulder, CO: Westview Press.

6. Peacock, Walter Gillis, Nicole Dash, and Yang Zhang. 2006. "Sheltering and Housing Recovery following Disaster." Pp. 258–274 in *Handbook of Disaster Research*, edited by H. Rodríguez, E. L. Quarantelli, and R. R. Dynes. New York: Springer.

7. Terranova, Andrew M., Paul Boxer, and Amanda Sheffield Morris. 2009. "Changes in Children's Peer Interactions following a Natural Disaster: How Pre-disaster Bullying and Victimization Rates Changed following Hurricane Katrina." *Psychology in the Schools* 46(4): 333–347.

8. Barry, Dan. 2006. "Lives Suspended on Gulf Coast, Crammed into 240 Square Feet." *New York Times*, June 14, p. A-1.

9. Browne provides a detailed account of the implications for family life of living in the small, 240-square-foot FEMA trailers. See Browne, Katherine E. 2015. *Standing in the Need: Culture, Comfort, and Coming Home after Katrina.* Austin: University of Texas Press.

10. During our first visit to their trailer, we noted that Deirdre and Daniel had only a flat sheet on top of their beds—no fitted sheet, no pillow cases, and no blankets. After the visit, we mailed them a box of bedding and several other supplies for the trailer. In appendix B we describe how we identified and attempted to respond to unmet needs among some of the families in our study.

11. Admittedly, we also felt somewhat unsafe—at certain times—in the trailer park where Deirdre and her family lived in Baton Rouge. For a description of how we handled safety concerns while in the field, see appendix B.

12. From a 2006 survey of the trailer parks completed by the aid agency International Medical Corps, as cited in Lauten, Anne Westbrook, and Kimberly Lietz. 2008. "A Look at the Standards Gap: Comparing Child Protection Responses in the Aftermath of Hurricane Katrina and the Indian Ocean Tsunami." *Children, Youth and Environments* 18(1): 158–201.

13. Pardee, Jessica W. 2012. "Living through Displacement: Housing Insecurity among Low-Income Evacuees." Pp. 63–78 in *Displaced: Life in the Katrina Diaspora*, edited by L. Weber and L. Peek. Austin: University of Texas Press.

14. Research shows that parental worries and associated rules about not playing outside due to actual or perceived dangers are common in U.S. neighborhoods that are plagued by crime and violence. This is one strategy that parents, like Deirdre in our study, use to protect their children. For more on this phenomenon, see Rosier, Katherine Brown. 2000. *Mothering Inner-City Children: The Early School Years.* New Brunswick, NJ: Rutgers University Press.

15. Pardee, 2012.

16. Berggren, Ruth E., and Tyler J. Curiel. 2006. "After the Storm—Health Care Infrastructure in Post-Katrina New Orleans." *New England Journal of Medicine* 354(15): 1549–1552; Gray, Bradford H., and Kathy Hebert. 2007. "Hospitals in Hur-

ricane Katrina: Challenges Facing Custodial Institutions in a Disaster." *Journal of Health Care for the Poor and Underserved* 18(2): 283–298; Griffies, W. Scott. 2010. "Health Care Infrastructure Post-Katrina: Disaster Planning to Return Health Care Workers to Their Home Communities." *Psychiatric Services* 61(1): 70–73.

17. Casserly, Michael. 2006. "Double Jeopardy: Public Education in New Orleans before and after the Storm." Pp. 197–214 in *There Is No Such Thing as a Natural Disaster: Race, Class, and Hurricane Katrina*, edited by C. Hartman and G. D. Squires. New York: Routledge.

18. Dewan, Shaila. 2007. "Road to New Life after Katrina Is Closed to Many." *New York Times*, July 12, p. A-1.

19. Fieldnotes are an important part of qualitative research. These involve detailed descriptions of settings and interactions that provide rich context for the data. Fieldnotes are time-consuming to write, as a one-hour visit may produce 10 pages of text, for example. For a detailed discussion on the methodological value of fieldnotes, see Emerson, Robert M., Rachel I. Fretz, and Linda L. Shaw. 1995. *Writing Ethnographic Fieldnotes*. Chicago: University of Chicago Press. In the passage included in this chapter, we have removed some of the fieldnotes because of space constraints. For example, Lori had written more detailed descriptions of her cab driver on the way to the motel, the man who worked at the front desk, the look of the pool area, and the scene on the street when she and Daniel emerged to go have some lunch.

20. Researchers conducting longitudinal studies tend to experience challenges tracking their participants over long periods of time. They thus employ several methods to identify their whereabouts over time. One such approach is to have individuals give an address and phone number of an extended family member or friend who is likely to stay in one residence for the duration of the study; this method was not available to us as entire networks were displaced and were usually highly mobile. It is also particularly difficult to keep track of low-income families; families like the Taylors, for instance, did not have consistent phone service or places of employment to contact. We attempted to keep track of our participants by keeping in contact as much as possible with emails, phone calls, text messages, social networking sites, cards, and visits. We were worried at several points about "losing" the Taylor family, and thus went to great lengths to stay in contact with them. We address this issue in more detail in appendix B.

21. In May of 2011, we drove by this motel and saw that it was fenced off and closed down.

22. We are especially grateful for the advice and support that Professor Pamela Jenkins provided us during this period. She put us in contact with a highly proactive disaster housing aid worker who ended up trying to help the Taylor family.

23. For a more detailed discussion of the various and often confusing federal housing programs (such as Section 8 and Hope VI) and disaster-related housing programs (such as FEMA's Individuals and Households Program), see Pardee, 2012.

24. For a study that focuses specifically on the ways that family members pro-

vided support and/or contributed to strain in the post-Katrina recovery process, see Reid, Megan, and Corinne Reczek. 2011. "Stress and Support in Family Relationships after Hurricane Katrina." *Journal of Family Issues* 32(10): 1397–1418.

25. We met this school janitor—an African American man in his late 50s or early 60s—during one of our visits to New Orleans. It was apparent how much he cared about Daniel and the entire Taylor family. We often had these sorts of heartwarming encounters with individuals who had come to know the Taylors and wanted to help them out.

26. For a discussion of the mental health implications of unstable housing contexts, especially for low-income renters, see Merdjanoff, Alexis A. 2013. "There's No Place like Home: Examining the Emotional Consequences of Hurricane Katrina on the Displaced Residents of New Orleans." *Social Science Research* 42: 1222–1235.

27. For more information on the educational impacts of Katrina, see Children's Defense Fund. 2009. "What It Takes to Rebuild a Village after a Disaster: Stories from Internally Displaced Children and Families of Hurricane Katrina and Their Lessons for Our Nation." http://www.childrensdefense.org/child-research-data -publications/data/rebuild-village-hurricane-katrina-rita-children.pdf. Accessed on April 13, 2013; Southern Education Foundation. 2007. "Education after Katrina: Time for a New Federal Response." Atlanta: Southern Education Foundation.

28. See Terranova et al., 2009.

29. Ibid.

30. Barrett, Edith J., Carrie Y. Barron Ausbrooks, and Maria Martinez-Cosio. 2008. "The School as a Source of Support for Katrina-Evacuated Youth." *Children, Youth and Environments* 18(1): 202–236.

31. "As of 2006, New Orleans ranked 8th nationally for the percentage of its population living in poverty. And according to change.org, some 60 percent of New Orleans residents say they have to choose between buying food and paying utility bills. Researchers at the Congressional Hunger Center report that there are only 20 grocery stores in New Orleans, compared to 30 before Katrina, which means the average grocery store in New Orleans serves 16,000 people—twice the national average. Not having a full-service grocery store in neighborhoods ultimately costs these communities millions of dollars in 'grocery leakage'—money people spend outside the community for food." http://newsone.com/1540235/americas-worst -9-urban-food-deserts. See also Rose, Donald et al. 2009. "Deserts in New Orleans? Illustrations of Urban Food Access and Implications for Policy." Ann Arbor: University of Michigan National Poverty Center/USDA Economic Research Service.

CHAPTER 4

1. Wolff, Edward. 2010. "Recent Trends in Household Wealth in the United States: Rising Debt and the Middle-Class Squeeze." Levy Economics Institute. Working Paper no. 589. New York: Bard College.

2. Fothergill, Alice. 2004. *Heads above Water: Gender, Class, and Family in the Grand Forks Flood*. Albany: State University of New York Press; McCoy, Brenda, and Nicole Dash. 2013. "Class." Pp. 83–112 in *Social Vulnerability to Disasters*, 2nd ed., edited by D. S. K. Thomas, B. D. Phillips, W. E. Lovekamp, and A. Fothergill. Boca Raton, FL: CRC Press.

3. Wood Harper, Dee, and Kelly Frailing, eds. 2010. *Crime and Criminal Justice in Disaster*. Durham, NC: Carolina Academic Press.

4. Quarantelli, E. L. 2007. "The Myth and the Realities: Keeping the 'Looting' Myth in Perspective." *Natural Hazards Observer* 31(4): 2–3.

5. Fischer, Henry W. 1998. *Response to Disaster: Fact versus Fiction and Its Perpetuation*. Lanham, MD: University Press of America.

6. Quarantelli, E. L. 2008. "Conventional Beliefs and Counterintuitive Realities." *Social Research* 75 (3): 873–904.

7. Frailing, Kelly, and Dee Wood Harper. 2012. "Fear, Prosocial Behavior, and Looting: The Katrina Experience." Pp. 101–121 in *Crime and Criminal Justice in Disaster*, 2nd ed., edited by D. W. Harper and K. Frailing. Durham, NC: Carolina Academic Press.

8. Weems, Carl F., Brandon G. Scott, Donice M. Banks, and Rebecca A. Graham. 2012. "Is TV Traumatic for All Youths? The Role of Preexisting Posttraumatic-Stress Symptoms in the Link between Disaster Coverage and Stress." *Psychological Science* 23(11): 1293–1297.

9. Herbert, Christophe F., and Alain Brunet. 2010. "Social Networking Sites in the Aftermath of Trauma." Pp. 85–96 in *Internet Use in the Aftermath of Trauma*, edited by A. Brunet, A. R. Ashbaugh, and C. F. Herbert. Amsterdam: IOS Press; Hjorth, Larissa, and Kyoung-hwa Yonnie Kim. 2011. "The Mourning After: A Case Study of Social Media in the 3.11 Earthquake Disaster in Japan." *Television and New Media* 12(6): 552–559.

10. For a discussion of the size and scope of the diaspora, see Weber, Lynn, and Lori Peek. 2012. "Documenting Displacement: An Introduction." Pp. 1–20 in *Displaced: Life in the Katrina Diaspora*, edited by L. Weber and L. Peek. Austin: University of Texas Press.

11. Steffen, Seana Lowe, and Alice Fothergill. 2009. "9/11 Volunteerism: A Pathway to Personal Healing and Community Engagement." *Social Science Journal* 46: 29–46.

12. For a description of the bias and mistreatment that some Katrina survivors endured, see Peek, Lori. 2012. "They Call It 'Katrina Fatigue': Displaced Families and Discrimination in Colorado." Pp. 31–46 in *Displaced: Life in the Katrina Diaspora*, edited by L. Weber and L. Peek. Austin: University of Texas Press.

13. Newman, Katherine. 1999. *Falling from Grace: Downward Mobility in the Age of Affluence*, 2nd ed. Berkeley: University of California Press.

14. Fothergill, 2004.

15. Tobin-Gurley, Jennifer, Lori Peek, and Jennifer Loomis. 2010. "Displaced Single Mothers in the Aftermath of Hurricane Katrina: Resource Needs and Re-

source Acquisition." *International Journal of Mass Emergencies and Disasters* 28(2): 170–206.

16. Peek, Lori. 2010. "Age." Pp. 155–185 in *Social Vulnerability to Disasters*, edited by B. D. Phillips, D. S. K. Thomas, A. Fothergill, and L. Blinn-Pike. Boca Raton, FL: CRC Press; Rowe, Cynthia L., and Howard A. Liddle. 2008. "When the Levee Breaks: Treating Adolescents and Families in the Aftermath of Hurricane Katrina." *Journal of Marital and Family Therapy* 34(2): 132–148; Temple, Jeff R., Patricia van den Berg, John F. Thomas, James Northcutt, Christopher Thomas, and Daniel H. Freeman. 2011. "Teen Dating Violence and Substance Use following a Natural Disaster: Does Evacuation Status Matter?" *American Journal of Disaster Medicine* 6(4): 201–206.

17. For further discussion of how Katrina affected the educational experiences of displaced students, see Peek, Lori, and Krista Richardson. 2010. "In Their Own Words: Displaced Children's Educational Recovery Needs after Hurricane Katrina." *Disaster Medicine and Public Health Preparedness* 4(3): S63–S70.

18. Lauten, Anne Westbrook, and Kimberly Lietz. 2008. "A Look at the Standards Gap: Comparing Child Protection Responses in the Aftermath of Hurricane Katrina and the Indian Ocean Tsunami." *Children, Youth and Environments* 18(1): 158–201. In this article, Lauten and Lietz describe focus groups they conducted with 700 children from New Orleans. Sixty percent of the children interviewed had witnessed a shooting or murder prior to the hurricane. Moreover, nearly half had seen a drug sale and 42 percent had seen physical violence between a man and a woman.

19. Stephens, Nicole M., Stephanie A. Fryberg, Hazel R. Markus, Camille S. Johnson, and Rebecca Covarrubias. 2012. "Unseen Disadvantage: How American Universities' Focus on Independence Undermines the Academic Performance of First-Generation College Students." *Journal of Personality and Social Psychology* 102(6): 1178–1197.

20. In terms of employment, studies find that college graduates earn more income over their lifetimes, are employed in more desirable jobs, and are much less likely to suffer from extended bouts of unemployment. College graduates also have better health outcomes than nongraduates. For a comprehensive review of the literature on the power of a college degree see Hout, Michael. 2012. "Social and Economic Returns to College Education in the United States." *Annual Review of Sociology* 38(1): 379–400; Looney, Adam, and Michael Greenstone. 2012. "Regardless of Cost, College Still Matters." Washington, DC: The Hamilton Project. http://www.hamiltonproject.org/papers/regardless_of_the_cost_college_still_matters/. Accessed on July 1, 2013.

21. Rosier, Katherine Brown. 2000. *Mothering Inner-City Children: The Early School Years*. New Brunswick, NJ: Rutgers University Press.

22. "Westbank" means the west side of the Mississippi River. However, in the New Orleans area, the river bends in such a way that the Westbank is actually *south* of the river and the city, and the Eastbank is *north* of the river and includes the city. Residents do not typically refer to an area being north or south of the river; they always use the terms "Westbank" and "Eastbank," even when parts of the Westbank

are actually east of some parts of Eastbank. As one might imagine, this is often confusing to nonresidents and newcomers.

23. Peek, 2010.

24. Nossiter, Adam. 2006. "After the Storm, Students Left Alone and Angry." *New York Times*, November 1.

25. For a review of the many challenges of displacement, see Esnard, Ann-Margaret, and Alka Sapat. 2014. *Displaced by Disaster: Recovery and Resilience in a Globalizing World*. New York: Routledge. See Weber and Peek, 2012.

CHAPTER 5

1. According to the Greater New Orleans Community Data Center (GNODC), nearly 21 months after Katrina, only 45 percent of Orleans Parish schools had reopened. See GNODC. 2007. "The Katrina Index: Tracking Recovery of New Orleans and the Metro Area." Monthly Report, June 14. New Orleans: GNODC.

2. Handel, Gerald, Spencer Cahill, and Frederick Elkin. 2006. *Children and Society: The Sociology of Children and Childhood Socialization*. New York: Oxford University Press.

3. Peek, Lori, and Alice Fothergill. 2009. "Parenting in the Wake of Disaster: Mothers and Fathers Respond to Hurricane Katrina." Pp. 112–130 in *Women, Gender, and Disaster: Global Issues and Initiatives*, edited by E. Enarson and D. Chakrabarti. New Delhi: Sage.

4. Fussell, Elizabeth. 2012. "Help from Family, Friends, and Strangers during Hurricane Katrina: Finding the Limits of Social Networks." Pp. 150–166 in *Displaced: Life in the Katrina Diaspora*, edited by L. Weber and L. Peek. Austin: University of Texas Press.

5. Fussell, Elizabeth. 2005. "Leaving New Orleans: Social Stratification, Networks, and Hurricane Evacuation." New York: Social Science Research Council. http://understandingkatrina.ssrc.org/Fussell/. Accessed on March 8, 2013.

6. Fussell, 2012.

7. Six months after the storm, in February 2006, a survey of families displaced to trailers and hotels found that 21 percent of school-age children were either not attending school or had been absent for more than 10 days during the previous month. See Abramson, David, and Richard Garfield. 2006. "On the Edge: Children and Families Displaced by Hurricanes Katrina and Rita Face a Looming Medical and Mental Health Crisis." National Center for Disaster Preparedness. New York: Mailman School of Public Health, Columbia University.

8. Fothergill, Alice, and Lori Peek. 2006. "Surviving Catastrophe: A Study of Children in Hurricane Katrina." Pp. 97–130 in *Learning from Catastrophe: Quick Response Research in the Wake of Hurricane Katrina*. Boulder: Institute of Behavioral Science, University of Colorado.

9. Weber, Lynn and Lori Peek. 2012. "Documenting Displacement: An Intro-

duction." Pp. 1–20 in *Displaced: Life in the Katrina Diaspora*, edited by L. Weber and L. Peek. Austin: University of Texas Press.

10. Fothergill and Peek, 2006; Fothergill, Alice, and Lori Peek. 2012. "Permanent Temporariness: Displaced Children in Louisiana." Pp. 119–143 in *Displaced: Life in the Katrina Diaspora*, edited by L. Weber and L. Peek. Austin: University of Texas Press.

11. Tobin-Gurley, Jennifer, and Elaine Enarson. 2013. "Gender." Pp. 167–198 in *Social Vulnerability to Disasters*, 2nd ed., edited by D. S. K. Thomas, B. D. Phillips, W. E. Lovekamp, and A. Fothergill. Boca Raton, FL: CRC Press.

12. Fothergill, Alice. 2004. *Heads Above Water: Gender, Class, and Family Life in the Grand Forks Flood*. Albany: State University of New York Press.

13. Lareau, Annette. 2003. *Unequal Childhoods: Class, Race, and Family Life*. Berkeley: University of California Press.

14. Calarco, Jessica McCrory. 2011. "'I Need Help!': Social Class and Children's Help-Seeking in Elementary School." *American Sociological Review* 76: 862–882.

15. Corsaro, William. 2014. *The Sociology of Childhood*, 4th ed. Los Angeles: Sage.

16. By December 2005, more than 185,000 refrigerators had been removed from curbsides by the U.S. Army Corps of Engineers, the federal agency in charge of removing debris. See O'Driscoll, Patrick. 2005. "Cleanup Crews Tackle Katrina's Nasty Leftovers." *USA Today*, December 11. In total, more than 53 million cubic yards of debris were removed from the curbsides of private property by the Army Corps of Engineers and other public works contractors. See Luther, Linda. 2008. "Disaster Debris Removal after Hurricane Katrina: Status and Associated Issues." Congressional Research Service (CRS) Report for Congress. Washington, DC: CRS.

17. The mothers had good reason to be worried. In flooded areas, sediment left behind by floodwaters was an average of 0.5-cm thick and public health officials were highly concerned about the lead, arsenic, and other carcinogens it contained. Extensive examination of soil samples showed that flooding resulted in the deposit of arsenic-contaminated sediments that exceeded both the Environmental Protection Agency and Louisiana Department of Environmental Quality soil-screening levels in numerous areas throughout New Orleans. Researchers also demonstrated that 18 months after Katrina, arsenic contamination was still a problem at 33 percent of the school sites that had reopened and 13 percent of the playgrounds. For a full report, see Rotkin-Ellman, Miriam, Gina Solomon, Christopher R. Gonzales, Lovell Agwaramgbo, and Howard W. Mielke. 2010. "Arsenic Contamination in New Orleans Soil: Temporal Changes Associated with Flooding." *Environmental Research* 110(1): 19–25. For a comprehensive review of environmental risks of living in New Orleans, including chapters on various forms of environmental injustice, see Bullard, Robert D., and Beverly Wright, eds. 2009. *Race, Place, and Environmental Justice after Hurricane Katrina: Struggles to Reclaim, Rebuild, and Revitalize New Orleans and the Gulf Coast*. Boulder, CO: Westview Press.

18. Many social scientists have pointed out that race and class are often corre-

lated with elevation in the city, meaning that neighborhoods which were predominantly home to black families were more likely to flood than areas populated by mostly white, middle-class ones. This widely cited claim, however, has been disputed by some scholars. Nonetheless, there does seem to be a correlation between race, class, and the subsequent impacts of the flooding of New Orleans. See Logan, John R. 2005. "The Impact of Katrina: Race and Class in Storm-Damaged Neighborhoods." Providence, RI: Brown University. http://www.s4.brown.edu/Katrina /report.pdf. Accessed on July 1, 2013.

19. For research on the various ways that children and youth may influence their parents' decision making in the aftermath of disaster, see Peek, Lori, Bridget Morrissey, and Holly Marlatt. 2011. "Disaster Hits Home: A Model of Displaced Family Adjustment after Hurricane Katrina." *Journal of Family Issues* 32(10): 1371–1396.

20. Litt, Jacquelyn. 2012. "'We Need to Get Together with Each Other': Women's Narratives of Help in Katrina's Displacement." Pp. 167–182 in *Displaced: Life in the Katrina Diaspora*, edited by L. Weber and L. Peek. Austin: University of Texas Press.

21. For a statement on how the loss of amenities weighed on families after Katrina, see Wieberg, Steve, Dennis Cauchon, and Laura Parker. 2005. "Three Families with One Question: What Do We Do Now?" *USA Today*, September 7. For detailed statistical assessments of the effect of the loss of amenities on families' decisions to return to New Orleans, see Groen, Jeffrey A., and Anne E. Polivka. 2010. "Going Home after Hurricane Katrina: Determinants of Return Migration and Changes in Affected Areas." *Demography* 47(4): 821–844.

22. Robertson, Campbell. 2011. "Smaller New Orleans after Katrina, Census Shows." *New York Times*, February 4, p. A-11.

23. In January 2006, the Orleans Parish School Board dismissed 7,500 teachers and public school employees. Shortly after, the Louisiana state legislature voted to move 107 underperforming schools to the state-run Recovery School District. For a review of the effects of this decision on teachers, see Vanacore, Andrew. 2011. "Decision Pending on Mass Firing of New Orleans Public School Teachers after Hurricane Katrina." *Times-Picayune*, August 29.

24. Ten months after the storm, city health officials reported that suicide rates in New Orleans were nearly triple what they had been prior to Katrina. See Saulny, Susan 2006. "A Legacy of the Storm: Depression and Suicide." *New York Times*, June 21. Six years after Katrina, suicide rates remained persistently higher than pre-Katrina levels; see Spiegel, Alix. 2010. "Traces of Katrina: New Orleans Suicide Rate Still Up." *National Public Radio*, August 30.

25. Public health officials in New Orleans reported persistent increases in suicide, high-risk behaviors, and depression among children and youth in the years following Katrina. See Guarino, Mark. 2009. "New Orleans' 'Katrina Generation' Struggles with Drugs and Depression." *Christian Science Monitor*, May 13.

26. New Orleans has been known as "the city that care forgot" since at least the 1930s. It is unknown who coined the term.

27. For discussions of the gendered nature of social networks in disaster pre-

paredness and response, see Klinenberg, Eric. 2002. *Heat Wave: A Social Autopsy of Disaster in Chicago*. Chicago: University of Chicago Press; Tobin-Gurley and Enarson, 2013.

28. A February 2006 survey of families displaced to trailers or hotels in Louisiana found that these households had moved an average of 3.5 times during the six months following Katrina. Many of the surveyed parents said that they allowed a lag time between the move and re-enrollment of their child in school due to the difficulties involved in resettlement. Children in families who moved multiple times were the most likely to be frequently absent or not enrolled in school. See Abramson and Garfield, 2006, p. 3. Researchers also found that children experienced between 1 and 11 school changes over a three-month period following Hurricane Katrina, with an average of three moves per child. See Lauten, Anne Westbrook, and Kimberly Lietz. 2008. "A Look at the Standards Gap: Comparing Child Protection Responses in the Aftermath of Hurricane Katrina and the Indian Ocean Tsunami." *Children, Youth and Environments* 18(1): 158–201.

29. Cutter, Susan L., Christopher T. Emrich, Jerry T. Mitchell, Bryan J. Boruff, Melanie Gall, Mathew C. Schmidtlein, Christopher G. Burton, and Ginni Melton. 2006. "The Long Road Home: Race, Class, and Recovery from Hurricane Katrina." *Environment* 48(2): 8–20.

CHAPTER 6

1. Sociologist William Anderson was one of the first to argue that scholars have not attended carefully enough to the ways that children and youth are active in imaginative endeavors after disasters. Among other things, he rightly notes, they may create songs, jokes, games, poetry, riddles, art, and plays to process the event and ultimately contribute to their own healing and the recovery of others. See Anderson, William A. 2005. "Bringing Children into Focus on the Social Science Disaster Research Agenda." *International Journal of Mass Emergencies and Disasters* 23(3): 159–175.

2. When we use the term "institution," we are using it in its broadest sense, not in the strict sociological sense (which refers to a socially constructed entity with groups of roles and expected behaviors, such as the institution of the family or the media).

3. Tierney, Kathleen J., Michael K. Lindell, and Ronald W. Perry. 2001. *Facing the Unexpected: Disaster Preparedness and Response in the United States*. Washington, DC: Joseph Henry Press.

4. Brodie, Mollyann, Erin Weltzien, Drew Altman, Robert J. Blendon, and John M. Benson. 2006. "Experiences of Hurricane Katrina Evacuees in Houston Shelters: Implications for Future Planning." *American Journal of Public Health* 96(8): 1402–1408.

5. Fothergill, Alice, and Lori Peek. 2006. "Surviving Catastrophe: A Study of

Children in Hurricane Katrina." Pp. 97–130 in *Learning from Catastrophe: Quick Response Research in the Wake of Hurricane Katrina*. Boulder: Natural Hazards Center, Institute of Behavioral Science, University of Colorado; Peek, Lori, and Alice Fothergill. 2006. "Reconstructing Childhood: An Exploratory Study of Children in Hurricane Katrina." Quick Response Report no. 186. Boulder: Natural Hazards Center, University of Colorado.

6. Quarantelli, Enrico L. 1995. "Patterns of Sheltering and Housing in U.S. Disasters." *Disaster Prevention and Management* 4(3): 43–53.

7. The American Red Cross and several other organizations run shelters under a mandate from the U.S. Congress. Research has found that approximately 20 percent of all evacuees in disasters go to this type of temporary housing. Most shelters close after a few days, but in the most catastrophic events, they may stay open for weeks or even months. In Hurricane Katrina, over 1,000 shelters opened in many states, sheltering over 1 million survivors well into the fall of 2005. In the relief phase, after the presidential disaster declaration, FEMA assists with temporary housing to ensure that survivors receive housing in a safe and functional environment. See Phillips, Brenda. 2010. *Disaster Recovery*. Boca Raton, FL: CRC Press; Tierney et al., 2001.

8. Trailers provided by the government after disasters are not without their problems. They can be too small and cramped for the number of family members who must live in them and during warm days they can be sweltering, almost unbearably hot, inside. Their tin roofs amplify every rainstorm, so that the noise inside is frighteningly loud, especially for those who just survived a hurricane. Survivors are often placed in trailer parks with hundreds of other displaced people who are strangers, making it difficult to create a community and feel safe. Kai Erikson, in his classic book on the Buffalo Creek flooding disaster in the 1970s, was the first to argue that the placement of complete strangers in post-disaster trailer parks led to the destruction of community and to feelings of isolation and despair among residents. See Erikson, Kai T. 1976. *Everything in Its Path: Destruction of Community in the Buffalo Creek Flood*. New York: Simon and Schuster.

In the Gulf Coast, additional issues came to light. Many children and their families were becoming ill in the smaller, travel-size FEMA trailers. Residents reported increased asthma, headaches, and nausea, and ultimately lawsuits were filed because of the health problems thought to be caused by the formaldehyde in the trailer materials. See Hsu, Spencer S. 2007. "FEMA Knew of Toxic Gas in Trailers." *Washington Post*, July 20; Kunzelman, Michael. 2012. "$42.6 Million FEMA Trailer Settlement Approved." *Associated Press*, September 27.

9. In addition to Habitat for Humanity, a notable post-Katrina housing solution was the "Katrina Cottages," small (308–1,800 square feet) residential units that were safe, affordable, and able to be quickly built. Part of the "Tiny Home Movement," these houses could be constructed from Katrina Cottage "kits," and were welcomed by many after Katrina, but opposed by some, who worried they would lower property values.

10. Rosier, Katherine Brown, and William A. Corsaro. 1993. "Competent Parents,

Complex Lives: Managing Parenthood in Poverty." *Journal of Contemporary Ethnography* 22: 171–204.

11. Barrett, Edith J., Carrie Y. B. Ausbrooks, and Maria Martinez-Cosio. 2008. "The School as a Source of Support for Katrina-Evacuated Youth." *Children, Youth and Environments* 18(1): 202–236.

12. For a discussion of some of the ways that teachers and school administrators helped displaced students, see Peek, Lori, and Krista Richardson. 2010. "In Their Own Words: Displaced Children's Educational Recovery Needs after Hurricane Katrina." *Disaster Medicine and Public Health Preparedness* 4(3): S63–S70.

13. Other research in different contexts has also found that the educational impacts of disaster can be minimal when various personal and institutional protective factors are in place in school settings. See, for example, Pérez-Pereira, Miguel, Carolina Tinajero, María Soledad Rodríguez, Manuel Peralbo, and José Manuel Sabucedo. 2012. "Academic Effects of the Prestige Oil Spill Disaster." *Spanish Journal of Psychology* 15(3): 1055–1068.

14. Some research has shown that boys have a harder time establishing new connections in new communities, have more "rough" gender expectations than girls, and may fight or otherwise engage in more delinquent behavior. For a review of this literature, see Crosnoe, Robert, and Monica Kirkpatrick Johnson. 2011. "Research on Adolescence in the Twenty-First Century." *Annual Review of Sociology* 37: 439–460.

15. On racial segregation and its impact on relationships, see, for example, Dalmage, Heather M. 2000. *Tripping on the Color Line: Black-White Multiracial Families in a Racially Divided World*. New Brunswick, NJ: Rutgers University Press; Echenique, Federico, and Roland G. Fryer. 2007. "A Measure of Segregation Based on Social Interactions." *Quarterly Journal of Economics* 122(2): 441–485; Moody, James. 2001. "Race, School Integration, and Friendship Segregation in America." *American Journal of Sociology* 107(3): 679–716; Quillian, Lincoln, and Mary E. Campbell. 2003. "Beyond Black and White: The Present and Future of Multiracial Friendship Segregation." *American Sociological Review* 68(4): 540–566.

16. Frankenberg, Erica, and Chungmei Lee. 2002. "Race in American Public Schools: Rapidly Resegregating School Districts." Civil Rights Project. Cambridge, MA: Harvard University; Reardon, Sean F., Elena Tej Grewal, Demetra Kalogrides, and Erica Greenberg. 2012. "Brown Fades: The End of Court-Ordered School Desegregation and the Resegregation of American Public Schools." *Journal of Policy Analysis and Management* 31(4): 876–904.

17. For a discussion of the role of the black church in the aftermath of Katrina, see Jenkins, Pamela. 2012. "After the Flood: Faith in the Diaspora." Pp. 218–230 in *Displaced: Life in the Katrina Diaspora*, edited by L. Weber and L. Peek. Austin: University of Texas Press. For a description of chronically disadvantaged communities and the black church during non-disaster times, see Rosier, Katherine Brown. 2000. *Mothering Inner-City Children: The Early School Years*. New Brunswick, NJ: Rutgers University Press.

18. Ibid.

19. Pipa, Tony. 2006. "Weathering the Storm: The Role of Local Non-Profits in the Hurricane Katrina Relief Effort." Non-profit Sector Research Fund Working Papers Series. http://www.aspeninstitute.org/sites/default/files/content/docs/NSPP Nonprofits%2520and%2520Katrina.pdf. Accessed on March 25, 2013.

20. Furstenberg, Frank, Jr. 1990. "How Families Manage Risk and Opportunity in Dangerous Neighborhoods." Paper presented at the 85th Annual Meeting of the American Sociological Association, Washington, DC. As quoted in Rosier and Corsaro, 1993, p. 172.

CHAPTER 7

1. Previous research has shown that separation from parents in the immediate aftermath of a major disaster is associated with increased symptomology for post-traumatic stress and other mental health disorders in children and adolescents. For example, according to Osofsky et al. (2009), children separated from parents after Katrina were 1.5 times more likely to experience negative mental health symptoms than those children not separated from parents. For further information on this phenomenon, see Garrett, Andrew L., Roy Grant, Paula Madrid, Arturo Brito, David Abramson, and Irwin Redlener. 2007. "Children and Megadisaster: Lessons Learned in the New Millennium." *Advances in Pediatrics* 54: 189–214; McFarlane, Alexander C. 1987. "Family Functioning and Overprotection following a Natural Disaster: The Longitudinal Effects of Post-Traumatic Morbidity." *Australia and New Zealand Journal of Psychiatry* 21(2): 210–218; Osofsky, Howard J., Joy D. Osofsky, Mindy Kronenberg, Adrianne Brennan, and Tonya Cross Hansel. 2009. "Posttraumatic Stress Symptoms in Children after Hurricane Katrina: Predicting the Need for Mental Health Services." *American Journal of Orthopsychiatry* 79(2): 212–220.

2. Newman, Katherine S. 1999. *No Shame in My Game: The Working Poor in the Inner City.* New York: Knopf and the Russell Sage Foundation.

3. Furstenburg, Frank F. 2007. "Should Government Promote Marriage?" *Journal of Policy Analysis and Management* 26: 956–960.

4. Peek, Lori, and Alice Fothergill. 2008. "Displacement, Gender, and the Challenges of Parenting after Hurricane Katrina." *National Women's Studies Association Journal* 20(3): 69–105; Tobin-Gurley, Lori Peek, and Jennifer Loomis. 2010. "Displaced Single Mothers in the Aftermath of Hurricane Katrina: Resource Needs and Resource Acquisition." *International Journal of Mass Emergencies and Disasters* 28(2): 170–206.

5. Fictive kin is defined as non-relatives whose bonds are strong and intimate. These bonds sometimes are more meaningful than those with biological relatives. See Litt, Jacquelyn. 2012. "'We Need to Get Together with Each Other': Women's Narratives of Help in Katrina's Displacement." Pp. 167–182 in *Displaced: Life in the Katrina Diaspora*, edited by L. Weber and L. Peek. Austin: University of Texas Press;

Stack, Carol B. 1974. *All Our Kin: Strategies for Survival in a Black Community*. New York: Harper and Row.

6. Before Katrina, the majority of the public schools in New Orleans were old and in need of repair. The school system also had high levels of corruption and mismanagement, including concerns about bankruptcy and several indictments of school employees for fraud and theft. Academically, New Orleans students were failing to meet national standards: 70 percent of eighth graders were not proficient in math and 74 percent were not proficient in reading. Merrow, John. 2005. "New Orleans Schools before and after Katrina." *PBS Newshour*, November 1, 2005. http://www.pbs.org/newshour/bb/education/july-deco5/neworleans_11-01.html. Accessed on July 1, 2013.

7. During the 2002–2003 academic year, only 5.5 percent of fourth graders and 6 percent of eighth graders in Orleans Parish scored at the "advanced" or "mastery" level in reading on the Louisiana Educational Assessment Program (LEAP) tests. During the same academic year in Lafayette Parish, 18.3 percent of fourth graders and 23.9 percent of eighth graders scored at or above the mastery level in reading on the LEAP test. Although rates of reading proficiency in Lafayette were low, they were more than three times higher than the rates in New Orleans and above the state average. See Agenda for Children. 2011–12. "Louisiana Kids Count: Data Book on Louisiana's Children." New Orleans: Annie E. Casey Foundation.

8. In 2001, 39.6 percent of the student body in the Lafayette Parish school district belonged to minority racial-ethnic groups and 46.4 percent of students qualified for free or reduced lunch. In the Orleans Parish school district, 96.1 percent of students belonged to racial-ethnic minority groups and 74.6 percent qualified for free or reduced lunch. See Swanson, Christopher B. 2004. "Who Graduates? Who Doesn't? A Statistical Portrait of Public High School Graduation, Class of 2001." Washington, DC: Urban Institute.

9. In 2001, the graduation rate in Lafayette Parish was 68.4 percent, four percentage points higher than the state average. The graduation rate is not available for the Orleans Parish school district for that year due to data limitations and reporting problems, but it is believed to be much lower. See Swanson, 2004.

10. Barrett, Edith J., Carrie Y. Barron Ausbrooks, and Maria Martinez-Cosio. 2008. "The School as a Source of Support for Katrina-Evacuated Youth." *Children, Youth and Environments* 18(1): 202–236; Peek, Lori, and Krista Richardson. 2010. "In Their Own Words: Displaced Children's Educational Recovery Needs after Hurricane Katrina." *Disaster Medicine and Public Health Preparedness* 4(3): S63–S70; Reich, Jennifer, and Martha E. Wadsworth. 2008. "Out of the Floodwaters, but not Entirely on Dry Ground: Experiences of Displacement, Adjustment, and Trauma in Adolescents following Hurricane Katrina." *Children, Youth and Environments* 18(1): 354–370.

11. Peek, Lori, Bridget Morrissey, and Holly Marlatt. 2011. "Disaster Hits Home: A Model of Displaced Family Adjustment after Hurricane Katrina." *Journal of Family Issues* 32(10): 1371–1396; Fothergill, Alice, and Lori Peek. 2012. "Permanent

Temporariness: Displaced Children in Louisiana." Pp. 119–143 in *Displaced: Life in the Katrina Diaspora*, edited by L. Weber and L. Peek. Austin: University of Texas Press.

12. Much has changed in the years since our initial visit to this elementary school, when it was still uncommon to find security measures such as those we witnessed. The change has come largely in response to an outbreak of school shootings at elementary, middle, and high schools in the United States and, to a lesser extent, other nations around the world. In particular, since the Newtown, Connecticut, elementary school shooting in 2012, many U.S. elementary schools have implemented additional security measures, such as keeping front doors locked at all times and installing security cameras throughout school facilities.

13. Lareau, Annette. 2003. *Unequal Childhoods: Class, Race, and Family Life*. Berkeley: University of California Press.

14. The playground space at Powell was built by volunteers working with KABOOM!, a national nonprofit dedicated to building child-friendly play spaces. After Katrina, KABOOM! constructed 136 new playgrounds in the Gulf Coast area. http://kaboom.org/press_release/fifth_anniversary_hurricane_katrina_national_non_profit_kaboom_helps_children_recover. Accessed on June 27, 2013.

15. Kroll-Smith, Steven, Vern Baxter, and Pamela Jenkins. 2015. *Left to Chance: Hurricane Katrina and the Story of Two New Orleans Neighborhoods*. Austin: University of Texas Press.

16. Post-disaster, renters tend to be among the groups that struggle the most to return to their home communities due to damage to the housing stock and other factors. Renters are classified as a highly vulnerable group for negative outcomes in disaster settings. See Blinn-Pike, Lynn. 2010. "Households and Families." Pp. 257–278 in *Social Vulnerability to Disasters*, edited by B. D. Phillips, D. S. K. Thomas, A. Fothergill, and L. Blinn-Pike. Boca Raton, FL: CRC Press; Comerio, Mary C. 1998. *Disaster Hits Home: New Policy for Urban Housing Recovery*. Berkeley: University of California Press; Morrow, Betty Hearn. 1999. "Identifying and Mapping Community Vulnerability." *Disasters* 23(1): 1–18.

17. For a discussion of the importance of friendships and peer relationships among children and youth, see Corsaro, William. 2014. *The Sociology of Childhood*, 4th ed. Los Angeles: Sage.

18. See pp. 148–150 in Adler, Patricia A., and Peter Adler. 1998. *Peer Power: Preadolescent Culture and Identity*. New Brunswick, NJ: Rutgers University Press.

19. Fine, Gary Alan. 1987. *With the Boys: Little League Baseball and Preadolescent Culture*. Chicago: University of Chicago Press.

20. Adler and Adler, 1998; Harris, Judith Rich. 1995. "Where Is the Child's Environment? A Group Socialization Theory of Development." *Psychological Review* 102: 358–389.

21. See Peek et al., 2011, for a description of how post-disaster adjustment processes may vary between adults and children.

CHAPTER 8

1. People living in conditions with high levels of uncertainty and risk, such as undocumented immigrants or children and families displaced following disasters, feel as if their "lives are in limbo." Bailey and colleagues (2002) and Mountz et al. (2002) refer to this condition as "permanent temporariness" and document how living such a life can lead individuals to resist developing new relationships or getting involved in new activities since it is unclear how long they will be in a particular setting. It also can result in frustration, stress, disillusionment, depression, and changes in identity. We have written on this topic elsewhere, and have shown that for some of the children of Katrina, living "lives in limbo" meant that every place felt unstable, transitional, and impermanent. For more on this concept, see Bailey, Adrian J., Richard A. Wright, Alison Mountz, and Ines M. Miyares. 2002. "(Re)producing Salvadoran Transnational Geographies." *Annals of the Association of American Geographers* 92(1): 125–144; Fothergill, Alice, and Lori Peek. 2012. "Permanent Temporariness: Displaced Children in Louisiana." Pp. 119–143 in *Displaced: Life in the Katrina Diaspora*," edited by L. Weber and L. Peek. Austin: University of Texas Press; Mountz, Alison, Richard Wright, Ines Miyares, and Adrian J. Bailey. 2002. "Lives in Limbo: Temporary Protected Status and Immigrant Identities." *Global Networks* 2(4): 335–356.

2. For a discussion of the role that siblings may play in caring for one another in disaster, see Babugura, Agnes A. 2008. "Vulnerability of Children and Youth in Drought Disasters: A Case Study of Botswana." *Children, Youth and Environments* 18(1): 126–157.

3. Burr and Klein (1994) hypothesize five models of family recovery from various highly stressful situations: In the *roller-coaster model*, families experience an initial deep decline following the stressful event and then gradually begin to recover. Although a pathway toward recovery is assumed, the model accounts for the fact that families may achieve different recovery states, which vary upward and downward over time. The *mixed model* entails an increase in functioning immediately after a crisis followed by a subsequent decline. The *increase model* is characterized by families who experience increases in the quality of family functioning, and no marked decline, after a crisis. Conversely, the *decrease model* is evidenced by a steady and consistent decline in family functioning, with no discernible improvements. Finally, families who experience neither decreases nor increases in functioning exemplify the *no change model*. See Burr, Wesley R., and Shirley R. Klein. 1994. *Reexamining Family Stress: New Theory and Research*. Thousand Oaks, CA: Sage. For a study applying the Burr and Klein model and focusing on the recovery patterns experienced by families displaced by Katrina, see Peek, Lori, Bridget Morrissey, and Holly Marlatt. 2011. "Disaster Hits Home: A Model of Displaced Family Adjustment after Hurricane Katrina." *Journal of Family Issues* 32(10): 1371–1396.

4. Within Clinton's family, there is a history of significant drug use and addic-

tion. All of Karen's siblings were addicted to drugs, and one brother died of a drug overdose and was found in a New Orleans park.

5. Individuals and organizations created online registries and used websites, online message boards, and other Internet technologies to help locate missing people throughout Katrina. For a review of this phenomenon, see Laituri, Melinda, and Kris Kodrich. 2008. "Online Disaster Response Community: People as Sensors of High Magnitude Disasters Using Internet GIS." *Sensors* 8: 3037–3055; Macias, Wendy, Karen Hilyard, and Vicki Freimuth. 2009. "Blog Functions as Risk and Crisis Communication during Hurricane Katrina." *Journal of Computer-Mediated Communication* 15(1): 1–31; Palen, Leysia, Starr Roxanne Hiltz, and Sophia B. Liu. 2007. "Online Forums Supporting Grassroots Participation in Emergency Preparedness and Response." *Communications of the ACM* 50(3): 54–58.

6. Green, Bonnie L., Mindy Korol, Mary C. Grace, Marshall G. Vary, Anthony C. Leonard, Goldine C. Gleser, and Sheila Smitson-Cohen. 1991. "Children and Disaster: Age, Gender, and Parental Effects on PTSD Symptoms." *Journal of the American Academy of Child and Adolescent Psychiatry* 30(6): 945–951; Peek, Lori. 2010. "Age." Pp. 155–185 in *Social Vulnerability to Disasters*, edited by B. D. Phillips, D. S. K. Thomas, A. Fothergill, and L. Blinn-Pike. Boca Raton, FL: CRC Press; Shannon, Mitsuko P., Christopher J. Lonigan, A. J. Finch, Jr., and Charlotte M. Taylor. 1994. "Children Exposed to Disaster: I. Epidemiology of Post-Traumatic Symptoms and Symptom Profiles." *Journal of the American Academy of Child and Adolescent Psychiatry* 33(1): 80–93; Sprung, Manuel. 2008. "Unwanted Intrusive Thoughts and Cognitive Functioning in Kindergarten and Young Elementary School-Age Children following Hurricane Katrina." *Journal of Clinical Child and Adolescent Psychology* 37(3): 575–587.

7. Emergency shelters for evacuated populations are often unprepared to respond to the needs of young children, which increases the stress on families trying to keep them safe from harm. For example, during previous disasters in the U.S., general population shelters were found to lack safeguards to prevent the spread of infectious diseases commonly transmitted among children. Moreover, shelters lacked adequate play areas and children were often left unsupervised, increasing the risk for child abuse or kidnapping. See Garrett, Andrew L., Roy Grant, Paula Madrid, Arturo Brito, David Abramson, and Irwin Redlenter. 2007. "Children and Megadisaster: Lessons Learned in the New Millennium." *Advances in Pediatrics* 54: 189–214; Fothergill and Peek, 2012.

8. When parents and caregivers experience depression or other mental health issues following a disaster, children's mental health is negatively impacted. For example, see Scaramella, Laura V., Sara L. Sohr-Preston, Kristin L. Callahan, and Scott P. Mirabile. 2008. "A Test of the Family Stress Model on Toddler-Aged Children's Adjustment among Hurricane Katrina Impacted and Nonimpacted Low-Income Families." *Journal of Clinical Child and Adolescent Psychology* 37(3): 530–541; Scheeringa, Michael S., and Charles H. Zeanah. 2008. "Reconsideration of Harm's Way: Onsets and Comorbidity Patterns of Disorders in Preschool Children

and Their Caregivers Following Hurricane Katrina." *Journal of Clinical Child and Adolescent Psychology* 37(3): 508–518; Spell, Annie W., Mary Lou Kelley, Jing Wang, Shannon Self-Brown, Karen L. Davidson, Angie Pellegrin, Jeannette L. Palcic, Kara Meyer, Valerie Paasch, and Audrey Baumeister. 2008. "The Moderating Effects of Maternal Psychopathology on Children's Adjustment Post-Hurricane Katrina." *Journal of Clinical Child and Adolescent Psychology* 37(3): 553–563; Weems, Carl F., and Stacy Overstreet. 2008. "Child and Adolescent Mental Health Research in the Context of Hurricane Katrina: An Ecological Needs-Based Perspective and Introduction to the Special Section." *Journal of Clinical Child and Adolescent Psychology* 37(3): 487–494.

9. Barry, Dan. 2006. "Lives Suspended on Gulf Coast, Crammed into 240 Square Feet." *New York Times*, June 14, p. A-1.

10. The Robert T. Stafford Disaster Relief and Emergency Assistance Act, PL 100-707, was signed into law November 23, 1988. It constitutes the statutory authority for most federal disaster response activities especially as they pertain to FEMA. For more on the Stafford Act, see http://www.fema.gov/pdf/about/stafford _act.pdf. Accessed on March 2, 2014. For more on recovery time trajectories, see Phillips, Brenda D. 2009. *Disaster Recovery*. Boca Raton, FL: CRC Press.

11. Smith, Gavin P. 2012. *Planning for Post-Disaster Recovery: A Review of the United States Disaster Assistance Framework*. Washington, DC: Island Press.

12. Bohrer, Becky. 2007. "FEMA to Close Post-Katrina Trailer Parks." *Washington Post*, November 29; Eaton, Leslie. 2007. "FEMA Sets Date for Closing Katrina Trailer Camps." *New York Times*, November 29, p. A-20; Whoriskey, Peter. 2007. "'We Called It Hurricane FEMA': Trailer Park Was Quickly Emptied." *Washington Post*, March 12.

13. Peek, 2010.

14. Abramson, David, Tasha Stehling-Ariza, Richard Garfield, and Irwin Redlener. 2008. "Prevalence and Predictors of Mental Health Distress Post-Katrina: Findings from the Gulf Coast Child and Family Health Study." *Disaster Medicine and Public Health Preparedness* 2(2): 77–86; McLaughlin, Katie A., John A. Fairbank, Michael J. Gruber, Russell T. Jones, Joy D. Osofsky, Betty Pfefferbaum, Nancy A. Sampson, and Ronald C. Kessler. 2010. "Trends in Serious Emotional Disturbance among Youths Exposed to Hurricane Katrina." *Journal of the American Academy of Child and Adolescent Psychiatry* 49(10): 990–1000.

15. In many ways, Aaron and Brandi illustrate the "authoritarian" and "authoritative" parenting styles, respectively, as theorized by the psychologist Diana Baumrind in the 1960s and still widely used today in understanding parenting. The authoritarian style is characterized as punitive, very strict, high on parental control and physical discipline, and showing little warmth. The authoritative style incorporates limits, control, and guidance, but also warmth, reasoning, and support. See Baumrind, Diana. 1968. "Authoritarian versus Authoritative Parental Control." *Adolescence* 3: 255–272.

CONCLUSION

1. O'Keefe, Phil, Kenneth Westgate, and Benjamin Wisner. 1976. "Taking the Naturalness out of Natural Disasters." *Nature* 260: 566–567.

2. Gault, Barbara, Heidi Hartmann, Avis Jones-DeWeever, Misha Werschkul, and Erica Williams. 2005. "The Women of New Orleans and the Gulf Coast: Multiple Disadvantages and Key Assets for Recovery, Part 1. Poverty, Race, Gender, and Class." Washington, DC: Institute for Women's Policy Research.

3. Ehrenreich, Barbara, and Frances Fox Piven. 1984. "The Feminization of Poverty." *Dissent* 31(2): 162–170; Peake, Linda J. 1997. "Toward a Social Geography of the City: Race and Dimensions of Urban Poverty in Women's Lives." *Journal of Urban Affairs* 19: 335–361; Edin, Kathryn, and Maria Kafalas. 2005. *Promises I Can Keep: Why Poor Women Put Motherhood before Marriage.* Berkeley: University of California Press; Hays, Sharon. 2004. *Flat Broke with Children: Women in the Age of Welfare Reform.* New York: Oxford University Press.

4. In our work, we predominantly focused on how social disadvantages— poverty, homelessness, food insecurity, and so forth—piled up in children's lives, ultimately leading to increasingly high levels of cumulative vulnerability. Psychologists and other public health experts have examined how mental health challenges may accumulate in children's lives. For example, Lai and colleagues assessed children's symptoms of posttraumatic stress (PTS) and depression after Hurricane Ike. They found that children who were simultaneously experiencing symptoms of PTS and depression had poorer recovery, had more severe symptoms, and faced more recovery stressors overall than children who were experiencing PTS only or depression only. See Lai, Betty S., Annette M. La Greca, Beth A. Auslander, and Mary B. Short. 2014. "Children's Symptoms of Posttraumatic Stress and Depression after a Natural Disaster: Comorbidity and Risk Factors." *Journal of Affective Disorders* 146(1): 71–78.

5. For more discussion of bullying of displaced children and youth after Katrina, see Fothergill, Alice, and Lori Peek. 2012. "Permanent Temporariness: Displaced Children in Louisiana." Pp. 119–143 in *Displaced: Life in the Katrina Diaspora*, edited by L. Weber and L. Peek. Austin: University of Texas Press; Peek, Lori. 2012. "They Call it 'Katrina Fatigue': Displaced Families and Discrimination in Colorado." Pp. 31–46 in *Displaced: Life in the Katrina Diaspora*, edited by L. Weber and L. Peek. Austin: University of Texas Press; Terranova, Andrew M., Paul Boxer, and Amanda Sheffield Morris. 2009. "Changes in Children's Peer Interactions following a Natural Disaster: How Predisaster Bullying and Victimization Rates Changed following Hurricane Katrina." *Psychology in the Schools* 46(4): 333–347.

6. Pina and colleagues found that greater helpfulness from extrafamilial sources of social support, including professional support services, predicted lower levels of child-rated symptoms of posttraumatic stress disorder, anxiety, and depression among Katrina-exposed youth. Pina, Armando A., Ian K. Villalta, Claudio D. Ortiz, Amanda C. Gottschall, Natalie M. Costa, and Carl F. Weems. 2008. "Social Sup-

port, Discrimination, and Coping as Predictors of Posttraumatic Stress Reactions in Youth Survivors of Hurricane Katrina." *Journal of Clinical Child and Adolescent Psychology* 37(3): 564–574.

7. Lareau, Annette. 2011. *Unequal Childhoods: Class, Race, and Family Life*, 2nd ed. Berkeley: University of California Press.

8. There has been an eightfold increase in the use of the term "resilience" in the literature over the last two decades. For a discussion of the implications of the rise of the use of resilience in research and practice, see Ager, Alastair. 2013. "Resilience and Child Well-Being: Public Policy Implications." *Journal of Child Psychology and Psychiatry* 54(4): 488–500.

9. Bonanno, George A., and Erica D. Diminich. 2012. "Positive Adjustment to Adversity: Trajectories of Minimal-Impact Resilience and Emergent Resilience." *Journal of Child Psychology and Psychiatry* 54(4): 378–401.

10. For statements from mental health researchers regarding how post-disaster recovery trajectories are associated with symptoms of posttraumatic stress, see La Greca, Annette, Betty S. Lai, Maria M. Llabre, Wendy K. Silverman, Eric M. Vernberg, and Mitchell J. Prinstein. 2013. "Children's Postdisaster Trajectories of PTS Symptoms: Predicting Chronic Distress." *Child and Youth Care Forum* 42(4): 351–369; Self-Brown, Shannon, Betty S. Lai, Julia E. Thompson, Tia McGill, and Mary Lou Kelley. 2013. "Posttraumatic Stress Disorder Symptom Trajectories in Hurricane Katrina Affected Youth." *Journal of Affective Disorders* 147(3): 198–204; Weems, Carl F., and Rebecca A. Graham. 2014. "Resilience and Trajectories of Post-traumatic Stress among Youth Exposed to Disaster." *Journal of Child and Adolescent Psychopharmacology* 24(1): 2–8.

11. Weems and collaborators assessed posttraumatic stress disorder symptoms at 24 months and again at 30 months after Hurricane Katrina among a sample of ethnic minority children enrolled in fourth through eighth grades. They found that younger age (as well as being female and having continued disrepair to a child's home) predicted elevated symptoms among the sample. Weems, Carl F., Leslie K. Taylor, Melinda F. Cannon, Reshelle C. Marino, Dawn M. Romano, Brandon G. Scott, Andrew M. Perry, and Vera Triplett. 2010. "Posttraumatic Stress, Context, and the Lingering Effects of the Hurricane Katrina Disaster among Ethnic Minority Youth." *Journal of Abnormal Child Psychology* 38(1): 49–56.

12. For a review of gendered expectations and how they influence behavior among children and youth, see Crosnoe, Robert, and Monica Kirkpatrick Johnson. 2011. "Research on Adolescence in the Twenty-First Century." *Annual Review of Sociology* 37: 439–460.

13. Weems et al., 2010.

14. Low-income African American boys from disadvantaged neighborhoods, in particular, face extreme struggles and challenges during non-disaster times, and we also observed how these characteristics intersected and influenced outcomes for this particular group in our work. For a detailed discussion of this phenomenon and the negative role of the criminal justice system in the lives of black youth and

adults, see Alexander, Michelle. 2012. *The New Jim Crow: Mass Incarceration in the Age of Colorblindness*. New York: New Press.

15. For calls for more child- and youth-centered research, see Anderson, William A. 2005. "Bringing Children into Focus on the Social Science Disaster Research Agenda." *International Journal of Mass Emergencies and Disasters* 23(3): 159–175; Peek, Lori. 2008. "Children and Disasters: Understanding Vulnerability, Developing Capacities, and Promoting Resilience." *Children, Youth, and Environments* 18(1): 1–29.

16. Mitchell, Tom, Katharine Haynes, Nick Hall, Wei Choong, and Katie Oven. 2008. "The Roles of Children and Youth in Communicating Disaster Risk." *Children, Youth and Environments* 18(1): 254–279; Mitchell, Tom, Thomas Tanner, and Katharine Haynes. 2009. "Children as Agents of Change for Disaster Risk Reduction: Lessons from El Salvador and the Philippines." Working Paper no. 1. Brighton, UK: Children in a Changing Climate, Institute of Development Studies; Plan International with World Vision International. 2009. "Children on the Frontline: Children and Young People in Disaster Risk Reduction." London: Plan International UK; Tanner, Thomas. 2010. "Shifting the Narrative: Child-Led Responses to Climate Change and Disasters in El Salvador and the Philippines." *Children and Society* 24(4): 339–351.

17. Pugh, Allison, J. 2014. "The Theoretical Costs of Ignoring Childhood: Rethinking Independence, Insecurity, and Inequality." *Theory and Society* 43: 71–89.

18. Ronan, Kevin, and David Johnston. 2005. *Promoting Community Resilience in Disasters: The Role for Schools, Youth, and Families*. New York: Springer.

19. Mitchell et al., 2008.

20. Peek and Fothergill, 2008.

21. For a detailed description of the role of media coverage in inducing stress reactions among some disaster-exposed children, see Weems, Carl F., Brandon G. Scott, Donice M. Banks, and Rebecca A. Graham. 2012. "Is TV Traumatic for All Youths? The Role of Preexisting Posttraumatic Stress-Symptoms in the Link between Disaster Coverage and Stress." *Psychological Science* 23(11): 1293–1297.

22. For overviews of how gender may influence preparedness, response to, and recovery from disasters, see Enarson, Elaine. 2012. *Women Confronting Natural Disasters: From Vulnerability to Resilience*. Boulder, CO: Lynne Rienner; Enarson, Elaine, and P. G. Dhar Chakrabarti, eds. 2009. *Women, Gender, and Disaster: Global Issues and Initiatives*. New Delhi: Sage; Enarson, Elaine, Alice Fothergill, and Lori Peek. 2006. "Gender and Disaster: Foundations and Directions." Pp. 130–146 in *Handbook of Disaster Research*, edited by H. Rodriguez, E. L. Quarantelli, and R. Dynes. New York: Springer.

23. Corsaro, William. 2014. *The Sociology of Childhood*, 4th ed. Los Angeles: Sage.

24. While this point seems to contradict our finding that children were bullied after Katrina, it is important to point out that this teacher is referring to a classroom of New Orleans children—all of whom evacuated, were displaced, and then

returned to the city. The instances of bullying that we documented were in situations where children who were displaced were attending unfamiliar schools in new cities and towns, and were bullied by children who were not from New Orleans.

25. Kids Rethink New Orleans Schools. See http://therethinkers.com/. Accessed on July 24, 2013.

26. David, Emmanuel. 2008. "Cultural Trauma, Memory, and Gendered Collective Action: The Case of Women of the Storm following Hurricane Katrina." *National Women's Studies Association Journal* 20(3): 138–162.

27. Vietnamese American Young Leaders Association (VAYLA). See http://www .vayla-no.org/. Accessed on July 24, 2013.

28. Abramson, David, and Lori Peek. 2013. "SHOREline: A Youth Empowerment and Post-Disaster Recovery Program." *Canadian Risk and Hazards Network HazNet Newsletter* 5(1): 15–17.

29. For a statement on the importance of evaluating disaster education programs for children, as well as other youth-oriented initiatives, see Johnson, Victoria A., Kevin R. Ronan, David M. Johnston, and Robin Peace. 2014. "Evaluations of Disaster Education Programs for Children: A Methodological Review." *International Journal of Disaster Risk Reduction* 9: 107–123.

30. Other researchers have documented how disasters can mobilize individuals and groups—such as women, people of color, and other marginalized populations— who were not politically active prior to the disaster experience. For a discussion of women becoming civically engaged and politically active after a flood disaster, see Fothergill, Alice. 2004. *Heads above Water: Gender, Class, and Family in the Grand Forks Flood*. Albany: State University of New York Press.

31. Interestingly, childcare providers who have worked in multiple different disaster contexts also report that children made up spontaneous games where they, too, would re-enact evacuations from hurricanes, wildfires, and other hazardous events. See Peek, Lori, Jeannette Sutton, and Judy Gump. 2008. "Caring for Children in the Aftermath of Disaster: The Church of the Brethren Children's Disaster Services Program." *Children, Youth and Environments* 18(1): 408–421.

32. For a description of a project dedicated to encouraging youth to share their stories of recovery through creative means, see Cox, Robin, and Lori Peek. 2013. "Creating Recovery: A New Canadian-U.S. Participatory Project on Youth Empowerment after Disaster." *Canadian Risk and Hazards Network HazNet Newsletter* 4(2): 9–10.

33. Fritz, Charles E., and Mathewson, John H. 1957. "Convergence Behavior in Disasters: A Problem in Social Control." Committee on Disaster Studies, Disaster Research Group. Washington, DC: National Research Council, National Academy of Sciences.

34. Steffen, Seana Lowe, and Alice Fothergill. 2009. "9/11 Volunteerism: A Pathway to Personal Healing and Community Engagement." *Social Science Journal* 46: 29–46.

35. Li, Yiyuan, Hong Li, Jean Decety, and Kang Lee. 2013. "Experiencing a

Natural Disaster Alters Children's Altruistic Giving." *Psychological Science* 24(9): 1686–1695.

36. For an examination of the effects of social exclusion post-disaster, see Peek, Lori. 2011. *Behind the Backlash: Muslim Americans after 9/11*. Philadelphia: Temple University Press. For a discussion of barriers to opportunities to help others, see Lowe, Seana, and Alice Fothergill. 2003. "A Need to Help: Emergent Volunteer Behavior after September 11." Pp. 293–314 in *Beyond September 11: An Account of Post-Disaster Research*, edited by J. L. Monday. Boulder, CO: Natural Hazards Center, University of Colorado.

37. Lowe and Fothergill, 2003, p. 308.

APPENDIX A

1. Thorne, Barrie. 2009. "'Childhood': Changing and Dissonant Meanings." *International Journal of Learning and Media* 1(1): 19–27.

2. Ibid.

3. Office of the United Nations High Commissioner for Human Rights. 1989. "Convention on the Rights of the Child: Part 1, Article 1." http://www2.ohchr.org /english/law/crc.htm. Accessed on September 11, 2011.

4. Bartlett, Sheridan. 2008. "The Implications of Climate Change for Children in Lower-Income Countries." *Children, Youth and Environments* 18(1): 71–98.

5. Peek, Lori. 2010. "Age." Pp. 155–185 in *Social Vulnerability to Disasters*, edited by B. D. Phillips, D. S. K. Thomas, A. Fothergill, and L. Blinn-Pike. Boca Raton, FL: CRC Press.

6. Peek, Lori, and Laura M. Stough. 2010. "Children with Disabilities in the Context of Disaster: A Social Vulnerability Perspective." *Child Development* 81(4): 1260–1270.

7. Thorne, Barrie. 1993. *Gender Play: Girls and Boys in School*. New Brunswick, NJ: Rutgers University Press.

8. Moore, Valerie Ann. 2002. "The Collaborative Emergence of Race in Children's Play: A Case Study of Two Summer Camps." *Social Problems* 49(1): 58–78.

APPENDIX B

1. Anderson, William A. 2005. "Bringing Children into Focus on the Social Science Disaster Research Agenda." *International Journal of Mass Emergencies and Disasters* 23(3): 159–175.

2. During the fall 2005 semester, Alice was starting her third year at the University of Vermont, beginning a much-anticipated research semester for junior faculty that was going to allow her the time to wrap up several ongoing projects. Lori was a new assistant professor, with plans to turn her dissertation into a book.

3. Fothergill, Alice, and Lori Peek. 2006. "Surviving Catastrophe: A Study of Children in Hurricane Katrina." Pp. 97–130 in *Learning from Catastrophe: Quick Response Research in the Wake of Hurricane Katrina*. Boulder: Institute of Behavioral Science, University of Colorado.

4. Upon reflection, we should have told our respondents sooner that we were planning to write a book about their experiences. We were not trying to hide this fact; we just did not want to set up false expectations in case a book did not materialize. Once we were certain, however, that we had enough data to write a book, we started sharing this with the children and adults in the study. We quickly realized that having such a tangible "product" from the research helped better explain our work and also differentiated us from journalists and social workers.

5. We thank University of Vermont undergraduate student Stephanie Fakharzadeh for inviting us to hand-deliver her senior thesis on the benefits of school gardens and the "edible schoolyard" model to the New Orleans charter school where she did her research. This task gave us the opportunity to see the circumstances she so vividly described firsthand.

6. Emerson, Robert M., Rachel I. Fretz, and Linda L. Shaw. 1995. *Writing Ethnographic Fieldnotes*. Chicago: University of Chicago Press.

7. In her essay describing ethnographic research methods, Annette Lareau recommends that fieldnotes be written within 24 to 48 hours of observation (and before any other observation period is scheduled). Although we tried to follow the "Lareau rule," we found that sometimes this simply was not possible due to time constraints and the packed schedule that we always maintained while in the field. When we could not develop full fieldnotes, we tried, at minimum, to get an outline of the day typed up, and then we established which of us would write up those fieldnotes upon return after the field visit. For a discussion of writing effective fieldnotes, see Lareau, Annette. 1996. "Common Problems in Field Work: A Personal Essay." Pp. 195–236 in *Journeys through Ethnography: Realistic Accounts of Fieldwork*, edited by A. Lareau and J. J. Shultz. Boulder, CO: Westview Press.

8. Ibid.

9. On one occasion, when we were visiting a childcare center in New Orleans, the director asked us not to take photos (after Lori took her camera out of her bag) because the center had had a bad experience with visitors taking video—unbeknownst to the staff—and then posting it for public viewing on YouTube. Moments like these served as reminders to us to be respectful and to make sure to ask permission before recording children or adults in any form—video, audio, photographic, or otherwise.

10. As the reader might imagine, given the discussion of photos throughout the book and in this appendix, we accumulated hundreds of photos over the seven years of this research. Many of those pictures of the children and families were absolutely beautiful. We promised from the beginning, however, to never publicly use the photos that showed their faces. This was a tough decision, in some ways, as we recognize how powerful images can be in telling stories. But, given our goals and ethical stance

on protecting respondent identities and honoring our commitment to confidentiality, in the end, we decided to keep the photos for our own research purposes and to give to the respondents as gifts, but never to share them any further.

11. Krueger, Richard A. 1988. *Focus Groups: A Practical Guide for Applied Research*. Newbury Park, CA: Sage.

12. We have previously argued that the ideal focus group size is three to five participants, so that all voices are heard. See Peek, Lori, and Alice Fothergill. 2009. "Using Focus Groups: Lessons from Studying Daycare Centers, 9/11, and Hurricane Katrina." *Qualitative Research* 9(1): 31–59. Cindy Dell Clark argues that small groups, such as a triad, work especially well for young children, around ages 6 and 7, who would not do as well with a larger group. See Clark, Cindy Dell. 2011. *In a Younger Voice: Doing Child-Centered Qualitative Research*. New York: Oxford University Press.

13. Eder, Donna, and Laura Fingerson. 2002. "Interviewing Children and Adolescents." Pp. 181–201 in *Handbook of Interview Research*, edited by J. F. Gubrium and J. A. Holstein. Thousand Oaks, CA: Sage.

14. For a description of long-term ethnography with children, and specific discussion of the difference that physical size can make, see Corsaro, William A. 2005. *I Compagni: Understanding Children's Transition from Preschool to Elementary School*. New York: Teachers College Press.

15. Peek and Fothergill, 2009, "Using Focus Groups."

16. Most of the children in our study had never been interviewed before for research purposes, and therefore were unaware of how the qualitative interview would progress. A few had been interviewed for school newspapers or as part of classroom projects, but even in these cases, the qualitative interviews we conducted tended to be different and more extended than what the children had experienced previously.

17. Peek and Fothergill, 2009.

18. Johnson, Alan. 1996. "It's Good to Talk: The Focus Group and the Sociological Imagination." *Sociological Review* 44: 517–538.

19. For an overview of methodological approaches used to study children in the aftermath of three catastrophic events, see Pfefferbaum, Betty, Carl F. Weems, Brandon G. Scott, Pascal Nitiéma, Mary A. Noffsinger, Rose L. Pfefferbaum, Vandana Varma, and Amarsha Chakraburtty. 2013. "Research Methods in Child Disaster Studies: A Review of Studies Generated by the September 11, 2001, Terrorist Attacks; the 2004 Indian Ocean Tsunami; and Hurricane Katrina." *Child and Youth Care Forum* 42(4): 285–337.

20. We thank Professor Cynthia Reyes at the University of Vermont for this valuable interview advice.

21. Clark, 2011.

22. See, for example, Danby, Susan, Lynette Ewing, and Karen Thorpe. 2011. "The Novice Researcher: Interviewing Young Children." *Qualitative Inquiry* 17(1): 74–84.

23. Hesse-Biber, Sharlene Nagy, and Michelle L. Yaiser. 2004. *Feminist Perspectives on Social Research*. Oxford: Oxford University Press.

24. Working as a team had many advantages, although occasionally it created

some mild confusion. Because we were always together (and we look somewhat alike—we are both tall, thin white women with long brunette hair), our participants often got us mixed up. They would sometimes ask if we were sisters, which led to much joking between us and the respondents. Sometimes the participants would get confused about who lived where ("Now, Alice, are you in Colorado or are you the one from Vermont?"). It gave us a chance to share a bit about our personal lives as we interacted with those in our study.

25. Like Lareau, 2003, Katherine Brown Rosier also sent a five-dollar bill in birthday cards to her participants. We only discovered this at the close of our research, but were glad to know that others had followed a similar protocol. See Rosier, Katherine Brown. 2000. *Mothering Inner-City Children: The Early School Years*. New Brunswick, NJ: Rutgers University Press.

26. The use of social media raised some confidentiality concerns, as "friend lists" are public on these sites. We tried to manage these concerns by never posting anything about the research project on the family members' pages. We also did not "friend" any of the study participants under the age of 18.

27. We would have had hundreds more transcripts if all interviews had been audio recorded, but they were not; this was due primarily to logistical issues and the spontaneous nature of some interviews, especially those that occurred when we were shopping, walking, or eating, for example, or in certain settings, such as stores or churches.

28. We worked with Sandy Grabowski, a professional transcriptionist, for the duration of this project. We would contact her at least a month in advance before we were heading into the field, so we could notify her of our schedule and also get on her calendar. Doing this was important, as Sandy would hold a spot for us in her transcribing queue, and thus she was always able to accommodate our time line and to return the transcripts to us rapidly. It also helped to work with the same transcriptionist throughout, because Sandy became quite familiar with culturally and geographically specific expressions that those outside the region are often not accustomed to. Her professionalism and attentiveness to detail improved the overall quality of the transcribed data that we received, and we remain grateful.

29. Lori's graduate and undergraduate research assistants at Colorado State University helped us with many of these tasks. For example, they scanned files, assisted with some of the transcription of the audio files, searched for literature on our behalf, found vital statistics, and otherwise helped us to construct a more complete picture of our research settings and participants.

30. Rubin, Herbert J., and Irene S. Rubin. 2012. *Qualitative Interviewing: The Art of Hearing Data*, 3rd ed. Thousand Oaks, CA: Sage.

31. Corsaro, 2005.

32. In addition, as some families were acquaintances of Alice's sister Anne, we had to be careful not to discuss any privileged information with her. We felt it was fine, however, for us to answer their general queries about Anne or her family, when we were asked.

33. We used Olympus recorders for this study, at the recommendation of our

professional transcriptionist. Our recorders had built-in USB devices. This meant we had one less cord to carry with us, and that we could plug the recorder directly into our laptop computer and download the files as soon as we were done with an interview. This ensured that we would not lose the interview and also allowed us to send off the digital files to our transcriptionist so she could begin transcribing, even as we were still in the field.

34. For a discussion of this particular ethical issue, see Browne, Katherine E., and Lori Peek. 2014. "Beyond the IRB: An Ethical Toolkit for Long-Term Disaster Research." *International Journal of Mass Emergencies and Disasters* 32(1): 82–120.

35. We often planned the interview before the meal out as we found that it worked better to do the interview first. Otherwise, respondents would start "catching us up" during the meal, when we did not have the recorder out and running. It was generally just better to complete the interview, then to continue the conversation during the meal.

36. Fothergill, Alice. 2003. "The Stigma of Charity: Gender, Class, and Disaster Assistance." *Sociological Quarterly* 44(4): 659–680.

37. Professors are often sent review copies of textbooks, for no charge, from publishers. Some professors request the books, and sometimes they are sent unsolicited. There is some unease about whether or not it is ethical for professors to then sell the books to independent book buyers who frequent departments looking for college textbooks to purchase and then resell. Some departments pool the money they receive from the book buyers (for a department coffee fund, for example), and other professors keep the money for their own personal use. Some refuse to sell the books at all. We decided that we would sell the books that we received unsolicited (we never requested the books) and use the money for our study participants. Those funds went toward things like purchasing groceries for families, buying meals when we would eat out together with families, and paying for laundry. Because we had been unable to secure other sources of funding for these expenses, we felt this was a good use of the book funds. We kept a log of when we sold the books, how much we received, and when we took and used the money on our research trips. We found that the few book buyers we worked with were enthusiastic about the use of the funds, and often would ask how the children were recovering when they would stop to buy additional books. Sometimes, they would even contribute an extra $10 or $20 to help out.

APPENDIX C

1. An earlier version of this appendix was published here: Fothergill, Alice, and Lori Peek. 2014. "Lessons from Katrina: Recommendations for Fostering More Effective Disaster Preparedness, Response, and Recovery Efforts for Children and Youth." *Canadian Risk and Hazards Network HazNet Newsletter* 5(2): 4–9.

2. Bronfenbrenner, Urie. 1986. "Ecology of the Family as a Context for Human Development: Research Perspectives." *Developmental Psychology* 22(6): 723.

3. Peek, Lori, and Alice Fothergill. 2008. "Displacement, Gender, and the Challenges of Parenting after Hurricane Katrina." *National Women's Studies Association Journal* 20(3): 69–105.

4. Quarantelli, Enrico L. 1995. "Patterns of Sheltering and Housing in U.S. Disasters." *Disaster Prevention and Management* 4(3): 43–53.

5. Self-Brown and collaborators found that positive peer social support served as a significant and positive protective factor for Katrina-exposed youth. See Self-Brown, Shannon, Betty S. Lai, Julia E. Thompson, Tia McGill, and Mary Lou Kelley. 2013. "Posttraumatic Stress Disorder Symptom Trajectories in Hurricane Katrina Affected Youth." *Journal of Affective Disorders* 147(3): 198–204. Overstreet and colleagues highlight research that has shown the negative effects of disruptions in children's peer and social networks. See Overstreet, Stacy, Alison Salloum, Berre Burch, and Jill West. 2011. "Challenges Associated with Childhood Exposure to Severe Natural Disasters: Research Review and Clinical Implications." *Journal of Child and Adolescent Trauma* 4(1): 52–68.

6. McLaughlin, Katie A., John A. Fairbank, Michael J. Gruber, Russell T. Jones, Joy D. Osofsky, Betty Pfefferbaum, Nancy A. Sampson, and Ronald C. Kessler. 2010. "Trends in Serious Emotional Disturbance among Youths Exposed to Hurricane Katrina." *Journal of the American Academy of Child and Adolescent Psychiatry* 49(10): 990–1000.

ABOUT THE AUTHORS AND SERIES EDITOR

ALICE FOTHERGILL is an associate professor of sociology at the University of Vermont in Burlington. She an editor of the first and second editions of *Social Vulnerability to Disasters* and author of *Heads Above Water: Gender, Class, and Family in the Grand Forks Flood.*

LORI PEEK is an associate professor of sociology and codirector of the Center for Disaster and Risk Analysis at Colorado State University in Fort Collins. She is the coeditor of *Displaced: Life in the Katrina Diaspora* and author of the multiple award-winning *Behind the Backlash: Muslim Americans after 9/11.*

KAI ERIKSON, SERIES EDITOR, is Professor Emeritus of Sociology and American Studies at Yale University. He is a past president of the American Sociological Association, winner of the MacIver and Sorokin Awards from the ASA, author of *A New Species of Trouble: Explorations in Disaster, Trauma, and Community,* and his research and teaching interests include American communities, human disasters, and ethnonational conflict.

INDEX

Page numbers in italics refer to figures and illustrations

as equal opportunity events, 4; poor families, 7, 21, 23, 45, 51, 64–66, 110, 136, 154, 284n5; and post-disaster trajectories, 33–34, 81, 93, 119, 194, 197, 200, 205; and resource depth, 26–27, 119, 123; school segregation, 7; and social networks, 119; working-class, 31, 50, 72, 84, 93, 110, 136, 158, 250, 253; working poor, 27, 125

climate change, 21

confidentiality. *See* methodology

creative arts, 26, 118–119, 209, 218–219, 239–242, 271, 293n1; art and drawings, *13*, 28, 103, *110*, *113*, 113–114, 121, *153*, *162*, 175, *176*, 209, 218, 238–241, *241*, *242*, 243–245; music and singing, 40, 63, 101, 118, 122, 141–142, 209, 218, 272; poetry, 121–122, 143, 218; theater and drama, 19, 63, 118, 139–140, 199, 272; writing, 28, 118, 121, 140, 218, 272–273. *See also* methodology

crime: children as witnesses to, 7, 82, 289n18; looting, 73–75, 85; in post-Katrina New Orleans, 41, 67, 74–75, 117, 164–165, 185. *See also* safety; violence, acts of

criminal justice system, 67, 164, 303n14

cultural capital, 25–27, 124, 197, 200–201

cumulative vulnerability: defined, 20–25; and post-disaster declining trajectory, 37–39, 67, 92–93, 97, 120, 145, 196–199, 302n4; stages of, 23, *24*, 25. *See also* vulnerability

Dallas, Texas, 186–192

declining trajectory, 13, 33–34, 37–39, *38*, 67–68, 85–86, 93–95, 120, 145, 194, 196–199. *See also* post-disaster trajectories

Denver, Colorado, 9, 77–87, 91–92, 157, 214

disaster planning recommendations: extracurricular activities sphere, 273; family sphere, 269–270; health and well-being sphere, 273–274; peers/friendships sphere, 272–273; school sphere, 270–272; shelter and housing sphere, 270

disasters: Bangladesh slum fire (2004), 29; Buffalo Creek flooding (1972), 294n8; Haiti earthquake (2010), 22, 29; Hurricane Cindy (2005), 30, 283n51; Hurricane Gustav (2008), 185–186; Hurricane Ivan (2004), 102, 104; Hurricane Rita (2005), 1, 75, 128; Indian Ocean earthquake and tsunami (2004), 29; Japan earthquake and tsunami (2011), 29; and myth of children as helpless victims, 4, 194, 206; and myth of children's resilience, 4, 194; and myth of disasters as equal opportunity events, 4, 194; Pakistan flood (2010), 22; and political activism, 305n30; scholarship, xii–xiii; Sichuan, China earthquake (2008), 22, 220. *See also* Hurricane Katrina; post-disaster trajectories; violence, acts of

displacement, 9, 11, 18, 24–25, 93, *94*, 95, 219; advantages in, 105–111, 119, 161, 164; and education, 57–58, 60–62, 77–78, 134–140, 161; and income levels, 93; multiple, 18, 34, 40, *46*, 58, 77, 85, 93, *94*, 120, 147, 151–152, 163, 187, 198–199, 203, 293n28; and race, 48; and receiving communities, 9, 34, 37, 44, 58–59, 78–80, 93, 198, 233, 271; statistics, xii, 6–7

educational attainment of parents, 42, 70, 157, 163

education and schools, 40, 42, 44–45, 48, 50, 53, 55, 57–63, 70, 77–82, 97–98, 100–102, 106, 109–110, 115, 123, 137, 149–150, 156–161, 182–183, 200; and advocates, 62, 134–139, 141–143; attendance and performance, 57–63; behavior problems, 159–160, 164, 168; and bullying, 58, 60, 68, 198, 205, 214, 272, 302n5, 304n24; and class status, 84–85, 110, 136, 158; college graduates and employment, 289n20; curriculum, post-disaster, 114, 137; dismissal of teachers, 292n23; dropping out, 22, 85, 280–281nn23–24; first-generation college students, 84–85; and food/

health issues, 284n4; grades and test scores, 149, 157, 159, 160, 164; New Orleans public schools, 7, 157–159, 161, 290n1, 296nn6–9, 298n12, 298n14; percentage of displaced children not attending school, 290n7; racial segregation and integration, 27, 100, 123, 135, 138–139, 157, 189, 201; and receiving communities, 37, 44, 58–59, 78–80, 143, 233, 271; and residential mobility, 280n23, 293n28; and safety, xiv, 22–23, 60, 62, 158–159; yearbooks, 217. *See also* spheres of children's lives

employment, 40–42, 48, 53, 57, 63–67, 91–92, 170–172, 179–181, 183, 185, 187–190

Environmental Protection Agency (EPA), 114

evacuation: barriers to, 6, 23, 31, 151, 196–197, 203, 284n5; and children's capacities, 30–31, 206–221, 283n52; decision-making, 43, 71–72, 102–105, 122–123, 151, 163; examples of, 1–3, 42–45, 71–76, 103–111, 122–123, 151, 163, 174–175, 200; and resource depth, 200; statistics, xii, 6

extracurricular activities, 19, 62–63, 70, 78, 84, 92, 118–119, 134–135, 137–139, 141–143, 149, 155–157, 162, 189–190, 192–193, 199, 203. *See also* creative arts; spheres of children's lives

family: as anchors, 168–169, 174, 186, 192, 202; death in, 40–41; extended, 88–89; family friends, 101–104, 108–110, 112, 114–115, 117, 173–177, 191; family violence, 7, 22, 280n21, 289n19, 300n7; fathers, 69, 101, 102, 104, 105, 106, 107–117, 123, 149, 151–156, 161, 163–165, 188; grandparents, 82–83, 86–87, 148, 150–153, 155–157, 159, 161, 165, 264; mothers, 73, 75–83, 86–87, 91, 101, 108–110, 117, 148–149, 154–155, 158–161, 166; pets, 20, 102, 104, 117, 122, 162, 206; relationships, 79, 82–83, 87, 150, 152–153; reunification, 177–178; separation, 23, 53, 55, 64, 75, 81, 154–

155, 173, 186–187, 192, 197, 202–203, 269, 296n1; siblings, 16, 29–30, 41–45, 48–50, 52–57, 60, 62–64, 65–67, 70–73, 75, 77, 80, 82, 86–87, 91, 101, 103, 109, *110*, 114, 147, 169–177, 180–193, 202, 211, 214, *242*, 301n15. *See also* spheres of children's lives

family recovery, models of, 299n3

federal disaster declarations, US, 6, 21

Federal Emergency Management Agency (FEMA) trailers, 1, 48–54, 53–55, 60, 65, 90, 122, 127–133, 158, 180–186, 261–262, 285n10, 294n8; descriptions of, 15–16, 49, 181–182, 285n10; locations, 59–61, 125, 129, 181–182; regulations for, 48–49, 133, 183–184; and safety concerns, 49–50, 133, 182, 262, 285n11; size, 49

fictive kin, 156, 296n5

finding-equilibrium trajectory, 13, 97–99, 102, 118–120, 122–125, 145, 194, 199–202. *See also* post-disaster trajectories

fluctuating trajectory, 13, 34, 145–147, 149–150, 167–170, 183, 186, 191–193, 194, 202–205. *See also* post-disaster trajectories

food insecurity, 53, 57, 65–68

foster care, 6

friendship. *See* spheres of children's lives

gatekeepers, 228–229

gender: and "appropriate behaviors," 212–213; and bullying, 60; and caregiving, 109, 172, 205, 212–213; and children's capacities/caretaking, 103, 212–213; and cumulative vulnerability, 23, 303n14; imbalance in post-Katrina New Orleans, 117; and integrated schools, 139; and post-disaster trajectories, 205; and preparedness, 304n22; and relationships/connections, 119, 295n14; role of, for researchers, 254–255; and socialization, 167; and social position, 194

Habitat for Humanity. *See* housing

health and health care, 29, 41, 42, 51, 53,

and race, 248–250, 253–254; recording and capturing children's voices, 238–244, 257–258, 309n27, 309n33; samples of adults, 237–238; samples of children, 8–9, 9, 248–250; secondary sample, 8, 9; and "snowball sample," 256; and social class, 253–254; and social media, 309n26; tertiary sample, 8–9, 9; tracking methods, 250–251; and vulnerability/needs of participants, 258–261, 284n3, 285n10, 309n25
music and singing, 40, 63, 101, 118, 122, 141–142, 209, 218, 272

Nagin, Ray, 43
natural disasters. *See* disasters
New Orleans, Louisiana: car ownership, 283n50, 284n5; Charity Hospital, 51–52; as "the city that care forgot," 117, 292n26; Covenant House, 56, 64; poverty in, 29, 51, 196, 287n31; Powell Elementary School, 157–159, 161, 298n12, 298n14; public schools, 7, 290n1, 296nn6–9; return to, after Katrina, 73–76, 112, 114–118; shelters, 41, 43–46, 47–48, 53, 56–57; Superdome, 2, 20, 30, 175, 208; and violence witnessed by children, 82, 289n18; Westbank and Eastbank, 289n22
New York City, 45, 47
nonprofit organizations, 140–142

parenting styles, 301n15
peers. *See* spheres of children's lives
Plan International, 29, 279n5
poetry, 121–122, 143, 218
post-disaster trajectories, xii–xv, 33, 195, 196, 196–205; and advocates, 32, 34, 97–98, 127–143, 147, 194, 199–201; and anchors, 192–193, 199; and age, 81–82, 85–86; and college, 85; and cumulative vulnerability, 37–39, 67, 92–93, 97, 120, 145, 196–199, 302n4; declining trajectory, 13, 33–34, 37–39, 38, 67–68, 85–86, 93–95, 120, 145, 194, 196–199; defined, 33–35, 37, 97, 145; and evacuation experiences, 122–123, 197; and

financial stability, 99, 118–119; finding-equilibrium trajectory, 13, 97–99, 102, 118–120, 122–125, 145, 194, 199–202; fluctuating trajectory, 13, 34, 145–147, 149–150, 167–170, 183, 186, 191–193, 194, 202–205; and institutions, 124; and length of emergency period, 119–120; and level of displacement, 119; and misalignment, 34, 149–150, 170, 176, 202; and race, 67; and resource depth, 97, 102, 106–111, 116, 119–120, 123–124, 199–201; and social networks, 119–120, 123, 198, 200; and structural disadvantages, 198–199, 203
posttraumatic stress disorder (PTSD), 90, 258, 296n1, 302n4, 302n6, 303n11
poverty, 45; and absent fathers, 154; and absent mothers, 170–173; "basement of extreme poverty," 40–41; children of color, 7, 64–66, 196, 198, 205, 278n32; and "daily disasters," 7; and disasters, 21, 23; and education, 110, 136; and evacuation, 284n5; in New Orleans, 29, 51, 196, 287n31; parental advocacy and, 142; pre-Katrina, 29, 51, 67, 196; and resilience, 204 ; working poor, 27, 125
Pre-Katrina housing, examples of, 41–44, 69–70, 103, 107, 113, 163–165

race: and criminal justice system, 67, 164, 303n14; and cumulative vulnerability, 23, 67, 82; and education, 7, 138–139, 182, 271–272, 297n8; and evacuation, 291n18; and friendships, 138; and Katrina deaths, 276n13; and myth of disasters as equal opportunity events, 4; and New Orleans, 89, 117, 163–164, 196; and post-disaster trajectories, 34, 194, 205–206; and prejudice/bullying, 45, 58, 60, 80, 198; and religious institutions, 47–48, 139; and research samples, 8, 11, 21, 34, 249; and resource depth, 26–27; role of for researchers, 253–254; and social networks, 41 receiving communities, 9, 34, 37, 44, 58–59, 78–80, 93, 198, 233, 271

Red Cross. *See* American Red Cross

religious institutions: as advocates, 139–40; church shelters, 15–16, 45, 174–182, 215, 228

resilience, xiv, 27, 97, 198, 202; defined, 204; myth of, 4; scholarship, xiv, 303n8

resource depth, 34, 98–99, 102, 105–106, 110–111, 123, 194, 200; and class, 26–27, 119, 123; and families, 269; and post-disaster trajectories, 97, 98–99, 102, 105–111, 116, 118–120, 123–124, 194, 199–201

resource mobilization, 25, 27–28, 34, 97, 125, 131, 142, 201; and conduit for resources, 124–125, 128–136, 139–142; model of, 27. *See also* advocates; institutions as agents of support

Robert T. Stafford Disaster Relief and Emergency Assistance Act, 183, 301n10

safety, 50, 60, 86, 90, 93, 126, 269–270, 272, 274; during Katrina and evacuation, 30–31, 43–44, 103, 105, 111, 122–123, 174, 208, 211–212; and FEMA trailers, 50, 133, 182, 262, 285n11; and gender, 117; and post-Katrina housing, 54, 70, 73, 106, 123, 148, 164–165; and pre-Katrina housing, 37, 41; and schools, xiv, 22–23, 60, 62, 158–159; and shelters, 48, 50, 126, 200

safety nets, 119, 123, 156, 219

Save the Children, 21, 29

schools. *See* education and schools

shelters, 43–46, 48, 50, 126, 177–180, 200, 213, 215, 237; in Baton Rouge, 43–46, 177–180, 213, 215, 237; in churches, 15–16, 45, 178–182, 215, 228; in New Orleans, 2, 20, 30, 41, 43–46, 47–48, 53, 56–57, 175, 208. *See also* housing

SHOREline program, 216

single-parent families, 23, 69, 81, 123, 129, 154–155, 180, 196–197, 199, 213

social capital, 25–26, 110, 123, 200–201, 211

social media, 76, 186, 218, 251, 272, 309n26

sociology of childhood, 4–5

spheres of children's lives, *17*, 17–20, 269–274; extracurricular activities, 19, 62–63, 70, 78, 84, 92, 118–119, 134–135, 137–139, 141–143, 149, 155–157, 162, 189–190, 192–193, 199, 203; family, 18, 33–35, 41–46, 63–67, 69–81, 86–90, 97–99, 122–123, 148–156, 170–172, 176–178, 183–188, 269; health (physical and emotional), 6, 19–21, 42, 53, 65–67, 77–79, 117–118, 130–131, 135, 141, 273; housing and neighborhood, 18, 23, 37, 66–70, 44–57, 106–107, 114–116, 128–134, 138–139, 158–159, 162–170, 209–210, 270; misalignment, 145–150, 167–168, 170, 202–203; peers and friends, 19, 25, 40, 62, 69, 71, 75–78, 81–85, 88–92, 101, 107, 110–111, 114, 116, 118, 129–130, 133–134, 136–140, 148, 149–150, 165–167, 178, 180–182, 186–190, 213, 272; school, 18–19, 44–45, 57–63, 77–86, 97–98, 100–102, 109–110, 134–139, 156–161, 182–183, 271

Stafford Act. *See* Robert T. Stafford Disaster Relief and Emergency Assistance Act

Students of the Storm, 216

suicide. *See* mental health

theater and drama, 19, 63, 118, 139–140, 199, 272

UNICEF, 29

United Nations: Convention on the Rights of the Child, 223; International Disaster Risk Reduction Day, 29

Vicksburg, Mississippi, 103, 105

Vietnamese American Youth Leaders Association (VAYLA), 216

violence, acts of: 9/11, terrorist attacks of, xii, 7, 21, 220; attitudes toward, 167; children at risk of, 22; children witnessing, 7, 82, 289n18; Columbine

High School shooting; (1999), 22; in neighborhoods, 198; New Orleans, post-Katrina, 117, 164–165; Oklahoma City bombings (1995), 22; Sandy Hook Elementary School shootings (2012), 22, 298n12

vulnerability: and age, 21–22, 90, 185; and children's capacities, 28–31, 206; in developing countries, 22; and gender, 23, 117, 303n14; pre-disaster, 23, 32–33, 98, 113, 123, 196–197, 202, 270; and resource depth, 25–28; and social disadvantages, 20–21, 298n16, 302n4; and socioeconomic status, 20–21; and temporal components, 23–25. *See also* cumulative vulnerability; post-disaster trajectories

Women of the Storm, 216

World Vision, 29

writing, creative, 28, 118, 121, 140, 218, 272–273

Xavier University, 83–86

youth: defined, 223–224; and motherhood, 91–92; and relationships, 82, 89–92, 208. *See also* children